BREAKING BREAD

with FATHER DOMINIC 2

Reise

Merry Christmas 2002
and
Happy Breaking Bread

Mom

FATHER DOMINIC GARRAMONE, OSB

First Edition
Fourth Printing

ISBN 0-9674652-1-4

Printed in the United States of America by Inland Press/Inland Book, Menomonee Falls, Wisconsin.

KETC
3655 Olive St.
St. Louis, MO 63108

Visit the *Breaking Bread With Father Dominic* Web site at *http://www.breaking-bread.com*. Instructional videotapes from the *Breaking Bread With Father Dominic* television program may be ordered at 1-800-293-5949.

Breaking Bread With Father Dominic is underwritten by Fleischmann's Yeast.

TABLE OF CONTENTS

Table of Contents

Editor:
Terri Gates

Art Director:
Jennifer Garrett

Recipe editor:
Barbara Gibbs Ostmann

Illustrator:
Michael Neville

Cover photo:
Scott Raffe

"Why spend your money for what is not bread;
your wages for what fails to satisfy? Heed me, and
you shall eat well, you shall delight in rich fare."

(Isaiah 55:2)

Introduction

How to Use This Book

Like my first volume, this cookbook has been written with the beginning baker in mind. At the same time, I'm sure bread lovers of every level of experience will enjoy the recipes that follow, and there are tips for more accomplished bakers as well. Here are some important things to remember.

Ingredients

I've tried to develop recipes that don't have exotic or expensive ingredients. My monastery is on the outskirts of a small city that fortunately has three very large grocery stores with a good selection of flours, herbs, spices and produce, but not everyone has such advantages. Whenever possible, I have tried to give alternatives to ingredients that may be hard to obtain.

If you are an experienced baker, you will probably feel comfortable making your own substitutions to suit your own taste—margarine for butter, more or less salt, dried cranberries instead of raisins, etc. Beginning bakers, however, would be better off trying the recipe at least once or twice exactly as it is presented, until they become comfortable with the method and have a good idea of what the result should be like.

I never specify bread flour for a recipe unless I have found that it is really necessary for a successful loaf. Bread flour is milled from a harder wheat with a higher protein content, which makes it ideal for breads with a long rising period (like sourdough or artisan breads) or for combination with whole grain flours like stone-ground wheat or rye. You may also substitute bread flour for all-purpose flour in many recipes, but I don't recommend it for batter breads or biscuits.

Whenever a recipe calls for eggs, use large eggs as I did when developing the recipes. Otherwise the proportion of liquid to dry ingredients will be wrong. I also use salted butter when butter is called for.

Yeast

If you are a regular viewer of our program, I'm sure you have heard me say that the number one problem people have with bread baking is killing the yeast. All of the yeast bread recipes in this book use active dry yeast, either the regular or the fast-rising variety. There are specific techniques and temperatures for each type of yeast, so please be sure to follow the directions carefully.

Regular active dry yeast is "proofed" by mixing it with a liquid that is warmed to a temperature of between 100 and 110 degrees. Fast-rising yeast (also called "instant yeast") is mixed with a portion of the dry ingredients. Then the liquid is heated to 120 to 130 degrees and stirred into the mixture.

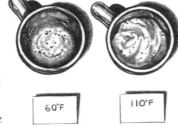

I highly recommend buying a digital instant-read thermometer, which is available not only at specialty shops but also at some discount stores and supermarkets. They generally cost between $10 and $15, which is a small price to pay for consistent results!

KNEADING

The best way to learn to knead dough is to watch your grandma do it from the time you are 5 years old, and then somewhere around

age 10 to ask her to teach you. But it is never too late to learn, even if you are a grandma yourself and just starting to bake bread!

Begin with the slightly flattened dough on a lightly floured counter in front of you. Take hold of the edge farthest from you and fold the dough toward you, pulling the dough back on itself. Using the heels of your hands, push the dough away from you in a rolling motion as you press down slightly. Turn the dough one quarter and repeat.

Try to establish a comfortable rhythm—fold, push, turn; fold, push, turn—that makes you feel like you're working with the dough and not against it. Especially, don't press down too hard or the dough will tend to tear and stick to your hands.

BAKING SHEETS AND PANS

When a recipe calls for a baking sheet, use the thickest metal jelly-roll pan you can find. There are baking sheets that have a double bottom with an air pocket in between, which helps keep the bottom of the bread from darkening too quickly. You can also get the same effect by setting one jelly-roll pan inside another and laying the loaf on top.

Standard loaf pans come in two sizes: medium (8 $\frac{1}{2}$ x 4$\frac{1}{2}$ x 2 $\frac{1}{2}$ inches) and large (9x5x3 inches). I generally prefer the medium-size pan, because I think the amount of dough in these recipes fits them better. But you can use the larger ones, too—it's just that sometimes the dough will not fill the pan quite so well, and the loaf may not quite develop the height you want.

Several recipes in the book call for mini-loaf pans. The ones I use have a nonstick surface and measure 5 $\frac{3}{4}$ x 3 $\frac{1}{2}$ x 2 inches. I have about a dozen of them and have bought them everywhere from gourmet cooking schools to the flour aisle of our local food mart. So I'm sure you'll have no trouble locating them.

Once you get some experience in baking don't hesitate to experiment with different pans: stoneware, ceramic, glass, coffee cans, etc. Remember that when using glass pans, the baking temperature should be lowered 25 degrees.

BREAD MACHINE RECIPES

I love getting my hands in the dough during bread baking, and I urge people to do the same. But, if because of time or other constraints, a bread machine is the only way you can get a decent loaf of bread in your house, God bless you! Whenever possible, this cookbook includes a bread machine version of recipes for those who prefer that method.

Look for the symbol and make sure you're using the appropriate recipe. While the ingredients will be similar for the two versions, the amounts may be quite different.

HERBS AND SPICES

REFLECTION

The abbey herb garden is just outside the west door of the kitchen, so it's easy for me to obtain fresh herbs for my breads and other dishes. The garden is designed in three sections: ornamental and fragrant herbs are in the more formal center section, flanked on one side by the sprawling mints and catnip that I grow for tea, with the culinary herbs closest to the kitchen door. The neatly arranged sections of chives, basil, marjoram and parsley inspire me just as much as cookbooks and magazine articles with glossy photos.

As every herb gardener knows, one of the fringe benefits of growing these useful plants is that you get to enjoy them several times, rather than just once as you add them to the cook pot. The variegated colors and textures of herbal foliage delight the eye, and the scent of herbs accompanies every step of the baking process, from the garden to the chopping block to the oven, and finally to the table. Even weeding an herb garden is more pleasurable as you brush against each plant and release the heady aroma of basil, lavender's sweet perfume, or the spicy fragrance of thyme.

Sometimes, pulling a loaf of herb bread out of the oven is almost as rewarding as eating it. Once when I was testing the recipe for Tomato Basil Focaccia for my first cookbook, I had a group of teenagers in the kitchen with me. When the kitchen timer went off, they all gathered around to see the results of our experimentation. As I pushed the peel into the oven and removed an especially impressive loaf, golden brown and adorned with fresh rosemary, my young friend Josh exclaimed, "Dude—that is like, the most beautiful thing I've ever seen—in my life!"

You don't have to have an extensive garden to enjoy fresh herbs in your breads—a few plants in pots can supply you with seasonings all summer long, and the produce section of many grocery stores now carry fresh herbs year round. I can't guarantee that your family and friends will be quite so impressed by your baking as Josh was, but I'm sure they'll appreciate you preparing the recipes in this next section.

SOUTHERN SWEET POTATO BREAD

Yield: 1 loaf.

1 ½ cups **HODGSON MILL Naturally White Flour**

1 cup **granulated sugar**

2 ¼ teaspoons **baking powder**

1 ¼ teaspoons **salt**

1 teaspoon **pumpkin pie spice**

2 **eggs**

½ cup **vegetable oil**

⅓ cup **sour cream**

1 teaspoon **vanilla extract**

1 cup mashed cooked **sweet potato**

1 cup chopped **pecans**

Preheat oven to 350 degrees.

Sift flour, sugar, baking powder, salt and pumpkin pie spice into a medium mixing bowl. Beat eggs in another bowl. Add oil, sour cream, vanilla and sweet potato; beat well. Add egg mixture to flour mixture; stir until just blended. Do not overmix. Fold in pecans.

Pour batter into a well-greased 9x5x3-inch loaf pan. Bake in preheated 350-degree oven 60 to 70 minutes, or until top is golden brown and a cake tester inserted into the center of the loaf comes out clean. Remove from pan and let cool on wire rack at least one hour before slicing. This bread is best if sliced the next day.

Note: *We sometimes have baked sweet potatoes for supper. I ask the cooks to put a few aside for me to peel and mash. One large baked sweet potato will yield about 1 cup mashed product. You can use the canned variety, too—I have, with excellent results.*

If you don't have pumpkin pie spice on hand, you can substitute ¼ teaspoon ground nutmeg and 1 teaspoon ground cinnamon.

Bread Break

I'm not a big fan of sweet potatoes; I don't like their texture on my tongue. However, this traditional quick bread from the American South is a delicious way to use leftover cooked sweet potatoes. Sweet potatoes also are used to flavor a variety of Southern yeast breads and rolls.

I made this bread for our back-to-school faculty picnic. I sliced six loaves and arranged the slices in concentric circles on a huge, round tray with a bowl of sweet (unsalted) butter in the center. There was very little leftover for breakfast the next day. So don't be afraid to make a double batch.

Yield: 12 biscuits.

Bread Break

I had read recipes calling for herbes de Provence for years without really finding out what the herb mix was. I was surprised to discover that I had everything I needed in my own garden! Most of the ingredients were in my culinary garden, just outside the west door of the monastery kitchen. The sage and lavender came from the garden by our print shop, where I have three huge lavender bushes. They bloom twice a year, thanks to vigorous pruning after the first blooms are spent.

The biscuits make a delicious accompaniment for everything from soup to roast pork. If you prefer a lighter biscuit, you can omit the whole wheat flour and replace it with an equal amount of white, but I like the rustic appearance and texture that graham flour adds.

1 ½ cups **HODGSON MILL Naturally White Flour**

½ cup **HODGSON MILL Whole Wheat Graham Flour**

1 tablespoon **granulated sugar**

2 teaspoons **baking powder**

1 teaspoon **herbes de Provence** (see note)

½ teaspoon **salt**

½ cup solid **vegetable shortening**

1 cup **milk**

Preheat oven to 425 degrees.

Combine white flour, whole wheat flour, sugar, baking powder, herbes de Provence and salt in a medium mixing bowl; stir to mix well. Cut in vegetable shortening using a pastry blender or two knives. Add milk; stir until just blended.

Drop batter by tablespoons onto a lightly greased baking sheet. Bake in preheated 425-degree oven 12 to 15 minutes, or until lightly browned. Remove from baking sheet and let cool slightly on wire racks. Serve warm.

Note: You easily can make your own herbes de Provence and keep the mixture on hand in the pantry. If you have your herb blend already prepared, these fragrant drop biscuits can be mixed and baked in less than half an hour, making them ideal for serving to last-minute guests.

Herbes de Provence is made by combining five or more of the following: basil, fennel, sage, thyme, rosemary, oregano, marjoram, savory, mint, lavender. If you buy a commercial mix, it's generally best to choose a domestic blend rather than one imported from Europe; the imported blends are often less fresh and might have inferior flavor.

It's easy to make your own. Here's a combination I like:

Herbes de Provence

*2 tablespoons dried **basil***
*2 tablespoons dried **thyme***
*2 tablespoons dried **sage***
*2 tablespoons dried **savory***

*2 tablespoons ground **fennel seeds***
*1 tablespoon dried **rosemary***
*1 tablespoon dried **lavender flowers***

Combine herbs in a jar with a tight-fitting lid. Store at room temperature. Shake well or stir before using.

Makes about $^1/_2$ cup herb mixture.

Tip: *For the best flavor, use whole leaves of thyme, savory and rosemary; grind the mixture with a mortar and pestle just before use. The flavor will be stronger and the mixture will keep longer.*

BACON DILL BREAD

Yield: 1 large or 2 regular loaves.

Bread Break

Dill is not a flavoring I much care for, except in pickles, but our Brother Nathaniel finds it irresistible. Monasteries are like other families — the cook can't always make what he likes best! — so I developed this bread flavored with dill and bacon. You'll often see recipes for "dilly bread" that use cottage cheese for moistness and sautéed onions for flavor. I find that the bacon in my version is less overwhelming of the dill. I avoid adding caraway seeds for the same reason.

You'll notice that there's no oil in this recipe. Between the bacon and the cheese, there's plenty of fat to enrich the dough. If you use low-fat or fat-free products, the dough will not be as soft and smooth, but the bread will still be delicious.

½ cup warm **water**

2 packages **FLEISCHMANN'S Active Dry Yeast**

2 teaspoons **brown sugar**

1 cup **milk**

1 cup **cottage cheese**

2 tablespoons chopped fresh **dill** or 1 tablespoon dried

1 ½ teaspoons **salt**

5 to 6 cups **HODGSON MILL Naturally White Flour**, divided

14 to 16 strips **bacon**, cooked, drained and crumbled (⅔ cup)

Combine water, yeast and brown sugar in a small bowl; stir to dissolve. Let stand 5 to 10 minutes, or until foamy.

Put milk and cottage cheese in container of electric blender; blend until smooth. Transfer to a saucepan and heat until mixture is warm (100 to 110 degrees).

Pour warm milk mixture into a large mixing bowl. Add yeast mixture, dill and salt. Add 2 cups of the flour; stir until thoroughly incorporated. Add bacon; mix thoroughly. Add 3 cups of the flour, one cup at a time, mixing thoroughly after each addition.

Turn out dough onto a lightly floured surface. Knead 6 to 8 minutes, adding small amounts of the remaining 1 cup flour as needed to keep dough manageable. After kneading, dough should be somewhat soft rather than stiff, but only slightly sticky.

Oil the surface of the dough and put dough in the rinsed mixing bowl. Cover with a towel and let rise in a warm, draft-free place 45 to 60 minutes, or until doubled.

Punch down dough. Knead briefly to work out the larger air bubbles. Form dough into one large or two medium free-form loaves and place on lightly greased baking sheet(s), or divide dough into 2 pieces, shape into loaves and place in lightly greased 8 ½ x 4 ½ x 2 ½-inch loaf pans. (Note: Free-form loaves might not rise as high as loaves in a pan.) Cover and let rise for 20 to 30 minutes, or until nearly doubled.

While loaves are rising, preheat oven to 350 degrees. Bake loaves 40 to 50 minutes (or longer for one large free-form loaf), or until light brown and loaf sounds hollow when tapped. Remove from pans and let cool on wire racks.

Note: You can fry the bacon, drain it, and then crumble it, or you can cut the bacon into small pieces and then fry and drain it. Either way works fine for the recipe, although with the latter technique I find myself more inclined to nibble!

I often bake this bread in a round 2-quart baking dish, but there's just a little too much dough to fit. So I remove enough dough to fill a mini-loaf pan. That way I can have a sample loaf for my helpers when the bread comes out of the oven, and the large loaf to serve the community.

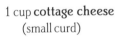

BACON DILL BREAD

Bread Machine

Yield: 1 (1 ¹/₂-pound) loaf.

1 cup **cottage cheese** (small curd)

2 **eggs**

1 teaspoon **brown sugar**

1 tablespoon finely chopped fresh **dill** or 1 ¹/₂ teaspoons dried

³/₄ teaspoon **salt**

¹/₄ teaspoon **baking soda**

About 7 strips **bacon**, cooked, drained, crumbled (¹/₃ cup)

2 ¹/₂ cups **HODGSON MILL Best for Bread Flour**

1 ¹/₂ teaspoons **FLEISCHMANN'S Bread Machine Yeast**

Add cottage cheese, eggs, brown sugar, dill, salt, baking soda, bacon, flour and yeast to bread machine pan in order suggested by the manufacturer. Select **basic cycle; light** or **medium color setting**.

Note: Cottage cheese is the main liquid ingredient. Check the dough in the bread machine pan after the initial kneading to adjust dough consistency. Adjust dough by adding 1 tablespoon flour if the dough is too moist or 1 tablespoon milk or water if the dough is too dry.

CHEDDAR CHIVE BREADSTICKS

Yield: 16 breadsticks.

Bread Break

These braided breadsticks are an attractive addition to a buffet table when served standing up in a tall basket or stoneware crock.

The process of rolling and braiding is time consuming, so you'll probably want to enlist the help of family and friends. If you're working alone or you're pressed for time, you can skip the braiding altogether. Simply roll the dough into a 16x8-inch rectangle and use a pizza cutter or sharp knife to cut it into 16 strips. Place the strips on the greased baking sheets and proceed as directed.

3 ½ cups **HODGSON MILL Naturally White Flour,** divided

1 package **FLEISCHMANN'S RapidRise Yeast**

1 teaspoon **salt**

1 cup **milk**

2 tablespoons **olive oil**

4 ounces **sharp Cheddar cheese,** shredded (about 1 cup)

½ cup snipped fresh **chives**

1 **egg**, beaten

Sesame seeds (optional)

Butter, melted (optional)

Combine 2 cups of the flour, yeast and salt in a medium mixing bowl; stir to mix. Combine milk and oil in a small saucepan; heat to 120 to 130 degrees, stirring occasionally. Add warm milk mixture to flour mixture; stir until smooth. Add cheese and chives; mix thoroughly. Add 1 cup of the flour; mix until thoroughly blended.

Turn out dough onto a lightly floured surface. Knead 5 minutes, adding small amounts of the remaining ½ cup flour as needed to make a smooth, elastic dough. Cover dough and let rest 10 minutes.

Divide dough into 16 equal portions. Divide each portion into 3 pieces; roll each piece into a thin rope, 10 to 12 inches long. Braid 3 ropes together, trimming the ends as needed. Place braided breadsticks on lightly greased baking sheet; cover and let rise in a warm, draft-free place 30 minutes, or until almost doubled.

About 15 minutes before the end of rising time, preheat oven to 375 degrees. Brush risen breadsticks with beaten egg and sprinkle with sesame seeds. Bake 20 to 25 minutes, or until golden brown. Remove from baking sheet and place on wire racks. Brush with melted butter. Let cool briefly before serving.

Note: Go to the deli and choose a very sharp Cheddar, then shred it yourself for these breadsticks. The prepackaged, pre-shredded Cheddar is just too bland. If you don't have fresh chives, you can substitute 1 teaspoon onion powder. In addition to topping the breadsticks with melted butter, you can sprinkle them with garlic powder, but they have plenty of flavor on their own.

CHEDDAR CHIVE BREADSTICKS

Yield: 16 breadsticks.

1 cup **milk**

¹/₄ cup **water**

2 tablespoons **olive oil**

1 teaspoon **salt**

3 cups **HODGSON MILL Best for Bread Flour**

1 cup shredded **sharp Cheddar cheese** (about 4 ounces)

¹/₂ cup snipped fresh **chives**

2 teaspoons **FLEISCHMANN'S Bread Machine Yeast**

1 **egg** beaten with 1 tablespoon **water**, for egg glaze

Sesame seeds (optional)

Butter or **margarine**, melted (optional)

Add milk, water, oil, salt, flour, cheese, chives and yeast to bread machine pan in the order suggested by manufacturer. Select **dough/manual cycle**.

When cycle is complete, remove dough from machine to lightly floured surface. Divide dough into 16 equal portions. Divide each portion into 3 pieces; roll each piece into a 10-inch-long rope. Braid 3 ropes together; pinch ends to seal. Place braided breadsticks on a greased baking sheet. Cover and let rise in a warm, draft-free place about 30 minutes, or until almost doubled in size. Brush with egg glaze; sprinkle with sesame seeds.

Bake in a preheated 375-degree oven 20 to 25 minutes, or until golden brown. Remove from baking sheet and place on wire racks. Brush with melted butter. Let cool slightly before serving.

FRUITED SWEET POTATO BREAD

Yield: 4 mini-loaves.

Bread Break

Sweet potatoes are used to flavor a variety of quick breads and yeast breads in traditional Southern cooking. Because sweet potatoes were similar to the yams of their native lands, newly arrived slaves from Africa found comfort in a familiar food and incorporated it into their cooking.

This might seem like a lot of ingredients, but the marvelously complex and subtle blend of flavors in this bread is exquisite. The aroma is so tempting that the first time I made it, the scent drew four different monks to the kitchen to investigate.

As an afternoon snack, this bread is delicious served with honey butter, accompanied by Darjeeling or Earl Grey tea.

$^{1}/_{4}$ cup ($^{1}/_{2}$ stick) **butter**, softened

1 cup **granulated sugar**

2 **eggs**

$^{1}/_{3}$ cup **orange juice**

$^{1}/_{2}$ cup **applesauce**

1 cup mashed cooked **sweet potato**

2 $^{1}/_{4}$ cups **HODGSON MILL Naturally White Flour**

2 teaspoons **baking powder**

$^{1}/_{2}$ teaspoon **baking soda**

$^{1}/_{2}$ teaspoon **salt**

1 $^{1}/_{2}$ teaspoons ground **cinnamon**

$^{1}/_{2}$ teaspoon ground **nutmeg**

$^{1}/_{2}$ cup **raisins**

1 cup chopped **walnuts**

Preheat oven to 350 degrees.

Combine butter, sugar and eggs in a medium mixing bowl; mix until well blended. Add orange juice, applesauce and sweet potato; beat well. Sift in flour, baking powder, baking soda, salt, cinnamon and nutmeg; stir until just blended. Fold in raisins and walnuts.

Divide batter among four well-greased 5 $^{3}/_{4}$ x 3 $^{1}/_{2}$ x 2-inch mini-loaf pans. Bake in preheated 350-degree oven 35 to 40 minutes, or until tops are golden brown and a cake tester inserted in the center of the loaf comes out clean. Remove from pans and let cool on wire racks.

Note: Many sweet potato bread recipes call for a cup of raisins, but I think that's too sweet and overwhelms the orange and apple flavors. You could substitute pecans for the walnuts, if you prefer. If you don't have mini-loaf pans, bake this bread in a 9x5x3-inch loaf pan for 60 to 65 minutes.

ANJ'S HAYSTACK ONION RINGS

Yield: About 10 haystacks, each serves 2 to 3 people.

Vegetable oil, for frying

1 (12-ounce) package
**Don's Chuck Wagon
Onion Ring Mix** (see note)

1 cup **HODGSON MILL
Naturally White Flour**

³/₄ cup **HODGSON MILL
Yellow Corn Meal**

1 teaspoon **salt**

1 teaspoon **onion powder**

1 teaspoon **paprika**

1 teaspoon **garlic powder**

1 teaspoon **black pepper**

¹/₂ teaspoon **dry mustard**

10 to 20 large Vidalia or other
sweet **onions**, thinly sliced

Heat vegetable oil to 350 degrees in a deep fryer. You will need a basket that fits inside the deep fryer to prepare this recipe.

Combine dry onion ring mix (do not add liquid), flour, cornmeal, salt, onion powder, paprika, garlic powder, pepper and dry mustard in a large mixing bowl; stir to mix well.

Add thinly sliced onions to the breading mixture; toss or stir until onions are thoroughly coated. Put enough dredged onions in deep-fryer basket to fill it a little more than half full. To prevent spattering, slowly lower the basket into the hot oil. Fry onions 3 to 5 minutes, or until golden brown. Lift out basket and gently shake off excess oil; let drain briefly. Turn haystack out all at once onto a serving plate lined with paper towels. Serve at once. Repeat procedure for each haystack.

If you don't use all the breading at one time, carefully sift out any remaining onion pieces from leftover breading. Discard onion pieces. Store breading in an airtight container in the refrigerator for up to several weeks.

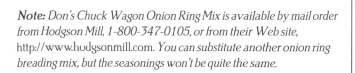

Note: Don's Chuck Wagon Onion Ring Mix is available by mail order from Hodgson Mill, 1-800-347-0105, or from their Web site, http://www.hodgsonmill.com. You can substitute another onion ring breading mix, but the seasonings won't be quite the same.

Bread Break

One of the pleasures of attending fairs and festivals is sampling foods you might not get at other times of the year: corn dogs, elephant ears, lemon shake-ups and more. My family really enjoys haystack onion rings, which are not really rings at all, but thin slices of onion all jumbled together with a spicy breading. When fried in a basket and turned out onto a plate, they resemble a haystack. My sister Angela decided she wanted to reproduce them, and after weeks of experimentation, came up with this recipe.

The onions really have to be thinly sliced for this recipe to work. My sister uses the slicing attachment in her food processor. A grater will not work, but the slicing side of some larger box graters does OK. I sharpened the blades on an old-fashioned cabbage slicer and it worked great.

HEARTY AND WHOLESOME

P eople often ask me, "What do you do to develop recipes?" Well, when I'm working on a classic bread like brioche or pumpernickel, I research recipes in cookbooks and on the Internet, then adapt them to suit my own taste with plenty of input from my confreres and friends, who are always willing to serve as taste testers. A few recipes just happen spontaneously, based on what needs pruning in the herb garden (like Italian Onion Herb Bread, page 51), or what's leftover from supper (like Southern Sweet Potato Bread, page 11). But many recipes are the result of arduous trial and error, sometimes requiring several attempts to get the flavor and texture just right. And for these latter recipes, I rely on the help of my good friend Mike the Deli Guy.

Mike owns and manages Klein's Cafe and Market in nearby Peru, Illinois. The cafe serves a wide variety of sandwiches on breads like grilled sourdough, multigrain with toasted sunflower seeds, and raisin walnut. Naturally, the Deli Guy really knows what breads will make a unique and flavorful sandwich, and I rely on his educated palate when developing my own recipes. So once a week for the past year, Mike has been coming out to the abbey kitchen to help me test new creations.

This weekly collaboration has produced many of the recipes in this cookbook, as well as several new items on the cafe menu. Some nights we bake as many as five different kinds of bread (and some really delicious mocha almond biscotti!). But even better, Mike and I have become close friends as a result of the time we've spent up to our elbows in dough. We've both been enriched by our friendship, and I was especially honored when Mike and his fiancee, Kim, asked me to preside at their upcoming wedding.

I've told people for years that bread brings us together, even people who might not otherwise have been connected, and makes us into more than we could have been by ourselves. The recipes in this section reflect that truth, combining different flours and flavors to create foods that nourish both body and soul.

PUMPERNICKEL BREAD

Yield: 1 large or 2 small loaves.

¹/₂ cup **bread crumbs**, toasted dark

¹/₃ cup **HODGSON MILL Yellow Corn Meal**

2 cups hot **water**

¹/₄ cup warm **water**

1 teaspoon **brown sugar**

2 packages **FLEISCHMANN'S Active Dry Yeast**

¹/₄ cup **molasses**

¹/₄ cup **vegetable oil**

2 tablespoons **cider vinegar**

1 **egg**

1 tablespoon **salt**

2 tablespoons **HODGSON MILL Vital Wheat Gluten**

2 tablespoons **instant coffee granules**

1 tablespoon **unsweetened cocoa powder**

3 ¹/₂ cups **HODGSON MILL Whole Grain Rye Flour**, divided

2 to 2 ¹/₂ cups **HODGSON MILL Best for Bread Flour**, divided

Cornmeal, for dusting baking sheet

Combine bread crumbs, cornmeal and hot water in a large mixing bowl; mix thoroughly. Let cool to lukewarm. Meanwhile, combine warm water, brown sugar and yeast in a small bowl; stir to dissolve. Let stand 10 minutes, or until foamy.

Add molasses, oil, vinegar, egg and salt to cornmeal mixture; stir with a heavy wooden spoon until blended. Stir in yeast mixture, wheat gluten, coffee granules and cocoa powder; mix well. Stir in 2 cups of the rye flour. Let dough rest 5 minutes. Add remaining 1 ¹/₂ cups rye flour; stir until flour is thoroughly incorporated. Add 1 cup of the bread flour, mixing the dough with your hands. The dough will seem very sticky and won't hold together very well, but be patient.

Turn out dough onto a well-floured surface. Knead 12 to 15 minutes, adding small amounts of the remaining 1 to 1 ¹/₂ cups bread flour as needed to keep the dough manageable. Finished dough will be sticky, slightly elastic and very stiff. Oil surface of the dough and put in the rinsed mixing bowl. Cover with a dish towel and let

Bread Break

This is not a bread for the faint of heart! The dough is very sticky and heavy, and requires a lot of kneading. If you prefer hearty, dense pumpernickel to the fluff found in most groceries, you'll be glad you made the effort. Many of my confreres of German or Polish background were delighted when I started experimenting with pumpernickel. My first few attempts at pumpernickel were incredibly dense and heavy, but the brethren gamely ate three loaves of failure before I got to this success. They were surprised to discover, as I was, that this bread has so many unusual ingredients. Legend has it that it was originally developed during a shortage of white flour, so other dry ingredients were added as extenders. It is not as dark as many commercial pumpernickels, which are almost always artificially colored.

rise in a warm, draft-free place 60 to 75 minutes, or until doubled.

Punch down dough. Knead about 1 minute. Form dough into a large round loaf or two oblong loaves; place on a baking sheet that has been liberally dusted with cornmeal. Cover and let rise about 45 minutes, or until nearly doubled.

About 15 minutes before end of rising time, preheat oven to 375 degrees. Bake 55 to 60 minutes for large loaf, or 35 to 40 minutes for smaller loaves, or until crust is hard and loaves sound hollow when tapped. They will not sound as hollow as other breads because pumpernickel is a rather dense bread. Remove from pans and let cool on wire racks. Slice thin to serve.

Note: Some pumpernickel recipes call for mashed potatoes, but I find that makes the dough a little too dense. The use of toasted bread crumbs adds to the unique texture. To make your own bread crumbs, finely grind bread; spread crumbs on ungreased baking sheet and bake in a preheated 350-degree oven 15 to 20 minutes, or until they are slightly darker than graham crackers. Be careful not to let them burn. You can use white, whole wheat or rye bread for the crumbs. If you use leftover pumpernickel, the bread will be correspondingly darker.

Because this bread is so dense, it doesn't toast very well. Be sure to slice it thin, whether for a sandwich or as an accompaniment to a meal. Try it with a deli meat sandwich, or with a strong Havarti cheese and cold beer.

PUMPERNICKEL BREAD

Bread Machine

Yield: 1 round loaf.

1 cup plus 2 tablespoons **water**

2 tablespoons **vegetable oil**

2 tablespoons **molasses**

1 tablespoon **cider vinegar**

1 **egg**

1 ½ teaspoons **salt**

1 ½ cups **HODGSON MILL Whole Grain Rye Flour**

1 ¼ cups **HODGSON MILL Best for Bread Flour**

1 tablespoon **HODGSON MILL Vital Wheat Gluten**

¼ cup **dry bread crumbs**

2 tablespoons **HODGSON MILL Yellow Corn Meal**

1 tablespoon **instant coffee granules**

1 ½ teaspoons **unsweetened cocoa powder**

2 teaspoons **FLEISCHMANN'S Bread Machine Yeast**

Cornmeal, for dusting baking sheet

Add water, oil, molasses, vinegar, egg, salt, rye flour, bread flour, wheat gluten, bread crumbs, cornmeal, coffee granules, cocoa powder and yeast to bread machine pan in the order suggested by manufacturer. Select **dough/manual cycle**.

When cycle is complete, transfer dough from machine to a lightly floured surface. Shape dough into a ball. Place ball on a baking sheet that has been greased and liberally dusted with cornmeal. Cover and let rise in a warm, draft-free place about 1 hour, or until doubled in size.

Bake in a preheated 375-degree oven 30 to 35 minutes, or until done. Remove from baking sheet and let cool on wire rack.

SEEDED BARLEY BREAD

Yield: 1 large or 2 medium loaves.

Bread Break

Our Father James' favorite food is what he calls "dark bread," that is, any bread made with whole grain flours. He eagerly devours whole wheat and pumpernickel, as well as this barley bread. His love for this particular bread was illustrated when I made a large round loaf of Seeded Barley Bread late one night, intending to serve it at lunch the next day. After morning prayer I wandered out into the kitchen with my cup of coffee, only to discover that a huge slab had already been cut from the loaf, evidently well before breakfast! Knowing Father James' propensity for early rising, I knew immediately who the culprit was. But how can you scold someone who so obviously appreciates your efforts? Lately I have noticed that more of the brethren are eating multigrain breads so sometimes I have to make as many as 10 loaves at a time.

This bread could be considered among the popular "artisan" breads, which are characterized by a long, slow

SPONGE:

1 ½ cups warm **water**

1 ½ cups **barley flour**

½ cup **HODGSON MILL Whole Wheat Graham Flour**

1 package **FLEISCHMANN'S Active Dry Yeast**

DOUGH:

1 cup warm **milk**

2 teaspoons **salt**

2 tablespoons **HODGSON MILL Vital Wheat Gluten**

¼ cup **vegetable oil**

¼ cup **molasses**

⅓ cup coarsely chopped **sunflower kernels**

3 tablespoons **flaxseed**

3 to 3 ½ cups **HODGSON MILL Best for Bread Flour**, divided

For sponge: Combine warm water, barley flour, whole wheat flour and yeast in a large non-metallic bowl; mix thoroughly. Cover with a towel and let stand in a warm, draft-free place 2 to 6 hours to ferment.

For dough: Tear sponge into pieces in the bowl. Add warm milk, salt, wheat gluten, oil and molasses; beat until smooth. Let stand 30 minutes. Add sunflower kernels, flaxseed and 2 cups of the bread flour; stir until well blended. Add the remaining 1 to 1 ½ cups bread flour, about ½ cup at a time, mixing thoroughly after each addition, until the flour is completely incorporated into the dough and you have a slightly sticky dough that is firm enough to knead.

Turn out dough onto a lightly floured surface. Knead 8 minutes, adding small amounts of flour as needed to keep dough manageable. After kneading, the dough should be somewhat soft rather than stiff, but only slightly sticky. Oil surface of dough, and put it in the rinsed bowl. Cover with a towel and let rise at room temperature 60 to 90 minutes, or until doubled.

Punch down dough. Knead briefly to work out the larger air bubbles. Form dough into one large or two medium free-form loaves and place on a lightly greased baking sheet, or shape dough into two loaves and place in lightly greased 8 1/2 x 4 1/2 x 2 1/2-inch loaf pans. Cover and let rise 30 to 45 minutes, or until nearly doubled.

About 15 minutes before end of rising time, preheat oven to 375 degrees. Bake 35 to 45 minutes, or until crust is brown and loaf sounds hollow when tapped. Remove from pans and let cool on wire racks.

Note: Barley is one of the earliest cultivated grains. It was commonly used for bread in biblical times. It makes a mild flour that is somewhat sweeter than wheat flour, sometimes even imparting a slightly nutty flavor to breads. In this loaf, the long rising period for the sponge adds a slight tang, resulting in a loaf of complex flavors and textures.

If you can find mini-sunflower kernels, there is no need to chop them. The flavor of the sunflower kernels becomes more pronounced when this bread is toasted.

rising period with a relatively small amount of yeast, sometimes as little as one teaspoon. Slow-rise breads have more flavor, so avoid the temptation to add more yeast or to speed up the process by adding sugar to the sponge.

Seeded Barley Bread

Yield: 1 (1 1/2-pound) loaf.

1 cup **water**

2 tablespoons **margarine** or **butter**

3 tablespoons **molasses**

1 teaspoon **salt**

1 1/2 tablespoons **flaxseed**

2 tablespoons **sunflower kernels**

1/2 cup **barley flour**

1 tablespoon **HODGSON MILL Vital Wheat Gluten**

2 1/4 cups **HODGSON MILL Best for Bread Flour**

1 1/2 tablespoons **nonfat dry milk powder**

1 1/2 teaspoons **FLEISCHMANN'S Bread Machine Yeast**

Add water, margarine, molasses, salt, flaxseed, sunflower kernels, barley flour, wheat gluten, bread flour, dry milk powder and yeast to bread machine pan in order recommended by the manufacturer. Select **basic cycle; light** or **medium color setting**.

Raisin Walnut Bread

Yield: 2 loaves.

Bread Break

This recipe was developed as a custom order for my buddy Mike the Deli Guy. At his shop he serves a scrumptious chicken salad on a raisin walnut bread that he orders from a bakery 70 miles away. He said he would prefer to bake his own bread, so we tried several different combinations of flours, oils and sweeteners until we settled upon this recipe. I usually prefer breads made with honey rather than molasses, but in this case the molasses really accentuates the rye and the raisins.

After we tried this bread with virtually every topping in the abbey kitchen, Mike decided he liked it best toasted and topped with his own chicken salad (of course!). I agree about the toasting, but I prefer to top it with strawberry-flavored light cream cheese. Make up a batch for yourself and find your own favorite.

1 cup lukewarm **milk**

1 cup lukewarm **water**

2 packages **FLEISCHMANN'S Active Dry Yeast**

2 tablespoons **light molasses**

2 cups **HODGSON MILL Whole Grain Rye Flour**, divided

2 tablespoons **vegetable oil** (I prefer canola)

1 ½ teaspoons **salt**

3 to 3 ½ cups **HODGSON MILL Best for Bread Flour**, divided

2 cups **raisins**

1 cup coarsely chopped **walnuts**

Combine milk, water, yeast, molasses and 1 cup of the rye flour in a large mixing bowl; stir to mix well. Let stand 5 to 10 minutes. Add oil and salt; mix well. Stir in the remaining 1 cup rye flour. Let dough rest 10 minutes; the rye flour will absorb moisture.

Add 3 cups of the bread flour, one cup at a time, mixing thoroughly after each addition. Turn out dough onto a lightly floured surface. Knead vigorously 8 to 10 minutes, adding enough of the remaining ½ cup bread flour to make a firm (but not stiff) dough that is slightly sticky. Lightly oil surface of dough, and put in the rinsed mixing bowl. Cover with a towel and let rise in a warm, draft-free place 60 to 75 minutes, or until doubled in bulk.

Punch down dough. Knead briefly to work out the larger air bubbles. Roll out dough to a thickness of about ½ inch. Sprinkle raisins and walnuts on top of dough. Fold the edges of the dough toward the center. Knead dough a few minutes to evenly distribute the raisins and walnuts. (At first the dough will be messy and seem to be falling apart, but be patient; it will all come together.)

Divide dough in half and shape each half into a loaf. Place loaves in lightly greased 8 ½ x 4 ½ x 2 ½-inch loaf pans. Cover with a towel and let rise 40 minutes, or until nearly doubled in bulk.

About 15 minutes before end of rising time, preheat oven to 350 degrees. Bake 35 to 45 minutes, or until loaves are golden brown and sound hollow when tapped. Remove from pans and let cool on wire racks.

Note: If you would prefer smaller loaves, divide the dough into four pieces and use mini-loaf pans. Bake at 350 degrees for 25 to 30 minutes. I like the smaller size for gift breads or for a light buffet.

RAISIN WALNUT BREAD

Yield: 1 (1 ½-pound) loaf.

½ cup **water**

½ cup **milk**

1 tablespoon **vegetable oil**

1 tablespoon **light molasses**

¾ teaspoon **salt**

1 ½ cups **HODGSON MILL Best for Bread Flour**

1 cup **HODGSON MILL Whole Grain Rye Flour**

1 ½ teaspoons **FLEISCHMANN'S Bread Machine Yeast**

1 tablespoon **HODGSON MILL Vital Wheat Gluten**

1 cup **raisins**

½ cup chopped **walnuts**

Add water, milk, oil, molasses, salt, bread flour, rye flour, yeast, wheat gluten, raisins and walnuts to bread machine pan in the order suggested by manufacturer.

Select **whole wheat/whole grain** or **basic/white bread cycle; light** or **medium/normal color setting**.

BANANA CRUNCH BREAD

Yield: 2 loaves or 4 mini-loaves.

Bread Break

The original version of this recipe came from my friend Jay, who loaned me his favorite cookbook, *Celebrations of Creations*, published by the Altar and Rosary Society of St. Roch's Church (now closed), in LaSalle, Illinois. The recipe, entitled "Healthy Bunch of Banana Bread," was typed on a piece of paper and tucked inside the book. The paper was much creased and stained with use.

Jay developed this recipe, and I adapted it somewhat, so that's why it has a new name. His version, by the way, included 1 cup chopped dates, soaked in boiling water for 5 minutes and drained.

I kept the book much longer than I intended, which meant that his mother didn't get his "famous" Christmas fruitcake for two years in a row, the lack of which, Jay says, has contributed to his mother's ongoing health!

3 cups **HODGSON MILL 50/50 Wheat Flour** (*see* note)

¼ cup **HODGSON MILL Wheat Germ**

½ cup **HODGSON MILL Cracked Wheat Cereal**

1 ½ teaspoons **baking powder**

1 teaspoon **baking soda**

1 teaspoon **salt**

⅔ cup **milk**

¾ cup **brown sugar**

¼ cup **honey**

7 very ripe **bananas**, peeled and mashed (about 2 ½ cups)

1 cup chopped **pecans**

Butter, melted (optional)

Preheat oven to 350 degrees.

Combine 50/50 flour, wheat germ, cracked wheat cereal, baking powder, baking soda and salt in a medium mixing bowl; stir to mix.

Combine milk, brown sugar and honey in a large mixing bowl; stir until well mixed. Add mashed bananas; mix thoroughly. Add flour mixture to banana mixture; stir until the dry ingredients are just moistened. Fold in pecans. The batter will be rather thick and stiff. Spoon batter into two greased loaf pans (8½ x 4½ x 2½ inches) or four greased mini-loaf pans (5¾ x 3½ x 2 inches).

Bake in preheated 350-degree oven 45 to 50 minutes for regular loaves or 35 to 40 minutes for mini-loaves, or until a cake tester comes out clean. Remove from pans and let cool on wire racks. If desired, brush tops of slightly cooled loaves with butter.

Note: If you've never made banana bread before, you may not know that "very ripe bananas" means "black, mushy, disgusting bananas that aren't good for anything else." The puree will not be pretty, but the finished product is delicious.

If you're wondering how to mash bananas, peel them first, place them in a bowl with steep sides, and use an old-fashioned potato masher to turn them into banana puree. The entire process, including washing the potato masher, takes less time than it takes to pull a blender out from under the counter, clear a space amid the debris, and plug it in.

This is not as cake-like as many banana breads. It's much denser, and the crust is quite crunchy from the wheat germ and cracked wheat. It's a nice change, and provides lots of fiber, too. You can substitute wheat bran for the wheat germ, or all-purpose (white) flour for some or all of the whole wheat.

You'll notice that there is no oil or butter in the recipe. The addition of $1/4$ cup vegetable oil, butter or sour cream does indeed improve the flavor of this bread, but this version is low-fat and more healthful.

HODGSON MILL 50/50 Wheat Flour is a mixture of half whole wheat flour and half unbleached white flour. You can substitute $1 1/2$ cups whole wheat flour and $1 1/2$ cups white flour for the 3 cups 50/50 flour.

Party Pasta Salad
With Lemon Herb Dressing

Yield: 20 servings.

Bread Break

I love pasta salad, and this recipe developed by my kitchen angel Bridget is especially good for a party or other large gathering. If you've never tried roasted peppers or artichoke hearts, this is a great introduction to new flavors.

Not realizing just how much this recipe yields, I once made a triple batch of Party Pasta Salad for Jeff and Todd Schmitt, two brothers who are alumni of the Academy, to serve at their annual end-of-summer party (the "Smitty Smackdown"). I had enough salad for their 30 guests, and fed the entire monastic community as well!

SALAD:

1 pound **HODGSON MILL Four Color Veggie Rotini Spirals**, uncooked

1 cup thinly sliced **red onion**

1 cup thinly sliced roasted **red peppers**

1 (6.5-ounce) jar marinated **artichoke hearts**, drained and cut into small pieces

1 pint **cherry** or **grape tomatoes**, cut in half

DRESSING:

1 cup **olive oil**

2 tablespoons grated **lemon peel**

2 tablespoons finely shredded fresh **basil**

1 tablespoon finely chopped fresh **dill**

$^{1}/_{2}$ cup **red wine vinegar**

1 tablespoon freshly ground **black pepper**

1 tablespoon **salt**

For salad: Cook pasta al dente according to package directions. Drain, rinse, and drain again. Combine pasta, red onion, red peppers, artichoke hearts and tomatoes in a large bowl; toss until evenly distributed.

For dressing: Combine olive oil, lemon peel, basil, dill, vinegar, pepper and salt in a jar with a tight-fitting lid. Shake to mix well.

Drizzle dressing over pasta salad. You want enough dressing to coat the ingredients but you don't want to oversaturate the pasta. Toss to mix well. Cover and refrigerate a few hours or overnight. Serve chilled. Refrigerate any extra dressing for later use.

Note: We used store-bought roasted red peppers to save time and effort. For an attractive presentation, cut the red onion and roasted red peppers in fine julienne, which means cut into matchstick-size pieces. Be careful not to overcook the pasta or it will turn into mush during mixing.

Heritage Breads

Ethnically speaking, I'm a bit of a mongrel. My father's parents were Italian and Danish, whereas my mother's father was Austrian and Grandma Tootsie was full-blood Irish. I often tell people I have the best of everything: Italian pasta, Irish potatoes, Austrian beer and Danish pastries!

All of the nationalities of my ancestors have influenced my experiences as a baker. I grow large plots of Italian herbs for Pull-Apart Garlic Bread and Italian Onion Herb Bread, and of course pizza is a perennial monastery favorite. But every Easter I make Austrian Povitica just like my great-grandmother Sardick did. When my grandmother Helen died this year, I felt privileged to receive a copy of her recipe for Danish kringle, written in her own hand, and I'm looking forward to trying it this Christmas. And Irish Soda Bread makes its way to the abbey table several times a year, in memory of all the McNulty relatives who have made it a family favorite.

Having a sense of family history and feeling connected to our ancestors are powerful forces within the human spirit. Every year I ask my students to research their names and find out as much as they can about their family history for a written report. Many students come back from meetings with older family members and enthusiastically recount stories about immigrant ships and covered wagons, show photos of family farms and first homes, and sometimes, if I'm lucky, get a sense of the bigger picture of history as well. "My great-grandpa helped build the Erie Canal!" one will say, and out will come the map to find just where that is, and why it was important.

But history isn't just about grand building projects, sweeping social changes and military victories. It's also about what people wore, and what kind of gardens they kept, and of course, what sort of bread went on the table. The recipes included in this section are from various ethnic traditions—French, Latino, Ethiopian, Irish—and have their place in history as well. Exploring your cultural heritage through bread can be the start of a lifelong journey of self-discovery.

BRIOCHE

Yield: 1 large loaf; about 12 to 16 servings.

1 package **FLEISCHMANN'S Active Dry Yeast**

1 cup **whole milk**, warmed

1/4 cup **granulated sugar**

4 1/2 cups **HODGSON MILL Naturally White Flour**, divided

4 **eggs**

1 **egg yolk**

1 1/4 teaspoons **salt**

1/2 cup (1 stick) **butter**, softened

1 **egg white** beaten with 1 tablespoon **water**, for egg wash

Granulated sugar, for sprinkling

Combine yeast and warm milk in a large mixing bowl; stir to dissolve. Stir in sugar and 1 cup of the flour. Let stand 15 minutes for yeast to develop. Add eggs, egg yolk and salt; mix well. Add 3 cups of the flour, 1 cup at a time, stirring thoroughly after each addition. The dough will be a very stiff batter, quite sticky.

Turn out dough onto a smooth surface (marble is ideal). Stretch and fold the dough over itself to develop the gluten network. Do this for 8 to 10 minutes, keeping hands lightly dusted with flour to keep the dough manageable. (I keep one hand dusted with flour and hold a bench knife, dough scraper or spatula in the other hand to manipulate the dough.) The dough will eventually become more cohesive, although still sticky. Add the remaining 1/2 cup flour if it's a particularly humid day.

Coat the surface of the dough with oil or butter and put dough in the rinsed mixing bowl. Cover with a towel and let rise in a warm, draft-free place 60 to 90 minutes, or until doubled.

Punch down dough. Knead in butter, about 2 tablespoons at a time, working quickly. There might be some butter visible that is not entirely incorporated, but that's OK. Put dough back in bowl, cover with a damp towel, and refrigerate at least 2 hours or overnight (this helps the dough firm up and become easier to shape).

Lightly grease a large brioche pan (or a 2-quart round baking pan or dish). Punch down dough and briefly knead to expel air

Bread Break

Many recipes for brioche have been simplified to make them more like your usual bread dough recipe. My version is more traditional than most. The first time you make brioche, you might be put off by how soft and sticky the dough is, but don't fret. Once you've worked the butter in and the dough has been refrigerated, it is pretty easy to work with. The hardest part is getting the little topknot to stay in the center of the loaf while it rises. Mine often slide off to one side, giving the brioche a slightly drunken appearance!

Once I knew what I was looking for, I had no trouble finding brioche tins in several different culinary shops. I even bought a stack of small ones in an antique mall that were incorrectly labeled as Jell-O molds! The pans come in a variety of sizes, and I even found one that is a fluted square instead the traditional round. But don't let a lack of special pans keep you from making these excellent little breads—just use standard or large muffin tins. You'll enjoy the bread so much that you'll be inspired to search for the traditional pans as well.

My confreres at St. Bede enjoy having small brioche for breakfast. Brioche is wonderful with unsalted butter and apricot preserves. Brioche doughnuts, however, are the absolute pinnacle of breakfast breads, in my opinion. Incredibly rich and quite addictive, they are the culinary equivalent of mortal sin wrapped in butter cream glaze. I got the idea for using brioche dough for doughnuts from *Blue Ribbon Breads* by Mary Ward and Carol Stine.

bubbles. Pull off one-fourth of the dough and set aside. Form the remaining three-fourths of the dough into a large ball; place in the prepared pan. Form the reserved dough into a small ball. Make an indentation in the top of the large ball and place the small ball on top. Cover and let rise 30 to 45 minutes, or until nearly doubled.

About 15 minutes before the end of rising time, place oven rack in lower third of oven and preheat oven to 350 degrees. Gently brush the top of the risen loaf with egg wash and sprinkle with sugar. Bake brioche 50 to 60 minutes, or until golden to dark brown. Remove from oven and let stand in pan about 30 minutes (this helps the loaf firm up and keeps it from collapsing when it is removed from the pan). Remove from pan and let cool on a wire rack.

~

VARIATIONS:

For small brioche: *After dough has been refrigerated and punched down, divide dough into 12 equal portions. Separate a piece about the size of a large olive from each portion; roll each piece into a ball. Place large balls in lightly greased brioche pans or muffin pans. Make an indentation in each large ball, and place a small ball on top. Cover and let rise until nearly doubled in size, about 30 minutes. Brush with egg wash and sprinkle with sugar. Bake in a preheated 350-degree oven 15 to 20 minutes, or until tops are golden brown. Remove from pans and let cool on wire racks. Makes 12 brioche.*

For doughnuts: *After dough has been refrigerated and punched down, roll out dough on a floured surface to a thickness of 1/4 inch. Use a doughnut cutter to cut out doughnuts and holes. Scraps can be kneaded together and rolled out a second time. Cover doughnuts and holes and let rise 25 to 30 minutes, or until nearly doubled. While doughnuts are rising, heat vegetable oil to 350 to 375 degrees. Fry doughnuts and holes two or three at a time about 2 minutes per side, or until golden brown. Drain on paper towels and let cool slightly. While doughnuts are still warm, dip into Butter Cream Glaze (recipe follows), turning to coat completely. Place on wire racks to let excess glaze drip off, then serve. Makes about 2 dozen doughnuts.*

Butter Cream Glaze

1 cup sifted confectioners' sugar
2 tablespoons butter, softened
2 to 3 tablespoons cream or milk

Combine confectioners' sugar, butter and cream in small bowl; stir until smooth. Makes about 1 1/8 cups glaze.

BRIOCHE

Bread Machine

Yield: 12 rolls.

$^{1}/_{2}$ cup **milk**

2 **eggs**

1 **egg yolk**

$^{1}/_{4}$ cup ($^{1}/_{2}$ stick) **butter** or **margarine**

$^{1}/_{2}$ teaspoon **salt**

2 $^{1}/_{4}$ cups plus 1 tablespoon **HODGSON MILL Best for Bread Flour**

2 tablespoons **granulated sugar**

1 $^{1}/_{2}$ teaspoons **FLEISCHMANN'S Bread Machine Yeast**

1 **egg white** beaten with 1 tablespoon **water**, for egg wash

Granulated sugar, for sprinkling

Add milk, eggs, egg yolk, butter, salt, flour, sugar and yeast to bread machine pan in the order suggested by manufacturer. Select **dough/manual cycle**.

When cycle is complete, remove dough from machine. Place in greased resealable freezer bag; refrigerate 2 to 24 hours.

Remove dough from refrigerator and place on floured surface. Divide into 2 portions, one about three-fourths of the dough and the other about one-fourth of the dough. Divide larger portion into 12 equal pieces; shape each piece into  a ball. Place balls in 12 well-greased 2 $^{1}/_{2}$-inch brioche pans or muffin cups. Divide the smaller portion of dough into 12 equal pieces; shape each piece into a ball. Make a deep indentation in center of each large ball; moisten indentation slightly with cold water. Press 1 small ball into each indentation. Cover and let rise in warm, draft-free place about 45 minutes, or until doubled in size.

Gently brush rolls with egg wash; sprinkle with sugar. Bake in a preheated 375-degree oven 15 minutes, or until golden brown. (If desired, reposition small balls after 5 minutes of baking.) Remove from pans and let cool on wire rack.

ETHIOPIAN AMBASHA

Yield: 3 (6-inch) round loaves.

Bread Break

Ambasha is an exotic bread with spices that are for the most part foreign to American palates. But don't let that keep you from finding ground fenugreek at your local health food store or gourmet shop and trying this bread. Serve it with honey as they do in Ethiopia.

I put it out for the monks one evening without telling them what it was. Some people really liked it, others found it a little off-putting. This recipe makes a relatively small amount so you won't have a lot of leftovers if the response is less than enthusiastic!

Try the recipe once as is. If you don't care for the flavor, the next time you make it try omitting the cardamom or replacing it with $1/8$ teaspoon ground cloves. I've also seen versions of ambasha with coriander and cinnamon accompanying the fenugreek.

1 package **FLEISCHMANN'S Active Dry Yeast**

1 $1/4$ cups warm **water**, divided

1 teaspoon **honey**

$1/4$ cup **vegetable oil**

1 $1/2$ cups **HODGSON MILL Whole Wheat Graham Flour**

2 teaspoons **salt**

1 teaspoon ground **fenugreek**

1 teaspoon ground **cardamom**

1 tablespoon ground **coriander**

1 $1/2$ to 2 cups **HODGSON MILL Naturally White Flour**

Combine yeast, $1/4$ cup of the warm water and honey in a medium mixing bowl; stir to dissolve. Let stand 5 to 10 minutes, or until foamy.

Add the remaining 1 cup warm water, oil and whole wheat flour; stir until thoroughly blended. Cover batter and let stand 15 minutes; the flour will absorb liquid and the yeast will develop.

Add salt, fenugreek, cardamom and coriander; stir until blended. Add white flour, $1/2$ cup at a time, stirring after each addition, until the dough pulls away from the side of the bowl and becomes workable. Turn out dough onto a lightly floured surface. Knead 5 minutes, adding small amounts of flour as needed to make an elastic dough with a smooth consistency that is slightly sticky. Oil the surface of the dough, then put it in the rinsed mixing bowl. Cover with a clean towel and let rise in a warm, draft-free place about 1 hour, or until doubled.

Punch down dough. Divide dough into 3 equal pieces. Roll each piece into a ball; flatten ball into a round, $1/2$- to $3/4$-inch thick. Place rounds on a lightly greased baking sheet. Cover with a towel and let rise 30 minutes, or until nearly doubled.

About 15 minutes before end of rising time, preheat oven to 400 degrees. Bake bread 30 to 35 minutes, or until loaves are lightly browned and sound hollow when tapped. Remove from baking sheet and let cool on wire racks. Serve warm.

Note: Once when I made ambasha, I had run out of whole wheat flour but I had some unprocessed miller's bran. I used 1 cup bran and 1 cup white flour for the initial batter, then used white flour for the rest of the recipe. The resulting dough was beautiful, with hearty-looking flecks of bran throughout.

ETHIOPIAN AMBASHA

Bread Machine

Yield: 2 small flat round loaves.

1 cup **water**

2 tablespoons **vegetable oil**

1 tablespoon **honey**

1 teaspoon **salt**

1/2 teaspoon ground **fenugreek**

1 1/2 teaspoons ground **coriander**

1/2 teaspoon ground **cardamom**

1 cup **HODGSON MILL Whole Wheat Graham Flour**

1 1/2 cups **HODGSON MILL Best for Bread Flour**

1 1/2 teaspoons **FLEISCHMANN'S Bread Machine Yeast**

Add water, oil, honey, salt, fenugreek, coriander, cardamom, flours and yeast to bread machine pan in the order suggested by the manufacturer. Select **dough/manual cycle**.

When cycle is complete, transfer dough from the machine to a lightly floured surface. Lightly knead dough 1 to 2 minutes. Divide dough in half. Roll each half into a ball and flatten each ball into a round, 1/2- to 3/4-inch thick. Place rounds on a lightly greased baking sheet. Cover with a towel and let rise in a warm, draft-free place 30 minutes, or until nearly doubled.

Bake in a preheated 400-degree oven 25 to 30 minutes, or until loaves are lightly browned and sound hollow when tapped. Remove from baking sheet and let cool on wire racks. Serve warm.

CUBAN BREAD

Yield: 2 loaves.

Bread Break

I have seen several different versions of Cuban bread, including one that calls for four tablespoons of yeast (nearly five packages), which seems to me a little excessive. But they all have a few things in common: extra yeast, a large proportion of salt, a cold oven to start, and a pan of hot water to help develop the crust.

One recipe I tested suggested brushing the loaves with cold water before they went into the oven. I did so, as gently as I could, and the loaves deflated, never to rise again. The taste was fine, but the loaves lacked the open-holed texture that characterizes *pan de cubana*.

I also discovered that $^3/_4$ cup of hot water in a pan on the bottom of the oven is just enough to achieve the perfect crust; most recipes don't specify the amount of water.

3 packages **FLEISCHMANN'S Active Dry Yeast**

4 teaspoons **brown sugar**

2 cups warm **water**

5 to 6 cups **HODGSON MILL Best for Bread Flour**, divided

1 tablespoon **salt**

Cornmeal, for sprinkling on baking sheet

1 **egg** or 1 **egg white** mixed with 1 tablespoon **water**, for egg wash

$^3/_4$ cup hot **water**

Combine yeast, brown sugar and warm water in a large mixing bowl; stir to mix. Stir in 2 cups of the flour; beat well. Let stand 10 minutes for yeast to develop. Stir in salt. Add remaining 3 to 4 cups flour, about 1 cup at a time, stirring after each addition, until a stiff dough forms.

Turn out dough onto a lightly floured surface. Knead 8 to 10 minutes, adding more flour as needed to keep dough manageable. Dough should be smooth, elastic and not sticky. Oil the surface of the dough and put it in the rinsed mixing bowl. Cover and let rise in a warm, draft-free place 45 to 60 minutes, or until doubled in bulk.

Punch down dough. Knead lightly. Form into two long loaves. Sprinkle cornmeal on a baking sheet; place loaves on baking sheet. Let rise, uncovered, 10 minutes.

Using a sharp knife or razor blade, make 3 or 4 diagonal slashes in the top of each loaf. Brush loaves with egg wash. Place on middle shelf of a cold oven. Place a shallow pan on the bottom shelf; pour hot water into pan. Set oven temperature at 400 degrees and bake 30 to 35 minutes, or until loaves are well browned and sound hollow when tapped. Remove from baking sheet and let cool on wire racks.

Note: For the best results, this recipe requires bread flour. All-purpose flour works, but it often produces a low loaf if it is not kneaded thoroughly.

Notice the absence of oil or butter in the dough, which makes the bread crustier. This bread is so good you won't have to worry much about leftovers, but if you think you'll use only one loaf within a day, don't freeze the other — just give it away!

This bread is outstanding as a base for quick broiler pizzas. Cut the loaf lengthwise, brush on pizza sauce and add toppings, then warm it under the broiler until the cheese starts to slightly brown. The crisp crust makes a delightful crunch as you bite into it. I also like Cuban bread as a base for submarine sandwiches.

CUBAN BREAD

Yield: 1 loaf.

1 cup plus 3 tablespoons **water**

1 ½ teaspoons **salt**

3 cups **HODGSON MILL Best for Bread Flour**

2 teaspoons **brown sugar**

2 teaspoons **FLEISCHMANN'S Bread Machine Yeast**

Cornmeal, for sprinkling on baking sheet

1 **egg** mixed with 1 tablespoon **water**, for egg glaze

³/₄ cup hot **water**

Add water, salt, flour, brown sugar and yeast to bread machine pan in the order suggested by manufacturer. Select **dough/ manual cycle**.

When cycle is complete, transfer dough to a lightly floured surface. Shape into a long loaf; taper ends by gently rolling back and forth. Place on a baking sheet that has been sprinkled with cornmeal. Let rise, uncovered, 10 minutes.

Using a sharp knife, make 3 or 4 diagonal slashes on top of loaf. Brush with egg glaze. Place on the middle shelf of a cold oven. Place a shallow pan on bottom shelf and add hot water to pan. Set oven temperature at 400 degrees and bake 30 minutes, or until done. Remove from pan and let cool on wire rack.

Yield: 1 round loaf.

Bread Break

Our community was "adopted" by an Irish woman named Marguerite Menne, who used to help out in our apple orchard. She also brought us freshly baked Irish soda bread, in spite of being teased regularly by Abbot David (himself descended from Irish immigrants). Both Abbot David and Marguerite have since died, so I make this soda bread in their memory.

Abbot David was superior of the abbey when I first started visiting St. Bede. I remember an interview with him during which I asked a lot of questions about what kind of work I might do if I joined the monastery. He patiently answered my questions, then finally smiled and remarked, "Remember, brother, we come to the monastery because we are seeking God, not because we are seeking employment."

This is the classic recipe for Irish soda bread: four simple ingredients, very little kneading, a slightly flattened shape, and a cross cut in the top. The flattened shape keeps it from being doughy in the center, and the cross keeps it from cracking during baking.

4 cups **HODGSON MILL Naturally White Flour**

1 teaspoon **baking soda**

¹/₂ teaspoon **salt**

1 ¹/₄ to 1 ¹/₂ cups **buttermilk**

Position an oven rack in center of oven. Preheat oven to 400 degrees.

Sift flour, baking soda and salt into a medium mixing bowl. Make a well in the center, and pour in most of the buttermilk. Stir, adding the remaining buttermilk as needed to make a loose dough.

Turn out dough onto a lightly floured surface. Knead lightly, just enough to make the dough smooth. Place dough on a lightly greased baking sheet and form into a flattened round, about 1- to 1 ¹/₂-inches thick. Cut a cross in the center of the top using a sharp knife dipped in flour.

Bake in preheated 400-degree oven 45 to 50 minutes, or until loaf sounds hollow when tapped on both top and bottom. Remove from pan and transfer to a wire rack. Cover with a clean, dry dish towel and let cool slowly.

Note: *It's best to allow soda bread to cool completely before slicing it. The loaf will continue to cook on the interior, even after it is removed from the oven. Because the dough is soft and rather sticky, I recommend using a sharp knife dipped in flour to cut the cross in the top. The floured knife will easily make the crease and will not stick. You can add 1 cup currants or raisins to the dough, if desired. (See Elegant Soda Bread, page 43.)*

ELEGANT SODA BREAD

Yield: 2 round loaves.

4 cups **HODGSON MILL Naturally White Flour**

1 teaspoon **baking soda**

2 teaspoons **baking powder**

1 teaspoon **salt**

3 tablespoons **granulated sugar**

1 ½ teaspoons ground **coriander**

2 cups **buttermilk**

Butter, melted (optional)

Preheat oven to 375 degrees.

Sift flour, baking soda, baking powder, salt, sugar and coriander into a medium mixing bowl. Gradually add buttermilk, stirring until smooth. The dough will be quite soft; do not overmix.

Divide dough in half. Using floured hands, form each half into a round, slightly flattened shape. Place in greased pie plates. Cut a cross in the center of the top using a sharp knife dipped in flour; the cross keeps the loaf from splitting during baking.

Bake in preheated 375-degree oven 45 to 60 minutes, or until bread sounds hollow when tapped on both top and bottom. Remove from pans and let cool on wire racks. While loaves are still hot, brush the tops with butter, if desired.

Note: If you omit the coriander, reduce the sugar to 2 teaspoons and add 1 (15-ounce) package raisins, you'll have my mother's favorite Irish soda bread recipe. She got it from Mrs. Jones, an Irish woman whose son was a priest who taught my mom in high school in Denver.

Mom used to make soda bread for the bake sale at St. Francis Hospital, which was always held the week before St. Patrick's Day. She'd tie a green ribbon through the cross to make it more attractive for the sale table, but she needn't have bothered. The people working behind the counter often bought it right out of her hand! (See Irish Soda Bread, page 42.)

Bread Break

When I was in my first year of priestly studies at St. Meinrad School of Theology, I often visited Louisville, Kentucky, about 70 miles away. On my first trip there with my friend John, we found a guide of the top 60 restaurants in the city. We decided that we would attempt to eat our way through the guide over the next four years, leaving out any place that required dressing up too much! Of course, we never got past the first 20, because we found a few we really liked and stuck with them.

One of these favorites was a classy but unpretentious place called Jack Fry's on Bardstown Road. They served a coriander soda bread with every entrée, and I used to eat baskets of it. They serve it still, freshly baked by their pastry chef, Robin Ferguson. Her version is richer than this one, using eggs and more sugar, plus a bit of melted butter.

The addition of coriander gives the bread an undercurrent of citrus that is subtle and exquisite.

Yield: 24 samosas.

Bread Break

These spicy, meat-filled buns are found in several countries, including Kenya, Turkey and Afghanistan. Afghan restaurants often serve these as appetizers, sometimes wrapped in puff pastry. I much prefer using bread dough, especially dough made with milk and a bit of sugar.

After several recipe tests with Mike the Deli Guy, I asked a group of monks to sample a batch of samosas and offer their reactions. Father Benedict came into the room and asked what they were eating. Father Philip described the spicy filling and suggested that Father Ben should try a bite. "I dunno," Father Ben demurred, "that doesn't sound very good." Father Philip replied, "Well, you don't have taste buds in your ears, do you? Eat one!" Good advice for whenever we encounter a new food.

$^1/_2$ recipe **Deep-Dish Pizza Dough** (page 53), risen once and punched down

1 pound **lean ground chuck**

4 cloves **garlic**, finely chopped

1 teaspoon **salt**

1 teaspoon ground **cardamom**

$^1/_2$ teaspoon ground **cumin seeds**

$^1/_2$ teaspoon **black pepper**

$^1/_8$ teaspoon ground **cloves**

$^1/_4$ cup **water**

1 large **green bell pepper**, chopped

1 large **onion**, chopped

Vegetable oil, for frying

Prepare dough according to recipe. Use half the dough for this recipe; save remaining half for another use.

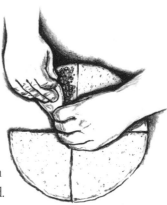

Combine ground beef, garlic, salt, cardamom, cumin seeds, pepper, cloves and water in a medium mixing bowl. Mix with hands until thoroughly blended.

Put meat mixture in a large skillet. Cook over medium heat, stirring frequently, until meat is brown and water is nearly evaporated. Add green pepper and onion; cook until pepper is slightly softened but still a bit crisp. Remove from heat and drain well.

Divide dough into 6 equal portions. Roll each portion into a circle about 8 inches in diameter. Using a sharp knife, cut each circle into quarters (or 4 wedges). In the center of each wedge of dough, place about 1 tablespoon meat mixture. Fold edge over to form a narrow triangle, and crimp edges with a fork to seal. (If you have trouble getting the dough to stick together, brush the edges lightly with water before sealing.)

Heat oil in a deep fryer to 350 degrees. Fry samosas, a few at a time, 2 to 3 minutes per side, or until golden brown. Drain on paper towels. Serve warm.

≈

Note: *Samosas can be baked like calzones instead of fried. Pierce the formed samosas with a fork several times, let rise 30 minutes, then bake in a preheated 425-degree oven about 20 minutes, or until golden brown. I find that the flavor of the spices really comes through in the baked samosas, although I like the appearance of the fried dough better.*

Samosas can be filled with just about anything from breakfast sausage to raw cauliflower, so feel free to adjust the spices or filling. For example, I've seen several recipes that call for 1 teaspoon ground cinnamon in the filling, as well as $1/2$ cup frozen peas added with the bell peppers and onions.

One half of any basic white dough recipe may be used (go ahead and mix up the whole batch and use the rest for pizza dough or baguettes).

BLACK BEAN SOUP

Yield: 4 to 6 servings.

Bread Break

In the past year I have developed a real appreciation for good black bean soup. It started when I was at a conference and went out to dinner with friends at one of those "all-you-can-eat-giant-salad-bar-with-great-soup" restaurants. Unfortunately, their corn bread was nothing special, but the black bean soup they served was excellent. So I decided I had to feature some recipe for it in our second season.

Not long after this, our Father Arthur put a page of recipes in my mailbox (my confreres do this all the time, much to my delight) that included one for black bean soup. I handed it over to my kitchen angel Bridget, who is a regular soup maven, and she adapted it for our use on the show and your enjoyment at home.

2 cups **dried black beans** (see note)

$^1/_4$ cup **olive oil**

1 cup finely chopped **onion**

$^1/_2$ cup finely chopped **carrot**

$^1/_2$ cup finely chopped **celery**

1 tablespoon finely chopped **garlic**

1 tablespoon ground **cumin**

$^1/_2$ teaspoon ground **allspice**

7 cups **water** or **vegetable stock**

2 tablespoons **tomato paste**

1 tablespoon **salt**

1 tablespoon freshly ground **black pepper**

OPTIONAL GARNISH:
Sour cream

Fresh **tomato salsa**

Rinse beans, then put in a large pot and cover with water. Let soak 24 hours. Drain well.

Heat olive oil in a large pot over high heat. Add onion, carrot, celery, garlic, cumin and allspice; cook, stirring occasionally, 5 minutes. Add drained beans and 7 cups water or vegetable stock. Bring to a boil. Reduce heat and simmer, uncovered, about 2 hours, or until beans are tender, adding water as necessary to keep beans covered. Stir occasionally.

Stir in tomato paste, salt and pepper. Taste and adjust seasonings.

If desired, garnish each serving with a dollop of sour cream topped with a spoonful of fresh tomato salsa.

Note: To make this soup using canned beans, omit the dried beans and the soaking step. Combine 4 (15- to 16-ounce) cans black beans, drained, with cooked vegetables and water; simmer 15 to 20 minutes, or until the flavors mix. Complete soup as directed.

HAUSTUS FAVORITES

REFLECTION

On Thursday nights my monastery has a community social called "haustus" (which comes from the Latin for "to be filled or satisfied"). We play cards or board games, listen to music, and enjoy food and drink, including my homemade pizza. Sometimes people are surprised to hear that monks have pizza parties, or that we play cards or watch sports on TV, or any number of activities like "normal" people. But monks need relaxation time as much as anyone, as is illustrated by the following story from a 5th-century monastic text: Once a hunter came upon St. Antony relaxing with the brothers. The hunter was shocked to see them just sitting around. The abbot said to him, "Put an arrow in your bow and shoot it." The hunter did so. Then Antony said, "Shoot another," and again the hunter complied. Then the old man said, "Shoot yet again." The hunter objected, "If I keep bending my bow I will break it." Abbot Antony replied, "It is the same with us. If we stretch the brothers continually, without measure, they will soon break. So sometimes we must relax to meet their needs."

The wisdom of the ancient monks is as pertinent today as it was then. We all need time for rest and relaxation, time for "holy leisure." Unfortunately, we often fill our free time with more busy-ness—clubs, sports, hobbies—all of them good in themselves, but not if they keep us from ever slowing down. I'm often guilty of this tendency, too, which is why I appreciate baking bread so much. It makes me slow down, stick around in one place longer, and spend quality time with my confreres, my family and friends, my students. Periodically in the course of making bread, one has to let the dough rest. The same is true for the baker.

If you want a reason to slow down and enjoy an evening with your family, give everyone a job preparing the dough and ingredients for the pizzas and sandwich breads in this chapter.

CIBATTA

Yield: 2 loaves.

STARTER:

³/₄ cup warm **water**

1 teaspoon **FLEISCHMANN'S Active Dry Yeast** (save the rest of the package for use in the dough)

1 cup **HODGSON MILL Best for Bread Flour**

Pinch **granulated sugar**

DOUGH:

About 1 ¹/₄ teaspoons **FLEISCHMANN'S Active Dry Yeast** (the remainder of the package used for the starter)

1 cup warm **water**

1 teaspoon **salt**

1 tablespoon **olive oil**

1 teaspoon **honey**

2 ¹/₂ cups **HODGSON MILL Best for Bread Flour**

For starter: Prepare the starter 6 to 12 hours ahead. Pour warm water into a large, non-metallic bowl and sprinkle yeast on top; stir to dissolve. Add flour and sugar; beat until smooth. Cover with plastic wrap and let stand in a warm place 6 to 12 hours.

For dough: Dissolve yeast in warm water in a small bowl; add to starter along with salt, oil and honey. Beat until smooth. Add flour (it's OK to add it all at once) and mix until thoroughly incorporated. The dough will be halfway between a batter and regular bread dough — hard to stir but too wet to knead.

Let mixture rest about 5 minutes, then beat and fold dough with a heavy wooden spoon, plastic dough scraper or heavy-duty rubber spatula for 5 minutes. Divide dough in half and place each piece in a heavily oiled bowl or serving platter. Cover with oiled plastic wrap and let rise in a warm, draft-free place 1¹/₂ to 2 hours, or until nearly tripled in bulk.

Heavily flour a baking sheet, and have extra flour available to dust your hands. Very carefully turn out one piece of dough (it will be extremely soft and sticky) onto the floured baking sheet, without deflating the air bubbles. Run your fingers along the

Bread Break

The word *cibatta* means "slipper," and this bread usually assumes that oblong shape. The dough is supposed to be very slack, having a high liquid content, so don't add more flour to make the dough more manageable. The wet dough produces a delightfully thin, crisp crust, and the long rising periods make the interior very soft, with large holes.

Father Ronald says cibatta reminds him of the breads they served at Sant'Anselmo in Rome. Closer to home, Hansen's, a sandwich shop in Peoria, Illinois, serves a chicken salad sandwich in a cibatta with both ends cut off, standing up vertically on the plate! I've also seen a rather squarish cibatta used for a grilled eggplant sandwich at the Pearl Bakery in Portland, Oregon. Their backroom bakers, Steve and Nick, showed me how to handle cibatta dough carefully to keep the air bubbles intact.

sides to plump the loaf and form the distinctive slipper shape. To make the more squarish "cushion" loaf, lift dough in center and allow ends to fold under. Repeat with second loaf on the same sheet. Let rise, uncovered, 30 minutes.

About 15 minutes before end of rising time, preheat oven to 400 degrees. Bake bread 30 to 35 minutes, or up to 40 minutes if you prefer a crisper crust. Remove from pan and let cool on wire racks.

This bread is best eaten on the day it is made, but if you must store it, use a waxed paper bag from the bakery rather than plastic, to keep the crust crisp.

Note: You really do need to use bread flour for this recipe to turn out well. Bread flour is milled from harder wheat with a higher gluten content, so it can stand up to the long fermentation process and keep its shape even in such a slack dough.

Italian Onion Herb Bread

Yield: 2 loaves.

2 tablespoons **vegetable oil**, divided

1/3 cup finely chopped **onion**

1 cup **milk**

1 to 2 tablespoons **dried Italian herb seasoning** (see note)

2 packages **FLEISCHMANN'S Active Dry Yeast**

1 cup warm **water**

1 tablespoon **brown sugar**, divided

2 teaspoons **salt**

5 1/2 to 6 cups **HODGSON MILL Naturally White Flour**, divided

Heat 1 tablespoon of the oil in a skillet. Add onion; cook and stir until onion is translucent but not browned. Remove skillet from heat. Add remaining 1 tablespoon oil, milk and Italian herb seasoning; stir to mix. Set aside to cool to lukewarm.

Combine yeast, warm water and a pinch of the brown sugar in a small bowl; stir to dissolve. Let stand 10 minutes, or until foamy.

Combine milk-onion-herb mixture and salt in a large mixing bowl; stir to mix. Stir in yeast mixture and the remaining brown sugar. Add 2 cups of the flour; mix thoroughly. Add 3 cups of the flour, one cup at a time, mixing well after each addition. Add as much of the remaining 1/2 to 1 cup flour, about 1/4 cup at a time, as needed to make a moderately stiff dough.

Turn out dough onto a lightly floured surface. Knead 6 to 8 minutes, or until dough is smooth, shiny and slightly sticky. Lightly oil the surface of the dough and place in the rinsed mixing bowl. Cover with a dish towel and let rise in a warm, draft-free place about 1 hour, or until doubled.

Punch down dough. Knead about 1 minute. Form dough into 2 long loaves and place on greased baking sheet or in greased "W" baking pan. Let rise 30 to 45 minutes, or until nearly doubled.

About 15 minutes before end of rising time, preheat oven to 375 degrees. Bake bread 45 minutes, or until loaves are golden

Bread Break

This bread sells very well at the Medieval Faire every year, mainly because the aroma of the finished loaves is so irresistible. The bread is good alongside any pasta dish, and is delicious sliced into rounds and served with salami and cheese. You can use sandwich loaf pans if you like, but I prefer to make long, Italian-style loaves, either on a baking sheet or in the "W" pans designed specifically for long, skinny loaves.

I'm often inspired to make this bread when the abbey herb garden is in desperate need of pruning. I ruthlessly trim garlic chives, lop off the top third of oregano plants, thin the parsley, and pinch back the basil until I have enough fresh herbs for a triple batch of dough. Then I ask the kitchen manager if we can change the supper menu from meatloaf to spaghetti and meatballs!

brown and sound hollow when tapped. Remove from pans and let cool on wire racks.

Note: *The first time you make this bread, use 1 tablespoon Italian herb seasoning and see if that's enough for your palate. If not, increase it to 2 tablespoons the next time. You can use any Italian herb seasoning you like, commercial or homemade.*

You can try other herb mixtures in this recipe, as well. I made it once with a combination of lovage, savory and parsley, and the community devoured six large loaves at a single meal!

If you are short on time, omit the onions and just warm the milk to 110 degrees before adding it to other ingredients along with the oil.

Bread Machine

ITALIAN ONION HERB BREAD

Yield: 1 (1 ½-pound) loaf.

3 teaspoons **vegetable oil,** divided

3 tablespoons finely chopped **onion**

½ cup plus 2 tablespoons **water**

½ cup **milk**

1 teaspoon **salt**

2 ¾ cups **HODGSON MILL Best for Bread Flour**

1 ½ teaspoons **brown sugar**

1 to 1 ½ teaspoons **Italian herb seasoning**

1 ½ teaspoons **FLEISCHMANN'S Bread Machine Yeast**

Heat 1 ½ teaspoons of the oil in a small skillet. Add onion; cook and stir until onion is translucent.

Add water, milk, remaining 1 ½ teaspoons oil, the onion mixture, salt, flour, brown sugar, Italian herb seasoning and yeast to bread machine pan in the order suggested by manufacturer. Select **basic cycle; medium/normal color setting.**

DEEP-DISH PIZZA DOUGH

Yield: Enough dough for 2 (14-inch) deep-dish pizzas or 4 (8- to 10-inch) pizzas.

1 cup warm **water**

1 package **FLEISCHMANN'S Active Dry Yeast**

2 tablespoons **granulated sugar**

1 cup warm **milk**

¼ cup **olive oil**

1 teaspoon **salt**

½ cup **HODGSON MILL Yellow Corn Meal**

4 ½ to 5 cups **HODGSON MILL Naturally White Flour**, divided

Combine warm water, yeast and sugar in a large mixing bowl; stir to dissolve. Let stand 5 minutes. Add warm milk, olive oil, salt, cornmeal and 3 cups of the flour; stir until well blended. Add 1 cup of the flour; mix with your hands until flour is thoroughly incorporated. Add remaining ½ to 1 cup flour, about ¼ cup at a time, mixing after each addition, until a soft dough is formed that pulls away from the sides of the bowl.

Turn out dough onto a lightly floured surface. Knead 6 to 8 minutes, adding small amounts of flour as needed to keep dough manageable. When finished, the dough should be slightly soft but should spring back when pushed. Lightly oil the surface of the dough and put in the rinsed mixing bowl. Cover with a towel and let rise in a warm, draft-free place 60 to 90 minutes, or until doubled.

Punch down dough. Knead about 1 minute. Oil the surface again and place back in bowl. Cover and let rise in a warm, draft-free place 60 minutes. (Or let rise in refrigerator for several hours. Let the dough stand at room temperature 30 minutes before proceeding.)

Punch down dough. Briefly knead. Divide dough in half. Each half is enough for 1 large (14-inch) deep-dish pizza or 2 medium (8- to 10-inch) pizzas. To save half of the dough for later use, tightly wrap dough in two layers of plastic wrap and refrigerate for 2 or 3 days.

Bread Break

I realize that enough dough for two 14-inch pizzas seems like a lot, but the dough keeps well in the fridge, and can be used for thick-crust pizza or be baked as loaves. The addition of ½ cup cornmeal gives this dough a unique texture and flavor, which my monastic brethren appreciate both as pizza crust and as sandwich bread. I doubt it will go to waste, but if you're worried about that, the recipe can be halved. For my monastic family, I have to double it!

Bread Machine

DEEP-DISH PIZZA DOUGH

Yield: Enough dough for 1 (14-inch) deep-dish pizza or 2 (8- to 10-inch) pizzas.

1 cup plus 1 tablespoon **water**

2 tablespoons **olive oil**

$^1/_2$ teaspoon **salt**

1 tablespoon **granulated sugar**

2 tablespoons **nonfat dry milk powder**

$^1/_4$ cup **HODGSON MILL Yellow Corn Meal**

2 $^1/_2$ cups **HODGSON MILL Best for Bread Flour**

2 teaspoons **FLEISCHMANN'S Bread Machine Yeast**

Add water, oil, salt, sugar, dry milk, cornmeal, flour and yeast to bread machine pan in the order suggested by the manufacturer. Select **dough/manual cycle**.

When cycle is complete, transfer dough from the machine to a lightly floured surface. If necessary knead in enough additional flour to make dough easy to handle.

Top dough with your favorite pizza toppings or follow the topping directions in the recipe for Deep-Dish Pizza (page 55).

DEEP-DISH PIZZA

Yield: 1 (14-inch) or 2 (8- to 10-inch) pizzas.

½ recipe **Deep-Dish Pizza Dough** (page 53)

1 pound **mozzarella cheese**, shredded (about 4 cups), divided

2 cups chopped **tomatoes**, drained

2 tablespoons finely chopped fresh **herbs** or 1 tablespoon dried (basil, rosemary, marjoram, etc.)

4 cloves **garlic**, finely chopped

1 pound **Italian sausage**, browned and drained (or, 5 Italian link sausages, broiled; cut into slices and then cut slices into quarters)

1 cup **tomato sauce** or **pizza sauce**

Grated **Romano cheese**

ANY OR ALL OF THE FOLLOWING TOPPINGS:

24 thin slices **pepperoni**

3 **green**, **red** and/or **yellow bell peppers**, seeded and cut into matchstick pieces

½ cup sliced or chopped **ripe (black) olives**

½ to 1 cup finely chopped **onion**

8 fresh **mushrooms**, sliced

12 **baby artichoke hearts**, halved

1 small **eggplant**, thinly sliced

Prepare Deep-Dish Pizza Dough according to recipe. Divide dough in half and use half for this recipe. Refrigerate the other half for another use.

Lightly grease a 14-inch deep-dish pizza pan (or two 8- to 10-inch pizza pans). Roll out dough to a circle about 1 inch wider than the pan. Place dough in pan and press to form bottom and sides of crust; the dough should come about halfway up the sides of the pan. Let dough rest 15 to 20 minutes. While dough is resting, preheat oven to 450 degrees.

Now, add toppings of choice. Begin with a layer of shredded mozzarella cheese (use about 2⅔ cups of the cheese; reserve the rest to put on top). Then add layers of tomatoes, herbs, garlic and sausage. Add any other desired toppings (see ingredient list for suggestions). Spoon tomato sauce over all. (I like to save the bell

Bread Break

Deep-dish pizza was popularized in the mid-1940s in Chicago as a one-dish casserole meal to help stretch the family budget, especially when meat was rationed but victory garden produce was plentiful.

I avoided making deep-dish pizza for many years because I thought it might be difficult, in spite of the fact that I had watched my mother make it for us in an ordinary lasagna pan. But the very first time I tried it for the brothers at the abbey, this deep-dish beauty came out of the oven looking like something that belonged on a magazine cover! You won't believe how easy it is until you try it.

peppers for the top layer, because they look so beautiful.) Top with reserved 1 1/3 cups mozzarella cheese and a generous sprinkling of grated Romano cheese.

Bake in preheated 450-degree oven 35 to 40 minutes (less for smaller pizzas), or until crust is golden and the top is melted and slightly browned. Remove from oven and let stand 5 to 10 minutes before serving.

Note: *The dough for this pizza is more enriched than for traditional thin-crust pizzas, and is somewhat more bread-like, so the bottom crust will not be crunchy. If you prefer a firmer crust, bake at 450 degrees 15 minutes, then lower the temperature to 375 degrees and bake 20 to 30 minutes. Loosely cover top with foil if the cheese or crust begins to brown too quickly.*

Metal and stoneware pizza pans are available (follow manufacturer's instructions for care and use). In a pinch, you can use heavy-duty cake pans.

Quattro Formaggio Pizza

Yield: 1 (12- to 14-inch) pizza.

$^1/_2$ recipe **Deep-Dish Pizza Dough** (page 53)

8 ounces **mozzarella cheese**, shredded (about 2 cups)

6 ounces **ricotta cheese**

4 ounces **provolone cheese**, shredded (about 1 cup)

2 ounces **Romano cheese**, grated (about $^1/_2$ cup)

1 **egg**

$^1/_2$ teaspoon ground **nutmeg**

$^1/_4$ cup snipped fresh **chives** or **garlic chives**

16 to 24 slices **plum tomato**

Salt

Freshly ground **black pepper**

Prepare Deep-Dish Pizza Dough according to recipe. Divide dough in half and use half for this recipe. Refrigerate the other half for another use.

Lightly grease a 14-inch deep-dish pizza pan (or two 8- to 10-inch pizza pans). Roll out dough to a circle about 1 inch wider than the pan. Place dough in pan and press to form bottom and sides of crust; the dough should come about halfway up the sides of the pan. Let dough rest 15 to 20 minutes. While dough is resting, preheat oven to 450 degrees.

Combine mozzarella, ricotta, provolone and Romano cheeses in a medium mixing bowl. Add egg, nutmeg and chives. Mix with hands until thoroughly blended. Spread cheese mixture evenly over pizza crust. Arrange tomato slices on top.

Bake in preheated 450-degree oven 15 minutes, or until cheese starts to brown. Season to taste with salt and pepper. Serve hot.

Bread Break

This is one of my favorite pizzas, especially when we have fresh homegrown tomatoes. Plum tomatoes are best, because they have more flesh and less juice, but other tomatoes work fine if you drain the slices for at least an hour before use.

Try to get a strongly flavored, well-aged provolone cheese. Don't be afraid to ask the deli worker for sample slices. You can experiment with other cheeses (Parmesan, Asiago, fontina, etc.) or vary the proportions. I prepare this pizza differently every time, depending upon what's in the fridge, and I'm never disappointed.

Big Ol' Batch o' Pizza Sauce

Yield: About 1 ½ gallons.

About 25 pounds **fresh tomatoes** (to produce 2 gallons tomato puree)

4 (12-ounce) cans **tomato paste**

1 tablespoon minced fresh **thyme**

1 tablespoon minced fresh **basil**

2 tablespoons minced fresh **chives**

2 tablespoons minced fresh **oregano**

4 cloves **garlic**, minced

½ teaspoon **black pepper**

¼ cup grated **Romano cheese**

¼ cup **granulated sugar** (optional)

1 to 2 teaspoons **salt** (optional)

Bread Break

At St. Bede we have a huge vegetable garden, faithfully tended by Brother Bede and Brother Luke. We get terrific fresh spinach, marvelously crisp green beans, and the best cantaloupes I've ever tasted. But like many gardeners, the brothers often bring in more tomatoes than we could possibly use. Because I make pizza so often and have plenty of fresh herbs, I decided to develop a recipe for a big ol' batch of pizza sauce that uses those giant, overripe tomatoes that might otherwise go to waste. The sauce can be frozen in single-serving containers for use all winter long.

The first time I tried to make pizza sauce, I didn't measure anything. I just threw in herbs, cheese and chopped onions until it looked right. The result was the most exquisite *spaghetti* sauce I have ever tasted — and which I have been unable to repeat, then or since.

The first step is to prepare the tomato puree. Remove stems, skins and seeds from very ripe tomatoes; cut tomatoes into 2-inch pieces. Process, in batches, in an electric blender or food processor until smooth. Transfer puree to a 9- or 10-quart stainless steel pot. Simmer, uncovered, over low heat, stirring occasionally, for three or four hours, or until reduced by half. Do not allow it to come to a full boil or it will scorch on the bottom; be patient.

Add tomato paste; mix thoroughly. (You might want to transfer the sauce to a smaller pot.) Add thyme, basil, chives, oregano, garlic, pepper and Romano cheese; stir to mix. Simmer, covered, 30 minutes. Add salt and/or sugar to taste.

Place the pot in a sink full of ice to cool the sauce. Divide sauce among freezer bags or other airtight plastic containers. Store in freezer until needed.

~

Note: *Pizza sauce is best made from plum tomatoes, but we grow the usual beefsteak variety, and that's what I've used for this recipe. If you use plum tomatoes, it won't take as long to reduce the mixture, and you might get a larger yield.*

If you have an old-fashioned food mill (and yes, you can still buy them), you won't have to remove the skins and seeds from the tomatoes. Just cut the tomatoes into pieces and process in the blender briefly — just a pulse or two. Then run the mixture through the food mill, which will strain out the skin and seeds and finish the puree.

Regarding the sugar and salt: Don't add it until the end of the final sim-
mering period, and taste the sauce first. Your tomatoes might be plenty
sweet, but a little sugar does take the edge off the acidic flavor that
some tomatoes have. The salt might not be necessary at all if you tend
to use salty pizza toppings such as sausage, pepperoni, bacon or
anchovies.

You can make this recipe over two or three days if you don't have sev-
eral hours of free time. Simmer the mixture for 2 hours, then cool the
pot of sauce in a sink full of ice. Cover the pot with plastic wrap and
refrigerate it for 1 or 2 days. During that time, the tomato pulp will set-
tle to the bottom. When you're ready to continue cooking, you'll be
able to skim the thin, watery juice off the top and speed up the reduc-
tion process. Just remember, cold sauce placed on a hot burner has to
be stirred more often to keep from scorching.

If you use dried herbs, cut the amounts in half. The flavor of dried chives
can be a little bland, so you might substitute 1 or 2 teaspoons onion
powder. The pepper, salt and sugar amounts will remain the same.

PARMESAN CREAM SAUCE

Yield: Enough to cover one 14-inch pizza.

Bread Break

I served my first white pizza, made with scallops and this cream sauce, to a group of volunteers who came to decorate the gym for a big fundraiser. The recipe was both a success and a failure: Everyone said the pizza was excellent and insisted I had to go make another, then everyone was so full that no more work got done on the project for the rest of the evening!

This sauce is delicious tossed with cooked pasta and served hot. You can add all sorts of flavors to the sauce — herbs, crumbled bacon, cooked onions, etc. However, my favorite use for the sauce is as a white pizza topping.

1 (8-ounce) package
   cream cheese

$^3/_4$ cup **milk**

$^1/_2$ cup grated
   Parmesan cheese

Black pepper, to taste

Ground **nutmeg**, to taste

$^1/_4$ cup finely chopped **fresh
   chives**, **garlic chives** or
   green onions (optional)

Cut cream cheese into cubes. Combine cheese cubes, milk and Parmesan cheese in top of a double boiler over simmering water. (You can use a 1-quart saucepan, but be careful not to have the heat too high or you'll scorch the sauce.) Stir mixture until smooth. Add pepper and/or nutmeg to taste (no more than $^1/_4$ teaspoon of either). If desired, stir in chives, garlic chives or green onions.

Note: I like to use this sauce as a pizza topping, along with scallops cooked with garlic and a light sprinkling of slivered almonds. For a large (12- to 14-inch) pizza, use $^1/_3$ to $^1/_2$ pound bay scallops; if you use the larger sea scallops, cut them into halves or quarters. Heat 2 tablespoons olive oil in a skillet; add scallops and 2 or 3 cloves garlic, finely chopped. Cook over medium heat, stirring frequently, until scallops just begin to turn opaque white. Remember, the scallops will get heated when the pizza bakes, so don't overcook them. Usually I dump the whole business — scallops, oil and all — into the cream sauce and stir. Then I reduce the heat and the mixture stays warm in the double boiler while I roll out the pizza dough. (I prefer a thinner crust for this style of gourmet pizza.) Spread the sauce evenly over the crust, then sprinkle $^1/_4$ cup slivered almonds over the sauce. Bake as usual. The cream sauce will brown slightly in a few places, rather than being evenly browned all over like a cheese pizza.

USING THE GOOD CHINA

W e had one minor disaster during the taping of the second season: When Josh was pulling my favorite stoneware bowl out of the soapy dishwater, it slipped out of his hands and broke against the metal sink. I came back to the prep kitchen, and he said he had something to apologize for and showed me the bowl in three pieces on the counter.

I was disappointed, of course, but I didn't yell, since throwing a fit wouldn't fix the bowl, and Josh felt bad enough already. But I didn't get upset for another reason. The bowl was handmade by my friend Jerry, who made much of the stoneware we use on the program. I had used this bowl several times a week for seven years. It had held hundreds of batches of dough that fed confreres, family and friends; had been used to make garlic bread for parties and pizza dough for haustus nights; had served as a faithful partner to my dough whisk when I developed the recipes for both seasons of the show. I would rather have it broken in the course of being used than keep it like a relic for years, only to maybe knock it off a shelf while I was dusting.

My mom and I have a running joke about people who keep things "for good"—like the "good china" or "my good earrings." We were in an antique shop and saw a beautiful beaded purse from the '20s. It was in mint condition, still in the original packaging. My mom exclaimed, "See, she kept it for good—and then she died!" Evidently, the day for "good" never came.

So I decided long ago to use the good china—my great-grandma Jensen's Limoges teacup and saucer for everyday tea, for example—and not to worry about whether it breaks. I use Jerry's stoneware bowls instead of plastic or stainless, and chop herbs with an antique mezzaluna. It's not that I'm careless with valuables or unsentimental about heirlooms. It's just that I don't believe in waiting for "good" to come; the time for good is now. I suspect great-grandma Jensen would want it that way.

This chapter focuses on breads that can be served with coffee at the kitchen table or with tea in the parlor. And for heaven's sake, use the good china!

REFLECTION

BASIC SWEET DOUGH

Yield: 1 recipe of dough.

3 1/2 to 4 cups **HODGSON MILL Naturally White Flour**, divided

1 package **FLEISCHMANN'S RapidRise Yeast**

1 teaspoon **salt**

1 cup **half-and-half** or **light cream**

1/4 cup (1/2 stick) **butter**

1/3 cup **granulated sugar**

1 **egg**, beaten

1/2 teaspoon **vanilla extract**

Sift 2 cups of the flour, yeast and salt into a large mixing bowl; stir until well blended.

Place half-and-half, butter and sugar in a saucepan; heat until butter is nearly melted. Let cool to 120 to 130 degrees.

Add half-and-half mixture to flour mixture; beat well. Add egg and vanilla; stir until blended. Add 1 cup flour; stir until thoroughly incorporated. Gradually add enough of the remaining 1/2 to 1 cup flour to make a soft dough that is rather sticky.

Turn out dough onto a lightly floured surface. Knead 3 minutes, or until the dough is a consistent texture. Cover with a slightly damp towel and let rest 10 minutes.

Use Basic Sweet Dough as directed in one of the following recipes, or in other recipes.

~

Bread Break

We often have guests at the monastery, assiduously cared for by our guest master, Father Marion. Visiting priests, oblates of the abbey, men and women on retreat, and monk's relatives frequently join us for prayers, Mass and meals. These visitors sometimes express the hope that I'll be baking "something special" during their stay, and I find that this Basic Sweet Dough makes it easy to accommodate them. The dough is so quick and versatile that I can create a dramatic breakfast bread with whatever's on hand in the kitchen. If we're out of half-and-half, I substitute whole milk enriched with a bit of sour cream.

Both the Lattice Braid and the Swedish Tea Ring are quite rich and should be served only on special occasions rather than as an "everyday" breakfast.

BASIC SWEET DOUGH

Yield: 1 recipe of dough.

1 cup **half-and-half** or
    light cream

$^1/_4$ cup ($^1/_2$ stick) **butter**

1 **egg**

$^1/_2$ teaspoon **vanilla extract**

5 tablespoons
    granulated sugar

1 teaspoon **salt**

4 cups **HODGSON MILL
    Naturally White Flour**

2 $^1/_2$ teaspoons
    **FLEISCHMANN'S Bread
    Machine Yeast**

Add half-and-half, butter, egg, vanilla, sugar, salt, flour and yeast
to bread machine pan in the order suggested by the manufacturer. Select **dough/manual cycle**.

When cycle is complete, remove dough from the machine to a
lightly floured surface. If necessary, knead in enough additional
flour to make dough easy to handle. Use as directed in Lattice
Braid (page 65), Swedish Tea Ring (page 66), Nested Eggs (page
67), Chanukah Jelly Doughnuts (page 79) or other recipes.

Tip: *Instead of a homemade filling or preserves, you could substitute
1 (12-ounce) can ready-to-use filling for pastries, cakes and desserts
(such as Solo).*

LATTICE BRAID

Yield: 1 loaf; about 12 slices.

1 recipe **Basic Sweet Dough**
  (either regular or bread
  machine, page 63 or 64)

½ cup **preserves** or **jam**
  (not jelly)

ICING:

1 cup **confectioners' sugar**

¼ teaspoon **vanilla extract**

2 tablespoons **milk** or
  light cream

Dash **salt**

Roll out dough on lightly floured surface to make a 16x12-inch rectangle. Spread preserves (your favorite flavor) lengthwise down the center third of the dough. Using a sharp knife, cut each outer third of the dough—plain dough not covered with preserves—into 16 (1-inch wide) diagonal strips, cutting from edge of dough to edge of the preserves. Fold the dough strips over the preserves, alternating left and right, to make a "braid." Tuck in the ends of the last strips to seal.

Carefully transfer loaf to a lightly greased baking sheet. Cover and let rise in a warm, draft-free place 45 minutes, or until nearly doubled.

About 15 minutes before end of rising time, preheat oven to 350 degrees. Bake loaf 20 to 25 minutes, or until lightly browned. Use large spatulas to remove loaf from pan and place it on a wire rack to cool.

While loaf is cooling, prepare icing. Combine confectioners' sugar, milk, vanilla and salt in a small bowl; stir until smooth. While loaf is still warm, drizzle icing over top. Serve warm.

Bread Break

The lattice braid is such an easy technique to learn that I have used it often with beginners, including a group of teenagers in a maximum-security correctional facility in Texas. They weren't quite sure what to make of a baker monk in tennis shoes, but their breads all turned out beautifully, and we even made homemade butter to spread on the fresh loaves.

You can use any flavor of jam or preserves, or even canned pie filling. My friend Moira sent me homemade fig preserves last Christmas. I made a double layer of filling with orange-flavored cream cheese topped with the fig preserves and golden raisins. The flavor combination was truly exquisite.

SWEDISH TEA RING

Yield: 1 tea ring; about 20 servings.

Bread Break

Personally, I find this tea ring a little too sweet (I think it's the dates that make it so) and would tend to reduce both the granulated and brown sugar in the filling by half. But I was overruled by the response of my fellow monks, who devoured an entire ring the first time it appeared at breakfast. Several confreres objected strenuously to my changing anything, especially Father Marion, who had three slices. So I leave it up to you to decide.

¹/₄ cup **granulated sugar**

¹/₄ cup **brown sugar**

¹/₂ cup chopped pitted **dates**

¹/₂ cup **raisins**

¹/₂ cup chopped **walnuts**

¹/₂ teaspoon ground **cinnamon**

¹/₈ teaspoon ground **nutmeg**

1 recipe **Basic Sweet Dough** (either regular or bread machine, page 63 or 64)

3 tablespoons **butter**, softened

Icing (optional; see **Lattice Braid**, page 65)

For date filling, combine granulated sugar, brown sugar, dates, raisins, walnuts, cinnamon and nutmeg in a bowl; toss or stir to mix.

Roll out dough on a lightly floured surface to make a 20x15-inch rectangle. Brush dough with butter, leaving a ¹/₂-inch border all around the edge. Evenly spread the date filling on buttered dough. Starting at the long edge, tightly roll up dough as for a jelly roll. Pinch seam to seal. Shape roll into a ring. Place ring seam-side down on a lightly greased baking sheet. Using a pair of sharp scissors, cut about three-fourths of the way through the ring at 1-inch intervals. Pull out each segment and slightly twist to expose the swirl of filling. Cover and let rise in a warm, draft-free place 45 minutes, or until nearly doubled.

About 15 minutes before end of rising time, preheat oven to 350 degrees. Bake ring 25 to 30 minutes, or until lightly browned (ring will not brown much near the center). Remove from pan and let cool on a wire rack. If desired, brush the still-warm ring with icing (see Lattice Braid for icing recipe).

Nested Eggs

Yield: 8 nests.

1 recipe **Basic Sweet Dough**
(either regular or bread
machine, page 63 or 64)

8 **eggs** in the shell, uncooked,
dyed or plain

1 **egg** mixed with 2 tablespoons
water, for egg wash

Sesame seeds

Divide dough into 16 equal
portions. Roll each portion
into a rope about 12 inches
long. Twist two ropes together,
then form the twisted rope
into an oval; trim excess
dough as necessary to make a continuous twist. Save the
trimmed excess dough and roll it out to form a bottom for the
"nest"; place the oval twist on top of the rolled-out dough. Place
an uncooked egg (still in the shell) in the nest — you can color
the eggs for Easter or Christmas, if you wish. Place the nest on a
lightly greased baking sheet. Repeat with remaining dough and
eggs. Cover and let rise in a warm, draft-free place 30 to 45 minutes, or until nearly doubled.

About 15 minutes before the end of rising time, preheat oven to
350 degrees. Brush the dough (but not the eggs) with egg wash;
sprinkle dough with sesame seeds. Bake 20 to 25 minutes, or
until golden brown. Remove from pan and let cool on racks.

Bread Break

I made these Nested Eggs for
Easter and they were a
charming addition to the
buffet table. They are a bit
time consuming, and you
might want to have help
rolling the dough into ropes
and forming the nests.

You can serve these little
breads for breakfast or
lunch. Be sure to use
uncooked eggs; while the
dough is baking, the egg
cooks perfectly.

The Greeks make a similar
bread for Easter. It is flavored
with anise seed and baked
in a large ring with five eggs,
dyed bright red, nestled in
the twisted braid. It makes a
dramatic centerpiece for the
Easter dinner table.

ENGLISH MUFFIN BREAD

Yield: 3 to 4 mini-loaves or small cylindrical loaves.

Bread Break

I enjoy an English muffin as an afternoon snack rather than as a breakfast bread. When I saw a set of stoneware baking crocks at my buddy Rusty's shop, I knew I had to develop a recipe for English muffin bread. I suspect you could use 15-ounce cans for a round form if you can't find stoneware crocks, but it might affect the baking time.

English muffin bread seems to be quite popular in many bed-and-breakfast inns, and more bakeries are carrying it, so there are lots of versions of this recipe out there. Bread machine and microwave versions abound, but many of the recipes I've seen in cookbooks or on the Internet seem almost indistinguishable from ordinary white bread, and some have way too much salt. I think you'll enjoy this version, which is fast and easy and develops the lovely large holes that catch melted butter and jam so well.

This bread is actually better if served after it has cooled

3 cups **HODGSON MILL Naturally White Flour**

1 package **FLEISCHMANN'S RapidRise Yeast**

2 tablespoons **granulated sugar**

1 teaspoon **salt**

$^{1}/_{4}$ teaspoon **baking soda**

1 cup **milk**

$^{3}/_{4}$ cup **water**

Cornmeal, for sprinkling on pan and batter

Combine flour, yeast, sugar, salt and baking soda in a medium mixing bowl; stir to mix. Combine milk and water in a saucepan; heat to 120 to 130 degrees. Add milk mixture to flour mixture and beat well for about 5 minutes. It will make a slightly stiff batter. Let batter rest 10 minutes.

Grease four 5 $^{3}/_{4}$ x 3 $^{1}/_{2}$ x 2-inch mini-loaf pans or four 3 $^{1}/_{2}$ x 4-inch stoneware baking crocks and sprinkle with cornmeal. Stir down batter. Spoon batter into prepared pans or crocks. Pans should be about half-filled with batter. Lightly sprinkle cornmeal on top of batter. Cover with a light towel and let rise in a warm, draft-free place 20 to 30 minutes, or until batter nearly reaches the top of the pan.

While batter is rising, preheat oven to 400 degrees. Bake bread 30 minutes; if loaves begin to brown too quickly, loosely cover with aluminum foil. Remove from pans and let cool on wire rack.

Note: If you'd like something a little more bread-like, add another cup of flour (some of the brethren at St. Bede prefer it that way). You also can substitute 1 cup whole wheat flour for 1 cup of the white flour — my favorite version. Depending on kitchen conditions, yeast and other factors, you may get four loaves, or you may only get three. Just be sure to fill the pans halfway.

English Muffin Bread

Yield: 1 (1 ½-pound) loaf.

½ cup **water**

½ cup **milk**

1 teaspoon **salt**

2 ¾ cups plus 2 tablespoons **HODGSON MILL Best for Bread Flour**

2 tablespoons **granulated sugar**

1 ½ teaspoons **FLEISCHMANN'S Bread Machine Yeast**

¼ teaspoon **baking soda**

Add water, milk, salt, flour, sugar, yeast and baking soda to bread machine pan in the order suggested by manufacturer. Select **basic cycle; medium/normal color setting**.

completely — at least three hours. If you bake it in the evening, you can leave the loaves out overnight, covered lightly with a clean, dry towel. There's no need to stay up waiting for the bread to cool, and it will be ready to serve in the morning. It is excellent toasted, of course.

When I made this bread in the studio during taping and shared it with the crew, every single one of them asked for the recipe, and several people came back the next day and said they'd made it for their families. So it's sure to become one of your favorites as well.

Lemon Raisin Buns

Yield: 12 buns.

Bread Break

This recipe was inspired by an old recipe for the sweet buns that were served in the Moravian Church during the services. The lemon flavor is rather subtle. If you wish, you can use the juice and grated peel of two lemons, or add 1 teaspoon lemon extract.

Often during taping I have to bake sample loaves the night before to use on camera the next day. One night I was alone in the studio baking these lemon buns and because they smelled so good coming out of the oven, I felt compelled to share with somebody. So I tracked down the overnight cleaning crew and gave them some for their midnight coffee break. But that's typical of bakers—the harder we work, the more we want to share.

3 to 3 ¹/₂ cups **HODGSON MILL Naturally White Flour**, divided

1 package **FLEISCHMANN'S RapidRise Yeast**

¹/₂ teaspoon **salt**

¹/₄ teaspoon ground **mace** (or **nutmeg**)

¹/₂ cup **milk**

¹/₄ cup **honey**

¹/₄ cup **water**

2 tablespoons **butter**

1 **egg**, beaten

Grated **peel** and **juice** of 1 large **lemon**

¹/₂ cup **raisins**

Melted **butter** and **granulated sugar**, for topping

Place 2 cups of the flour in a medium mixing bowl. Add yeast, salt and mace; stir until well blended. Combine milk, honey, water and butter in a small saucepan; heat over medium heat, stirring frequently, until butter is nearly melted and mixture is 120 to 130 degrees. Add milk mixture to flour mixture; stir until well blended. Add egg, lemon peel and lemon juice; mix well. Add 1 cup of the flour; stir until flour is thoroughly incorporated.

Turn out dough onto a lightly floured surface. Knead 2 or 3 minutes, adding small amounts of the remaining ¹/₂ cup flour to keep the dough manageable. Dough will be soft and rather sticky because of the honey. Cover dough with a towel and let rest 10 minutes. The dough will firm up and become easier to handle.

Flatten dough until it is about ¹/₂-inch thick. Sprinkle raisins on top. Fold sides of dough to the center, over the raisins. Knead about 3 minutes, or until raisins are evenly distributed, adding small amounts of the remaining flour as needed to make an elastic dough.

Divide dough into 12 portions; roll each portion into a ball. Place balls in greased standard-size muffin pans (2 ¹/₂ x 1 ¹/₄-inch cups). Cover and let rise in a warm, draft-free place about 1 hour, or until doubled.

About 15 minutes before end of rising time, preheat oven to

350 degrees. Bake buns 15 to 20 minutes, or until lightly browned. Remove from pans and let cool on wire racks 10 minutes. While buns are still warm, brush with melted butter and roll in granulated sugar. These are best served warm.

Note: When I was first experimenting with this recipe, I was using amounts sufficient to make 24 small buns, which seemed like too many for the average family (although about right for my monastic family). Then I tried making 12 large buns, but that made for almost too hearty of a serving. (Abbot Roger said that he could barely finish one, and that he was full all morning!) So I halved the recipe, which should be plenty for breakfast or for tea.

 Bread Machine

LEMON RAISIN BUNS

Yield: 12 buns.

1/2 cup **water**

1/2 cup **milk**

1/4 cup **honey**

1 **egg**

2 tablespoons **butter** or **margarine**

Juice of 1 medium **lemon** (about 2 tablespoons)

1/2 teaspoon **salt**

3 1/4 cups plus 2 tablespoons **HODGSON MILL Best for Bread Flour**

1/2 cup **raisins**

Grated **peel** of 1 medium **lemon** (about 1 1/2 teaspoons)

1/4 teaspoon ground **mace** (or **nutmeg**)

1 1/2 teaspoons **FLEISCHMANN'S Bread Machine Yeast**

Melted **butter** and **granulated sugar**, for topping

Add water, milk, honey, egg, butter, lemon juice, salt, flour, raisins, lemon peel, mace and yeast to bread machine pan in the order suggested by manufacturer. Select **dough/manual cycle**.

When cycle is complete, transfer dough from machine to a lightly floured surface. Divide dough into 12 equal portions; roll each portion into a ball. Place balls in greased standard-size muffin pans (2 1/2 x 1 1/4-inch cups). Cover and let rise in warm, draft-free place about 1 hour, or until doubled in size.

Bake in a preheated 350-degree oven 15 to 20 minutes, or until done. Remove from pans. Brush with melted butter and roll in sugar. Serve warm.

Classic Scones

Yield: About 12 scones.

3 ½ cups **HODGSON MILL Naturally White Flour**

½ cup **granulated sugar**

1 tablespoon **baking powder**

½ teaspoon **salt**

¾ cup (1 ½ sticks) **butter**

¾ cup **raisins** or **currants**

1 **egg**

¾ cup **milk**

Whole milk or **cream**, for brushing

Preheat oven to 375 degrees.

Sift flour, sugar, baking powder and salt into a medium mixing bowl. Using a pastry blender or two knives, cut in butter until the mixture resembles coarse crumbs. Stir in raisins. Make a well in the center of the mixture. Mix egg with milk in a small bowl; pour egg mixture into the well. Blend with a wooden spoon, then mix with hands to make a smooth, soft dough. Do not overknead.

Roll out dough on a floured surface to a thickness of ½ inch. Use a floured 3-inch biscuit cutter to cut out rounds. Dough scraps can be rolled out a second time. Place rounds on a lightly greased baking sheet. Lightly brush with milk or cream.

Bake in preheated 375-degree oven 10 to 15 minutes, or until very lightly browned. Serve warm.

Note: At a traditional British-style tea, scones are served with clotted cream and preserves. Making clotted cream is a long process and a bit fussy. Put 2 cups heavy (whipping) cream in a stainless steel or nonstick shallow pan and let stand at room temperature 6 hours, or overnight. Place on very low heat, so that the cream maintains a constant temperature of about 180 degrees. It must never boil, or it will be ruined. After several hours, you'll see small rings or bumps forming on the surface of the cream. Remove from heat, cool in a pan of ice until it reaches room temperature and store in the refrigerator for at least 3 hours. Skim off the thick, clotted cream and serve it on scones or fresh berries.

Clotted cream is also called Devonshire cream and is sometimes available from import shops. In a pinch, serve scones with whipped unsalted butter.

Bread Break

These are the classic scones of traditional afternoon tea, but they're delicious anytime you serve them. I first had them when I invited my friend Cindy, a fellow teacher at St. Bede Academy, to my office for tea during our third hour free period. She brought scones, clotted cream and homemade strawberry preserves. When I first tasted that combination, I knew I had to learn how to make scones. Cindy and I were collaborating on the drama department's fall theater program, and we discovered that production meetings with tea and scones were more, well, productive!

Sometime later I discovered that we were in good company. I was reading choreographer Agnes de Mille's *Dance to the Piper*, and was delighted to discover that she and composer Aaron Copland met over tea and scones to collaborate on the groundbreaking American ballet *Rodeo*.

CHOCOLATE SCONES

Yield: 8 scones.

Bread Break

If you worry that your family won't like scones (they can seem a bit dry and they're not as sweet as brownies), have no fear. I have served these Chocolate Scones to everyone from monks to parents to freshmen boys, and everyone has declared them excellent.

Although I never made these on camera during the second season, I accidentally sent this recipe with a batch of others intended for the cookbook. But when I tried to retrieve it, station personnel vigorously objected. Just another example of the power of chocolate!

1 ³/₄ cups **HODGSON MILL Naturally White Flour**

¹/₄ cup **unsweetened cocoa powder**

¹/₂ cup **granulated sugar**

2 teaspoons **baking powder**

¹/₄ teaspoon **salt**

¹/₂ cup (1 stick) **butter**, cold, cut into small pieces

¹/₃ cup **semisweet chocolate morsels**

¹/₂ cup **heavy** or **whipping cream**

1 **egg**, beaten

1 teaspoon **vanilla extract**

Preheat oven to 400 degrees.

Sift flour, cocoa powder, sugar, baking powder and salt into a medium mixing bowl; stir thoroughly. Using a pastry blender or two sharp knives, cut butter into flour mixture until it resembles coarse crumbs. Stir in chocolate morsels.

Combine cream, egg and vanilla in a small bowl; whisk until well blended. Add cream mixture to flour mixture; stir with a wooden spoon until just moistened. Do not overmix.

Turn out dough onto a lightly floured surface. Knead gently 8 or 10 strokes. Place dough on lightly greased baking sheet and pat into a flattened circle about 8 inches in diameter. Using a large knife or long spatula, cut circle into 8 wedges, but do not separate the pieces.

Bake in preheated 400-degree oven 15 to 20 minutes. The scones should be firm on the edges but still soft in the middle. Remove from baking sheet and let cool on a wire rack. Cut into wedges before serving.

Scones can be served warm or cool, with clotted cream (page 73) or butter and preserves.

Note: *For a special touch, I like to decorate scones with melted almond bark (white chocolate). After baking, leave the scones in a circle (do not separate into wedges). Melt 1 ounce almond bark on medium power in the microwave oven. Stir in $^1/_4$ teaspoon shortening. Use a decorator's bag to pipe the almond bark in a zigzag pattern on each wedge. Cut into wedges at the table as you serve tea. If you don't have almond bark, you could use semisweet chocolate morsels.*

To make these scones extra-special, divide the dough into two pieces and pat each piece into an 8-inch circle. Place one dough circle on the baking sheet; spread raspberry or strawberry preserves on dough. Top with remaining dough circle. Using a large knife, cut circle into 8 wedges, wiping knife clean after each cut, but do not separate the pieces. Bake as usual.

ORANGE POPPY SEED SCONES

Yield: 16 scones.

There are hundreds of scone recipes out there, with every imaginable flavoring: berries, raisins, onions, cheese, even bacon. Once you've made a few scone recipes, you can try experimenting with your own favorite flavors. I chose this version because it sounded good to my buddy Greg one night when we were testing the Seeded Barley Bread (page 26). He had never tried scones before, but it was a match made in heaven. He ate four that night and took the rest of the batch home.

One thing I especially appreciate about scones is how simple the method is, and they bake quickly, too. I often make two batches of scones during the time I have a yeast bread in its first rise. One batch will go to the abbey table, while my kitchen helpers and I share the other as we clean the kitchen. I find that it's easier to get volunteers if you feed them well!

2 ½ cups **HODGSON MILL Naturally White Flour**

½ cup **granulated sugar**

1 tablespoon **baking powder**

3 tablespoons **poppy seeds**

½ teaspoon **salt**

½ cup (1 stick) **butter**, cold, cut into small pieces

1 **egg**

⅔ cup **orange juice**

Grated **peel** of one medium **orange** (about 1 teaspoon)

Preheat oven to 350 degrees.

Sift flour, sugar, baking powder, poppy seeds and salt into a medium mixing bowl. Using a pastry blender or two knives, cut butter into flour mixture until it resembles coarse crumbs. In a separate bowl, beat egg with orange juice and grated peel. Add egg mixture to flour mixture and stir until just mixed.

Shape dough into a ball and divide in half. Place each half on a lightly greased baking sheet and pat into a circle about 8 inches in diameter. Using a large knife or long spatula, cut each circle into 8 wedges, but do not separate the pieces.

Bake in preheated 350-degree oven 15 to 20 minutes, or until lightly browned. Remove from pans and let cool briefly on wire racks. Cut into wedges and serve warm.

Note: The first time I made these, I accidentally omitted the orange peel. Although the scones were moist and tender, they had very little flavor. So be sure to include the grated orange peel when you make them. Fresh orange peel makes a rather tart scone (my preference) whereas dried orange peel is a bit more mellow.

Holiday Baking

One thing I especially appreciate about our life at St. Bede is that the brethren are very careful to keep Advent and Christmas as two separate seasons. Advent has a noble simplicity in the abbey, decorated primarily by what I call "the adornment of expectation," as daily we listen to the prophetic texts of the Hebrew Scriptures. On the first Sunday of Advent, an Advent wreath made of fresh ever-greens appears in the refectory (the monastery dining room), traditionally made by the person who most recently joined the community. But no other decorations go up until a day or two before Christmas, so we don't get caught up in the so-called "hustle and bustle" of the holidays.

It never fails to astonish me when people say things like, "I never bake anymore—except during the holidays, of course." When I hear that, I usually ask them, "Do you mean to tell me that the only time you bake is during the busiest time of the year? What are you doing the rest of the year?" The answer, of course, is that people consider baking an important part of their holiday traditions. So from Thanksgiving to New Year's Day, they make time in the kitchen a top priority.

But what about other festivals throughout the year? Wouldn't it be nice to have baking traditions that accompany other holidays, like Groundhog Day, Shrove Tuesday or Fourth of July? I myself have a personal tradition of spending time in the woods harvesting wild grapevine on Columbus Day, and then baking herb bread for supper. Why not make time for baking something special for the last day of summer, or start a tradition that on the first day that snow cancels school, you'll be in the kitchen with the kids?

Many holidays throughout the year have special ethnic breads associated with them. In the pages that follow, you'll find breads for Christmas, as well as for Chanukah, Epiphany, Mardi Gras and the Mexican Day of the Dead. I hope they inspire you to create your own baking traditions.

Chanukah Jelly Doughnuts

Yield: 12 to 16 doughnuts.

1 recipe **Basic Sweet Dough**
(either bread machine or
regular, page 63 or 64)

About ⅓ cup **jam** or
preserves (raspberry,
strawberry or other flavors)

Vegetable oil, for frying

Confectioners' sugar

Prepare dough according to recipe directions. Roll out dough on a lightly floured surface to a thickness of ¼ inch. Use a floured 3-inch biscuit cutter to cut out rounds.

Put 1 to 2 teaspoons jam in the center of one round; lightly brush the outer edge with water. Place a second round on top (you might need to stretch it out slightly to cover the little mound of jam) and crimp the edges with the tines of a fork. Place on lightly greased baking sheet. Repeat with remaining rounds and jam. Cover and let rise in a warm, draft-free place about 30 minutes, or until almost doubled.

While doughnuts are rising, heat oil to 350 to 375 degrees. Fry doughnuts 2 or 3 minutes per side, or until golden brown. Fry only two or three at a time, or the temperature of the oil will drop too quickly and the doughnuts will become soggy. Drain on paper towels, then sprinkle on all sides with confectioners' sugar. These are best if served warm, but they will keep overnight as well.

~

Note: Be sure you seal the edges of the doughnut carefully, or it will open up while it is frying and spill the jam into the hot oil.

Confectioners' sugar is the traditional topping for these doughnuts, but I suspect you could use granulated sugar or a butter cream glaze as well. I was told that strawberry and raspberry are the most common flavors sold by the street vendors, but I imagine apricot jam or fig preserves would be just as good.

Bread Break

Potato pancakes (latkes) and a braided challah loaf are the traditional Chanukah foods in this country, but I'm told by my Jewish friends that jelly doughnuts fried in oil are sold on street corners in Jerusalem during the feast. Chanukah celebrates the liberation of the temple from the occupying Syrian army under Antiochus IV in the 2nd century B.C. According to legend, a small amount of oil, all to be had in the city, miraculously burned in the sanctuary's lamp stand for eight nights. So, a sweet treat fried in oil seems appropriate.

STOLLEN

Yield: 3 large loaves.

Bread Break

Stollen is a traditional German bread served at Christmas. I have yet to see any explanation as to why it has its unique "folded-over" shape, but every recipe I've seen specifies it, so I have followed suit.

This recipe came from Father Arthur's mother, Mrs. Schmit, who sent me a photocopy of the original recipe from a 1930s newspaper. She also graciously sent me a sample loaf, so I could have some idea of my final goal. Unfortunately, the recipe wasn't entirely clear in its directions. It took me several tries and three phone calls to Mrs. Schmit before I even came close to her original, and even then I fell somewhat short of the ideal. But that's typical of bakers — we never feel we quite measure up to those who went before us. The people we mentor will probably feel the same about us!

I know this seems like a huge batch — 8 to 10 cups flour! — but that's what the

2 packages **FLEISCHMANN'S Active Dry Yeast**

2 cups lukewarm **milk**

8 to 10 cups **HODGSON MILL Naturally White Flour**, divided

1 pound (4 sticks) **butter**, softened

1 cup **granulated sugar**

4 **eggs**

Grated **peel** of 1 large **lemon** or **orange**

1 cup coarsely chopped **candied cherries**

1 ½ cups coarsely chopped **dried mixed fruit**

1 ½ cups coarsely chopped **almonds**

Butter, melted

Confectioners' sugar icing (page 65 or your favorite recipe)

Sliced **almonds, candied cherries** or **dried mixed fruit**, for garnish

Combine yeast and lukewarm milk in a small bowl; stir to dissolve. Stir in 1 cup of the flour. Let stand 5 to 10 minutes.

Combine butter and sugar in a large mixing bowl; beat until fluffy. Add eggs, one at a time, beating well after each addition. Add the yeast mixture and lemon peel; stir until blended. Add the remaining 8 to 9 cups flour, one cup at a time, until you have a soft dough that pulls away from the sides of the bowl.

Turn out dough onto a lightly floured surface. Knead until smooth and elastic, adding small amounts of flour to keep the dough manageable. Do not overknead; the dough should be soft rather than stiff. Cover and let rise in warm, draft-free place 60 to 90 minutes, or until doubled in bulk.

Combine candied cherries, dried fruit and almonds in a bowl; add a little flour and toss to coat. This helps keep the fruit and nuts from sticking together.

Punch down dough. Knead briefly to expel large air bubbles. Flatten the dough. Sprinkle dredged fruits and nuts on top of dough. Fold corners of dough up and over the fruits and nuts. Knead until fruits and nuts are evenly distributed in the dough.

Divide dough into 3 (or more) portions. Roll out one portion into an oblong about 1-inch thick. Press down the center of the dough with the edge of your hand, to make a crease. Brush melted butter on top of dough. Fold dough over itself, along the crease, making a long, folded loaf. Place loaf on greased baking sheet and brush melted butter on the top. Repeat for remaining portions of dough. Cover and let rise 30 to 45 minutes, or until doubled.

About 15 minutes before end of rising time, preheat oven to 350 degrees. Bake stollen 35 to 45 minutes, or until done. Loosely cover tops of loaves with foil if they brown too quickly. Remove from baking sheets and let cool on wire racks. While loaves are still slightly warm, drizzle confectioners' sugar icing on loaves and garnish with nuts or fruits.

original recipe called for. Besides, I figure if you're going to bake for the holidays, you might as well bake enough to share. I can assure you that with Mrs. Schmit's stollen recipe, whatever you bake will be eaten. Every year after the abbey's Christmas Midnight Mass, we invite the congregation to our student refectory for a reception. Last year I put out one very large stollen, thinking that with so many other foods on the buffet table, one loaf would be plenty. It was reduced to crumbs within minutes, and I had to rush back to the kitchen and ice another one, which also disappeared rapidly.

Bread Machine

STOLLEN

Yield: 1 (1 ½-pound) loaf.

½ cup **milk**

½ cup (1 stick) **butter** or margarine

1 **egg**

2 ⅓ cups **HODGSON MILL Best for Bread Flour**

¼ cup **granulated sugar**

1 teaspoon grated **lemon peel**

1 ½ teaspoons **FLEISCHMANN'S Bread Machine Yeast**

⅓ cup chopped **dried mixed fruit**

¼ cup chopped **candied cherries**

⅓ cup chopped **almonds**

Butter, melted

Confectioners' sugar icing (page 65 or your favorite recipe)

GARNISH (OPTIONAL):

Chopped **dried mixed fruit**

Chopped **candied cherries**

Chopped **almonds**

Add milk, butter, egg, flour, sugar, lemon peel and yeast to bread machine pan in the order suggested by manufacturer. Select **dough/manual cycle**.

When cycle is complete, transfer dough from machine to a lightly floured surface. Knead in mixed fruit, cherries and almonds. Roll dough into a 1-inch-thick oblong. Press down the center of the dough to make a crease. Brush melted butter on top of dough. Fold dough over itself along the crease, making a long, folded loaf. Place on greased baking sheet; brush with melted butter. Cover and let rise in a warm, draft-free place 30 to 45 minutes, or until doubled in size.

Bake in a preheated 350-degree oven 25 to 30 minutes, or until done. Remove from baking sheet and let cool slightly on wire rack. Meanwhile, prepare confectioners' sugar icing. Drizzle icing over still-warm stollen. If desired, sprinkle chopped fruit, cherries or nuts on top.

Pan d'Oro

Yield: 1 loaf; 10 to 12 servings.

1 package **FLEISCHMANN'S Active Dry Yeast**

¼ cup warm **water**

1 ¼ cups **granulated sugar**

¼ cup (½ stick) **butter**, softened

4 **eggs**

¾ cup **whole milk**

1 ½ teaspoons **lemon extract** (optional)

½ teaspoon **salt**

3 ½ cups **HODGSON MILL Naturally White Flour**

Sifted **confectioners' sugar**, for sprinkling

Combine yeast and warm water in a small bowl; stir to dissolve. Let stand 5 to 10 minutes, or until foamy. Combine sugar and butter in medium mixing bowl; mix until well blended. Add eggs; beat well. Add yeast mixture, milk, lemon extract and salt; mix well. Add flour; beat for 200 strokes. Cover and let rise in a warm, draft-free place 60 to 75 minutes.

Stir down batter. Transfer batter to a greased star-shaped pan d'oro pan (it should fill the pan about halfway). Let rise 20 to 30 minutes, or until batter reaches within 1 inch of the top of the pan.

While batter is rising, preheat oven to 400 degrees. Bake 45 minutes, or until a cake tester comes out clean. Set pan on a wire rack and let loaf cool in pan for at least an hour before removing it from pan. There will be a slight bulge on the bottom of the loaf; trim this off as needed to make a flat bottom. Sprinkle loaf with sifted confectioners' sugar.

Note: I always use a vegetable cooking spray to grease the pan d'oro mold, because it's easier to get into the small points that way. However, some of the cheaper brands of cooking spray can cause overbrowning, especially on the bottom of the mold (which becomes the top of the loaf). Depending on the type of grease used and the thickness of the mold, you might need to reduce the oven temperature to 375 degrees and bake the loaf a bit longer.

Bread Break

Although *pannetone* is the traditional Christmas bread in Italy, *pan d'oro* (golden bread) is gaining popularity. It was recommended to me by native Italians as well as by fellow monks who studied in Rome. Pan d'oro makes a dramatic addition to a holiday buffet table. It can be served for brunch as well as dinner.

Although it is cake-like in texture, don't expect pan d'oro to be as sweet as the usual lemon cake. It is traditionally baked in a tall, star-shaped pan, available at specialty shops. It also can be baked in regular loaf pans, brioche molds or a Bundt (fluted tube) pan. You might have to adjust the baking time if the pans you use are smaller than the one called for in the recipe.

BLINY

Yield: 36 to 42 (4-inch) pancakes.

Bread Break

Bliny (the singular is blin) are yeasted buckwheat pancakes served on Shrove Tuesday in Russia. It is traditional for wives to serve them to their mothers-in-law and vice versa. Some recipes call for a higher proportion of liquid, making a thin pancake much like a crepe. I must admit to a certain provincial prejudice and say I prefer them thicker, like good old American flapjacks. But you might try omitting some of the white flour to see what you prefer.

The only drawback to these pancakes is their color. The buckwheat gives them a gray tint on the interior. But there's nothing unappealing about the flavor or the texture of bliny, and you might want to enjoy them year-round and not just for Shrove Tuesday.

1 package **FLEISCHMANN'S Active Dry Yeast**

1 teaspoon **granulated sugar**

1/4 cup warm **water**

2 cups warm **milk**

3 tablespoons **vegetable oil**

1/2 teaspoon **salt**

1 cup **HODGSON MILL Buckwheat Flour**

3/4 cup **HODGSON MILL Naturally White Flour**

3 **eggs**, separated

Butter

Combine yeast, sugar and warm water in a small bowl; stir to dissolve. Let stand 5 to 10 minutes, or until foamy.

Combine yeast mixture, milk, oil and salt in a large mixing bowl. Stir in buckwheat flour and white flour; beat until smooth. Cover and let rise in a warm, draft-free place about 1 hour, or until doubled.

Stir down batter. Add egg yolks and beat until incorporated. Beat egg whites in a bowl until soft peaks form, then gently fold egg whites into the batter.

In a greased skillet over medium heat, make pancakes using a scant 1/4 cup batter per pancake; batter will spread 3 or 4 inches in diameter. Cook pancakes until bubbles in the batter pop but do not close up; turn and cook other side until golden. Remove from skillet, butter both sides of each pancake, and place on a baking pan or cookie sheet; keep warm in a preheated 200-degree oven while you cook the remaining batter.

GINGERBREAD WAFFLES

Yield: 3 large waffles.

1 ¹/₂ cups **HODGSON MILL Naturally White Flour**

¹/₄ cup **granulated sugar**

1 ¹/₂ teaspoons **baking powder**

¹/₂ teaspoon **baking soda**

¹/₂ teaspoon **salt**

¹/₂ teaspoon ground **cinnamon**

¹/₂ teaspoon ground **ginger**

¹/₄ teaspoon ground **nutmeg**

³/₄ cup **milk**

¹/₄ cup **vegetable oil**

¹/₄ cup **molasses**

2 **eggs,** separated

Sift flour, sugar, baking powder, baking soda, salt, cinnamon, ginger and nutmeg into a large mixing bowl. Combine milk, oil, molasses and egg yolks in a medium bowl; stir to mix. Add milk mixture to flour mixture; stir until dry ingredients are just moistened. Whisk egg whites in a bowl until soft peaks appear. Gently fold egg whites into batter.

Cook on a preheated waffle iron until browned, following manufacturer's directions for time and temperature.

Note: Here's a tip for whisking egg whites: Using a cold bowl helps speed up the process, so if you know you're going to make waffles in the morning, put a small mixing bowl in the fridge the night before.

This recipe uses the same spices as gingerbread and can be served with many different toppings. Try them with the usual butter and syrup, or with a warm fruit compote (use canned pie filling in a pinch), or with a dollop of French vanilla ice cream.

Bread Break

Waffles are traditional Mardi Gras fare because they help use up the eggs and butter that were forbidden during Lent in certain times and localities during the Middle Ages. But don't reserve this recipe just for Mardi Gras. Try serving them at a Christmas family brunch or a special birthday breakfast in bed.

We rarely have waffles in the monastery, and when we do, they are usually the frozen variety. So when I'm on the road for a special appearance or media tour in association with the show, a big Belgian waffle with warm syrup is a real treat. It's hard to make fresh waffles for my big family, but you'll have no trouble making special waffles for your family and friends with this easy recipe. It has a lot of ingredients, but the method itself is quite simple. To save time in the morning, measure out and sift the dry ingredients the night before.

Yield: 1 cake; 8 to 12 servings.

Bread Break

People tend to think of King Cake as a Mardi Gras tradition. In fact, it was originally a part of the Epiphany or Twelfth Night celebration at the end of the Christmas season. A bean, coin or other trinket was hidden in a rich cake or bread, and the person who got that slice was declared the "Lord of Misrule" or king of the feast. Sometimes, two cakes were made, one for the men and one for the women, so that both king and queen were crowned.

My version of King Cake is based on the Spanish tradition of an orange-flavored yeast bread rather than the French butter-and-egg cake. I added the chocolate nuggets as a treat for each person sharing the cake, and I shaped it as a crown to reflect its original association with the Magi of Matthew's gospel. Having the cake already divided into sections helps prevent fights over whose slice contains the prize.

DOUGH:

1/2 cup **sour cream**

1 tablespoon **solid vegetable shortening**

Grated **peel** and **juice** of 1 medium **orange**

2 1/2 cups **HODGSON MILL Naturally White Flour**, divided

1 package **FLEISCHMANN'S RapidRise Yeast**

1/4 cup **granulated sugar**

1 teaspoon **salt**

1/2 teaspoon ground **nutmeg**

1/4 teaspoon ground **cardamom**

1 **egg**

7 to 11 **milk chocolate nuggets with almonds**, unwrapped

Coin or **trinket**, wrapped in parchment paper

TOPPING:

Butter, melted

Granulated sugar

8 to 12 **candied cherries** or **gumdrops**

Combine sour cream, shortening, orange peel and orange juice in a medium saucepan; stir. Heat until shortening melts. Remove from heat and let cool to 120 to 130 degrees.

Sift 1 cup of the flour, yeast, sugar, salt, nutmeg and cardamom into a medium mixing bowl; stir with a fork to mix. Stir sour cream mixture into flour mixture; beat about 3 minutes, or until thoroughly mixed. Beat in egg. Stir in the remaining 1 1/2 cups flour; mix until all the flour is incorporated.

Turn out dough onto a lightly floured surface. Knead 3 minutes. Cover dough with a damp towel and let rest 10 minutes.

Lightly grease a 9-inch ring mold or tube pan. Divide the dough into 8 to 12 pieces, depending upon the number of servings you want. Flatten each piece into a circle about 3 inches in diameter. Reserve one dough circle for the coin or trinket. Place one chocolate nugget in the center of one dough circle; wrap dough around chocolate by pulling up the sides and pinching the top to

form a teardrop shape (this forms the points of the crown). Repeat with remaining dough circles and chocolate nuggets. Wrap the coin or trinket (wrapped in parchment paper) in the reserved dough circle.

Evenly space the pieces, point-side up, in the prepared ring mold. Cover with a towel and let rise in a warm, draft-free place about 1 hour, or until doubled in size.

About 15 minutes before end of rising time, preheat oven to 350 degrees. Bake cake 25 to 30 minutes, or until golden brown. Let cool in pan about 30 minutes, then remove from pan and place on wire rack. Brush all sides with melted butter and sprinkle with granulated sugar. Garnish points with candied cherries or gumdrops, using toothpicks or a small amount of frosting to secure them.

Note: *If you use toothpicks to attach the candied cherries, be sure to remove them before serving the cake to small children, and warn older guests as well.*

PAN DE MUERTOS

Yield: 1 loaf.

Bread Break

This bread is a traditional part of All Saints' Day and All Souls' Day celebrations in Mexico. There are dozens of variations for this bread, which is taken to the cemetery along with other foods and flowers for a symbolic meal with those who are buried there. Not a morbid or sorrowful affair, the Day of the Dead is a time for celebrating the memory of beloved family members with special treats like this bread. Pan de Muertos has a cake-like quality to it, and is delicious all by itself, without butter or other toppings.

When I was testing this recipe, I took a batch to one of the Spanish classes in the Academy. I saw one of the students later that day, and she confided to me, "Someone brought that 'dead bread' last year, but yours was lots better!"

STARTER:

1 package **FLEISCHMANN'S Active Dry Yeast**

1/4 cup warm **water**

1/2 cup **HODGSON MILL Naturally White Flour**

1 **egg**

DOUGH:

4 **eggs** (reserve one yolk for egg wash)

1/3 cup **granulated sugar**

1/2 teaspoon **salt**

1/2 cup (1 stick) **butter**, melted

Grated **peel** and **juice** of one medium **orange**

4 1/2 cups **HODGSON MILL Naturally White Flour**, divided

1 **egg yolk** (reserved from 4 eggs) mixed with 1 tablespoon **water**, for egg wash

Melted **butter** and **granulated sugar**, for topping

For starter: Combine yeast and warm water in a small bowl; stir to dissolve. Let stand 10 minutes, then stir in flour and egg. Cover and let develop for 30 to 60 minutes.

For dough: Crack eggs into a large mixing bowl, reserving 1 egg yolk for egg wash. Beat eggs well. Add starter to beaten eggs; mix until smooth (you might need to use an egg beater). Add sugar, salt, melted butter, orange peel and orange juice; mix well. Add 3 cups of the flour, one cup at a time, mixing thoroughly after each addition. Add remaining 1 1/2 cups flour, about 1/4 cup at a time, mixing after each addition, until a soft dough forms that pulls away from the sides of the bowl.

Turn out dough onto a lightly floured surface. Knead 5 minutes, adding small amounts of flour as needed to keep dough manageable. When finished, the dough should be soft but should spring back when pushed. Lightly oil surface of dough, and put in the rinsed mixing bowl. Cover with a towel and let rise in a warm, draft-free place 60 to 90 minutes, or until doubled.

Punch down dough. Pull off about one-fourth of the dough and set it aside. With the remaining dough, form a low, round loaf, about 2 inches thick. Place loaf on a lightly greased baking sheet. Divide the reserved dough into 5 equal portions. Use one portion to form a smooth ball; place ball in the center of the loaf (this is meant to suggest a skull).  Divide each remaining portion in half; roll each of the 8 pieces into a rod, about 4 inches long. Flatten the ends slightly (these represent the bones). Place the bones in a circle radiating out from the skull (like spokes on a wheel), or arrange them in four crosses equally spaced around the center. Brush the bottom of each bone with a little water if you have trouble getting it to stick to the loaf. Cover and let rise in a warm, draft-free place 30 to 45 minutes, or until nearly doubled.

About 15 minutes before end of rising time, place rack in lower third of oven and preheat oven to 350 degrees. Brush risen loaf with egg wash. Bake 35 to 40 minutes, or until loaf is golden brown and sounds hollow when tapped on the bottom. Remove from baking sheet and let cool on a wire rack 30 minutes. Brush loaf with melted butter and sprinkle generously with sugar.

Note: *You can use this dough to form 2 to 4 smaller loaves. In some parts of Mexico, the bread is shaped like people or animals.*

Bread Machine

Pan de Muertos

Yield: 1 loaf.

STARTER:

2 teaspoons **FLEISCHMANN'S Bread Machine Yeast**

¹/₄ cup warm **water** (100 to 110 degrees)

¹/₂ cup **HODGSON MILL Best for Bread Flour**

1 **egg**

DOUGH:

4 **eggs** (reserve one yolk for egg wash)

¹/₂ cup (1 stick) **butter**

2 tablespoons **orange juice**

¹/₂ teaspoon **salt**

3 ¹/₂ cups **HODGSON MILL Best for Bread Flour**

¹/₃ cup **granulated sugar**

2 teaspoons grated **orange peel**

1 **egg yolk** (reserved from 4 eggs) mixed with 1 tablespoon **water**, for egg wash

Melted **butter** and **granulated sugar**, for topping

For starter: Dissolve yeast in warm water in a small bowl. Let stand 10 minutes. Stir in flour and egg. Cover and let stand 30 to 60 minutes.

For dough: Add starter, eggs, butter, orange juice, salt, flour, sugar and orange peel to bread machine pan in the order suggested by manufacturer. Select **dough/manual cycle**.

When cycle is complete, transfer dough from machine to a lightly floured surface. Set aside one-fourth of dough. With remaining dough, form a flat, 2-inch-thick round loaf. Place loaf on greased baking sheet. Divide reserved dough into 5 portions. Use 1 portion to form a smooth ball; place ball in the center of the loaf. Divide each of the remaining 4 portions in half, making 8 pieces. Roll each piece into a rod, about 4 inches long; flatten ends slightly. Arrange rods in 4 crosses, equally spaced around the center. Cover and let rise in a warm, draft-free place 30 to 45 minutes, or until almost doubled in size.

Brush top of loaf with egg wash. Bake in a preheated 350-degree oven 30 minutes, or until done. Remove from baking sheet and transfer to a wire rack. While still warm, brush with melted butter and sprinkle generously with sugar.

FASTNACHTS

Yield: 24 doughnuts.

¹/₃ cup **vegetable oil**

¹/₃ cup **granulated sugar**

¹/₄ cup **sour cream**

2 **eggs**

3 cups **HODGSON MILL Naturally White Flour**

2 teaspoons **baking powder**

Vegetable oil, for frying

Cinnamon sugar, for coating

Combine oil, sugar, sour cream and eggs in a medium mixing bowl; beat with a wire whisk for 2 minutes.

Sift flour and baking powder into a large mixing bowl; stir until thoroughly combined. Add egg mixture; stir until just combined. With dough still in bowl, gently knead 8 or 10 strokes. Let dough rest 5 minutes.

Heat oil to 350 to 375 degrees. Pat or roll out dough on a lightly floured surface to a thickness of about ¹/₄ inch. Cut dough into 3x2-inch rectangles; cut a short slit down the center of each rectangle. Fry in hot oil a few at a time, 2 or 3 minutes per side, or until golden brown. Drain on paper towels, then toss in cinnamon sugar to coat. Best if served fresh and warm.

Note: You can use egg substitute and low-fat sour cream for a less calorie-intensive version, but that seems to defeat the purpose of Fat Tuesday in my view. But do please use vegetable oil for frying rather than the traditional lard.

For cinnamon sugar, combine ¹/₂ cup granulated sugar and 1 table-spoon ground cinnamon; increase amounts proportionately as need-ed. Instead of cinnamon sugar, you can use plain granulated sugar or confectioners' sugar. Unsugared, the doughnuts are a bit bland, but are much improved by dunking them in tea sweetened with honey.

Bread Break

The real name for these doughnuts is *Fastnacht kuchen*. Fastnacht is the German word for the day before Ash Wednesday, which is when these fried doughnuts are traditionally served. There are as many different recipes for these Shrove Tuesday doughnuts as there are German grand-mothers. The majority of them are made with a yeast dough containing mashed potatoes, some with as many as a dozen ingredi-ents. The more complex Pennsylvania Dutch ver-sions of fastnachts are excellent and well worth the effort, but I offer here the simplest possible recipe. They are easily made fresh, but the doughnuts also will keep well until the follow-ing morning.

Kids in the Kitchen

I was blessed to grow up in a baking home. My mother baked bread and cookies for as long as I can remember, as did my grandmother, who lived with us from the time I was 5. We kids were always in the kitchen with them, and I can honestly say I don't ever recall either of them saying, "Get out of my way!" Instead, we were put to *work.*

The kitchen was where we learned our numbers ("I need six cups of flour—who's going to count for me?") as well as fractions ("What's three-fourths of a cup times two?") and how to tell time ("This will bake for 35 minutes—what time will it be when it's ready to come out of the oven?"). We loved beating eggs and sifting flour, and when you got tall enough, you would be asked to turn on "the Cookie Lamp." This magical kitchen accessory was a small wall light with an old-fashioned glass shade that, when turned on, "kept the cookies from burning" (at least, according to my superstitious Irish grandmother).

We didn't have a lot of money when I was growing up. We wore hand-me-downs and shopped at garage sales and considered it a "fling" when we could order a large sundae with extra nuts at the ice cream shop. But we were, and still are, a very happy family, with a whole new generation of kids in the kitchen. Those times we spent measuring, mixing and baking gave us memories to treasure forever and a reason to share them with our own children (even as a monk with 95 "kids" in his freshman religion classes!).

The recipes that follow are all kid-tested and are sure to provide an opportunity for you to make some great memories with the youngsters in your life. As one friend of mine put it after she made bread with her three children for the first time, "The kitchen is a mess, but the house smells wonderful, and we're enjoying homemade bread, so I couldn't be happier."

Quick Pretzels

Yield: 24 pretzels.

1 package **FLEISCHMANN'S Active Dry Yeast**

1 tablespoon **brown sugar**

$1/4$ cup warm **water**

$1 \frac{1}{2}$ cups warm **milk**

$1 \frac{1}{2}$ teaspoons **salt**

$4 \frac{1}{2}$ to 5 cups **HODGSON MILL Naturally White Flour**, divided

1 **egg**, beaten

Kosher or **coarse salt** (optional)

Combine yeast, brown sugar and warm water in a large mixing bowl; stir to dissolve. Let stand 5 to 10 minutes, or until foamy. Stir in warm milk and salt. Stir in 4 cups of the flour, one cup at a time.

Turn out dough onto a lightly floured surface. Knead 5 minutes, adding as much of the remaining $1/2$ to 1 cup flour as needed to form a smooth, elastic dough that is slightly sticky. Cover with a towel and let rest 5 minutes.

Preheat oven to 425 degrees.

Cut dough into 24 pieces. Roll each piece into a 12- to 14-inch rope. Twist each rope into a pretzel shape and place on lightly greased baking sheet. Brush tops of pretzels with beaten egg and sprinkle with salt.

Bake in preheated 425-degree oven 12 to 15 minutes, or until pretzels are golden brown. Remove from baking sheet and let cool briefly on wire racks. Serve warm.

Note: You can make these pretzels with water, but I like the flavor and texture of milk-based pretzels better. Serve the pretzels warm with pizza sauce or cheese sauce for dipping.

If you divide the dough into fewer portions, you can make larger pretzels. Just be sure that all the pretzels on one baking sheet are the same size, so that they will bake in the same amount of time.

Bread Break

Pretzels get their name by a circuitous route. They were originally meant to be a Lenten bread, made with only water, flour, yeast and salt. The classic shape is meant to suggest arms crossed in prayer, which gave rise to their Latin name, *bracaella*, "little arms." This word became *bretzel* in Old German, which eventually shifted to pretzel.

I have made these basic pretzels with people of all ages, and everyone loves them. The freshmen in our high school especially enjoy making pretzels and eating them fresh out of the oven. I made these with my nephew Jordan's second-grade class and they turned out beautifully, so don't hesitate to try making pretzels with children of any age.

Bread Machine

QUICK PRETZELS

Yield: 8 pretzels.

$^3/_4$ cup **milk**

$^1/_4$ cup **water**

$^3/_4$ teaspoon **salt**

2 cups **HODGSON MILL Best for Bread Flour**

1 $^1/_2$ teaspoons **brown sugar**

1 $^1/_2$ teaspoons **FLEISCHMANN'S Bread Machine Yeast**

1 **egg**, beaten

Coarse salt (optional)

Add milk, water, salt, flour, brown sugar and yeast to bread machine pan in the order suggested by manufacturer. Select **dough/manual cycle.**

When cycle is complete, transfer dough from machine to lightly floured surface. Divide dough into 8 equal pieces. Roll each piece into 14-inch rope. Curve ends of each rope to make a circle; cross ends at top. Twist ends once and place over bottom of circle. Place pretzels on greased baking sheet. Brush tops with beaten egg and sprinkle with salt.

Bake in a preheated 425-degree oven 12 to 15 minutes, or until golden brown. Remove from baking sheet and let cool briefly on wire racks. Serve warm.

MUSTARD GARLIC PRETZELS

Yield: 12 large pretzels.

1 package **FLEISCHMANN'S Active Dry Yeast**

$1/4$ cup warm **water**

Pinch **granulated sugar**

1 $1/4$ cups lukewarm **milk**

2 tablespoons **vegetable oil**

2 tablespoons **granulated sugar**

$1/4$ cup spicy Dijon-style **mustard**

1 teaspoon **dried thyme**

1 teaspoon **salt**

4 to 4 $1/4$ cups **HODGSON MILL Naturally White Flour**, divided

3 quarts **water**

1 tablespoon **baking soda**

1 **egg white** mixed with 1 tablespoon **water**, for egg wash

GARLIC-CHEESE TOPPING:

$1/2$ cup grated **Parmesan cheese**

2 teaspoons **garlic powder**

Combine yeast, warm water and pinch sugar in a small bowl; stir to dissolve. Let stand 5 to 10 minutes, or until foamy. Combine milk, oil, 2 tablespoons sugar, mustard, thyme and salt in medium mixing bowl; stir to mix. Add yeast mixture; mix well. Add 3 cups of the flour, 1 cup at a time, mixing thoroughly after each addition. Add enough of the remaining 1 to 1 $1/4$ cups flour to make a moderately stiff dough.

Turn out dough onto a lightly floured surface. Knead 5 minutes. Lightly oil the surface of the dough and put in the rinsed mixing bowl. Cover and let rise in a warm, draft-free place 60 to 75 minutes, or until doubled.

Punch down dough. Knead lightly to work out the larger air bubbles. Let dough rest 10 minutes.

Divide dough into 12 equal pieces. Roll each piece into a rope about 18 inches long. Shape ropes into pretzels (see illustration on page 95). Place pretzels on lightly greased baking sheets and let rise 15 minutes. While pretzels are rising, preheat oven to

Bread Break

I know this recipe looks like a lot of work, but once you taste these freshly made marvels, you'll never eat a mall pretzel again! They would be just as popular at a Super Bowl party as at a child's sleepover.

The average Dijon-style mustard isn't sturdy enough for this recipe, so choose one with a little more bite to it. I've seen gourmet shops with shelves of different mustards, and hundreds are available on the Internet. In a pinch, I add extra horseradish and garlic to whatever's in the fridge.

450 degrees. Bake pretzels 5 minutes, then remove from oven. Reduce oven temperature to 350 degrees.

Bring 3 quarts water to a boil in a deep skillet, pan or pot. Dissolve baking soda in boiling water. Lower 3 or 4 pretzels at a time into the boiling water; let boil 1 minute, then turn pretzels over and boil 1 minute. Gently remove pretzels from water with tongs or slotted spoon; place on paper towels to drain. Repeat until all pretzels have been boiled.

Place boiled, drained pretzels on well-greased baking sheet, about ¹/₂-inch apart. Brush pretzels with egg wash. Bake in pre-heated 350-degree oven 20 to 25 minutes, or until golden brown. Prepare garlic-cheese topping by mixing Parmesan cheese and garlic powder. About 5 minutes before the pretzels are ready to come out of oven, sprinkle the tops with garlic-cheese topping. Remove from pans and let cool slightly on wire racks. Serve warm.

✍

Note: The advantage of the added flavorings in this recipe is that it eliminates the need for messy dips. But if you want more traditional pretzels, you can omit the mustard and thyme (the amount of flour will be a bit less, too) and top them with coarse salt just after the egg wash. Of course, the dough is simple enough that you could make a batch of each and have a taste test.

Use greased baking sheets rather than parchment paper. The damp pretzels stick to the paper and get misshapen in the process. I discovered this with my first trial batch, which also didn't have enough mustard.

Leftover pretzels are just fine the next day. Reheat them in a preheated 200-degree oven 10 or 15 minutes. You can use the microwave oven, of course, but it might make them a bit tough.

MUSTARD GARLIC PRETZELS

Bread Machine

Yield: 8 large pretzels.

$^1/_2$ cup plus 2 tablespoons **milk**

$^1/_4$ cup **water**

1 tablespoon **vegetable oil**

2 tablespoons spicy Dijon-style **mustard**

$^1/_2$ teaspoon **salt**

2 cups plus 2 tablespoons **HODGSON MILL Best for Bread Flour**

1 tablespoon **granulated sugar**

1 $^1/_2$ teaspoons **FLEISCHMANN'S Bread Machine Yeast**

$^1/_2$ teaspoon **dried thyme**

3 quarts **water**

1 tablespoon **baking soda**

1 **egg white** mixed with 1 tablespoon **water**, for egg wash

GARLIC-CHEESE TOPPING:

$^1/_4$ cup **grated Parmesan cheese**

1 teaspoon **garlic powder**

Add milk, water, oil, mustard, salt, flour, sugar, yeast and thyme to bread machine pan in the order suggested by manufacturer. Select **dough/manual cycle**.

When cycle is complete, transfer dough from machine to a lightly floured surface. Divide dough into 8 equal pieces; roll each piece into an 18-inch rope. Curve the ends of each rope to make a circle; cross ends at top. Twist ends once and place over bottom of circle. Place pretzels on greased baking sheets. Let rise 15 minutes. Bake in a preheated 450-degree oven 5 minutes; remove from oven. Reduce oven temperature to 350 degrees.

Bring 3 quarts water to a boil in a deep pan or pot. Dissolve baking soda in boiling water. Reduce heat to a simmer. Add pretzels to water, one at a time. Do not crowd the pan. Simmer 1 minute, turn, and simmer another 1 minute. Remove with slotted spoon; place on paper towels to absorb excess moisture. Place on greased baking sheets and brush with egg wash.

Bake in preheated 350-degree oven 10 minutes. Prepare

garlic-cheese topping by mixing Parmesan cheese and garlic powder. Remove pretzels from oven and sprinkle with garlic-cheese topping. Return pretzels to oven and bake 5 minutes, or until done. Serve warm.

≫

LIZARD PEPPER BREAD

Yield: 12 pieces.

1 package **FLEISCHMANN'S RapidRise Yeast**

2 ¹/₂ to 3 cups **HODGSON MILL Naturally White Flour**, divided

¹/₂ cup **HODGSON MILL Yellow Corn Meal**

2 teaspoons **brown sugar**

¹/₂ teaspoon **salt**

¹/₄ teaspoon **baking soda**

1 cup **salsa** (preferably hot and spicy)

¹/₄ cup **sour cream**

¹/₂ cup grated **pepper jack cheese**

Sift yeast, 2 cups of the flour, cornmeal, brown sugar, salt and baking soda into a medium mixing bowl. Combine salsa and sour cream in a microwave-safe dish or saucepan; heat in microwave oven or on stove top to 120 to 130 degrees. Pour salsa mixture into flour mixture; stir until thoroughly blended. Stir in grated cheese. Add enough of the remaining ¹/₂ to 1 cup flour, about ¹/₂ cup at a time, to make a soft dough.

Turn out dough onto a lightly floured surface. Knead 5 minutes. Cover with a damp towel and let rest 10 minutes.

Roll out dough on a well-floured surface to a thickness of about ¹/₄ inch. Cut out lizard shapes using a cookie cutter; place on lightly greased baking sheets. Knead dough scraps together with 1 tablespoon water, then roll out and cut. Cover lizards with a dry towel and let rise in a warm, draft-free place 30 to 45 minutes, or until doubled.

About 15 minutes before end of rising time, preheat oven to 400 degrees. Bake breads 20 minutes, or until slightly darkened.

Remove from baking sheets and let cool slightly on wire racks before serving. their soup!) or serve them on the side — they're great for wiping the soup bowl clean.

~~~

Note: I only roll the dough out twice; more than that and the breads get a bit stiff. After the second rolling, break the scraps into small pieces and place them on a separate baking sheet; they'll bake faster than the larger breads. Use them as croutons for soup or salad, or as a part of a Mexican party mix.

For children, you might want to use a milder salsa and Cheddar cheese. The resulting breads will taste a lot like those little goldfish snacks.

LIZARD PEPPER BREAD

Yield: 12 pieces.

1 cup **salsa** (hot and spicy)

¼ cup **sour cream**

½ teaspoon **salt**

2 ½ cups **HODGSON MILL Best for Bread Flour**

½ cup **HODGSON MILL Yellow Corn Meal**

½ cup grated **pepper jack cheese**

2 teaspoons **brown sugar**

¼ teaspoon **baking soda**

2 teaspoons **FLEISCHMANN'S Bread Machine Yeast**

Add salsa, sour cream, salt, flour, cornmeal, cheese, brown sugar, baking soda and yeast to bread machine pan in the order suggested by manufacturer. Select **dough/manual cycle.**

When cycle is complete, transfer dough from bread machine to a lightly floured surface. Roll dough to ¼-inch thickness. Cut out lizard (or other) shapes with a cookie cutter. Place on greased baking sheets. Cover and let rise in a warm, draft-free place 30 to 45 minutes, or until doubled in size. Bake in a preheated 400-degree oven 20 minutes, or until done. Let cool slightly before serving.

~~~

KIDS' PIZZA CUPS

Yield: 12 minipizzas.

Bread Break

These pizza cups are ideal for children's parties because they're fast to make; the dough is ready in 20 minutes, and the pizzas bake in 15 minutes. Better still, each child can choose the toppings he or she wants. No more fighting over who wants onions and who wants pepperoni!

Kids love helping with this recipe. The older ones can make the dough, while little ones can roll out the dough or fill the cups. My sister Eileen says a child of 8 or 9 is able to roll out circles without getting too frustrated. She bakes with my nephew Jordan all the time, so she should know.

DOUGH:

1 package **FLEISCHMANN'S** RapidRise Yeast

1 tablespoon **granulated sugar**

1 teaspoon **salt**

3 to 3 ½ cups **HODGSON MILL Naturally White Flour**, divided

1 cup **skim milk**

1 tablespoon **vegetable oil**

TOPPINGS (SEE NOTE):

Grated **mozzarella cheese**

Pizza sauce

Other toppings of choice (**sausage, pepperoni, bell peppers, onions**, etc.)

For dough: Sift yeast, sugar, salt and 2 cups of the flour into a medium mixing bowl; stir with a fork to mix well. Heat milk in a saucepan to 120 to 130 degrees. Pour milk and oil into flour mixture; stir until well blended. Add 1 cup of the flour; mix with your hands until flour is thoroughly incorporated. Add as much of the remaining ½ cup flour, about 1 tablespoon at a time, as is needed to form a soft dough that pulls away from the sides of the bowl.

Turn out dough onto a lightly floured surface. Knead 5 minutes, adding more flour as needed to keep dough manageable. When finished, the dough should be slightly soft but should spring back when pushed. Cover dough with a damp towel and let rest 10 minutes. The dough is now ready to use.

To assemble minipizzas: Preheat oven to 425 degrees. Lightly grease two Texas-size or jumbo muffin pans (3 x 1½-inch muffin cups).

Divide dough into 12 equal pieces. Roll each piece into a circle 6 inches in diameter. Use dough circles to line the individual muffin cups. Press dough into the bottom and up the sides of each cup; dough should come about three-fourths of the way up the sides.

Fill each minipizza with the following layers: 2 tablespoons grated mozzarella cheese; 1 tablespoon pizza sauce; 2 tablespoons combination of other toppings (pepperoni, sausage, onion, green bell pepper, etc.); 1 tablespoon pizza sauce; 1 tablespoon grated mozzarella cheese.

Bake in preheated 425-degree oven 12 to 15 minutes, or until crust is browned and cheese is melted and slightly browned. Let stand in pan 5 minutes before serving.

Note: A pound of grated cheese and two 8-ounce cans of pizza sauce is enough for 12 pizza cups. The amounts of the other toppings are variable, depending on how much you use of each. A pound of sausage, browned, is ample. If you use pepperoni, cut the slices into quarters first. Be sure to chop vegetables smaller than usual.

To make it easier to form the individual cups, drape the rolled out circle of dough over an inverted 1-cup dry measure and press to form the appropriate shape. Use the handle of the measuring cup to turn it over into the muffin cup, remove measuring cup, and press dough to the sides of the muffin cup. Try it — it's easy and fast!

You can use standard-size muffin pans (2 1/2 x 1 1/4-inch muffin cups), but they hold so little that the pizzas are more like hors d'oeuvres. That seems like a lot of fuss to me.

KIDS' PIZZA CUPS

Yield: 12 minipizzas.

DOUGH:

1 cup **milk**

¹/₄ cup **water**

1 teaspoon **salt**

3 cups **HODGSON MILL Best for Bread Flour**

1 tablespoon **granulated sugar**

2 teaspoons **FLEISCHMANN'S Bread Machine Yeast**

TOPPINGS:

1 (8-ounce) package **grated mozzarella cheese**

1 ¹/₂ cups **pizza sauce**

¹/₄ cup sliced and quartered **pepperoni**

¹/₄ cup coarsely chopped **onion**

¹/₄ cup coarsely chopped **green bell pepper**

Add milk, water, salt, flour, sugar and yeast to bread machine pan in the order suggested by manufacturer. Select **dough/manual cycle.**

When cycle is complete, transfer dough from machine to a lightly floured surface. Divide dough into 12 equal portions. Roll each piece into a 6-inch circle. Lightly grease Texas-size jumbo muffin pan (3x1 ¹/₂-inch muffin cups). Use dough circles to line the individual muffin cups. Press dough into the bottom and up the sides of each cup; dough should come about three-fourths of the way up the sides.

Fill each minipizza with the following layers: 2 tablespoons grated mozzarella cheese; 1 tablespoon pizza sauce; 2 table-spoons combination of other toppings (pepperoni, sausage, onion, green bell pepper, etc.); 1 tablespoon pizza sauce; 1 table-spoon grated mozzarella cheese.

Bake in a preheated 425-degree oven 12 to 15 minutes, or until done. Serve warm.

HONEY SPICE BREAD

Yield: 1 large round loaf or 2 or 3 canape loaves.

1 package **FLEISCHMANN'S Active Dry Yeast**

1/4 cup warm **water**

1 cup **milk**

1/4 cup (1/2 stick) **butter**, melted

1/2 cup **honey**

2 teaspoons ground **cinnamon**

2 teaspoons ground **coriander** (optional)

1 1/2 teaspoons **salt**

1/4 teaspoon ground **cloves**

4 to 5 cups **HODGSON MILL Best for Bread Flour**, divided

Combine yeast and warm water in a small bowl; stir to dissolve. Let stand 5 to 10 minutes, or until foamy.

Combine milk and melted butter in a medium mixing bowl; stir to mix. Stir in honey, cinnamon, coriander, salt, cloves and 1 cup of the flour. Add yeast mixture; stir until well blended. Add 3 cups of the flour, one cup at a time, mixing thoroughly after each addition.

Turn out dough onto a lightly floured surface. Knead, adding as much of the remaining 1 cup flour as needed to make a soft, slightly sticky dough that is smooth and elastic. Oil the surface of the dough and put in the rinsed mixing bowl. Cover with a clean towel and let rise in a warm, draft-free place about 1 hour, or until doubled. Punch down dough. Follow one of the shaping directions.

For canape molds: Canape molds are baking tins that produce bread in different shapes; that is, when the bread is sliced, each slice is shaped like a heart, a star, etc. The molds usually have a detachable top and bottom, to make it easy to remove the bread after baking. The tins are simple enough for children to use, and kids love making mini-PBJ sandwiches with the shaped slices. Follow manufacturer's instructions regarding amount of dough in each mold, oven temperature and baking times. But you may want to experiment a little bit; for example, the instructions for my set of baking molds said to bake at 375 degrees for 50 to 60 minutes, and I have never had to bake them more than 45. Canape molds are baked standing up in the oven, so be sure you have

Bread Break

The inspiration for this bread was an Ethiopian bread in Mariana Honig's *Breads of the World*, which continues to be one of my favorite bread books. I guess my American palate didn't care for the proportions of the flavors, because I've altered the amounts for all the spices. My experimentation with this bread, incidentally, yielded one of my first truly spectacular flops — a bread so bland and shapeless that I couldn't bear to put it out on the table!

When I got a result I liked, I followed my usual custom of tasting it with every condiment, spread and cheese in the entire kitchen. I was surprised and delighted by how good this bread tastes with peanut butter. Combining the exotic spices with a favorite like peanut butter might encourage kids to expand their tastes. If your kids are a bit fussy, have them smell the different spices in the jar before you add them; some kids might not care for the coriander or the cloves.

adequate oven height before starting the recipe. When the breads come out, the two end slices might be a bit overdone, but don't let that distress you. Just cut them off and enjoy the rest of the loaf.

For a round loaf: Form dough into a smooth ball and place in a lightly greased 3-quart baking dish or other ovenproof pan. Cover with a clean towel and let rise about 45 minutes, or until doubled. About 15 minutes before end of rising time, preheat oven to 350 degrees. Bake loaf 40 to 50 minutes, or until loaf is golden brown and sounds hollow when tapped. The honey might make the crust brown too quickly; if this happens, loosely cover the top of the loaf with aluminum foil and move the pan to a lower shelf in the oven. Remove foil for the last few minutes of baking. Remove from pan and let cool on a wire rack.

Note: This dough is easy to work with for sculpture bread. Choose easy animals at first (a turtle or a teddy bear, for example) and work your way up to alligators, mermaids and angels.

HONEY SPICE BREAD

Yield: 1 (1 ¹/₂-pound) loaf.

1 cup plus 2 tablespoons **milk**

1 tablespoon **butter**

1 ¹/₂ tablespoons **honey**

³/₄ teaspoon **salt**

1 ¹/₂ teaspoons ground **cinnamon**

¹/₄ teaspoon ground **cloves**

¹/₂ teaspoon ground **coriander**

3 cups **HODGSON MILL Best for Bread Flour**

1 ¹/₂ teaspoons **FLEISCHMANN'S Bread Machine Yeast**

Add milk, butter, honey, salt, cinnamon, cloves, coriander, flour and yeast to bread machine pan in the order suggested by the manufacturer. Select **basic cycle; medium/color settings.**

TV Series Episodes

Bread Machine Recipes

General Index

About the Author

TERRI GATES

Father Dominic Garramone, a priest and a Benedictine monk, says that his favorite thing about bread is that "you can't eat it alone."

He has been baking bread since his childhood in Peoria, Illinois, where he grew up among four sisters and brothers. He discovered that his baking avocation fits in well at St. Bede Abbey, the monastery where Father Dom lives in nearby Peru, Illinois. He has a large kitchen in which to experiment with recipes, and 34 fellow monks who are willing taste testers.

Father Dom teaches freshman religion at the monastery's coed college preparatory school, and directs students of all ages in the school's theatrical productions. He often invites students to join him in the kitchen, where Father Dom teaches lessons about responsibility, friendship, family and self using as examples the complex interaction of flavors and chemistry inherent in baking bread.

Father Dominic entered the monastery in 1983 when he was 22 years old. He graduated summa cum laude from St. Mary's College in Winona, Minnesota, and earned two Master's degrees, also summa cum laude, from St. Meinrad School of Theology in southern Indiana.

About St. Bede Abbey

My community of St. Bede Abbey is a Benedictine monastery found in the farmland and wooded bluffs west of Peru, Illinois. The community was established in 1890 as a priory of St. Vincent's Archabbey in Latrobe, Pennsylvania, and became an independent abbey in 1910. We live according to the Gospel of Christ and the Rule of St. Benedict, meeting for common prayer at morning, noon and evening, as well as for daily Mass. We also spend part of each day in private prayer and spiritual reading, so we're truly blessed to live in a more rural setting, with woods and gardens surrounding the monastery.

The 35 members of the St. Bede community are men of wide-ranging age and experience, from the junior brother still in his studies to the elderly and retired man who approaches death after more than 50 years of worship and service to the Lord. As I'm sure you can tell from the "monk stories" I tell on my program, we have plenty of colorful personalities to make life interesting!

Our work is varied, but includes a high school, parish ministry, spiritual direction and manual labor. The abbey orchard has over 1,200 apple trees, and is open for business from mid-August to early November—our cider is especially good, and has taken top honors at the Illinois Specialty Growers Convention. We have about a dozen beehives, and honey from the abbey apiary is in demand throughout the Illinois Valley. A busy print shop is also on the monastery premises. Within the monastic community, members perform a variety of services: business manager, candle maker, barber, plumber, electrician, gardener, organist, sculptor, writer, singer, auto mechanic and, of course, baker!

St. Bede Abbey welcomes men and women who wish to visit the monastery or spend time on retreat, but we really prefer for people to contact us first rather than just dropping by. If you would like to find out more about St. Bede, check out our Web site at *http://www.theramp.net/stbede/index.html.* To find out how you can support us in the works of our mission, you can write to: Office of Mission Advancement, St. Bede Abbey, Peru, IL 61354.

The Research-Based Argument Essay

Lucy Calkins, Mary Ehrenworth, and Annie Taranto

Photography by Peter Cunningham

HEINEMANN ◆ PORTSMOUTH, NH

This book is dedicated to my grandfather, who taught me to teach while teaching me to cook. —Annie

This book is dedicated to Jackson Ehrenworth, whose argument skills are daunting. —Mary

This book is dedicated to Kelly Boland, who has led so much of our work in argument writing. —Lucy

This book is also dedicated to our friends from CBAL at ETS (Randy Bennett, Paul Deane, Mary Fowles, Yi Song, Kasey Jueds), whose research in argument inspired us all.

Heinemann
361 Hanover Street
Portsmouth, NH 03801–3912
www.heinemann.com

Offices and agents throughout the world

© 2013 by Lucy Calkins and Mary Ehrenworth

The authors and publisher wish to thank those who have generously given permission to reprint borrowed material:

Excerpt from "Spelling," a poem by Margaret Atwood. Reproduced with permission of Curtis Brown Ltd., London on behalf of Margaret Atwood. Copyright © Margaret Atwood 1981. Used also by permission of Larmore Literary Agency.

Excerpt from "How to Write an Argument Essay," Bellevue Writing Lab. Reprinted by permission of Davina Ramirez.

Cataloging-in-Publication data is on file with the Library of Congress.

ISBN-13: 978-0-325-04743-0
ISBN-10: 0-325-04743-X

Production: Elizabeth Valway, David Stirling, and Abigail Heim
Cover and interior designs: Jenny Jensen Greenleaf
Series includes photographs by Peter Cunningham, Nadine Baldasare, and Elizabeth Dunford
Composition: Publishers' Design and Production Services, Inc.
Manufacturing: Steve Bernier

Printed in the United States of America on acid-free paper
21 20 19 18 17 EBM 2 3 4 5 6

Acknowledgments

THERE ARE HUNDREDS of teachers and students who piloted this teaching, and we are grateful to each and every one. The notebook pages and drafts that were sent to us, the feedback on lessons, and the research on student growth was invaluable. We are so lucky to work with communities of generous and dedicated educators. There are a few classrooms and individuals who especially contributed to the research of this unit of study. They include Marcie Von Beck and her fifth-grade students at Thurgood Marshall Elementary School, Seattle; the fifth-grade students at PS 134, Brooklyn, and their literacy coach, Jen McMorrow; Valerie Panzella and her fifth grade at PS 22, Staten Island; Simone Hampton at PS 54, Brooklyn; Katie Clements and Alex Messer at PS 321, Brooklyn; and the entire fifth-grade team at PS 197 in Brooklyn.

We can't say enough about how energizing it has been to rub shoulders with the team from CBAL (Cognitively Based Assessment of, for, and as Learning) at ETS. Randy Bennett, Paul Deane, Mary Fowles, Yi Song, and Kasey Jueds shared research, cosponsored retreats, studied student work, and generally raised the level of our knowledge. Many of the lessons in this unit were made more expert and authentic because of their advice. It's such a pleasure to work across disciplines and organizations with generous colleagues.

This book was written collaboratively by a team that involves others, beside ourselves, and the ideas in the book were coauthored by an even larger group. Kelly Boland plays a lead role in all of our work with opinion/argument writing. She developed and piloted talk protocols for debate, coauthored the curriculum, helped to design templates for inquiry minilessons, and wrote a good portion of this book. Hareem Khan also helped write and revise, bringing her special verve and a deep grounding in debate. Kate Montgomery helped with every aspect of the manuscript, from talking through the logic to drafting

sessions to streamlining the writing. From early discussions to drafting of curricular plans to piloting work in schools, many TCRWP staff developers also shared in this research. Of all of these, Audra Robb deserves special mention because she has been invested in the unit of study and in the performance assessments that were designed specifically for it from the start.

In this final book in the series, there are also some key people at Heinemann whose role in this process especially factored in during the final stages of production and who deserve a big salute. Elizabeth Valway has organized, translated, and entered changes to every page and every last word as requested—even taking the time to think through and make the additional changes resulting from the original changes, before they even occurred to us. Sarah Fournier, editorial coordinator at Heinemann, has been managing the flow of permissions and contracts and student writing—which is an enormous amount of work for thirty-three simultaneously occurring projects. She has also served as both editor and project manager for the online resources for every grade. She has been unfailingly reliable, always gracious, and impeccable in her care of us. Teva Blair, lead editor, has parented the entire effort. And Abby Heim has not only been the producer, but has also been our counselor, manager, and champion. Of course, leading all of these people is Kate Montgomery, who has always been, for us, the leading light at Heinemann.

The class described in this unit is a composite class, with children and partnerships of children gleaned from classrooms in very different contexts, then put together here. We wrote the units this way to bring you both a wide array of wonderful, quirky, various children and also to illustrate for you the predictable (and unpredictable) situations and responses this unit has created in classrooms across the nation and world.

—Lucy, Mary, and Annie

Contents

BEND III Writing for Real-Life Purposes and Audiences

Registration instructions to access the digital resources that accompany this book may be found on p. ix.

Welcome to the Unit

THE FREEDOM TO ARGUE is one of our most important freedoms. As long as we can write and talk to create change, we have a precious freedom indeed. This is the glory of participatory democracy. It is no wonder, then, that when the effort was made to unite all fifty states around common standards, argument was featured in those standards. Argument is part and parcel of what it means to be a citizen in a democracy. That is, when you teach your students to argue with logic as well as passion (and to listen to and read the arguments of others, testing them for their logic and credibility), you teach them to become discriminating and credible, influential and engaged. You teach not only a skill but an identity and a way of life that is essential in a democracy.

Of course, argument is also essential to the academy, the university, and knowledgeable professionals everywhere. Nothing is more important than the ability to weigh conflicting views and to decide thoughtfully on one's own position, and then to articulate that position in ways that are convincing to others. Think, for example, about your response to any of the new developments in the field of education: the push for privatization, the effort to evaluate teacher proficiency through test scores and other measures, the world-class state standards themselves. The teaching profession relies on you and your colleagues being knowledgeable about these developments and speaking out in ways that are compelling and credible. As Diane Ravitch, former assistant secretary of education and a leading educational historian, said recently at a keynote to Teachers College Reading and Writing Project principals, "Politicians are—and must be—followers. They follow public opinion. So the future of education is in your hands." We must use our skills in argument writing to have a voice in the greatest makeover of public education that this nation has ever seen!

Clearly, the goals of this unit are big ones; it is rigorous work. As argument writers, students are expected to structure their writing so that it includes claims that are supported by reasons that are backed by evidence. As part of this, you'll teach your students to sort, weigh, and order evidence. They'll learn to suspend judgment, to read critically, to note-take, to build an argument, and to revise and rethink and rebuild. You'll pay particular attention to helping your students create an organizational structure in which ideas are logically grouped to support the writer's purpose. Students will have been working on this goal for years, and by now, you'll be able to tap that acquired expertise so they can easily think inside the structures they take on.

Because your students will enter this unit positioned to meet the fifth-grade standards, and because the expectations of middle school students are facing them, this unit goes well beyond the fifth-grade standards alone. For example, while those standards ask for students to organize their writing in logical groupings, you'll take the emphasis on logic further. The goal of your unit can be summarized this way: teach students to argue logically by teaching them to analyze texts, to weigh evidence, and to consider logical reasoning. You will reach up to the seventh-grade standards, even, by teaching students to consider two important elements—audience appeal and counterargument.

Of course, for students to write argument texts well, they need to draw on their entire skill set as writers (not just as persuasive writers). In this unit, you will convey to students the expectation that they plan and rehearse their writing; collect, sort, and select from an abundance of specific information; assess their writing using checklists; study and emulate the work of mentor writers; draw on a host of revision and editing strategies as well as knowledge of good writing to improve their drafts; meet publishing deadlines; and help each other within a community of writers. This work will stand on the shoulders of all the work your students have been doing up until now (a goal of all units, but one that is particularly essential here). With all the opinion and argument writing they have done across the grades, we feel they are ready to reach forward, and we want to send them on with the greatest possible powers as writers.

You will put a new emphasis on partner talk within this unit of study and demonstrate that one productive way to talk is to deliberately take different positions and engage in an information debate. You'll teach your students debating moves. As they engage in debates, you'll help them argue not with emotion and folk knowledge, but with evidence and logic. Then as your students write, too, you will help them to shift from offering personal opinions and preferences to staking claims and backing those claims with reasons and evidence.

Threading throughout this entire unit is an emphasis on critical reading, which supports the fifth-grade reading standard that focuses on using reasons and evidence to support particular points in a text and drawing evidence from literary or informational texts to support analysis, reflection, and research.

Finally, like other fifth-grade units, this unit also supports efficiency, taking students through more than one round of writing and providing them with multiple opportunities to write "flash-drafts." In this way, they learn to write powerfully in short periods of time, transferring writing skills developed through slower, deeper work into more compressed time frames. That work, what the standards describe as "planning, revising, editing, rewriting," using technology for research and for publishing, is inherent in this unit, as in prior units.

OVERVIEW OF THE UNIT

At the start of the unit, students will investigate and write argument essays about whether or not chocolate milk should be served in schools. As students explore that issue, they'll read texts, both digital and print, exploring the reasons for and against flavored milk in schools. These resources can be found in the online resources.

You may be surprised by the fact that we assign students a topic for the first portion of this unit. We've struggled with this as well and tried teaching the unit in many different ways to offer students choices and still provide them the support we think is important. After great deliberation, we hold

that the demands on students are sizeable and that students' work during the first portion of this unit is best supported when they are able to work with a carefully constructed text set of articles and videotapes. Although there is nothing magical about the issue of whether chocolate milk should or should not be served in elementary schools, many hundreds of teachers have piloted this unit using that topic and the corresponding text set of materials, and therefore we have been able to work the kinks out of these. You can, of course, choose an alternative topic. The unit is constructed so that the topic is almost a case in point, and another topic could be substituted. Should you decide to select another topic, you can find alternative text sets on our website (www.readingandwritingproject.com).

In the unit's first bend, as students explore the issue of whether chocolate milk should be served, you will guide them to understand that to develop a solid argument, they need to research both sides of an issue, postponing a quick, premature conclusion until the actual evidence is cumulated and reviewed. Once students have studied texts—both print and digital—that advance different perspectives on the issue, you will teach them to consider the warrant behind arguments in those texts, reading these critically. Students will then begin to plan and write their own arguments, and for now, this will lead them to draft letters to the principal on this whole-class topic.

To write persuasive letters, students will draw on all they know about structuring persuasive essays. You will also teach them to cull evidence from sources and to analyze their data. As part of this work, you'll show them how to interpret the data from the texts they are reading, analyzing the numbers and doing the math. The writing process, in this instance, is a process of composing an argument, and you'll coach students to make decisions about which information to quote and which to paraphrase and about ways to set the context for the evidence they ultimately decide to include in their letters.

The second bend begins with a response from the principal in which she invites students to further research whether or not chocolate milk should be in schools and to craft position papers, or argument essays, to be presented to panels of administrators, parents, and cafeteria workers. With their charge set, students will return to research, thinking about the possible systems for note-taking they might employ and then selecting the one that works best for them. Then too, they'll look at the research with a more critical eye. They are more knowledgeable on the topic, more adept at noticing the author's perspective as well as conflicting information.

As students move toward drafting, they will look across the data they have gathered throughout the unit and evaluate it, deciding which evidence they will use to bolster their claims. They'll look for flaws in their logic and revise their work to make their arguments more sound. Students will also entertain counterclaims, stating and debunking the other side, and will attend carefully to the perspectives of their audience, thinking through the roles the individuals in the audience hold in the world and therefore the evidence they would find most compelling.

For the final bend of the unit, writers will draw on all they know about writing to take a stand in the world. They'll write another argument essay, this time about a topic of their choosing, to contribute to a public conversation. Students will think about what they want to change in the world, or what they want people to think differently about, and embark on their research, gathering texts as well as finding new sources of evidence, conducting interviews and surveys of their own. With their deadline in mind, students will make plans for their own writing, outlining the work they still need to do and how they intend to get it done, applying all they have learned about argument writing. Students will also carry their knowledge of narrative writing into argument, using real or imagined moments to make their point, and they'll learn not to generalize their evidence, but rather to accurately portray the data, to make effective cases.

ASSESSMENT

As with all the units in this series, prior to launching the unit, you will want to assess your students' grasp of the kind of writing they'll be doing—in this case argument writing. Establishing a baseline will help you to tailor your teaching to meet the needs of your students as well as provide students with the chance to monitor their own progress throughout the unit, setting goals and evaluating their growth by putting their subsequent pieces next to their first.

Just as in prior units, you will want this assessment to be accurate, a true representation of the work that students can do all on their own. You'll want to give students the following prompt, which reminds them of the expectations inherent in argument writing, and then step back and let them write.

"Think of a topic or issue that you know and care about, an issue around which you have strong feelings. Tomorrow, you will have forty-five minutes to write an opinion or argument text in which you will write your opinion

or claim and tell reasons why you feel that way. When you do this, draw on everything you know about essays, persuasive letters, and reviews. If you want to find and use information from a book or another outside source, you may bring that with you tomorrow. Please keep in mind that you'll have forty-five minutes to complete this, so you will need to plan, draft, revise, and edit in one sitting."

As in prior on-demand writing tasks, you will want to list the qualities of argument writing you expect students to include in their pieces. You could say or display the following.

"In your writing, make sure you:

- Write an introduction
- State your opinion or claim
- Give reasons and evidence
- Organize your writing
- Acknowledge counterclaims
- Use transition words
- Write a conclusion"

This on-demand task will give you vital information about students' current knowledge of persuasive writing as a genre—its purpose, craft, and structure. You'll also find out how your students write when they write about something about which they know a lot and care deeply. This will be important knowledge, because this unit of study focuses on a lot of text-based research. That means that sometimes what looks like writing difficulty is really reading trouble. The students may not deeply comprehend the texts, which makes it impossible to write well about them. This task, therefore, will let you see how a student writes when reading is not an issue and will help you separate reading skills from writing skills.

Once students have completed the writing task, you will want to assess them with the Opinion/Argument Writing Learning Progression. Find where each individual piece of writing falls on the learning progression, and then look to see at which level the majority of the class stands. This information will help you tailor your whole-class instruction. To level each piece of writing using the learning progression, we recommend you read each student's piece and then look at the exemplar texts at several levels, thinking, "Which one most closely resembles my student's writing?" Once you've settled on a level for the writing, then look to the descriptors of that level to identify specific ways each child can improve. If a writer's essay is level 5, you and that writer can look at the descriptors of, say, elaboration, providing reasons and evidence for those reasons, and note whether the writing adheres to those. If so, tell that child—or your whole class, if this is broadly applicable—"You used to support your reasons by . . . ," and read the descriptors from the prior level "but now you are . . . ," and read the level 5 descriptor. "Can I give you a pointer about a way to make your writing even better? You could try . . . ," and read from the level 6 descriptor. You can even say, "Let me show you an example," and then cite a section of the level 6 exemplar text.

If, in prior units, you duplicated students' on-demand writing and taped it into their writing notebooks, you will want to do so again now. Your students should be familiar with the checklists by now, so you might ask them to assess their own on-demand writing, gathering a baseline. Then, as students dive into the work of this unit, they can work toward their self-set goals. They might put their on-demand writing side by side with their work inside the unit, looking to see if they have maintained the quality of their work as well as to see how their work is growing progressively stronger as they move through the bends.

At the end of the unit, you'll assess again. You could give the same task, on a different topic, with a different text set. We've found, though, that there is something very powerful for children in doing it again—using the same texts—and then laying their two pieces alongside each other and marking them up, annotating them, and showing off their new skills. It's just easier to see the new writing work when the research is the same.

GETTING READY

In this unit, research and knowledge are at the heart of student writing. To write well, they must be knowledgeable about the topic; they need several texts with which to work. So, as you prepare for this unit, you will need to select a class topic for all students to research and write about in the first two bends and then gather a text set, one that includes both print and digital texts and that includes texts that represent both sides of the issue. You also may choose to include some more nuanced texts for students to study as they grow more sophisticated at critical reading and more adept at navigating the art of argument.

We recommend studying the debate over chocolate milk in schools; the text set to support that can be found in the online resources. Prior to beginning, you will want to print the articles and make copies for the class (we recommend "Nutrition in Disguise" and "Chocolate Milk: More Harmful Than Healthful" to start). If you are able to show videos, they will add to your unit, but they are not essential. You might cue up videos on class computers for students to watch and take notes during independent writing; if you do that, we recommend "Sugar Overload" and "Flavored Milk: Tasty Nutrition."

Some of the teaching in this unit, much as in the unit before this one, is *implicit*. Students will learn by studying the arguments of others. You will want to have mentor essays for students to study as they write. We recommend using the drafts and essays highlighted throughout the unit, those written by Jack as a sixth-grader. These can be found in the online resources, and you will likely want to print them and make copies for students to refer to as they work.

ONLINE DIGITAL RESOURCES

A variety of resources to accompany this and the other Grade 5 Units of Study in Opinion, Information, and Narrative Writing are available in the online resources. To access and download all the digital resources for this grade-level set:

1. Go to **www.heinemann.com** and click the link in the upper right to log in. (If you do not have an account yet, you will need to create one.)

2. **Enter the following registration code** in the box to register your product: **WUOS_GR5**

3. Enter the security information requested, obtained from within your unit book.

4. Once you have registered your product it will appear in the list of "View my registered Online Resources, Videos, and eBooks." (Note: You only need register once; then each time you return to your account, just click the "My Online Resources" link to access these materials.)

(You may keep copies of these resources on up to six of your own computers or devices. By downloading the files you acknowledge that they are for your individual or classroom use and that neither the resources nor the product code will be distributed or shared.)

Investigating to Understand an Argument

IN THIS SESSION, you'll teach students that when argument writers begin to research a topic, they investigate and collect information about both sides of the issue.

GETTING READY

✔ Letter from the principal asking teachers to weigh in on whether or not chocolate milk should be served in schools (see Connection)

✔ T-chart for notes that has the heading "Chocolate Milk in School" prewritten at the top, and "For" on the left and "Against" on the right (see Teaching)

✔ Texts on hand for reading aloud or viewing: the article "Nutrition in Disguise: What the Midwest Dairy Council Has to Say about Chocolate Milk" or the original video *Flavored Milk: Tasty Nutrition* (see Teaching), and the article "Chocolate Milk: More Harmful than Healthful" or the video *Sugar Overload* (see Active Engagement)

✔ Large Post-its® and note cards (see Teaching and Active Engagement)

✔ Students' writers' notebooks and pens (see Teaching and Active Engagement)

✔ Example of student writing that shows the student noting bibliographic information (see Mid-Workshop Teaching)

✔ "How to Write an Argument" chart (see Share)

YOUR STUDENTS ARE GROWING UP in a millennium that will witness unprecedented change. In their short lives, your kids have seen Egypt run its first democratic election. Copenhagen hosted an international summit to protect the environment. NASA achieved its first landing on Mars. There has been trouble, too. Japan suffered a catastrophic nuclear meltdown. Syria experienced massacres in the tens of thousands as its people struggled for basic human rights: freedom from oppression and the choice of their own leaders.

When we look at what is going on in the world, and at how ordinary people in places around the world have suffered, we are reminded of what a gift it can be for our children to grow up in this country. They may not always like their political leaders. They may disagree with social and economic decisions that are made by their government. But they will always have an opportunity to express their views and argue for what they believe in. The children we teach will not fear violent reprisals if they raise their voices or build coalitions around important issues.

This unit of study aims to move your students dramatically forward with their argument skills—in writing most of all, but also in speaking and critical thinking. The overall goal of this unit of study is to teach students to be more persuasive and more analytic, able to weigh evidence, to follow lines of logic, and draw evidenced-based conclusions. Behind this goal is the hope that students will use their newfound skills of critical thinking and persuasion to do good in the world. There will be work, therefore, to help them become accustomed to listening to others, acknowledging complexity, suspending judgment, evaluating evidence, and imagining things not the way they are, but the way they *might* be, so that their opinions reflect an informed, fair perspective.

I'm reminded of a story that might explain the impetus of this particular unit of study and its stance. It's a visit that Walter Dean Myers, the noted children's author, made to one of our schools. Walter spoke of growing up as a foster child and struggling to keep his head above water in school. He spoke of writing books and only realizing after his father had died that his father never read them because he couldn't read.

Then Walter spoke about one of the most valuable lessons he learned from his father and his father's generation. That lesson was that the right to become powerful readers and writers, to express their ideas, to enter into debate and argument, was a right that men and women had given their lives to achieve for their children and grandchildren in this country. He spoke of Dr. Martin Luther King, Jr., and he said to the school children, "Don't you dare neglect this right, for it is not given to all, and it has been won with great courage."

"The overall goal of this unit of study is to teach students to be more persuasive and more analytic, able to weigh evidence, to follow lines of logic, and draw evidenced-based conclusions."

We forget, sometimes, that our students need to be inculcated with the knowledge that the right to argue is profoundly important. In this unit of study, therefore, students will develop skills at composing arguments about issues that directly affect them, for after all, that is how activists argue. We'll suggest that they begin with the issue of chocolate milk, which is embedded in issues of choice, authority, control, and the ethics of advertising. Across the unit, children will also investigate and argue issues that are of deep personal concern, no matter how quirky, so that they see that the point of this work is not just to make decisions about chocolate milk; it is to express their views convincingly on any matter that they care deeply about and have researched.

In Bend I, the focus is on moving students from opinion and preferences to evidence-based argument. This bend focuses on improving their skills at structuring argument essays and at collecting and incorporating evidence into what will ultimately be argument letters. In Bend II, students will bring the arguments they made in Bend I to a bigger audience and develop these into essays that are position papers and panel presentations. To do this, they will develop more focused and specific positions and weigh possible reasons, selecting the most relevant and evidenced-based. They will learn to critique the arguments that others make and in doing so, critique (and ultimately strengthen) their own arguments. In the final portion of this unit, students will do this work with more independence, each working on his or her own individual topic. Students will learn to find evidence, using interviews and surveys as well as reading to learn varied perspectives on a topic. This final bend focuses on agency and activism, as students shape their arguments to best affect decision makers and interested parties.

This unit of study brings together all of the reading and writing skills your students have studied for years, including the research and organizational skills of the last information unit, the expressive writing skills they learned in narrative, the writing about reading skills developed in literary essay, and the focus on reflection they honed in memoir. Moreover, it positions your students for the writing they will do in middle school and beyond and positions them to live as informed and engaged citizens.

Investigating to Understand an Argument

CONNECTION

Create a real-life mini-drama in which you motivate kids to weigh in on an issue that is relevant and accessible to them.

"Will you help me? I got a note from our principal today, asking me to weigh in on an issue. But I actually think this is something you know more about than I do, so I would love your advice. Ms. Granger wrote this." I opened an envelope, drew out a letter, and read:

> Dear Teachers,
>
> There has been some controversy about our policy of offering chocolate milk for school lunch. We need to make a decision about whether or not we should continue offering it in the cafeteria. Will you let me know what you think about this? Thank you!
>
> Sincerely,
>
> Ms. Granger

"So there it is. I need to let her know whether or not the school cafeteria should serve chocolate milk. For me, the question kind of came out of the blue—I haven't exactly been worrying about whether chocolate milk is or isn't a good thing to offer kids—so I've been carefully pondering this. And I realized you could help me think it through.

"What do you think? How would you answer Ms. Granger? Will you tell each other your thoughts? Turn and talk." The students talked for a moment and then I signaled for their attention.

As students jump to share opinions, caution them that these should be based on more than gut reactions. Opinions need to grow from consideration of evidence, which means suspending judgment.

"Here's the thing. It's not so hard to have an opinion. In fact, it's terribly easy to have an opinion. You just . . . have one. Right? '*I love* chocolate milk. That's my opinion.' Or '*No way. I don't even like* chocolate milk.' Your opinion is the first thing that comes to mind. You like chocolate, so why not serve it? Or you have a chocolate allergy, so no one should have it."

Teachers, this initial inquiry will thread its way throughout this book, so although we usually encourage you to alter anything to suit you, in this instance, if you alter the starting inquiry, you'll find that one decision has a ripple effect across a good deal of this unit.

It may surprise you that we channel students to all write about this one issue in lieu of giving them topic choice. After all, a principle that underlies much of workshop instruction is that writers choose what they want to say. The goal, however, is not to follow the Ten Commandments of Writing Workshop. Rather, the goal is to maximize opportunities for development, to accelerate growth. This unit is unique in part because the writing students will produce will not come from their personal expertise; rather, it is grounded in research. We have found that students are most successful in this genre if they spend some time working together on iterations of a class topic, gathering enough information about that topic to write well. Gradually, they'll diverge to more independent topic choices— and all along, their choice of thesis will be shaped individually.

"But here's the deal: what we think right away, or what we personally prefer—that's not the whole story! That isn't all there is to know or think about an issue.

"Our responsibility in the world is to try to understand more than ourselves. When we offer an opinion (especially when the consequences matter) we can't be self-centered or shallow about our answers. We can't only say what we think off the top of our heads. Our position needs to be considered carefully from different angles."

Point out that your students' initial opinions about the issue at hand provide them with starting points, and from here, they need to engage in the process of weighing evidence to develop considered arguments.

"When I asked you what you thought about serving chocolate milk and said, 'Turn and talk,' what you said to each other was really *a starting point* for an argument. Some of you started with a strong sense of 'I know where I stand on this,' and some with a sort of 'leaning' toward one response or another. Some of you started equally able to go either way. But before you answer Ms. Granger, you need to move from that starting point to a position that is what people call 'considered.' That is, an argument you've researched and developed.

"So back to the question: should we sell chocolate milk in the school cafeteria? Should it be banned? Ms. Granger wants help choosing a position on this issue."

❖ **Name your teaching point.**

"Writers, today I want to teach you that when you are composing an argument, you will need to collect evidence not to support what you first think about the issue, but instead, evidence that allows you to think through the various sides of the argument."

TEACHING

Direct students' attention to an introductory text on the topic that clearly supports one side of this issue, and offer some tips for ways to collect evidence.

"Let's start by giving this a try together. Then you can try it with a partner, and after that I'll send you off to finish collecting some evidence on your own for the rest of today. Tomorrow you'll fast-draft an argument for or against chocolate milk, which you can then send to Ms. Granger. That means that you'll use the evidence you collect today to support your position in your writing tomorrow."

"Since you will need evidence to build your arguments, you'll want to read some of the strong voices in this debate. There's a folder on each of your tables. To collect and organize information, you will each need to come up with a system for recording notes. Recall that in your research report unit, you collected information in booklets. You may end

It is an oversimplification to teach children that you build an argument by taking a position and backing it up with evidence when, really, first you consider the evidence, weighing all the data and sources, then you build a theory and test it out, revising it as you research. For now, simplifying lets you get started efficiently.

At the start of an argument unit of study, we generally provide children with texts that clearly support one side of the argument. By reading one clear position first, students can practice pulling out relevant evidence (this is harder than it seems). It is natural for someone to listen to a controversial and opinionated view on a topic and to react by thinking, "But that's just one side of the story." After reading (or hearing) one side of an argument, students will be apt to find themselves voicing the other sides, and that kind of critical thinking is exactly what we hope to affect. Across the unit, we progress from working with texts that are explicit and one-sided toward texts that are more nuanced.

To help students have the knowledge they need to write about this issue and yet to keep their focus on writing (as opposed to searching for sources), we suggest you provision them with a text set of relevant information. A few texts packed with information will do; students will need to return to the texts they have often, milking them for all they are worth. We encourage you to include some digital texts. As the unit progresses, students will end up living like magnets, finding more texts on the same topic, growing the text set across the unit. We have created a starter text set on chocolate milk that you might use. You can find the bibliography with links to the texts and videos in the online resources. 👆

up deciding to do this again. For now, I'm going to show you how I set up my notes, knowing that I'm collecting toward *both* sides of this argument." I turned to the chart paper and gestured for students to open their notebooks.

"I'm thinking that the information will address both sides of this question. Some of the facts will build an argument *for* chocolate milk in schools, and some will build an argument *against* chocolate milk in schools. It will be important to research both sides of this issue to make an informed argument. I'm going to label one page of my notebook 'For,' and the page across from it will be 'Against.' Then, as I go, I'll add things to one page or the other. You can figure out your own system as well." I put a few large blank Post-its on each side of my pages, ready to hold notes.

I gestured to two pages of chart paper, where I had made a large-scale version of my two notebook pages:

Chocolate Milk in Schools	
For	**Against**

Demonstrate taking notes on Post-its, which can be moved around later.

"The text we're going to read is called 'Nutrition in Disguise: What the Midwest Dairy Council Has to Say About Chocolate Milk.' It's no secret that the title of a piece often tells you what side the author supports. The title can give you a sense of the kind of evidence a piece will offer up. 'Nutrition in Disguise: What the Midwest Dairy Council Has to Say About Chocolate Milk.' Hmm. What do you expect? Will it argue *for* schools distributing chocolate milk or *against*?"

Children chimed that it would be *for* chocolate milk. "Writers, I heard many of you suggest we can expect to be working on the *for* page in our notebooks. I agree. I'll use these Post-its to write on so I can sort the details later. You might want to use this same collecting technique, or you may have another method you prefer. I'll give you just a moment to get whatever materials you have on hand ready.

"We won't read the whole text. For now, I want to make sure that you feel comfortable with this process: figuring out how to set up your notes to collect evidence on the different sides of an issue, quickly deciding what side an author is supporting, and gathering some details from what you read, as evidence in support of that side."

Demonstrate collecting evidence for one side of the issue, using any research skills that are common to your classroom.

"I expect this article will help me collect evidence that supports the 'Yes, chocolate milk in schools' position in this debate. You can collect evidence now as well, if you'd like." I read the start of the article, then paused.

You may choose to read aloud this text, or turn to the original video, which students find engaging and which you can watch in about two minutes. The video is available from the Midwest Dairy Association's website: www.midwestdairy.com.

Your students did a tremendous amount of research in the information writing unit so some of them will want to rely on note-taking systems that have worked for them. Some may choose, therefore, to record boxes and bullets in their notebook or to use note cards that they plan to tape into their notebook or keep in an envelope or folder. By suggesting a system, you guarantee that every student can get started, even ones who are not confident enough to draw on prior knowledge and experience to choose their own system. There will be time later in the unit to refine individual systems.

Notice that we introduce the concept that we're collecting evidence to support a position. Most state standards speak of this as a claim with reasons and evidence. We also emphasize the concept of taking a position in an argument in which there are different sides. Perhaps because it's a sports reference, children seem receptive to the notion of taking and defending a position.

"Nutrition in Disguise: What the Midwest Dairy Council Has to Say about Chocolate Milk"

If you secretly love chocolate milk, you're in for some happy news. Recently, the Midwest Dairy Association released an infomercial that argues chocolate milk is, according to nutritionist Melissa Dobbins, "nutrition in disguise."

In the infomercial, Ms. Dobbins, who introduces herself as a nutritionist for the Dairy Association and a mom, brings along three young friends to help her demonstrate that chocolate milk is a healthy part of a young person's diet. As Ms. Dobbins puts it, "The fact is, that chocolate and other flavored milks have the same 9 essential nutrients as white milk, and a small amount of added sugar compared to other beverages. Best of all, because they love the taste, some kids drink more milk when it's flavored."

When I paused, I jotted two simple notes, one stating that chocolate milk had nutrients, and another that chocolate milk got kids to drink more milk. I plastered these on the page that was *for* chocolate milk in schools in the enlarged chart-paper version of my notebook, muttering aloud as if thinking to myself, "Hmm, chocolate milk has all those nutrients. That seems important. And kids drink *more* milk when it's flavored, I bet."

I read a bit more of the text.

You only have to watch kids in the lunch line to see the truth of what Ms. Dobbins says. Given a choice, almost any child will choose chocolate milk over white. "We serve six or seven cartons of chocolate for each one of white milk at lunch," says Mrs. Rally, a server in a local elementary school cafeteria. "In fact it's pretty much only with breakfast cereal that any kid would choose white milk."

What's the attraction of chocolate milk? Well, if you haven't had any for awhile, give it a try. You'll have to admit that the creamy, smooth, chocolaty taste is truly delicious. But is it good for you? Ms. Dobbins says . . . yes. "Research shows that children who drink flavored milk meet more of their nutrient needs, do not consume more added sugar, fat, and calories, and are not heavier than non milk drinkers," says Ms. Dobbins.

"Hmm," I murmured. "Let's see, what details clearly support for (or against) chocolate milk here? Well, I guess that kids who drink chocolate milk don't consume more sugar, fat, or calories. That's really interesting. *I* assumed they definitely did. After all, chocolate milk has more calories. That's very interesting. Let me jot that down." I did.

"Let's stop now. You'll want to read the rest of it later; it will be in your folders so you can continue your research."

Debrief in a way that is transferable to another text, another day.

"Did you see what I did that you could try too? I took in the information from the text, thought about which side of the debate it helped, and wrote down that information in the right section of my notebook, so that I can use it later when I write my argument. I'm still not sure what my position will be, but I'm collecting information that this author presents—not my own feelings, but evidence from the text. Even if I had a hunch, like you might have had, about what my final position will be, I'm still keeping an open mind about it. Who knows what you'll learn as you research this topic! I'm sure you all got information from that part and wrote it down somehow in your notes as well."

The work that students will do in this unit is a far cry from the reports that many of us wrote when we were kids. These days, students read divergent perspectives on a topic to notice not only the varied perspectives but also the sources of information. They question the biases and the warrant behind the sources. They notice that the information from various sources can't always be synthesized into one amalgamated Ye Ole Report. Instead, the thoughtful reader is aware that reading is a bit like watching a boxing match in which different intellectual positions duke it out. The astute reader reads as one might watch a fight, thinking, "What's the fight about?" "What are the sides here?" "Who is winning?"

This consciousness is the end goal of this unit, not the starting point. Today's session is only Session 1. But you will see that this session orients students to expect something different than traditional reports.

In the new science frameworks (Next-Generation Science Standards), this discrepancy is sometimes referred to as "folk knowledge." One goal of research is to unsettle your folk knowledge, or prior understanding, in favor of a more researched stance. (See www.nextgenscience .org to see the draft standards.)

Your urge may be to finish reading entire texts in the minilesson so that your students comprehend these under your tutelage. Actually, though, you want to leave big chunks of the text for students to read on their own. Think of the minilesson as a sort of book introduction, or teaser, where you peak students' interest. Then, during independent time they can continue working on their own. Encourage them to finish texts you've introduced and then to turn to other texts in their folders. A reading list of videos and downloadable articles is included in the bibliography in the online resources, as is the full text of this article, which you'll use again in the following sessions. ✺

ACTIVE ENGAGEMENT

Invite students to give this a try. Reiterate the process you followed, and then set children up to glean more information from a different text. Do this by reading it aloud and stopping after a bit so students can talk with their partners and take more notes.

"Writers, let's give you a chance to really focus on this. The trick is to take in the text and then collect details that clearly support one side or the other of this issue. Let's look at a second text. It's titled 'Chocolate Milk: More Harmful than Healthful.' Quickly, which side of the debate do you think this supports? Thumbs up if you think it's *for* chocolate milk in schools. Thumbs down if you think it's *against* chocolate milk in schools." Almost all thumbs went down for the second one.

"Great. Reading something from the other side will keep us from getting stuck on one side. I'm going to read aloud the first part, and as I do so, try to catch some information and decide where it goes. When I stop, you'll have a chance to talk with your partner about the information you gleaned, showing each other exactly what you recorded and where you put that information." I read aloud.

"Chocolate Milk: More Harmful than Healthful"

Schools around the world serve chocolate milk—and kids love it. On a recent Australian newscast, investigative reporter Chloe Baker interviewed children about chocolate milk. "The only time I get chocolate milk is when I go to school only," one student told Ms. Baker, as her friends nodded. In fact, many children only get to have chocolate milk at school—but they get to drink a lot of it there. Some children consume as many as 10 or even 15 cartons of chocolate milk in a week at school. Baker noted that "it's an out-of-control problem."

Chocolate milk has a sky-high sugar content. One tiny carton of chocolate milk has approximately 30 grams of sugar. That is more than a can of soda—and you wouldn't see schools giving kids Coke. In fact, according to the Coca-Cola company, a mini-can, which contains 7.5 fluid ounces of soda, has only 25 grams of sugar. Thus, a small container of chocolate milk has approximately 20% more sugar than soda.

The students jotted notes, turned, and talked with their partners about the information they'd recorded.

"I can't believe how much sugar chocolate milk has!" Claire exclaimed. "I thought that other lady said it had hardly any added sugar. I don't know *what* to think now." She added "chocolate milk has more sugar than soda" to the *against* side of her chart and stared dubiously at her prior note, "chocolate milk has less sugar than soda," that was on her *for* side. (See the online resources to view Claire's chart.)

I reconvened the students. "Writers, Claire has raised an issue that I notice a lot of you are struggling with. That is, that these authors not only offer conflicting viewpoints; they even have conflicting information! Remember, one reason you're researching is that this issue is complicated; you'll have to find out more to form your own opinion. Later, when you're reading, you can investigate this information more."

Again, you can choose to read aloud or you can show the video, "Sugar Overload," which is available in the online resources.

In a think tank we participate in with members of a special branch of the Educational Testing Service (ETS) called Cognitively Based Assessment of, for, and as Learning (CBAL) that is researching, among other things, argument, we found that moving quickly from a text that supports one side of the argument to one that supports the other is strategic—and you can reinforce this strategy with your students later. When people only read material that supports one side of an argument for too long, once they finally begin to research the other side, they're so stuck in their thinking that they refuse to acknowledge the legitimacy of any evidence for the other side. Move right away to a text that supports the opposite viewpoint, and you'll both illuminate the authenticity of this argument, and you'll help your students suspend judgment.

Take advantage of how some of your students notice conflicting information, and use that to hammer home the notion of suspending judgment and diving into research. Also notice which students put details on the wrong side of the chart. This is an early indicator that they'll struggle with supporting a side. In fact, one reason this sorting exercise is so important early on in the unit is that it reveals right away which students need easier texts or help identifying evidence or both.

LINK

Remind writers that solid arguments require a well-rounded, considered understanding of the issue. Offer them more materials they can use to build their arguments, and let them know they'll fast-draft tomorrow.

"Writers, do you know some people in your life who are absolutely set in their ways, people for whom it would take a major miracle to even consider any other way of looking at things?" Many kids agreed with me; I'd struck a nerve. "It's frustrating to talk with a person who acts like," I made a stern face, crossed both arms, and acted like the protector of all truth. Then I added, "The truth is that *most* of us are like that about some things. We know what we think and don't want to even *hear* any other idea. The thing is, though, if we really want to be the wisest people we can possibly be, it's important to listen to alternate views, to consider other ideas.

"You can decide what kind of thinker you want to be. I hope that you learn that when it counts, it's best to postpone being 100% absolutely sure," and I again replayed the stern face, crossed arms, protector of all truth. "It is best to study the situation, to gather information from various perspectives, and *then* build a reasoned opinion—with evidence! Building solid arguments takes work.

"So although you may already be beginning to support a position on chocolate milk, I hope you are willing to consider alternate views. I've put a stack of articles about the pros and cons of chocolate milk in schools on each of your tables, and there are a couple of computers loaded up with some videos. I particularly recommend Jamie Oliver's *Sugar Overload* video! I also put a list in your folders, in case you want to read or download videos tonight. Use these materials to gather evidence and various points of view so that you can build reasoned arguments. Tomorrow you can fast-draft a response to Ms. Granger, using information from your research to defend your position. As you work today, remember to use all you know to help you, not just what you've learned today. Off you go!"

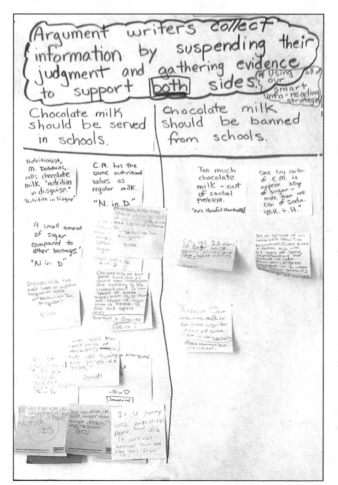

Sometimes, even when it seems blatant to us that a particular text weighs in as for or as against an issue, some students have a very hard time discerning this. For now, try providing kids with enough support that this confusion doesn't derail them. It helps to select articles that are not gray on an issue—making it easier to discern where the author stands—so what you've put in these folders, or the digital texts you've bookmarked, should be strategic. Later you can introduce sources that are more complex and nuanced.

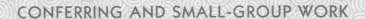

Coaching into Students' Research and Note-Taking

THE GOAL FOR THIS UNIT is for students to write argument *essays* that are logical and convincing, and for now, it is for them to write argument *letters* that are similarly logical and convincing: that is, once students learn one form of argument writing, they should be able to carry that across other forms. For their arguments to be solid, their writing needs a strong grounding in research. So, as your students take off out of the gate, you will want to help them to be attentive to the evidence that the articles provide them. "Instead of putting your feet up and reading these in a relaxed way, you need to be mining them for all the evidence you can glean. Pause a lot and think, 'What did I learn from the part I just read? Then jot down notes."

As you read over shoulders, there are a few things to watch for first. A fair number of your students will probably read an article about chocolate milk as if that article holds the final word, written by some omniscient source. Each bit of information in the article is seen as the gospel truth, and the students will have no problem synthesizing contradictory evidence from articles that come to competing conclusions, because these readers never even dream that the texts represent positions, and that their role as a reader is to weigh and judge alternate positions. They are accustomed to gleaning facts from texts and reassembling those facts from a collection of texts into their own "reports." Therefore these students will approach this work as if it is nothing

---

MID-WORKSHOP TEACHING   **The Source for Your Information Matters! Noting Bibliographic Information**

"Writers, look up here for a moment. If I told you that there was a note this morning on the principal's door that said 'Class 5C is the best,' and then I said, 'It was signed by me,' that would mean one thing. And what if I said there was a note on the principal's door this morning and it said, 'Class 5C is the best' and it was signed by your art teacher? That would mean something different, wouldn't it? And what if it was signed by the superintendent of our schools? Or by President Obama? My point is that a piece of information, or an opinion—5C is the best—means something different depending on who said that information.

"Knowing this should change how you take your notes. Claire noticed as she looked back at her Post-its that she wasn't sure which text her notes referenced or who the source was of her information. That would be like not knowing who put that sign on the principal's door!

"So Claire has begun to do something that college students do a lot. She is putting a note identifying the source text right beside her notes. See, Claire's Post-it says":

Chocolate milk has

- Protein
- Vit. A
- Vit. D
- Calcium

from Nutrition in Disguise

"That might be a useful strategy for all of you. You can invent your own system for where to record the text's name so that this works whether you are taking notes on Post-its, index cards, or in your notebook. And if others of you invent techniques that are really helpful to you—maybe a way to shortcut this—let us know so we can all learn from you!"

---

different than what they're accustomed to doing. These students absolutely need help understanding that the texts are position statements and that their job is to see those positions as different, and to compare and contrast them.

Then, too, you will probably find students who are treating this unit like a personal essay unit and are drawing on their own ideas, reactions, and opinions in their notes. You will be pleased that they are actively engaged in growing ideas, but you'll want to drive them away from personal preferences and anecdotes and back toward the texts they are reading. Acknowledge that when they wrote personal essays, they used personal anecdotes to support their claims, and then point out that they are engaged in a different kind of writing now, and let them know that this kind of writing requires writers to support their claims with research from sources.

There may be some students who seem determined to find evidence that supports their predetermined position, and to ignore everything else. They will fill in information for just one side of the debate. They won't record evidence that doesn't match their own preferences. In these cases, you could acknowledge that it seems as if those students are hunting for evidence to support their opinions, and again, let them know that there have been times when this is what they were taught to do. Explain that this unit of study is on research-based argument writing, and this asks for something different. "When you research, it is best to look at both sides before you even finalize your position," you might coach. "Since you have a lot of information about one side, and a leaning toward that side in the first place, you can think to yourself, 'I should deliberately try to find some research which approaches this differently.' Then you can deliberately look for texts that support a different view."

Then too, you might find that several students categorize information in ways that seem to you to suggest the students' are misreading the articles. For example, under a "Pro Chocolate Milk" heading, you may see that a student has listed evidence about the amount of sugar in chocolate milk, and about the harmful effects of sugar. If you notice one student has done this, assume that there are others who will have done it

as well, and take a quick scan of the room to find those students. In fact, research has shown that there are a whole group of students who do have trouble ascertaining a text's position on a topic, even when that position seems very clear to an adult.

If you have a group of students who struggle with this, then, don't be surprised. You might do some investigation. If you read the text aloud, do the students still have trouble? If you use a more blatant text (or add some extra words as you read the text aloud to make it more overtly one sided) do the students still struggle with this?

You'll want to work with this group. For starters, you may ask them to read and talk about the numbers in a text. They may, for example, be struggling to interpret percentages, and need you to remind them of some of the basic information about percentages—that percentages are fractions of one hundred. Or they may be struggling with numbers in a different way—if these students read that three out of five children drink chocolate milk, what does that mean to them? Once students better understand the information, you suggest they go back to their notes with their new understanding and see if they'd still categorize the information in the same way. Then, too, you can help students see that words have valences, and that some words suggest an author is putting a positive spin on something, other words suggest a negative spin.

You will find that many students are not sure whether information supports one side of an argument or another. If students are unsure of this, celebrate this. The truth is that reasons are generally supportive of one side or another, but evidence can usually be spun one way or another. The fact that there are four grams of added sugar in each serving of chocolate milk can be interpreted as excessive or as not so bad—after all, it's *only* four more grams that in plain milk. If students aren't sure where to put a piece of information like that, you might turn them back to the text and let them know that usually the author will have added a spin to the information. Suggest that they look at the text again and think, "Was this information treated as a positive or a negative in this article?"

Writers Use Evidence to Form and Build an Opinion

Ask writers to review the evidence they've gathered, decide tentatively on a side of the issue, and explain to a partner why they've made that decision.

"Writers, you've read and written down lots of evidence now for both sides of this issue. I've no doubt that you are beginning to see the position you want to take on this issue. To make an argument, people review the evidence and take a position based on all they know.

"Right now, will you look through the evidence you have gathered? Think about which pieces of evidence are especially convincing to you, and why. I've given you some flag Post-its. Mark the evidence that you think is really convincing, and be ready to talk about why that evidence is convincing to you."

I let students work a bit. Then I said, "Now, based on your evidence only (not your own personal preferences), will you decide whether (for the time being, because you'll collect more evidence) *the evidence suggests* that schools should serve chocolate milk or not?"

I left a bit of silence. Then, a few minutes later, I said, "Talk with your partner about the position that you're settling on, at least for now, and about the evidence that made the difference for you."

Listen in, coaching partners to press each other for reasons and evidence.

I listened to Natalie and Nora. Natalie began, "I think chocolate milk should be allowed in schools. What about you?"

I looked at Nora, signaling for her to talk back. When Nora started to say her own idea, not reacting to Natalie, I whispered to her. "Your partner just said her position, but she didn't say *why*. She didn't support it. You need to ask her for her reasons and to see what evidence she is relying on." Nora did as I suggested.

FIG. 1–1 Claire organized her notes.

Natalie thought for a few seconds, then launched into a defense. "Kids like to drink chocolate more than they like white milk. I do too. It's way better."

I looked up at Nora, as if to say, "So what will you say next?" and Nora nodded and pressed Natalie for her evidence and for her research.

Natalie scanned the pages in front of her and said, "I'm not the only one who thinks it's better. Seventy percent of milk kids drink at school is chocolate!"

"That's a lot," Nora replied. "But just because kids drink it doesn't mean they *should*. I'm not really sure." They sat quietly for a moment.

I prompted Nora to press Natalie for more reasons, whispering, "Ask her to give another reason," and then I moved on, but overheard, as I left, Natalie explaining that chocolate milk should be in schools because it has vitamin A and calcium. She concluded, "Those things are good for your body. Kids need them, so kids need chocolate milk."

Point out that students have just rehearsed the draft of their arguments that they'll write tomorrow. Ask them to write-in-the-air to explain, doing this as rehearsal for writing.

"Writers, do you realize that what you just talked about can be what you write about? By talking through your thinking you've started planning the fast-draft letter you'll write tomorrow to Ms. Granger. Will you try this talking again, this time bringing with you all you know about rehearsing for writing? You may want to explain your side point by point, listing across your fingers. You may want to take on a teaching voice, and try to remember that you are teaching your listener. You may want to think about boxes and bullets—your main argument and your reasons for it. Take a moment to gather your thoughts and prepare a bit more, and then turn and tell someone else, not your partner, the position you are taking and why. Go ahead."

I listened as Claire sat up tall, straightened her glasses, and in her best professorial voice, told Alex, "I *absolutely* think that chocolate milk should be served in schools." She put up her thumb. "It should be there because kids who drink it get more nutrients." She paused for a minute and continued, "They get calcium and vitamin D." She put up her pointer finger, "It should be there because kids will drink more milk. In the article I read it said that kids drink more milk when chocolate is there. When it's just plain they skip it."

I said, "Writers, let's record what we've done so far in writing argument, so that we can learn to do it again and again. Here is what we've done so far. I'll keep adding to this as we go."

You may notice students starting their claim as, "I think that. . . ." While this may seem like yet another personal opinion, in fact your students are now positioning themselves as experts. Their claim may, therefore, sound like, "I think that. . . ." Later in the unit, you'll address academic language, moving students from "I think that chocolate milk . . ." to claims such as "Research shows that chocolate milk. . . ."

This unit is designed to take students through the writing process several times. As they, and therefore you, cycle through the process, you will build upon this chart, not only adding additional bullets to the end of the chart, but also adding subbullets to the existing items on the chart. So, as you begin, you might want to think through how you will add to each of these as you go, possibly leaving room under each one so you can fill in more information as the unit unfolds.

SESSION 1 HOMEWORK

ENTERTAINING CONTRARY VIEWS: SUSPEND CLOSURE AND BE OPEN-MINDED

Writers, I talked to you today about choosing the kind of thinker you want to be. Remember I said that when someone with a view that is different than yours approaches you, you can be the kind of person who stands with your arms crossed, your face stern, your back up? We all have people in our lives who listen to *our* ideas like that, and I think none of us like it very much when we feel as if our listener's mind is made up before we even open our mouths. Tonight I'm going to ask you to read an article about chocolate milk that argues *the opposite* of what you believe, and I'm going to ask you to be a respectful, open-minded listener. Even if you really can't for the life of you imagine *any* view about chocolate milk other than your own, try your very hardest to be an open-minded listener. Make yourself say things back to the author like, "Good point!" and "That makes sense," and "I see what you mean."

This will mean that you end up taking notes on the side of this argument that will probably not be the side you argue. Though who knows, you might even end up finding your thinking gets changed. Tonight take home your folders. You can read the articles you started today, or others. If you have Internet at home, you might watch some of the videos. The links are inside the folders.

See the bibliography in the online resources for printable versions of these articles and links to the video clips.

Flash-Drafting Arguments

TODAY YOUR STUDENTS WILL WRITE FLASH-DRAFTS of letters to the school principal. You may quake at the idea. They don't seem ready! Some of them took paltry notes. Yesterday, as you looked over their shoulders, you noticed that a number of kids were still holding onto what seemed to be their personal preferences. You suspect that if you ask students to write quick drafts of argument letters, many will write about all the reasons why they, personally, do or do not like chocolate milk. You're instinct is to spend another day working with them on their note-taking.

We encourage you to move forward whether your kids seem ready or not. Moreover, we encourage you to resist a general temptation in this unit to teach one skill until your kids have all mastered it and only then progress to the next skill. For example, today you might find yourself tempted to make sure that each student has collected every citation there is to collect from the chocolate milk articles, and that they have recorded each source, before you proceed. That would mean teaching variations on a minilesson repeatedly, inching kids forward very slowly, holding them back from going ahead. We understand the temptation to do that, but the unit has been designed to follow an entirely different progression. You'd be better off letting your students approximate for now, and move on. Remember that your students have written persuasive essays before, as well as literary essays. This is not their first experience with persuasive writing—far from it.

Keep in mind also that although your students may not seem ready today to write flash-draft argument letters, they are by now accustomed to writing less than ideal texts straight away at the start of a unit. In their earlier research unit, after all, they wrote all-about reports on the Westward Expansion on the second or third day of the unit! In the fourth-grade essay unit, they each wrote a full essay on ice cream during the first day! So put aside your worries. It is okay that students won't have done a lot of research yet. They can't yet handle a whole lot of information anyhow. These letters are meant to be approximations.

This unit is designed to cycle students through multiple rounds of argument writing, with the expectation that they will not master much during their first round, but will, rather, garner a sense of the whole and of the process. Their second round of argument

IN THIS SESSION, you'll remind children that writers often use what they know about structuring an essay to help them quickly write a full, rough draft of their argument.

GETTING READY

✔ Seat children according to their stance on chocolate milk. All of the students arguing in favor should be on one side of the meeting area, in groups of three of four. All against should be on the other side, also in groups.

✔ "How to Write an Argument" chart (see Teaching and Active Engagement)

✔ A chart set up with the title "Schools Should Serve Chocolate Milk" on one side of the page and "Schools Should Not Serve Chocolate Milk" on the other (see Teaching and Active Engagement)

✔ Students' note cards from Session 1 (see Teaching and Active Engagement)

✔ Copies of the texts students read during Session 1 (see Teaching and Active Engagement)

✔ "A Position Statement Often Goes Like This" chart (see Teaching and Active Engagement)

✔ "Body Paragraphs Often Go Like This" one-day chart (see Teaching and Active Engagement)

✔ "Research-Based Arguments Essayists . . ." one-day chart (see Link)

writing will be stronger but will still contain a few gaps and problems. Their final round will show great strides! That is, this unit will provide repeated opportunities to engage in all the important aspects of writing argument letters and essays so that students become progressively more skilled and more efficient.

"We encourage you to resist a general temptation in this unit to teach one skill until your kids have all mastered it and only then progress to the next skill."

Flash-drafts provide a very effective window onto what students can do. You can't really tell how a young person is doing as a writer of argument from his or her notes alone. Some students take thin notes, but their flash-drafts convey a clear and convincing line of thinking. Other students take reasonable notes but are ill-equipped to write within a structure. If you wait until the final days of a unit to see students' actual essays, it will be too late to help those who needed help much earlier.

The standards expect that students make a transition from opinion to argument writing, but chances are that at the start of this unit, many of your children will still write the equivalent of "I love chocolate milk, that's why we should serve it at lunch." If, despite a first session that encourages students to ground their opinions in research, a number of your students are clinging tenaciously to a more personal and expressive style, it's important that you know this. Chances are this will be the case.

We've supported hundreds of teachers teaching this unit, and from that experience, we can assure you that in very little time, your students will read the backs of their drink containers suspiciously. If the work students do today is not that impressive, don't worry. Their growth, then, will be all the more stunning! And remember, the standards you will address are, in fact, standards for sixth-graders. Just by inviting your fifth-graders to begin tackling this challenging work, you are already ahead of the game.

Flash-Drafting Arguments

CONNECTION

Show students ways that the writing work they will be doing today is similar to the writing work they have done in the past—and will need to do in the future.

"Writers, yesterday one of you asked me the most interesting question, and I've been pondering it ever since. After you rehearsed your positions on chocolate milk a bit, and supported them with some evidence, Brian said, 'Are our letters going to be like literary essays?' Brian was right; the work you are doing now is similar to what you all did in your literary essays when you provided evidence from the story to support your ideas. Once you know how to support an idea with evidence in one kind of writing, you can do the same work in other kinds of writing.

Today is all about structure. Even though you'll be writing letters, not essays, the structure you use will be the same, so think back on what you know about essay structure."

❖ **Name the teaching point.**

"Today, I want to remind you that when a writer writes essays—personal, literary, argument, or otherwise—the writer often organizes her opinion and reasons into a boxes-and-bullets structure. And writers of any genre, once they have a rough idea of structure, often try to get the whole piece of writing down on the page quickly, roughly, and then go back to revise."

TEACHING AND ACTIVE ENGAGEMENT

Teach through guided practice. Take children through the process of planning an essay in which they state their opinion and support it.

"At the end of yesterday's writing workshop, you reviewed the evidence you had compiled and decided where you stand on the issue. Then you explained your position and some of your reasons to your partner. We talked yesterday about the fact that when you explained your reasons for deciding one way or another on the issue, you were rehearsing for writing—doing what argument writers do. Those conversations were powerful rehearsal work for the letters you are about to write to Ms. Granger today.

◆ COACHING

If students don't have any experience writing essays, you will certainly need to take an extra day, at least, to teach essay structure.

When you teach students a process that involves a few steps, you can demonstrate that process in the teaching component of a minilesson and then set children up to try the same process on their own later in the minilesson. This minilesson blurs those two components. When the process requires more steps than you can reasonably teach through demonstration, you can't say, "Watch me do these eight steps, then you do them." When teaching a multistep procedure, then, it is beneficial to teach through guided practice, as in this minilesson. Eventually, children will be able to work through this process, or one like it, on their own.

"Today, we'll be doing a version of essay boot camp, only it will be an argument-letter boot camp. Writers often take a short burst of time to draft, quickly, one beginning-to-end version of what they are going to write—just to see the *whole* shape of it. Then, writers go back and revise that flash-draft, with the whole piece of writing in mind. They can see where it is going and how it balances out that way. You have done this before in other kinds of writing, but it's increasingly complicated when you are bringing in everything from research, so I'll coach you again today in doing this. I've added planning in boxes-and-bullets format to our process chart. You'll notice that I've used the word *claim*. That's what writers often call the specific statement that expresses their position."

How to Write an Argument

- Collect evidence that allows you to think through various sides of an argument.
- Rehearse by explaining your position and listing your reasons point by point.
- Plan your claim and reasons into boxes-and-bullets structure.

Coach children to name their position, then list their reasons to a partner.

"Let's get started. I think you've all chosen your side of the issue: 'Should chocolate milk be served in schools?' Thumbs up if you have chosen your side.'" Thumbs shot up. Passions ran high on the topic!

"Now you need to plan how you'll support your position—how you'll build your argument. It will help to do this planning with a couple people who think as you do." I revealed chart paper on which I'd written two possible position statements inside boxes, one representing the *for* view, one the *against*.

Schools should serve chocolate milk.	Schools should not serve chocolate milk.

"Work with someone near you who shares your position to think of reasons you'll use to support the position. You can help each other without making your papers exactly match." While children started talking, I quickly added a place to insert three reasons as a part of each claim.

The more times students practice this routine of setting themselves up to write an essay (or a persuasive letter), the easier it will be for them to do this same work in future writing projects!

This process can take too long if you don't make an enormous effort to speed things up. Don't wait for all children to finish what they are doing before proceeding forward. When you channel kids to talk, use that time to jot things onto chart paper or to otherwise set yourself up for the next step.

Schools should serve chocolate milk	Schools should not serve chocolate milk
• because . . . (reason A) • because . . . (reason B) • because . . . (reason C)	• because . . . (reason A) • because . . . (reason B) • because . . . (reason C)

I did the same for the con claim. Then, I spoke over the hubbub, saying, "Start by restating your claim, and then state your reasons, like this," and I dictated one way to word the template, although it was empty of specifics. "'Chocolate milk should (should not) be banned in school because A, because B, and most of all, because C.' Go ahead."

As children rehearsed, I listened in, adding prompts and reminders as needed. Over the hubbub, I called, "If you are stuck on reasons A, B, and C, use your group to help you decide. You won't all have the same A, B, and C reasons. Make your own decisions!" When some students signaled they were done, I nudged them on, "Try it again, fixing your wording. Start from the claim and say the whole thesis, using your fingers to help you keep track of your reasons—one for each bullet."

Summarize the work the class has done, and then ask one child who is encountering problems others are facing, too, to state her claim and reasons. Recruit the class to help the one child in ways that provide universal help.

After no more than two or three minutes, I reconvened the class and said, "Okay, now you've all figured out the claim that will go at the start of your letter. You'll state your argument and quickly lay out your three reasons (probably all in one sentence, but maybe in a bunch of short sentences)." On a piece of chart paper I jotted a reminder about how thesis statements tend to go.

A Position Statement Often Goes Like This

I think   because [reason 1], because [reason 2], and because [reason 3].

I called on Alessandra to share her thesis, knowing that it illuminated a problem I saw many of the children having. Alessandra began tentatively, sensing her reasons might be problematic. "You should ban chocolate milk from schools because it is like eating candy and because it has too much sugar and because it is not good for you?" she said questioningly.

"Alessandra, I hear a little hesitation in your voice." Alessandra nodded.

"Well, I think the reasons are kind of all the same!" she added.

Notice that the process of writing a thesis statement entails practically a miniature version of the process of writing a whole essay.

Notice that the written version and the spoken ones do not match. One says "Schools should serve . . . ," and the other, "Chocolate milk should/should not be banned from schools . . ." This is my way of signaling to kids that there is not one right way to do this. By showing several alternate ways to do this work, I try to signal that I welcome yet other variations.

Timing is everything. You need to be quick about this. Your coaching should be plentiful. Obviously, you will respond to whatever you see and offer the sort of prompting your children need. It's important, however, that this section of the minilesson take no more than two or three minutes!

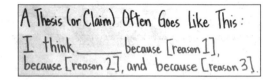

Look for common pitfalls here. For instance, you might listen for children who give reasons that do not directly support their idea (e.g., chocolate milk should be banned because the cafeteria always runs out of it and they need to order more). Sometimes reasons overlap (e.g., chocolate milk should be banned because it is too sweet; also because it is like eating candy). You might also listen for children who confuse reasons and evidence. Coach them to say "because" to get to reasons and "for example" when they are adding evidence.

Turning to the class, I asked, "Do you see how 'Chocolate milk has too much sugar' and 'Chocolate milk is like eating candy' and 'Chocolate milk is not good for you' are basically the same thing?" They nodded. "Let's help Alessandra come up with reasons that don't overlap. What is a very different reason chocolate milk should be banned? We need a reason that has nothing to do with sugar! Turn and talk."

Quickly, I reconvened them and asked Alessandra to share her new, revised reason. "Chocolate milk should be banned from schools because it makes kids not like the taste of regular milk," she said, beaming.

Channel members of the class to work with someone else who is arguing similarly to construct a first body paragraph by writing-in-the-air. Coach them to include at least two pieces of evidence.

"Writers, you have said aloud your claim and your reasons. You just wrote the thesis to your argument! Now work together with someone to talk through the first body paragraph of your letter. Start by writing-in-the-air. To do this, you'll add evidence to support your reasons. (This is where you say your first reason, explaining with examples and details.) Go!"

Channel children to refer to the article or their notes to cite evidence.

I noticed Robert glancing at the stack of articles and said, "I can tell that you are itching to look at the articles, Robert. That's super wise. You'll probably use your pencil to underline or box out important evidence as you find it." Then I said to the whole class, "Writers, Robert just came up with a wise idea. He's looking for evidence by rereading one of the articles, underlining the information he may want to include to support each of his reasons. Some of the rest of you might do that as well."

After a few minutes I said to the whole class, "Thumbs up if you have managed to say a lot about your first reason!" Many children signaled that they had collected evidence to support their first reason.

In literary essay, students learned to distinguish between reasons and examples. You may find it helpful to recall that work now.

One important reason we ask students to move from collecting evidence to writing an argument is because the structure of what a person plans to make shapes that person's research. We want to make sure that students are anticipating writing in a structured, claims-and-evidence, boxes-and-bullets, way. Today plunges students into that work, just as yesterday plunged them into developing evidenced-based opinions.

Take this opportunity to do some quick assessment. Once you have asked children to box out text evidence, watching what they do if you can. This will help you grasp which students understand the concept of text evidence. Some may sit with blank faces. Some may underline portions of the article that don't correlate to the point they are trying to make. Take note of misconceptions and struggles so you can plan to address them in the days ahead.

Channel students to move on, doing similar work both talking, writing-in-the-air, and writing on the second body paragraph.

"When you've said a lot about your first reason and the evidence that supports it, move on. Talk through your second body paragraph, and then talk through the next one." As children continued, I unveiled a chart that held a reminder on it of the ways essays tend to go.

Move around the carpet area, listening and interjecting with quick coaching. Then, ask one student to share, coaching her to raise the level of the work.

I listened as children recited essays to each other. Caroline's sounded like this.

> Chocolate milk should not be banned in schools. It should not be banned in schools because it has a lot of vitamins. Also, kids like the taste of it better than regular milk. The last reason chocolate milk should not be banned in schools is because kids and parents can make their own choices about what is best for them.
>
> One reason chocolate milk should not be banned in schools because it has a lot of vitamins. Chocolate milk has vitamin D, calcium, and protein. And a reason is that . . .

"Don't forget to use words like *for example*, and *another example*," I coached her, gesturing to the chart. "Try that last part again, this time using transition words such as *for example, another reason.*" Then, "Don't just say what you think. Pull actual examples from the text. It might help to start, 'In the text, it says . . .'"

I reconvened the class and asked one student to share his writing-in-the-air. As Ivan shared his first body paragraph, I gestured to the chart of transition words, setting him up to go from saying "One reason . . ." to "For example. . . ."

> Chocolate milk should not be banned from schools. One reason chocolate milk shouldn't be banned from schools is because it gives you nutrients. For example, chocolate milk has nine essential nutrients. It has calcium, vitamins A, D, protein and many more. Studies show that kids who drink fat-free flavored milk meet more nutrient needs.

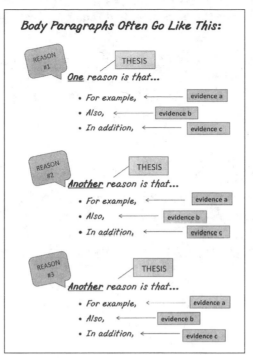

Body Paragraphs Often Go Like This:

REASON #1 — THESIS
One reason is that...
- For example, ← evidence a
- Also, ← evidence b
- In addition, ← evidence c

REASON #2 — THESIS
Another reason is that...
- For example, ← evidence a
- Also, ← evidence b
- In addition, ← evidence c

REASON #3 — THESIS
Another reason is that...
- For example, ← evidence a
- Also, ← evidence b
- In addition, ← evidence c

Of course, students' writing-in-the-air will allow you to assess their control of essay craft and structure. You can see at a glance what they've learned in prior units. Are they writing with a logical structure, quoting and paraphrasing from texts (they've done this with literary essays), composing introductions and conclusions? It's important to expect writers to carry what they've learned forward across all the writing they do—and, too, to teach toward transfer.

Debrief by naming what students have done that you hope they remember to do again—including when they are sent to their work areas to complete their letters.

"Writers, did you see the way that Ivan started off by saying his claim: 'Chocolate milk should not be banned from schools,' and then giving his first reason, 'because it gives you nutrients'? Then he gave specific evidence from the text to support his point. He even used words like *for example* to introduce his evidence. That is something you can all do!"

LINK

Channel children to write-in-the-air and to then flash-draft the essay they have rehearsed.

"Take another few minutes here on the rug to keep talking through your letter, and when you're sure you can write most of it, move to your writing spot. Once you start writing, you won't want to stop writing until the whole thing is done. You will only have about fifteen minutes to write the whole letter, so write up a storm! This is what writers do. They think it through or talk it through, figuring out how their piece will go, and then they get whatever they can on paper—quickly and without fussing over it. You can do this with any kind of writing at all. Writers do it all the time! Okay, get started talking and moving quickly into the fast-drafting."

Research-Based Argument Essayists...

- Prepare to collect information by suspending their judgment and gathering evidence that supports BOTH sides

- Prepare to draft by asking, "Which side do I stand on? What evidence supports my side?"

Students' Work Can Help You Plan for Future Teaching

ALWAYS, BUT ESPECIALLY AT THE START OF A UNIT, students' work provides you a window into what students know and can do. Today, if you take a peek over their shoulders, you will no doubt see issues with students' use of evidence, as well as with their control of essay structure.

Predictably, some students will make very few references to the nonfiction texts on chocolate milk that they read; instead, these students will rely almost exclusively on their own personal preferences. It takes some kids a while to realize that research-based argument writing differs in some key ways from personal essays. In the latter, students drew primarily on personal experience to support claims. To write argument essays, they will draw primarily on research. For some students, then, it is just a matter of teaching them to alter their writing style based on different tasks and expectations. For others, the reason they haven't referenced the nonfiction articles is that the texts were far too complex for them to read and understand and, therefore, too complex to cite. Often when students are writing about content, what manifests itself as writing trouble is really reading trouble. You'll want to find ways to make sure that students can access some sources of information so that they can use these to build arguments.

The flash-drafts that your students write today will show you what they know and remember about writing essays. Claire, for instance, jumbled her evidence for chocolate milk being nutritious, putting not just vitamins A and D, but also carbohydrates and added sugar as sources of nutrients. To help Claire, I had her get out the articles she was leaning on. Together, we underlined the evidence about nutrition, and I helped her by reading aloud the part that explained how vitamins are different from carbohydrates and sugar. I set Claire up to talk over the article with a partner, and then to review her evidence. As students' pencils race down the page, read over their shoulders and assess, as this will give you some insight into what may be causing trouble.

You will probably see that many or even most of your students begin their letters by diving immediately into their claims, their thesis statements. Their letters might look like Annie's.

Dear Ms. Granger,

Chocolate milks should be banned from schools. They should be banned from schools because they are unhealthy.

If you see this, you might want to tell these students that there are things writers do *before* elaboration—they hook the reader and they forecast the reasons the essay will explore.

(continues)

MID-WORKSHOP TEACHING
When You're Done, You've Just Begun

"Writers, can I have your eyes here for a moment? Mia has finished her flash-draft. Do you think she's putting her feet up on her desk, leaning back in her chair, surveying the scene, and eating Doritos? No way!

"You know the saying: 'When you're done, you've just begun.' That means that like Mia, you'll need to decide what to do once you reach the last line of your draft. Mia first pulled out her notes from yesterday and is looking to see if she put the information she'd recorded in the *against* column of her chart into her 'ban chocolate milk' draft. She's checking off each item that she used, and she is seeing if she can add to her draft information that she left out. She just pointed out to me that after this, she's probably going to reread the article to see if there is more information in it that she can bring to her letter, which makes a lot of sense to me. I expect some of you will decide to do similar work as well, if you finish your flash-draft."

Lila made a bit more of an effort to hook in her reader, but still she doesn't have much of an introduction.

> Do you think we should ban flavored milk? I certainly don't think so.

Of course, these students may not have included a broader introduction simply because you will not yet have mentioned the need for this, although they should remember this skill from their work on personal and literary essays. The much more important thing to notice is that neither of these students forecast the reasons they will be discussing in their text. Your teaching has strongly emphasized that a claim or thesis includes several reasons. The CCSS for fifth grade include the expectation that students lay out a logical progression for their argument, letting the reader know their reasons and what is to come. Kids who shortchange that work will shortchange their arguments. So you will want to insist that students begin their argument letters with a thesis, and that they remember that a position statement (or thesis) includes not just the claim, but also the main reasons that the author has for justifying this claim.

Then, too, you will also be on the lookout for children who are struggling with grouping and organization. Despite the extensive coaching in this session, there may be students who are still putting multiple reasons within one large paragraph or who are squishing all their information together without signaling when they move from one point to the next and the next. These children's essays feel like one long ramble about the pros or cons of chocolate milk. Over the next day or two, you'll probably need to cluster these children into small groups and reteach them the content of today's minilesson, helping them honor the boxes-and-bullets structure, forming one paragraph for each bulleted

reason. It might be helpful for them to cut apart the draft they've written and then tape each reason onto a separate sheet of paper so they can collect evidence to support each distinct part of their essay.

Before long you'll want to remind these students to orient the reader at the beginning of each body paragraph (by restating the opinion and the reason they'll be addressing) and to end each body paragraph with a bit of closure. It can help to teach them to use phrases like "All of this shows . . . " or "This proves . . . " to sum up the argument they presented in that particular body paragraph. Again, we suggest very concrete revision work, with strips of paper containing opening and closing sentences being taped onto the start and end of a paragraph.

Of course, the purpose of today is to get a quick draft out, so most of what you will be doing as you confer will be gathering data about what you'll need to do in the ensuing days. You will want to be sure to record your findings. You might find it helpful to make a chart with the categories you expect to see, and the students in need of that support on the right, like the table below.

Category	Students in need of support
• Introduction	• Annie • Lilia
• Organizing information into boxes and bullets	
• Orienting the reader (restating opinion and reason)	
• Closing body paragraph	

Writers Reread and Make Writing Plans

Let students know that writers often reread to identify the work they need to do next. Ask them to try this now, and forever after, whenever they reach a sort of milestone in their work.

"Writers, I wanted to let you know something at this point: whenever they reach a sort of milestone in the writing work, writers take a moment to step back and reread their writing. They reread and decide on the work they need to do next—not just what to write next, but *how* to go about the next part of their writing work. This is a point where writers make a lot of choices. Why don't you try that now—reread. Note parts of your letter that you really like or parts that need more work. Then get with your partner (not your like-minded group, but your writing partner) and talk about today's work and what you might do next and how you'll do it. Remember, when you talk together about writing, it is helpful to be very specific. Writers need to actually point to, actually mark, actually make notes on, exact lines in their writing."

Coach into students' work, channeling them to think not only about what they might add to their writing, what they might say next, but also to think about what they might do next. Coach them to plan their strategies.

As children reread, I skimmed a few of their drafts, including Claire's (see Figure 2–1).

I said to Claire, "As you get to be older, it's important for you to decide what writing work you need to do next. Can you think what you need to do to make this better? Not what to say, but what sort of work should you do, what strategies should you use?"

Claire thought for a moment and said, "I think I need to write more! I have more in my head that I didn't get down yet. Like, I did more research on the nutrients in milk."

"Claire, can you be specific? Can you mark on your writing where you will do more? And think about this: how will you get yourself to say more? Maybe you'll reread your notes or go back to a text? Or maybe you'll talk it through with a partner again? Make a plan!"

FIG. 2–1 Claire's bare-bones flash-draft showing her claim and reasons supported by hints of evidence from texts

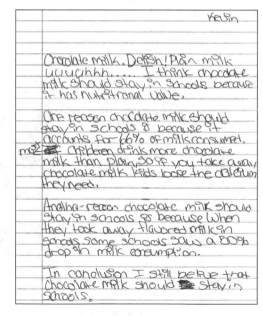

FIG. 2–2 Kevin supports his reasons with some evidence, incorporating a statistic into each body paragraph.

Then I said to the whole class, "Writers, Claire realized that she knew more than she had written. She has lots of reasons, but has just written a reason in a sentence and not said more or elaborated on her evidence. Instead of rereading her writing and thinking, 'What else should I *say*?' Claire did something really smart. She reread her writing and thought, 'What else should I *do*?" Now she's planning all these strategies she's going to do. She's going to reread her writing and make notes to herself about things to add and go back to her texts for evidence. Also she will read her writing to a partner to get help. Maybe some of the rest of you can think, like Claire did, 'What should I do next?'"

PLANNING FOR NEXT STEPS IN WRITING

Tonight, your homework is to give yourself an assignment. Decide on a strategy you think you should use next to take your work another step farther, just as Claire did in class today, and then record that strategy at the top of your notebook page in a self-assignment box or a to-do box. Then get started doing that work!

To think about what you need to do next, it will help if you recall what you know about the writing process. Writers say that the writing process is a cycle and that writers are always cycling between rehearsal, drafting, and revision. Think about the stage of the writing process that you're embarking on now, and think about what you know that writers do at that stage. Then get started!

Using Evidence to Build Arguments

Today's session aims to help students incorporate text evidence into their arguments. If you think of how often you've needed to remind students who are discussing books to refer to the texts when talking about them, and if you think of students' enduring resistance to Post-iting while they read or to referencing identified passages while they talk about a text, you'll probably agree with us that it's a wise thing to devote some time to teaching students to cite text evidence. This becomes particularly important in any school that is focused on implementing the world-class state standards, because the standards are making "text evidence" a mantra.

When you research students' habits for writing about reading, you'll often notice a surprising divergence. That is, they are reluctant to do any writing when they are reading fiction, as if they can't bear to interrupt their reading. Yet, given a nonfiction text, they often take too many notes, practically recreating the text by copying parts, underlining, and highlighting.

To teach students to ground their own opinions in research, you need to teach them the importance of developing systems for recording, collecting, and analyzing. The truth is that note-taking can be infinitely complex. Think for a moment about the mental work you do when you read a text to collect evidence that you may cite later. You, no doubt, keep in mind your ever-evolving vision of the final work. Your ability to foresee that final work helps you be strategic as you collect information and ideas. When you have an image in mind for what you will make, you can annotate the margins of a text with notes such as, "USE THIS—it's GREAT evidence."

Even if your students have written literary essays and research reports in which they incorporate text evidence and have been taught about quoting and paraphrasing, they'll be novices at this complex work. You'll probably see that those who did incorporate evidence into their letters to the principal lacked finesse at doing so. Chances are especially good that they will have made passing references to the evidence and not been specific about it. Their evidence may not have matched their claims, for example, or they will have cited it without even an attempt to analyze it. Some of the evidence will not have

IN THIS SESSION, you'll teach students that argument writers conduct research and provide evidence that supports their claim.

GETTING READY

- ✔ A sample letter that is missing text evidence. You may choose to use Jack's (see the online resources for a printable copy) or one of your own. Either provide copies for students or project it so that students can read along with you (see Teaching and Active Engagement).

- ✔ An article offering evidence that supports the claim in the sample letter you use to demonstrate. Either provide copies or project this so students can read it (see Teaching and Active Engagement).

- ✔ Index cards or spider leg strips of paper for students to use on the rug (see Teaching and Active Engagement)

- ✔ Students will need notebooks and something to write with (see Teaching and Active Engagement)

- ✔ "How to Write an Argument" chart (see Link)

- ✔ "Questions Writers Ask Themselves when Connecting Reasons and Evidence" chart (see Conferring and Small-Group Work)

- ✔ Written on chart paper: "Evidence: Thirty percent fewer people smoke in New York City this year than last year." (see Mid-Workshop Teaching)

- ✔ Enlarged copy of the Opinion Writing Checklist, Grades 4, 5, and 6 as well as individual copies for students (see Share).

- ✔ Colored pencils or markers (see Share)

- ✔ Student sample essay as well as adhesive labels containing goals from the Opinion Writing Checklist, Grades 5 and 6, copies for each student (see Homework)

actually matched the claim at all. Later in this unit, you'll help students learn to evaluate and analyze evidence, but for now, your goal is to encourage them to actually weave evidence into their arguments. We've found that this type of skill isolation is important—that when you try to teach a whole set of skills, such as incorporating evidence, quoting, citing, and evaluating relevance as one thing, it all starts to break down.

"To teach students to ground their own opinions in research, you need to teach them the importance of developing systems for recording, collecting, and analyzing."

So for today, you'll help students take notes in ways that allow them to incorporate evidence. To teach this, you'll provide a lot of coaching aimed at helping them become analytic note-takers rather than transcribers of tiring details. You'll help them learn that figuring out what's worth noting means reading and note-taking as *writers*. Students benefit from having their audience and genre in mind, and eventually their position, too. This knowledge acts as a kind of analytical lens, making parts of the text more relevant and significant. Today, you'll help students sharpen their lessons, and you'll help them develop systems for recording, collecting, and analyzing.

Using Evidence to Build Arguments

CONNECTION

Ask students to compare notes about their independent work.

I began by saying, "Writers, one of the most important things that you'll learn as writers is to set tasks for yourselves. That ability is going to carry you so far in high school and college—when you have to be in charge of your own deadlines. So before we get started on today's lesson, will you show your partners what you did last night for homework? What assignment did you give yourselves? How did it go?"

Tell students about a time when an argument was strengthened by gathering and including relevant evidence.

After regathering the writers and sharing a couple of examples of students' independent planning and work, I said, "Writers, when I was in high school, I desperately wanted to switch schools. The school I was attending just wasn't the right fit for me, and though I told my parents this again and again, they wouldn't budge. I realized that saying 'This school is not good for me. You should let me switch schools' was not convincing enough. I needed to make an *argument*. And to make an argument, I needed evidence. Relying on my own feelings and experience wasn't going to be enough. That's often true in arguments.

"My parents are busy people," I continued. "I knew that I couldn't bring them every brochure and article I collected on the school I wanted to attend. Instead, I had to do the work of a researcher. I pored over every bit of information I could find on the school I wanted to attend. I highlighted the parts that showed how wonderful that school was (for example, I found a statistic that said that over 50% of each graduating class went to great colleges, and one that recorded the average class size). This was really compelling evidence to present to my parents, because it wasn't just about how I felt. It was actual facts and information about how the school really would be better. After seeing my analysis, with all that focused evidence, they were convinced. I switched schools one month later!"

Make the connection between your story and argument writing.

"So listen to this. When I was remembering this story, I started thinking that making arguments on paper, like you are doing now, is exactly like making an argument in real life. Either way, a person needs evidence to bolster claims—to actually convince readers of something. My parents weren't budging on the school decision until I had gathered enough evidence to convince them that my new school choice was better."

SESSION 3: USING EVIDENCE TO BUILD ARGUMENTS

Remember, for homework last night, you invited writers to give themselves a self-assignment and then to do the work they decided they needed to do. As students talk, you might listen in and look for a writer who has done—or gestured toward doing—the work you're going to suggest the whole class do today. You might begin your lesson studying that student's work, or you might use your own example instead. It is important, however, to take this bit of time to recognize the independent work students did for homework. Of course, if you are pressed for time, you can leave this step out.

You might choose to use this analogy to hit home the fact that evidence is crucial to making a convincing argument. Better yet, you'll tell your own story of a situation in which you gathered, culled through, and chose the most compelling evidence to present in an argument.

❖ **Name the teaching point.**

"Today, I want to remind you that argument writers don't just say what they think personally. They give compelling evidence to prove their point. To do this, they pore over research materials, analyzing which evidence will really support their claim—perhaps the exact evidence that convinced them in the first place—and they often start by putting that evidence into their letters *in their own words.*"

TEACHING

Using the writing of a student not in your class, recruit your students to think about some tips they might give the writer to help him incorporate more text evidence.

"So, writers, I have a letter here that was written by a former student, Jack, when he was a sixth grader. I'm going to read it out loud to you. As I read, your job is to listen for evidence Jack has used and to see if you can think of ways to help him use more text evidence—facts and information from your research—to strengthen his argument. You've read some of the same things he has, so you should have some good ideas."

I read Jack's essay (see Figure 3–1) aloud.

The students enjoyed this spirited letter, but when they counted the amount of explicit text evidence, they discovered that it was almost nonexistent. "What do you notice, writers? Can you pull out any text evidence?"

"Well it has a few things that are like facts. He says it has vitamins and calcium. That's true," said Natalie.

"But—everyone think about this—is saying that chocolate milk has vitamins and calcium *really* text evidence, or is that just common knowledge, what we might call folk knowledge?" I pushed.

"Oh. I guess most people know that. That is sort of everyday stuff. He doesn't really have any evidence from research!" Natalie concluded.

Most state standards emphasize including specific quotations, and we'll address this soon. But the ability to paraphrase is also important. How many essays have you seen in which students simply copy huge chunks of text, without demonstrating understanding of that text evidence? By beginning with the strategy of paraphrasing—putting a portion of a text in their own words—you'll monitor and strengthen students' comprehension of the material they include.

Jack was actually a sixth-grader when he did this writing. The students know that Jack is a former student. We use his writing periodically throughout this unit, and you might decide to follow suit. It's lively writing that students will enjoy. You could also substitute the work of one of your own former students.

> Dear Ms. Granger,
>
> Schools should keep serving chocolate milk to us! I love chocolate milk, and my friends love chocolate milk! Everyone loves chocolate milk. They make strawberry milk as well, and they should serve that too. We should serve chocolate milk because it tastes good and because it has some good vitamins.
>
> Chocolate milk tastes like... chocolate! Who doesn't like chocolate? Everyone likes chocolate. Go to a Duane Reade or a Starbucks or a Dean and Delucca. What do you see at the counter, luring in the kiddies and the adult's? CHOCOLATE. chocolate makes us happy. School does not always make us happy. So keep serving chocolate milk. It is an oasis of sweetness. I think even the teachers would find they liked school more, if they drank more chocolate milk.
>
> In addition, chocolate milk has some stuff that's good for you. It has vitamins, and calcium. Put away those sodas and gatorade. Drink milk. Just exercise too, and the sugar will melt away, leaving only the happiness.
>
> Thank you,
>
> Jack

FIG. 3–1 Jack's letter has an impassioned claim but little explicit evidence from texts.

Demonstrate the process writers go through when searching for and fitting in relevant and supportive text evidence.

"That's a problem, right? Let me show you how I might go about helping Jack include some supportive evidence in his letter. First, I want to think of a source that is going to offer evidence in support of Jack's claim, that schools should keep serving chocolate milk. I've got it. Remember that article we read, 'Nutrition in Disguise'? I bet that will have some supportive evidence. Let's take a look at it. Let's skim it now, and be on the lookout for evidence—not just any evidence, but evidence that supports Jack's claim."

I modeled skimming the article, knowing that the students would also do so alongside me. As I skimmed, I thought aloud.

> "Nutrition in Disguise: What the Midwest Dairy Council Has to Say about Chocolate Milk"
>
> *If you secretly love chocolate milk, you're in for some happy news. Recently, the Midwest Dairy Association released an infomercial that argues chocolate milk is, according to nutritionist Melissa Dobbins, "nutrition in disguise."*
>
> *In the infomercial, Ms. Dobbins, who introduces herself as a nutritionist for the Dairy Association and a mom, brings along three young friends to help her demonstrate that chocolate milk is a healthy part of a young person's diet. As Ms. Dobbins puts it, "the fact is, that chocolate and other flavored milks have the same 9 essential nutrients as white milk, and a small amount of added sugar compared to other beverages. Best of all, because they love the taste, some kids drink more milk when it's flavored."*
>
> *"We serve six or seven cartons of chocolate for each one of white milk at lunch," says Mrs. Rally, a server in a local elementary school cafeteria. "In fact it's pretty much only with breakfast cereal that any kid would choose white milk."*
>
> *What's the attraction of chocolate milk? Well, if you haven't had any for awhile, give it a try. You'll have to admit that the creamy, smooth, chocolaty taste is truly delicious. But is it good for you? Ms. Dobbins says . . . yes. "Research shows that children who drink flavored milk meet more of their nutrient needs, do not consume more added sugar, fat, and calories, and are not heavier than non milk drinkers," says Ms. Dobbins.*

"Hmm, Ms. Dobbins is a nutritionist, so she should know. She says that chocolate milk has the same nutrients as regular milk. That might be a good one to flag. I'm going to write that down on a spider leg so that I can add it to the draft in the place that it fits best." I jotted:

> Ms. Dobbins, a nutritionist for the dairy association, says that chocolate milk has the same nine nutrients as regular milk.

Demonstrate that it helps to ask, "What is this piece of evidence mostly about?" as you consider which part of the draft it fits best.

"Let me reread this. What is this evidence mostly about? Well, seems like it's mostly about how chocolate milk is actually good for you. It has nutrients. So where would this fit best in Jack's draft, I wonder? Let me look." I skimmed the draft, continuing to think aloud. "Oh, look! This last paragraph is where Jack gives the reason that chocolate milk is good for you."

In addition, chocolate milk has some stuff that's good for you. It has vitamins, and calcium.

"I'll insert this piece of evidence right here, after 'It has vitamins, and calcium.' That seems like a good fit. Now let me go back to the article and see if I can find some more supportive evidence." I modeled going back to the text, skimming, and considering evidence.

"What about this: 'Ms. Dobbins says that kids love the taste.' That does support Jack's claim, but I don't know. Not all kids love the taste. I'm going to leave that one out."

Debrief, restating the steps you proceeded through to find and add evidence to the writing sample.

"So, you see what I'm doing, right? I'm reading the article and looking for evidence that supports Jack's claim. I'm thinking carefully about it to make sure that it's strong evidence and that it really *does* support Jack's claim. I'm writing it down somehow—not the exact words, but paraphrasing, writing the gist of the evidence in my own words. I chose to write on a spider leg, but you might find a system that works better for you. Then I'm going back to Jack's draft and figuring out what place in the draft is the best fit—where Jack is giving a reason that this evidence supports—and I'm sticking it in."

ACTIVE ENGAGEMENT

Rally students to continue this work in partnerships: scanning the article for relevant evidence and fitting it into the sample text.

"Let's keep going, but now *you're* in charge of helping Jack. What would you do to help him add some evidence into his piece? And where would you add it? Keep skimming this article looking for evidence that supports Jack's claim and reasons. When you find some, jot it down somehow. Remember to paraphrase. Just get the gist of it into your own words, and then think about where in Jack's draft that evidence would fit. What's it mostly about? Which of Jack's reasons does it support?"

As the students got to work, I circulated, offering support as needed, knowing that students would be grappling with a new multistep process. I noticed Sophia writing on a spider leg as I had done, while Ivan was writing his evidence on an index card.

After a few moments, I regathered the class and shared a few examples. Ivan had written down that kids who drink chocolate milk meet more of their nutrient needs. Sophia had written that research shows students who drink chocolate milk do not get more fat, sugar, or calories than other kids.

Students benefit from observing you take the time to mull this over. They will see that it is important to be thoughtful about including evidence. The point is for you to help students realize that one of the writer's bigger jobs is to make sure that the evidence actually connects to the claim, so that you don't just slap it in there willy-nilly. Therefore, when demonstrating the search for evidence, don't find the evidence right away and plop it seamlessly into the essay! Instead, make some common mistakes, such as repeating the same evidence under different reasons, putting in evidence that actually supports a counterclaim, or adding in unsupported evidence based on personal experience, so you can then correct yourself. A further note: when you look for evidence today, don't yet bring direct quotations or statistics into the text because we'll showcase both of those kinds of evidence soon. You'll want to save your thunder!

You will want to support students in developing systems for gathering this evidence and noting where in their letters it will go. It is for this reason that you demonstrate adding additional evidence on spider-leg slips of paper, taped on to the margins of the letter's first draft. Or you might show them how to write on index cards, noting the reason that the evidence supports. Then too, you might help students devise a system of jotting in the margins, perhaps putting a star in the margin of an article and a correlating star on the drafted letter where the evidence will be incorporated. Whatever the system, convey to your students that once you find the evidence, you hold onto it so it can be incorporated into later drafts.

LINK

Suggest that students reread drafts and, if necessary, add relevant evidence to strengthen their arguments.

"Writers, you are learning that argument writers develop claims by studying text evidence carefully and then they bring the exact evidence that convinced them in the first place into their writing. It's often helpful to review your argument and then review the evidence that the texts you read suggested. Often you'll find evidence that will strengthen your argument. Saying that evidence in your own words to support your claim and reasons will strengthen your argument. You know other ways to strengthen your writing as well, of course. You could revise your reasons and add evidence, you could use what you know about introductions or endings from writing other essays."

Keep in mind that today, you hope students draw on all they know to continue their work.

"Before you go off, please make yourself a work plan. You might find that the chart can help you." I pointed to the chart, "How to Write an Argument" (now with an added bullet and subbullet about evidence).

How to Write an Argument

- Collect evidence that allows you to think through various sides of an argument.
- Rehearse by explaining your position and listing your reasons point by point.
- Plan your claim and reasons into boxes-and-bullets structure.
- Use evidence to support your reasons.
  - Paraphrase, putting it in your own words.

Predictable Problems with Adding Evidence

ANTICIPATE THAT YOUR CHILDREN WILL BE FIRED UP after this minilesson. Substantiating a claim with evidence from research gives weight and importance to their work, and this is empowering. Excited and eager to back up their claims and reasons, children will pore over the texts they have, scouring for any piece of information they might incorporate.

You might see children piling evidence in on the heels of their reasons, as if hoping that the evidence will speak for itself. For example, Kevin said that chocolate milk should be banned from schools because health is important, and then, for evidence, he piled on fact after fact suggesting that many children today are overweight. In an instance such as this, Kevin assumed that readers grasp the implicit connections, inferring that chocolate milk is a problem because it adds to children's obesity and that overweight children have other health problems as well. You'll want to teach Kevin himself that it helps to ask themselves questions, and one of the most important questions is "So what?"

If Kevin asked the "So what?" question, he would perhaps realize that he needed to explain that chocolate milk adds to the weight problems and that the weight problems lead to an avalanche of other health problems. It is critical for children to learn that it is not enough to just to plop information in and zoom ahead. Writers need to specifically connect the evidence to the reason.

MID-WORKSHOP TEACHING   Writers Consider Not Only Quantity but Also Relevance of Text Evidence

"Writers, look up for a minute. You are including *so much* explicit evidence in your letters now. Your arguments are already more convincing than they were yesterday. Here's a question: thumbs up, how many of you have cited text evidence twice?" I asked. "Three times?" I took note of the sea of thumbs around the room.

"That's great. But writers, here's the thing. The evidence actually only works if you explain how it supports the reason. Let's practice. You be the judge; tell me if I've made my evidence support my reason. (I'm going to switch from chocolate milk in school to another topic.) Listen to my reason first."

I laid out a claim: "Cities should outlaw smoking in city buildings everywhere because then people will smoke less." Pointing to the easel, where I'd written the following, I read:

Evidence: Thirty percent fewer people smoke in New York City this year than last year.

"Does that evidence clearly support the reason? Or do I need to write something more, to explain it, so people see that it supports the reason?" Soon the class had agreed that more was needed, and the sentence strip was revised to include, "In New York City, a law was passed outlawing smoking in buildings and now, after that law, thirty percent fewer people smoke in New York City. This shows that the law outlawing smoking in city buildings has made a big difference."

"Do you see that just plopping down evidence isn't enough? Writers need to analyze how the evidence supports their reason and explain that thinking. That's unpacking the evidence!

"Now, writers, the challenge is to evaluate your own evidence, making sure your evidence supports your claim. Right now, turn to you partners and first say your reason—and then your evidence. Partners, you'll be the judges and let the writers know whether the evidence they've chosen fully supports their reason—or just a little bit."

You might say something like, "Evidence needs to be unpacked and explained. Writers connect the evidence to the reason, telling the reader why it matters and how it supports the point they are trying to make. Take a moment to think about why the information you have added matters. How does it connect to the point you are trying to make?" Kevin could turn and talk to a partner, orally rehearsing what he is going to add into his writing. You might begin a chart with questions children could ask each other as they do this work.

Questions Writers Ask Themselves when Connecting Reasons and Evidence

- Why is this important?
- How does it connect to the point?
- What are you trying to teach/show/make your reader believe?

If some children are plopping information in without relating it to their claims this may be a reading problem, not a writing problem. The conferring and small-group work section in Session 1 has ideas for how to work with kids on interpreting information. You might also turn to the related reading unit of study, Unit 3, Book 2, in Units of Study for Teaching Reading, Grades 3–5.

Another common situation that comes up when students begin stocking their writing with information is that some children believe they're paraphrasing, when really they're copying, taking language directly from the text—maybe only changing a word or two. I noticed this when I pulled up next to Sophia (see Figure 3–2).

What she had written was practically verbatim from "Nutrition in Disguise." She had changed "flavored milk" to "chocolate milk" and written out the word *nine*. "Sophia, this is great information in support of why chocolate milk should be in schools. But it sounds familiar. Have I heard that information somewhere else?" I asked. She nodded,

and I coached her to pull the article out, putting it side by side with her writing. I pointed out that it was virtually identical.

I reminded Sophia that the goal in paraphrasing is to put the information into your own words. "Sophia, when you're paraphrasing, you want to take the information and think, 'How else could I say this so that I'm not using the exact words from the article, but my own?' You might start by saying 'The text says . . . ' 'This means . . . ' Or 'The text says . . . Another way to say that is . . . '"

I knew that later we would, in fact, be inserting quotations. But for now, I was concerned that Sophia demonstrate her understanding of the text.

Sophia gave it a go. "The text says chocolate milk has nine essential nutrients. This means . . . " She paused, thinking about how to say it. "This means it has stuff that kids need." I noted that it was a good start, but a bit vague. "Writers want to keep the meat," I said. She tried it again. "This means it has a lot of things that kids need to live and grow." I asked her to reread the information and incorporate more into her writing. She tried it one more time, "This means it has lots of things that kids need, nine nutrients to be exact."

I coached her to continue this process, incorporating all the information from the quote. Through the process, Sophia had to draw upon other information that she learned from the text. Ultimately, she said, "Chocolate milk is really healthy. Kids need a ton of stuff to grow big and strong, and it's got what they need, nine nutrients to be exact. Sure, it's got some extra sugar, but not nearly as much as other drinks. Really, it's hardly any compared to other things like soda." She then revised her writing (see Figure 3–3).

The key to helping children learn to paraphrase is giving them an opportunity to redo the work many times, with each version less reliant on the original text. A small group of children can help each other in ways that resemble the help I gave Sophia.

chocolate milk should be in school because it is healthy. chocolate milk has the same nine essential nutrients as white milk, and a small amount of added sugar compared to other beverages.

FIG. 3–2   Sophia pulls information directly from the text, copying it almost entirely word for word.

Chocolate milk should be in school beasure it is healthy. It is packed with things that kids need to live and grow, nine nutrients to be exact. There is some extra sugar, but not as much as other drinks. Not nearly as much. It's hardly anything compared to stuff like soda.

FIG. 3–3   This revision conveys the important information without taking it directly from the text.

Setting Goals and Working toward Them

Remind writers that they have experience using checklists to set goals, and rally them to do this work in the context of their letters.

"You are all the kinds of writers who strive for excellence. In every unit of study, you dream big, aiming for the stars. Remember how you used the Information Writing Checklist to set ambitious goals and work toward them? Now you're going to use the Opinion Writing Checklist to do the same with your letters."

I revealed the Opinion Writing Checklists for Grades 4, 5, and 6, reminding students that they looked at this both when writing literary essays in fourth grade *and* when writing memoir.

Rally students to push themselves to use these checklists to set challenging goals that will significantly lift the level of their writing.

"I've put two checklists on your tables—one is for opinion writing that meets expectations for fourth grade, and one is for opinion writing that meets expectations for fifth or for sixth grade. Before this unit is over, most of you will accomplish most of the sixth-grade expectations. But we're just at the start of the unit, so you decide whether your writing fits more in the fourth- and fifth-grade checklist or if it fits more on the one that is a notch up. You know how to reread your writing and assess it, point by point."

Opinion Writing Checklist

	Grade 5	NOT YET	STARTING TO	YES!
Structure				
Overall	I made a claim or thesis on a topic or text, supported it with reasons, and provided a variety of evidence for each reason.	☐	☐	☐
Lead	I wrote an introduction that led to a claim or thesis and got my readers to care about my opinion. I got my readers to care by not only including a cool fact or jazzy question, but also figuring out was significant in or around the topic and giving readers information about what was significant about the topic.	☐	☐	☐
	I worked to find the precise words to state my claim; I let readers know the reasons I would develop later.			
Transitions	I used transition words and phrases to connect evidence back to my reasons using phrases such as *this shows that* … .	☐	☐	☐
	I helped readers follow my thinking with phrases such as *another reason* and *the most important reason*. I used phrases such as *consequently* and *because of* to show what happened.			
	I used words such as *specifically* and *in particular* in order to be more precise.			
Ending	I worked on a conclusion in which I connected back to and highlighted what the text was mainly about, not just the preceding paragraph.	☐	☐	☐
Organization	I grouped information and related ideas into paragraphs. I put the parts of my writing in the order that most suited my purpose and helped me prove my reasons and claim.	☐	☐	☐
Development				
Elaboration	I gave reasons to support my opinion that were parallel and did not overlap. I put them in an order that I thought would be most convincing.	☐	☐	☐
	I included evidence such as facts, examples, quotations, micro-stories, and information to support my claim.			
	I discussed and unpacked the way that the evidence went with the claim.			

"But here's the thing. Your goal is for your writing to make major strides forward during this unit. You know that the best sports coaches are very tough on their athletes. They don't let them get away with anything. Those coaches spot a sloppy move and they're on it! They call out, 'You can do better.' You need to be like a really tough coach. If you see a so-so introduction, don't say, 'Good enough.' Say, 'I can make this better. It's not up to my standard.' You'll be doing a lot more essay work during this unit, and if you don't aim for the sky, your essays will be mediocre. There are *always* things you can do to make your writing better and better and better. Expert sports coaches say, 'Practice doesn't make perfect. Perfect practice makes perfect.' So be tough on yourselves, and aim for perfect practice!"

Ask your students to use the Opinion Writing Checklists to set goals for themselves.

"Writers, the reason to do this self-assessing is so you can set goals for yourself. Will you look at the progress you need to make during this unit and set some goals for yourself? Use colored pencils or markers or whatever you have to make stars or fireworks beside goals you'll be especially aiming toward.

"*But* here is the last thing I need to say to you. My goal as a teacher is for every one of you to reach the end-of-sixth-grade column in as many ways as possible. This coming up unit is the steepest climb you will have made yet, and I do expect it will take your writing very, very far. So consider choosing items in that sixth-grade column for your goals."

FIG. 3–4 Students can write their names on Post-its, then stick these on the chart next to their goals.

PRACTICING IDENTIFYING WHAT IT LOOKS LIKE WHEN WRITING MEETS SPECIFIC GOALS

Writers, I'm going to distribute an essay (see Figure 3–5) that meets many sixth-grade goals, and I'm also giving you a few pages of the goals checklists that I've copied onto sticky labels so that you can peel off one goal at a time. Will you find examples of where the text I'm giving you matches the sixth-grade goals, and stick the label beside that place? This will allow you to annotate the model text I give you. Later in this unit, I'm going to give you this same page of goals (as well as a page of fifth-grade goals) on sticky labels, and I'm going to ask you to annotate *your own* essay. For now, my hope is that practicing this with someone else's writing will help you get a clear goal in mind for the work you aim to do in your letters.

Teachers, see Figure 3–5 (available in the online resources) for a printable sample essay you might use. The idea is that students will search the essay for goals and then peel those goals off of the label paper you've sent home and stick them in the appropriate place. Remember, your students are writing letters, but the central form is argument essays, whether they transform those into letters, position papers, petitions, or editorials.

①

The Secrets Of
Dairy Industry
By: Cecilia
5th Grade

Have you ever read a nutrition facts label on a chocolate milk carton? Most likely you have. Dairy companies tell us that chocolate milk is healthy and delicious. They tell us that it helps us refuel our bodies during a workout. That is what we want to hear. But is it the truth? No one has ever seen a commercial or read an advertisement for chocolate milk stating that chocolate milk is filled with fat, sugar, and calories. Dairy companies give us what we want to hear, but not necessarilly the truth. It's the only way to mask the fact that chocolate milk isn't healthy. They want us to by their products, and if schools stopped serving chocolate milk, they would lose

②

a lot of money. So what's the point in telling us the truth, anyway?

Chocolate milk isn't healthy. Although it has few vitamins, chocolate milk is also packed with sugar, fat, and calories. Chocolate milk has eight tablespoons of sugar in one of the eight ounce cartons they serve in schools! That's one tablespoons per ounce! A child drinking one carton [of chocolate milk] each school day will gain one pound in 14 weeks from chocolate milk alone...many children are drinking 2-4 cartons per day..." says Doctor Sarah Jane Schwarzenberg of MN-AAD's pediatric obesity task force. This may not seem like a lot, but in one year, a kid would gain five extra pounds, and in ten they would gain fifty. Recently, Jamie Oliver filled a wheelbarrow with sugar to represent the amount of sugar a kid gets from drinking

③

chocolate milk every day for a year. Ann Cooper calls chocolate milk "soda in drag". Even the "Got Milk?" corporation admits that chocolate milk has 31 more calories than white milk. Some very active kids can burn off the calories and fat with exercise, but most kids aren't very active. A lot of kids are overweight, and still drink chocolate milk. No matter how many vitamins, the bad stuff outweights them in chocolate milk.

Dairy companies want us to buy their products. All companies want us to buy their products. This is what's in their heads: money. NOT the health of American kids. The dairy industry has sponsored several studies in favor of chocolate milk. "Studies sponsored by the dairy industry show that when this happens overall milk consumption drops..." says Dana Woldow. The dairy industry

④

sponsored this and many others studies because they want to show us that chocolate milk should be kept in schools, and if chocolate milk is kept in schools, schools will buy it from them. Many dairy companies, such as "the Mid-Atlantic dairy association". These commercials are just ways to get us to buy their products, and it's working. But it needs to stop working!

If schools stopped serving chocolate milk, the dairy industry would lose a lot of money. Flavored milk accounts for 70% of milk served in US schools. This means that if the schools stopped serving chocolate milk, dairy companies would lose sales to schools. Overall milk consumption drops 37% when chocolate milk is removed. This means that sales to schools would also drop 37%,

⑤

resulting in money loss for the dairy industry. To them, there's no point in telling us the truth when they'd lose all that money by doing so.

It's true that many people who know about the amount of sugar, fat, and calories chocolate milk has still believe it's healthy. They think so because of the vitamins. But kids can get vitamins in plenty of other tasty and nutritious foods. Kids shouldn't depend on chocolate milk for health.

Although dairy companies give us what we want to hear, the truth is more important. Sure, it has vitamins, but it still isn't healthy. The only reason they tell us that it is because they want us to buy their products. If we stopped, they would lose a lot of money. But if the Dairy Association admitted admitted that chocolate milk isn't

⑥

healthy, kids in our country would be overall healthier. They need to think about the futures of American children. And if dairy companies aren't telling us the truth, what other food companies might also be lying?

FIG. 3-5   Cecilia's essay demonstrating the sixth-grade standards

Using Quotations to Bolster an Argument

WILLIAM ZINSSER (2006), in *On Writing Well*, has this to say about quoting the stakeholders in a story: "Somewhere in every drab institution are men and women who have a fierce attachment to what they are doing and are rich repositories of lore. Somewhere behind every storm sewer is a politician whose future hangs on getting it installed and a widow who has always lived on the block and is outraged that some damn-fool legislator thinks it will wash away. Find these people to tell your story, and it won't be drab."

When we start off writing about something new, we seek out experts and stakeholders in the field. We tune in to the commentary on the street, the official version as well as the insider's take on this, the marketing slogan as well as the consumer's experience. The best writers listen to a babble of different voices on a topic, and they select the most quotable of these, the voices with the greatest authority and experience and power.

In this session, you will teach students to mine different sources for specific quotations to strengthen their side of an argument. You'll want to teach them that a quotation can be strong because of who says it as well as because of the idea it conveys. In other words, you'll teach students to be selective in choosing who and what to quote.

Similarly, you'll teach your writers to weave a quote seamlessly into an argument instead of plopping it in merely for oomph. The most effective use of quotations occurs when a side-voice fits in exactly to reiterate, validate, or exemplify the existing argument.

You might also teach your writers to lop off the beginning or end (or both) of a long-winded quotation and use only the most pertinent portion. Citing is an art that, once perfected, will allow your students to go through words, through life, listening, equipped with a writer's radar for distinctive words and original ideas to add humanity and variety and authority to their own texts—spoken or written.

IN THIS SESSION, you'll teach students that argument writers add relevant quotes to make their arguments more potent, and you'll set them up to conduct an inquiry into what makes a quote powerful.

GETTING READY

✔ A chart set up with the title "What Makes a Quotation Powerful?" (see Teaching and Active Engagement)

✔ Transcript of a report on a school-yard event from an eyewitness to that event, enlarged for students to see (see Teaching and Active Engagement)

✔ Students' writers notebooks and pencils (see Active Engagement)

✔ "How to Write an Argument" chart (see Link and Share)

✔ Example of student writing that uses transitional phrases to move between quotes and the writer's own writing (see Mid-Workshop Teaching)

✔ "Phrases that Set Up Quotations" chart (see Mid-Workshop Teaching)

✔ A sample student letter—that names the source of the quote—enlarged on chart paper. You may decide to use Kennedy's (see Share)

✔ Markers and small chart paper (approximately three lines) for each group of students (see Share)

Using Quotations to Bolster an Argument

CONNECTION

Celebrate the gigantic step students took when they added more evidence to their letters.

"Writers, have any of you ever watched one of those reality shows on TV where they do a make-over? They start with something—maybe it's a house—that's dark and dreary. Then the trucks arrive, workers pour out, they race around, unloading, carrying, hammering, painting, and presto: the place is transformed into a miniature palace. I feel like your work yesterday went through one of those make-overs.

"We could have a display of 'used to be' and 'is now.' We'd show your first flash-drafts as examples of 'used to be.' Many of them were all about your personal preferences: 'I think chocolate milk is great because I love the taste!' The drafts in the 'is now' category—your revised flash-drafts—are far more grounded in research evidence.

"So far, your work has gone from being this good," I gestured knee high, "to being *this* good," I gestured shoulder high, "and so my job is to show you how to make it *this* good." I gestured sky high. "I've been thinking and thinking of what can make a really huge difference, and I've got a tip to give you, if you're willing." I checked that the kids were with me and continued.

Tell students that argument writers search their texts for quotations that will bring their side of the argument to life. Set them up to investigate particular kinds of quotations they might include and their purposes.

"Writers, when you write argument essays, as when you write stories and research reports, it helps to include the exact words that people say. You already know that in stories quotations can make a character come to life. In the same way, quotations can also make your view, your position, come to life.

"When you do your research, it's like you get a chance to listen in to the word on the street, to the insider talk behind the curtain. You learn a lot not just from the content you glean by researching, but also by the way people say things. Your reader wants to listen in as well.

"So, what makes a quotation powerful? You probably have some ideas about this already. After all, you not only have written research texts with quotations before, but you've also been alive! You live like a researcher all the time. You go home from school and recount specific moments, and you quote what people say. When you have an argument with a

It is important to let writers know that they have been changing in dramatic ways, because this suggests they are on a trajectory of growth that is promising. You want to always convey the message to students that with industrious effort, they can outgrow themselves, and that's the whole name of the game: getting better. It is probably true that their writing has undergone a transformation, so now is a good time to make a fuss about that.

Notice that this minilesson is an inquiry lesson, which means it is structured a bit differently than other minilessons. Inquiry minilessons don't have a teaching point that crystallizes the entire lesson, Instead, they have a key question.

The content of this session, and indeed this unit, is academic writing; it's advanced thinking. You'll want to teach this content by making it as accessible as possible. One way we do this is to borrow from everyday life to make your points.

friend or in your family, you've probably said, 'He said . . . ' or 'She said . . . ,' and then you gave some particularly strong quotation. But how does this work in the context of argument writing?"

❖ **Name the question that will guide the inquiry.**

"The question you'll be exploring, then, is this: what makes a quotation powerful?"

TEACHING and ACTIVE ENGAGEMENT

Introduce students to a text, in this case a recounting of an event, setting them up to investigate the way the reporter used quotations in important ways.

"To get us started I'll offer up a text—in this case a girl recounts what happened during a fight on the playground. Her account is full of quotations, and they make it powerful. Study her account and think about it to try to figure out how she has used quotations in powerful ways. I'll record what you figure out on chart paper.

"Here's the scene I want you to imagine. One girl has the scoop. She saw the fight on the playground. Here's what she reports about it. I'll pretend I'm the girl who saw it all!" I acted out a recounting of a fight as I read the text.

> *Sarah was so brave just now! She heard a bully say to a second grader, "You nerd!" That bully was wack.*
>
> *So Sarah called out to the bully, "Stop picking on little kids, will you?"*
>
> *I called, "You go, girl!" to Sarah. (You gotta have your friends' backs!)*
>
> *Someone else called, "Yes! Girl power!" I'm not sure who said that, but we were all cheering.*
>
> *Sarah went right up to the bully, and she said, "You don't scare me! You're just a bully." He didn't even argue! He took 3 steps and then another 2 steps, back! Then Sarah turned to the second graders and said, "We can't let bullies rule." They acted like she was their hero.*

Reread the transcript of the eyewitness report, asking students to turn and talk, noting instances when the reporter used quotations. Describe what the reporter was doing with quotes that they could do as well.

"I'm going to reread that scene, and this time I need you guys to hold your inquiry question in mind. The girl with the scoop has everyone listening intently partly because she uses quotations well. What is she doing that you could do, that every writer could do?" I showed a transcript of just the start of the account and read it aloud.

> *Sarah was so brave just now! She heard a bully say to a second grader, "You nerd!"*
>
> *So Sarah called out to the bully, "Stop picking on little kids, will you?"*
>
> *I called, "You go, girl!" to Sarah. (You gotta have your friends' backs!)*
>
> *Someone else called, 'Yes! Girl power!" I'm not sure who said that, but we were all cheering.*

Students will need to hear the text more than once, and see it, to really study quotations. Telling it once in a storytelling voice lets them engage with the text first emotionally. It will pull the students into the inquiry. Then you can unveil the text on chart paper or distribute copies.

Note that almost always when we are mining texts, we keep them brief. It's entirely possible to list more uses of quotations from this one segment than kids will possibly be able to internalize and do.

"Turn and talk, writers. What makes certain quotations powerful?" I listened in for a minute as partners shared their thoughts.

Collect student input on the chart, wording their observations in ways that are generalizable to other days, other texts.

I convened everyone after a few moments and asked for their observations. Claire offered, "The part where the kid says Sarah has got girl power was a powerful quote 'cause Sarah was really powerful to help the second-graders and . . . " Her voice trailed off.

I said, "I'm with you, Claire. It was great of Sarah to have that sort of courage, right? But for now, can we think specifically about the question? What makes the quotation powerful?"

Claire said, "It really gets your attention because it's . . . it's . . . unusual, it's surprising."

"I think you are onto something, Claire, because I bet a lot of things were being called out during the fight. Some kids were probably saying, 'Fight, fight,' and others were probably asking, 'What's going on?' But the reporter doesn't include every quotation, does she? She chooses the ones that stand out, that are surprising. Turn and tell each other if you see other examples of the reporter citing surprising quotations." As the children talked, I scrawled the first item on the list.

What Makes a Quotation Powerful?

- Choose quotations that are surprising, even shocking, to spice things up.
-
-

Return to the transcript again, asking students to identify more uses of quotations.

I reread the transcript again, asking for other observations about the way this girl had used quotes. Daniel offered, "The one telling this—the girl—told how somebody called 'You go, girl,' and that was surprising, like you said, but also after she told those words, she added her own thoughts when she said, 'You gotta have your friends' backs.' I like the way she said that. She made it into something bigger, a life lesson, sort of."

I jotted as the children talked.

Teachers, as you listen in to your students, you can be forming ideas about who to call on later to guide the lesson along and keep it as tight and focused as possible. That is, you are noticing who is stating key qualities that would benefit all students to hear. When you call on students you don't need to do it randomly. If you want students' contributions to add to the momentum of the lesson, you can make strategic choices.

Notice the way in which I keep children engaged and busy while taking a minute to record on the chart. If you do this often, you keep your minilessons lively and brief.

"We can't let bullies rule us!" Ivan practically shouted. "It's just like Daniel said. That's sort of a lesson. It's not explaining, it's just a lesson. And the words are just right."

"Writers, these are great tips. I'll add them."

LINK

Send students to work, suggesting they try out adding quotes to their drafts in meaningful ways. Remind them that they can use their note-taking system to help gather quotes.

"Writers, I bet you're eager to go back to your texts and try out adding quotes to support your reasons. You've got a lot of tools to help you. Remember, in your folders, you have your familiar texts on the debate over chocolate milk, and you have access to the videos as well.

"You may want to take a moment before you start to think about your system for gathering quotes. Yesterday you developed systems for gathering evidence from texts. You might use the same system today—index cards or writing stars in the margins to mark things—whatever was working for you. If you're reviewing a video, you can pause the video to make sure you're jotting the quotation down accurately. Don't forget that writers *also* paraphrase, putting the evidence into their letters in their own words. The big goal is to use evidence to prove your point, and I'm sure you'll all find lots of ways to try that out. I'm going to add quoting to our chart about how to write an argument as you go off."

How to Write an Argument

- Collect evidence that allows you to think through various sides of an argument.
- Rehearse by explaining your position and listing your reasons point by point.
- Plan your claim and reasons into boxes-and-bullets structure.
- Use evidence to support your reasons.
  - Paraphrase, putting it into your own words.
  - Quote, and then unpack the quote, showing how it relates to the claim.

What Makes a Quotation Powerful?
- Choose quotations that are surprising, even shocking, to spice things up
- Choose quotations that are life lessons, especially if the words are just right
- Explain what's important about the quotation

Teaching Children to Control Their Use of Quotations

AS I LOOKED AROUND THE ROOM, I noticed a handful of students were quoting large chunks of text, practically copying whole sections of the articles. Feeling a bit like a fisherman, I circled the room, signaling to any of the children who seemed to be copying text to join me for a quick meeting on the carpet. I also voiced over to all the writers, saying, "Writers, I notice many of you are practically quoting the *entire* source. You are selecting *huge* chunks of text to put into your essays. It is almost like when I read your letters to Ms. Granger, it feels as though I'm reading the articles themselves. It should feel like I'm reading your letter—your opinion, your reasons, your voice. Don't let quotes take over everything."

Once I'd collected writers who needed more instruction in selecting and honing quotes, I said to them, "You are totally wise to cite evidence, but you use the evidence to highlight points that you first make with your own voice, before you get another voice or two to chime in." I added that in general, the cited passages might be 5% of their text, or 10%, but not more. I coached students to look back at their essays and put their left index finger on the start of one quote and the right index finger on the end of that quote. They all quickly realized that at least for some sections of their letters, the proportion of the letter that came directly from sources was too large.

MID-WORKSHOP TEACHING   **Using Transitional Phrases between Writing and a Quotation**

"Writers, I was just looking at Daniel's piece, and he is doing some work that I think the rest of you might want to try. Daniel isn't just plopping quotations into the middle of his writing. He's transitioning between his own writing and the quotation with some transitional phrases. He's using phrases like 'In the article . . . ' and 'According to the video . . . ' to set up his quotation." I read a few lines from Daniel's first paragraph aloud, emphasizing the transitional phrases, and using an accented, intellectual voice that sounded a bit British.

In the article "Schools May Ban Chocolate Milk Over Added Sugar" it says . . .

According to a video on NBC News called "Milk Dud: Schools rule out chocolate milk," it states that . . .

"As you continue to incorporate quotations, remember that you don't want to just plop the words into your piece. To move between quotations and your own writing, you want to use words and phrases that make your position clear." I read Daniel's aloud again to demonstrate. The children giggled, but already I heard them whispering in their best accented voices, "Research indicates . . ." and "Evidence suggests. . . ." Then I gestured at the chart. "I have put up a chart of some phrases you might use."

Phrases that Set Up Quotations!

- According to the text . . .
- In the article/video . . .
- The text states . . .
- Research shows/indicates . . .
- Experts demonstrate . . .
- Evidence suggests . . .

"The key is, when writers quote," I coached, "they select only the most important lines. They think, 'Which exact words, which line or two that someone else wrote or said, should I include?' Then, they include those lines, and only those lines, in their essays. Then writers sometimes paraphrase or tell about the rest of what the passage conveyed."

I challenged students in the group to look at the paragraph that contained the largest proportion of quotes, and to cross out the parts of the quote that could be paraphrased, rewriting it in the writer's own words, so that only the most important part remained in quotations.

I pulled up next to one member of the small group, Stephen. He'd been alternating between rereading his writing and looking up as if ready to explode with frustration. He practically hauled me to his side with his exasperation, and so of course I began by asking him why he seemed so frustrated.

"I can't cut *any* of this out," he said. "It's impossible." Then he watched me scan his page and blurted out, "I already know you are going to say this is too long, but the reader needs to know it. That's why I put it in." I scanned his page, noting the very long quote.

> Chocolate milk should be in schools. It should be in schools because it has lots of nutrients. In the USA Today article it says, "Many, including the School Nutrition Association, American Academy of Pediatrics, American Dietetic Association, American Heart Association, and National Medical Association, argue that the nutritional value of flavored low-fat or skim milk outweighs the harm of added sugar. Milk contains nine essential nutrients including calcium, vitamin D and protein. A joint statement from those groups points to studies that show kids who drink fat-free flavored milk meet more of their nutrient needs and are not heavier than non-milk drinkers. 'Chocolate milk has been unfairly pegged as one of the causes of obesity,' said Julie Buric, vice president of marketing for the Milk Processors Education Program." This shows chocolate milk can be good for you too.

"Can you tell me why the reader needs to know all this information?" I asked.

"Well, it seems important that the reader know all these important people say chocolate milk is healthy and nutritional. I mean if doctors believe it, we should too. Then it seems like my reader should know what nutrients it has so they can see themselves that chocolate milk is pretty healthy. It's a lot more than sugar, you know." He continued on saying that it's important to know it doesn't lead to obesity because that shows that it's healthy.

"Stephen," I responded, "You are right. This is all important information. And it would be good for your reader to know. But you don't need to stuff all this into one paragraph. You can break into parts. It helps to think, 'What's this paragraph really about?' and then just use the part of the quote that supports the one reason you address in that paragraph."

To help him get started, I said, "What is this first paragraph about?"

He pointed to the first sentence, "It has lots of nutrients." I coached, "Now go back to the quote and put your finger under only the key sentences from the quote that support that claim, the sentences that show it has lots of nutrients."

Stephen went back and put his finger on the line that listed the nutrients. He also put a finger on the line that said kids reach more nutrient needs.

"Great! Those lines would be wonderful to support your reason. They do show that chocolate milk has lots of nutrients it is very healthy. Those lines can go right here."

Then I said, "Take a second to look at the lines that you didn't put your finger on. What do they discuss?" He told me that they talk about obesity and how fat kids get from sugar. "Right," I coached. "That's valuable information. But does that information support the reason that schools should sell chocolate milk because it has nutrients?" He shook his head no.

"Remember, writers select the information that best supports their point. They leave the rest out, or use it later when it suits another reason."

As I moved away from Stephen, I said this to the class, as a reminder. "Writers, eyes up here. It's beautiful to see you scouring the articles, looking for lines to lift into your letters. I want to let you know that writers can also pull quotations from digital texts. You can watch videos and jot down lines you want to quote. Some of you have watched videos at home on this subject, and some have been watching *Sugar Overload* on our computer. Just as you pull exact words from articles, you want to pull the exact words from the video, which can be hard. People talk faster than you think. So, you might rewind and watch a small part two or three times to get the words down exactly as they are said.

"You know that writers use repetition to highlight what's important so, you might also listen for phrases that are repeated. It's often easier to remember and get down something you hear more than once. There are a few videos bookmarked on the computer in the room, if you want to give it a try."

Introducing the Source, Explaining the Tie-In

Using the work of a student who has done so, engage students in a conversation about different ways to introduce and give background information on a source.

"Writers, can I have your eyes on me, please? Kennedy has remembered some important work from our information reports. Listen to this section of her writing, paying attention to the way she introduced the person she was quoting." I used my best "snobby voice" as I read:

> According to famous chef Jamie Oliver, "the sugar is coming and it just ain't stopping!"

"Did you notice the 'according to . . . ?' It makes Kennedy's position stronger, doesn't it? And Kennedy did something else as well. She included some background information on Jamie Oliver. She wrote, 'According to *famous* chef Jamie Oliver.' So she told us the source was Jamie Oliver *and* she told us he is a famous chef. There are other ways she could have tucked in background information on Jamie Oliver."

Using the same student work as an example, ask students to work together to come up with alternative ways to introduce the source.

"I'm going to pass out giant slips of chart paper and markers, and will you and the people near you come up with another way Kennedy could have worded this? Use two skills—your best 'set-up' phrases and anything about Jamie Oliver that might impress the reader." As I spoke, I distributed a slip of chart paper—only three lines long—and a marker pen to children sitting in each corner of the meeting area and to one or two to children in the center of the room as well.

Revealing a sheet of chart paper, I said, "I've written a chunk of Kennedy's text so you have some bigger context if you want it. You have two minutes to do this, so huddle quickly, come up with a good idea, and get it written out."

> One reason why schools should stop selling chocolate milk is because it has too much sugar. <u>According to famous chef Jamie Oliver, 'the sugar is coming and it just ain't stopping!'</u> When Jamie showed a school bus full of sugar, he makes you stop and think about how much sugar kids are getting from chocolate milk. It makes me realize that even though one bottle of milk might not have much, if you drink it all the time, it's a lot of added sugar.

Dear Ms. Granger,

    I believe chocolate milk should not be served in schools. Chocolate milk contains too much sugar. It is very unhealthy for students and schools should stop selling chocolate milk.

    One reason why schools should stop selling chocolate milk is because it has to much sugar. According to famous chef Jamie Olives, "the sugar is coming and it just ain't stopping!" When Jamie showed a school bus full of sugar, he makes you stop and think about how much sugar kids are getting from chocolate milk. It makes me realize that even though one bottle of milk might not have much, if you drink it all the time, it's a lot of added sugar.

    Another reason why I believe schools should stop serving chocolate milk is because school should be a place that promotes healthy habits. School is a place where we should learn good habits. Why would you give us sugary drinks? School is a place where we are learning to become better readers, writers, and thinkers. People who are thinkers, think about what they are eating and drinking.

    In closing, I think it would be cheaper to serve chocolate milk than juice but long term unhealthy kids turn into unhealthy adults. Would you want that on your conscious?

            Sincerely,
            Kennedy

FIG. 4–1 Noting background information introduces the source and helps the reader to understand why this person is an authority.

Soon children had displayed several alternative ways Kennedy could have given background information on the person she was quoting.

"The sugar is coming and it just ain't stopping," explains Jamie Oliver, a famous chef from California.

One person who thinks there is too much sugar is Jamie Oliver, who is a famous chef who has been hired to make lunches for kids in California's schools. He says, "The sugar is coming and it just ain't stopping."

Jamie Oliver, a famous chef, says, "The sugar is coming and it just ain't stopping."

I convened the students to admire this work. "Wow, see how you can give some information about the person you're quoting by saying their name, and then some information, set off by commas? Or you can almost give a little biography of the person, telling the us why this person is so important or reliable. Nice work, writers."

I gathered the class back together. "Writers, this is such important work. As you continue to write, think about not only the information, but also the source. I'll add that to the chart so we don't forget."

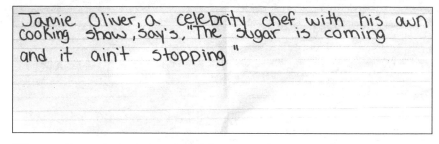

FIG. 4–2 These students broadened the context by stating that Jamie does more than advocate the school lunch.

> Jamie Oliver, a chef and nutrition expert, says, "the Sugar is Coming and it uin't Stopping"!"

FIG. 4–3 This group introduced the source and said why he is an authority on the issue, noting he is a nutrition expert.

How to Write an Argument

- Collect evidence that allows you to think through various sides of an argument.
- Rehearse by explaining your position and listing your reasons point by point.
- Plan your claim and reasons into boxes-and-bullets structure.
- Use evidence to support your reasons.
  - Paraphrase, putting it into your own words.
  - Quote, and then unpack the quote, showing how it relates to the reason.
  - Introduce the source and explain the connection.
  - Use "set-up" language (transitional phrases) to prop up your sources.

INTRODUCING INFORMATION AND NAMING SOURCES

For homework tonight, take some time to add more information into your letter, including direct quotations as well as other kinds of information. Will you also reread your draft of your letter and make sure that you have inserted identifying information that provides a bit of relevant information on all the sources of your quotations as well as any other information you paraphrased? As you do this, keep in mind that it's not just *people* who need to be introduced. If you know something about the newspapers or magazines or websites that you are referencing, you can also add in that sort of detail as well.

Redrafting to Add More Evidence

 **Dear** Teachers,

One question you will want to ask yourself in your teaching of writing, again and again, is "Are the students doing enough writing?" That is to say, it can be easy to get wrapped up in teaching students to add a little of this or a little of that, only to find that several days later they have only done just that—added a few sprinkles of text that don't substantially lift the level of their drafts. Ensuring that children have enough opportunities to write becomes even more complex in a unit like this one, where reading and research are integral to the process.

In the end, we know that stronger writing comes from repeated practice, and you'll want to offer children as many opportunities to draft letters (and later, essays), as possible. Today you will ask students to redraft their rough draft letters, incorporating the new evidence they've acquired over the past two days. In this way, you give them the opportunity to practice letter writing yet again, while simultaneously teaching them to write in ways that incorporate a wealth of information and research. You'll find as well that when students start fresh, they may be more likely to integrate new learning into their new drafts, as opposed to sprinkling in little bits here and there that give their writing a sort of patchwork feel.

MINILESSON

You'll probably want to begin by rallying children's excitement for today's writing. With older children, we often find that explaining the *why* of a particular lesson or strategy, the reason for the work of the day, helps garner a bit more excitement and engagement. You might begin with a small story. "Writers, a young man I know recently told me that he will be climbing Mount Denali in Alaska. Denali is the highest mountain peak in all of North America and climbs 20,320 feet above sea level! Can you imagine?" Continue on, "Here's the thing, though. Evan is not just going to climb the mountain by himself. He'll be dragging a sled full of 130 pounds of supplies he'll need to survive. And carrying a heavy pack." Pause, allowing the children to ooh and aah a bit over this. "It's one thing to climb a mountain. It's another thing entirely to do it with all those pounds of extra weight."

You might explain to children how writing a research-based essay can be a bit like mountain climbing. A few days ago they were only carrying a few pounds of weight—a few quotes, a bit of text evidence—and so the writing was much easier. Now, they are carrying pounds and pounds of evidence and quotes, gathered from their work across the past two days, and this makes writing their argument letters a bit more arduous—maybe not exactly like climbing a mountain dragging 130 pounds, but close!

Why the hyperbole? We want students to approach the task of drafting and redrafting with grit and energy rather than with frustration. We want them to see that starting again, rather than being a step back, is actually a step forward.

For your teaching point, you might say something like, "When you are not just writing a letter, but writing a letter in which you carry the cargo of evidence, you're doing ambitious, challenging work. It is not likely that your first draft will be your best effort. Chances are you'll want to reread that draft, decide what parts of it work and what parts don't work, and then plan and write another draft."

We recommend teaching through guided practice today, keeping your teaching time as short as possible so that students have ample time to draft. "Right now, you're going to get yourselves set up to begin new drafts," you might begin. "You could make the new draft practically the same as the old one, keeping the same reasons and the same structure for the draft, but you have a lot of new evidence to fit into your essay, and presumably you have some new thinking as well. So take some time to rewrite your claim and to rethink your reason. Write your claim in at least four other ways—just to push yourself to imagine that it could be said differently."

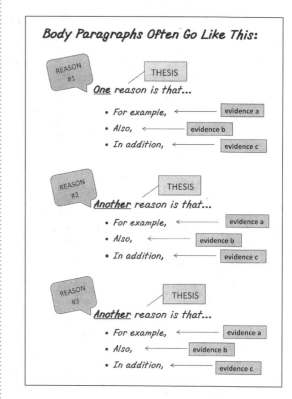

Body Paragraphs Often Go Like This:

REASON #1 → THESIS
One reason is that...
- For example, ← evidence a
- Also, ← evidence b
- In addition, ← evidence c

REASON #2 → THESIS
Another reason is that...
- For example, ← evidence a
- Also, ← evidence b
- In addition, ← evidence c

REASON #3 → THESIS
Another reason is that...
- For example, ← evidence a
- Also, ← evidence b
- In addition, ← evidence c

As students work, give them some tips. "Usually, a claim is better if it is bold and clear. It takes a strong position. A claim is better if you figure out exactly what you have to say." Again, let the students work, then consider giving another bit of coaching. "To write a strong claim, you need to think ahead to your evidence. You almost need to write the whole letter, in your mind, to make sure you have the goods you need to support your claim."

After students work a bit on their claim, you can channel them to do similar work with the plan for reasons that support their claim. "Writers often start this process by laying all of their evidence before them and sorting it into reasons that support their claims. The reasons you've developed may have changed as you've collected more evidence, or your evidence may now seem to better support slightly different reasons. One thing is for sure: it's worth it to rethink and revise your reasons—both what they are and their order. Will you do a drumroll, saving the most important reason for last? Or will you go for shock value, putting the most surprising reason first? Right now, will you take a few minutes to sort your reasons and evidence?" You'll want to make sure the students have enough room to lay their quotes, notes, and other evidence before them, so they can survey the terrain and prepare to rehearse.

As your students begin this process, give them tips to help nudge them along. "Writers, I've put our chart, 'Body Paragraphs Often Go Like This,' up in the meeting area to help you. You might make a little system for yourself, one that will help you keep track of which notes are going where. So, for instance, you might put a little *1* next to anything that will go in body paragraph number one, a *2* next to anything that will go in body paragraph number two, and so on. That's just one way to get yourselves organized. You might have another way. That's great! Just make sure that you are using some kind of system."

You might coach, saying, "Students, don't just grab any ol' reasons and pile them into your letter. All reasons are not equally important. You'll want to have a pile of rejected reasons lying beside you as you sort through possibilities and end up with only the very strongest."

After giving students a few minutes to re-sort and categorize the information they've gathered, you may want to channel them into a bit of rehearsal. As with any other writing genre, the students' writing will be infinitely more cohesive if you give them an opportunity to rehearse it orally before putting their pens to paper.

One option is to have students rehearse with partners, taking turns saying aloud the first body paragraph of their essay. If you choose this option, encourage partners to be helpful coaches, not just passive listeners, reminding their partners to carry forward all they know about good opinion writing, including using transition words, beginning new paragraphs with topic sentences, and tying evidence back to their opinion.

Rehearsing with partners takes some time, however, and it will be more efficient to coach writers to "talk to their paper," saying their essay aloud as they draw their finger down a sheet of loose leaf.

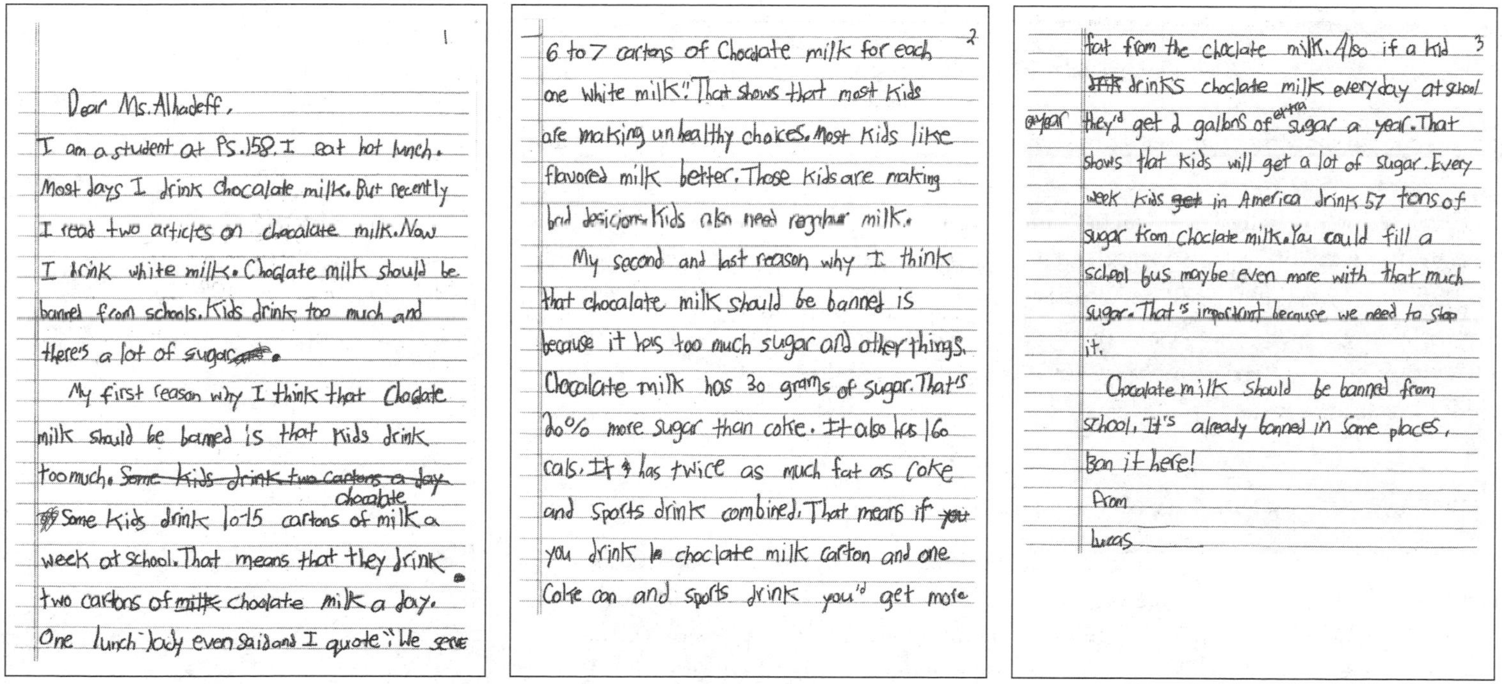
1

Dear Ms. Alhadeff,

I am a student at PS.158. I eat hot lunch. Most days I drink chocalate milk. But recently I read two articles on chocalate milk. Now I drink white milk. Choclate milk should be banned from schools. Kids drink too much and there's a lot of sugar.

My first reason why I think that Choclate milk should be banned is that kids drink too much. ~~Some kids drink two cartons a day.~~ Some kids drink 10-15 cartons of chocolate milk a week at school. That means that they drink two cartons of ~~milk~~ choclate milk a day. One lunch lady even said and I quote: "We serve

2

6 to 7 cartons of Chocolate milk for each one white milk." That shows that most kids are making unhealthy choices. Most kids like flavored milk better. Those kids are making bad desicions. Kids also need regular milk.

My second and last reason why I think that chocalate milk should be banned is because it has too much sugar and other things. Chocalate milk has 30 grams of sugar. That's 20% more sugar than coke. It also has 160 cals. It has twice as much fat as coke and sports drink combined. That means if ~~you~~ you drink a choclate milk carton and one Coke can and sports drink you'd get more

3

fat from the choclate milk. Also if a kid drinks choclate milk everyday at school they'd get 2 gallons of extra sugar a year. That shows that kids will get a lot of sugar. Every week kids ~~get~~ in America drink 57 tons of sugar from choclate milk. You could fill a school bus maybe even more with that much sugar. That's important because we need to stop it.

Chocalate milk should be banned from school. It's already banned in some places. Ban it here!

From
Lucas

FIG. 5–1 As Lucas drafted fast and furiously, he reread his piece for clarity, crossing out errors and rewriting as needed.

Dear Ms. Alhadeff,
Chocolate milk should be allowed in schools because it is "Nutrition in Disguise!" One reason is, it gives kids their 3 daily servings of milk. Another reason is, it has less than half the sugar added to Coka-Cola! The last reason is chocolate milk has the same nutrients as plain milk.

One reason chocolate milk should be in schools is, it gives kids their 3 daily servings of milk at school. For example, kids drink milk at home, but at school no one gives them their milk. They must choose for themselves. Some turn to chocolate milk, which can give them 1 out of their 3 daily servings of milk. They know it tastes good but it is also good for their health! This means that chocolate milk helps kids by giving them their daily milk at school.

Itzel

Another reason, why chocolate milk should be allowed is, research shows that chocolate milk has less than half the sugar added to Coka-Cola! For example, Ms. Dobbins, a nutritionist for the Dairy Association, proved that a mini can of Coka-Cola has 9 teaspoons of sugar and 39 grams of carbohydrates! When she she tested the small container of chocolate milk, it had 3 teaspoons of sugar and 24 grams of carbohydrates! This matters because studies proved that chocolate milk is much healthier that Coka-Cola.

The last reason, why chocolate milk should be allowed in schools is, it has the same nutrients as white milk. For instance, Chocolate milk and

white milk both have protein, vitamin A, vitamin D, calcium, and iron. This is important because, chocolate milk is just as healthy as white milk which means it is very healthy for kids.

Chocolate milk must be allowed in schools because it's nutritious! It gives kids their daily milk at school, it is much healthier than Coka-Cola, and it is just as healthy as plain milk. I hope that this has convinced you.

Sincerely,
Itzel

FIG. 5–2 Itzel uses comparative data to show chocolate milk is healthy, putting its nutritional value beside that of other drinks.

Once students have rehearsed the first half of their second drafts, you'll want to send them off to write quickly and efficiently. "Writers," you might say, "you've laid out and surveyed your newest research. You've planned and rehearsed for how your new drafts will go. You have a lot of new evidence to add as well, including specific quotations, snobby language, and transitions. Now, it's time to draft! I don't want to take up another second of your writing time!" Then, with a sense of urgency, send children off to redraft their letters, fast and furious on loose leaf paper.

CONFERRING AND SMALL-GROUP WORK

You won't want to interrupt children's writing today, but instead use this opportunity to survey the terrain and take note of what students are doing, to help you make informed decisions down the road. You might begin by listing a few predictable problems you anticipate children having. The learning progression will be helpful in informing some of what you might look for. We recommend making a simple chart for yourself, perhaps like this.

• The writing is sparse. Writer struggles to elaborate.	• The student's piece is not organized. Paragraphs overlap, repeat, or are a jumble of unrelated information.	• The writer's evidence does not align to the writer's claim.
• The essay is swamped with an overabundance of evidence.	• The writer's piece feels clunky and could benefit from transitional words and phrases.	• The writer rambles on about an idea, including too much of his or her personal thinking.

We recommend circulating around the room with this chart in hand, jotting children's names in the boxes that apply to them. So, for instance, if you notice Ari is writing long, convoluted paragraphs and could use a bit of work on organization, jot his name in the box along with others who need the same. In this short period of time, you've set yourself up for the small-group teaching you'll do tomorrow and throughout the unit.

Remember to study your strong writers as well, so you'll be ready to coach them. You might have a second chart like this:

• The writing is long and elaborated, but all parts are treated equally, as if of the same importance.	• The work is beginning to address a specific audience, and the writer is ready to designate that focus and rethink examples and direct address.
• The writer adds in a sense of the bigger context, and is ready to study how to embed the context and related research questions without overwhelming the piece.	• The writer shifts verb tense in the essay, naturally presenting evidence that is historical in past tense and evidence that is current in present. Writer is ready to study mentor texts for how writers shift tense and why in argument writing.

MID-WORKSHOP TEACHING

We recommend using today's mid-workshop teaching time to support stamina and velocity. Instead of one interruption, you may decide instead to coach children with a few purposeful voiceovers. "You should be on your second body paragraph by now," you might say. Or, "Don't just dive into a new body paragraph. Instead, begin by telling your reader what it will be about." And later, "Don't leave your evidence behind! You've collected all these beautiful quotes and worked to paraphrase particularly strong pieces of evidence. Make sure your evidence ends up in your draft!"

SHARE

For today's share, you might divide the children into four groups, one in each corner of the room, and in each corner, ask one or two children to read their letters aloud. You'll want to choose these children strategically, deciding on students who have written drafts that feel particularly strong and persuasive. The focus for the last few days has been evidence-based arguments, so you'll want to be sure that the children you select are, in fact, using evidence to bolster their claims. Because the students in this class had heard Claire's bare-bones flash draft a few days ago, she was one of the students we suggested might share now. You might look for children like Claire, with visible growth in their work due to planning and evidence.

 Ask the children who are listening to be *active listeners*. You may want to give them a copy of the Opinion Writing Checklist, channeling them to listen for ways a classmate achieves all the goals on that checklist and using it to give specific feedback. Of course, the real reason to do this is that by viewing another writer's work in relation to the checklist, writers themselves internalize those goals. Here is Claire's draft (see Figure 5–3).

After hearing this draft, Norah complimented, "I notice that you restated your reasons and your claim in the conclusion. You also added a little twist by saying that kids could slurp up the hidden nutrition. It was a cool image. It strengthened your position."

Ari noted that Claire used a variety of evidence to support her claim. "I see a quote and a list of nutrients and then some numbers," he said. "I think that I only use quotes. Maybe I could try a few things, like you did."

Ivan said, "I like your set-up, 'Melissa Dobbins, the Director of Nutrition Affairs at the Midwest Dairy Council.'"

As your students hear from other writers, they, much like Ari, will start to grow ideas for how they might revise their current drafts. Encourage them to write their ideas down so that they remember to do that work on future days. Before the workshop ends, encourage them to take out their notebooks and jot self-assignment boxes or note on the checklist what they plan to work on in their pieces.

Draft # 2

Chocolate milk should be served in schools. It sholud be served because it helps children meet their nutritional needs. In addition, It should be served because, more children drink milk because of the great taste.

One reason why chocolate milk should be served in schools is because children who drink flavored milk meet more of their nutritional needs. "Children who drink flavored milk meet more of their nutritional needs, do not consume more added sugar, calories, and fat, and are not heavier than non-milk drinkers" says Melissa Dobbins, the Director of Nutrition Affairs at the Midwest Diary Council. She also said that chocolate milk provides protien, Vitamins A, Vitamin D, and Calcium. When children drink chocolate milk, they are getting bts of nutrition.

Another reason why chocolate milk should be served in schools is because children will drink more milk because of the great taste. According to a study, when chocolate milk was dropped from shchool districts milk consumption dropped 35%. When chocolate milk is taken away children are not getting the nutrition from milk they need. Chocolate milk should be served in schools. Children won't be able to get the protien they need without it. Chocolate milk is hwy many children drink milk and slurp up the nutrition that is hidden inside of it.

FIG. 5–3 In her second draft, Claire uses quotes, facts, and statistics to support her claim.

HOMEWORK

You might say, "Writers, you have a new draft. Your work tonight is to get started revising it. You know so many revision strategies now. There are lots of different ways you could get started with this work. One thing to keep in mind is that revision strategies aren't genre-specific—meaning, as you revise your letters you might want to try using revision strategies that you used when you were revising other genres. You might, for example, read your letter as though you are a stranger, noticing places a stranger might scratch her head and say, 'Huh?' and then try to fix those places. You might instead (or also) try rereading to find 'the heart' of your piece. Instead of looking for the heart of the story, this time, you're looking for the heart of your letter. You might have a conversation with someone about the love of chocolate milk, and try out your reasons and evidence, listening for what seems particularly common in your conversations and for the questions that are raised. I'm sure you can remember other useful revisions strategies, too."

Good luck!

Lucy, Mary, and Annie

Balancing Evidence with Analysis

IN THIS SESSION, you'll teach students that writers analyze their evidence and explain their thinking, so that their own voice is powerful throughout their writing.

GETTING READY

✔ Images of layer cakes (Google images "layer cakes")—optional (see Connection)

✔ An excerpt of a student essay in which the child includes evidence but no analysis as well as the excerpt revised to include evidence and analysis (see Teaching)

✔ "Questions to Help Writers Analyze Evidence/Fortify Their Thinking" chart (see Teaching)

✔ "Ways to Push Our Thinking" chart (see Teaching and Conferring)

✔ Students' writing folders with the drafts of their letters (see Active Engagement and Share)

✔ "How to Write an Argument" chart (see Link)

✔ Pens, pencils, or thin-tipped markers in various colors (see Conferring)

✔ Example of a block quote to whittle down (see Mid-Workshop Teaching)

WHEN THEY REACHED THIS SESSION, some of the teachers who recently taught this unit began noting something that has caused its fair share of angst. By this point, students were beginning to back one side of an argument, to provide supporting reasons, and to fish for quotes to weave in. It looked like all the teaching of the past four sessions was sinking in. But the resulting writing was far from gratifying. Instead, draft upon draft of student work showed a lackluster uniformity, almost as if the essays had been cut from the same voiceless mold. Why was the voice vanishing?

Don Murray defines voice in *Writing to Deadline* as "The cry I made from the crib, the sounds I learned, the power of *I*. The grand ego from which all writers are bred." Many agree that it qualifies as the most elusive of all qualities to actually *teach* the writer. The fact is that children will lose and find their voice many times as they move beyond the crib, the nursery, the yard, and into the world—as they develop into *themselves*. Voice will deepen, become more thoughtful, as children learn when to lower it in a whisper and when to let it ring high. Although it's not unusual for writing to become robotic for a time, if you're finding that your writers' voices are vanishing from the page, it is time to take action and lure them back, stronger and more purposeful than before. This is the session to begin that work.

"I see the evidence and the quotes you're picking from the texts and the world around you," you will acknowledge. "But readers also need to know what *you* make of those quotes." There is a turning point at this part of the unit. We're emphasizing that it is important to strengthen the writer's voice while maintaining a well-informed expert perspective. The challenge is to help children find balance between the research or the evidence out there versus the opinions and personal experiences that can only bubble forth from the life that the writer knows best: his or her own.

Balancing Evidence with Analysis

CONNECTION

Tell a story of comparing layer cakes, showing some visuals to ignite students' interest and imply various balances of cake to frosting.

As students came in for the minilesson, they were surprised to see pictures of various layer cakes.

"Writers, have you ever been to a dinner where you can try different desserts? Well, last night, I was at a restaurant with a friend, and there was a whole case full of cakes, like these cakes." I gestured toward the images of cakes. "Imagine trying to decide between all these cakes!" I looked at the cake images again, as if paralyzed by indecision. The children, of course, were pointing to cakes they thought would be particularly good.

"Well, writers, my friend and I decided to order *three* slices of cake, so we could compare them.

"Here's what happened. We tried a bite of one cake, then a bite of another, then another, and we compared each one. The first one was a really dense cake, with only a tiny bit of frosting. We found that when we went to eat it the cake crumbled away. It definitely needed more frosting to bind it together! Then the second one was all this frosting, with hardly any cake to support it. And the third one was . . . just right!

"Here's what was just right about the third cake: it had just the right balance of cake and frosting."

"You might be wondering why I'm telling you about layer cake."

❖ **Name the teaching point.**

"Writers, today I want to teach you that a good argument is a bit like a layer cake—just the right balance of dense, researched evidence layered between rich thinking. To achieve this balance, you add your own thinking and explanations."

You might access these images and put them up on your Smart Board or simply print a couple from the Internet and tape them to your chart paper. Or if your technology is not being friendly, just draw a couple!

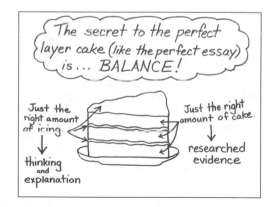

TEACHING

Offer two methods for developing thinking about evidence. Begin with a list of predictable strategies writers ask themselves.

"Writers, picture that your evidence is the cake part and your thinking is the frosting. The trick of this work is to not just plop more and more evidence into your writing. You have to remember to *explain* the significance of your evidence in order to bind it together the way frosting holds the cake together. This means really analyzing the evidence in your text and explaining your thinking.

"There are a couple of methods writers use to make sure to analyze evidence and get their thinking into their writing. One might be new to you, and one I'm sure you'll remember from writing other essays, and from the work you did in memoir. Let me show both to you, and then you can do some work to see which methods can help you become a more powerful writer."

Offer an anchor chart of predictable questions writers can ask to help them add their own thinking in response to text evidence.

"Writers, one method I use to analyze evidence is that I ask myself some predictable questions. These are the kinds of questions that writers who do research often ask themselves about their evidence." I displayed the chart that I had prepared earlier.

"Let me give you a quick example of how helpful these questions can be to a writer. You know the writer Jack? I remember, as he was writing, he was getting into a rut with including only evidence without any analysis. He had just written a bunch of facts, like this."

> There's one more reason why chocolate milk should be served in schools. The famous nutritionist showed that chocolate milk has a lot less sugar and carbohydrates than soda and power drinks like gatorade.

"Hmm, this does feel as if it's all cake and no frosting to bind it together, right? It's just piece of evidence, with no thinking. I imagine that as Jack was revising, he probably asked himself some of these questions. Listen to how his draft changed after he did this."

> There's one more reason why chocolate milk should be served in schools. The famous nutritionist showed that chocolate milk has a lot less sugar and carbohydrates than soda and power drinks like gatorade. So if kids get in the habit of drinking milk in school, then they'll probably skip the sodas outside of school. The famous nutritionist didn't actually say this as a fact, this is my interpretation, but it was the facts her kids pointed out about how soda has more sugar, that made me think of it.

Questions to Help Writers Analyze Evidence/Fortify Their Thinking

Why did I include this evidence?

How does this evidence relate back to my claim? CLAIM

What makes this particular quote or statistic so important? " " %.f

How is this evidence changing my thinking? Now I think...

Demonstrate asking and answering a couple of these questions. Be sure to highlight your extended thinking.

"I'm going to imagine now that I'm Jack asking myself one of the questions," I continued. I used one voice for asking questions and another for answering them. "What makes this particular quote or statistic so important?" I asked myself in a professorial voice.

"Well, I included this evidence about how that nutritionist said that chocolate milk has less sugar and carbohydrates in it because it makes chocolate milk seem much healthier than soda. I mean, everyone knows that soda isn't really good for you."

"Let me try another one," I said, switching back to my regular voice before asking in my professor voice, "How is this evidence changing my thinking?"

As Jack, I answered, "Well, if chocolate milk is healthier than soda, it makes me think it's a good thing for kids to have it in school because maybe they'll get in the habit of having it, and they'll like it so much they'll drink chocolate milk instead of soda at home, too. I wasn't thinking about that before, how it could change the choices kids' make outside of school. I should definitely write all of that down!"

Looking up and switching back to my regular voice again, I said, "Of course, I'm just guessing what Jack might have done. But he certainly could have asked himself these questions to get to that deep thinking he added into his draft."

It will be important for you to help kids think through the logistics of adding their thinking into their drafts. You might coach students to put a star where they want to insert that thinking and then actually write that thinking down in their notebook, or they could add spider legs, or use Post-its as they've done before. If students are working digitally they can add this thinking as insertions to their word-processed drafts. One note: if your students are working digitally, be sure to save each flash draft as its own document, both so students do truly start fresh and can write a lot with each new draft and so they can compare how their writing has grown and changed.

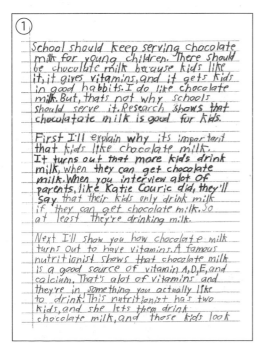

① School should keep serving chocolate milk for young children. There should be chocolate milk because kids like it, it gives vitamins, and it gets kids in good habits. I do like chocolate milk. But, thats not why schools should serve it. Research shows that chocolate milk is good for kids.

First I'll explain why its important that kids like chocolate milk. It turns out that more kids drink milk, when they can get chocolate milk. When you interview alot of parents, like Katie Couric did, they'll say that their kids only drink milk if they can get chocolate milk. So at least they're drinking milk.

Next I'll show you how chocolate milk turns out to have vitamins. A famous nutritionist shows that chocolate milk is a good source of vitamin A, D, E, and calcium. That's alot of vitamins and they're in something you actually like to drink! This nutritionist has two kids, and she lets them drink chocolate milk, and those kids look

② pretty healthy. One girl has really white teeth and shiny hair. This nutritionist works for the Dairy Association, so she must have studied how good milk is good for you.

There's one more reason why chocolate milk should be served in schools. The famous nutritionist showed that chocolate milk has alot less sugar and carbohydrates than soda, and power drinks like gatorade. So if kids get in the habbit of drinking milk in school, then they'll probably skip the sodas outside of school. The famous nutritionist didn't actually say this as a fact, this is my interpretation, but it was the facts her kids pointed out about how soda has more sugar, that made me think of it.

That's why we should keep serving chocolate milk at our middle school-it gets kids to drink milk, it gives us vitamins, and it builds good habbits. Now that's all clear, has an

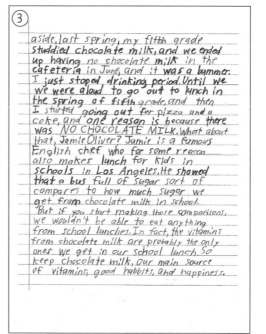

③ aside, last spring, my fifth grade studdied chocolate milk, and we ended up having no chocolate milk in the cafeteria in June, and it was a bummer. I just stoped drinking period. Until we were aloud to go out to lunch in the spring of fifth grade, and then I started going out for pizza and a coke, and one reason is because there was NO CHOCOLATE MILK. What about that, Jamie Oliver? Jamie is a famous English chef who for some reason also makes lunch for kids in schools in Los Angeles. He showed that a bus full of sugar sort of compares to how much sugar we get from chocolate milk in school. But if you start making those comparisons, we wouldn't be able to eat anything from school lunches. In fact, the vitamins from chocolate milk are probably the only ones we get in our school lunch. So keep chocolate milk, our main source of vitamins, good habbits, and happiness.

FIG. 6–1 Jack's evidence and his analysis of the evidence

"Writers, do you see how asking some predictable questions might have helped Jack develop explanations for why this evidence was so important, and after he added those things in, his own voice became even stronger?"

Shift to reminding students of the work they have done previously with thought prompts, as another method to extend their thinking.

"Let's give you a chance to try this work. Before we do, though, I'm sure you recall another familiar method for pushing your thinking about ideas. Remember the thought prompts you used for essay and memoir? Turn and talk to your neighbor about some of those that helped you to push yourselves as you develop your thinking. Remember, we used phrases like 'In other words . . . ,' and 'This shows. . . .'

After listening in, I revealed a familiar chart and said, "If you come up with other phrases that help push your thinking— either just now, or as you write your letters—make sure to add them to the chart.

"Let me try this now, to start thinking of ways to balance out my letter so that it's not just evidence. If I said, 'This makes me realize . . . Well, this evidence about chocolate causing happiness makes me realize that food isn't just about nutrients. It's also about emotions and how it makes us feel. So maybe chocolate milk could be helpful emotionally.'" I looked up as if surprised. "Well, that was some added thinking too! So for me, both these methods are helpful—asking myself questions and using these prompts."

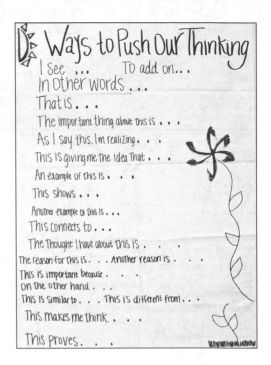

ACTIVE ENGAGEMENT

Give students a chance to try this work, emphasizing how their talk is rehearsing the thinking they can add to their letters.

"Let's give you a chance to try this work, writers. Can you look at your letter right now with your partner? And can you put your finger on one place in your letter where you really used a lot of evidence or where the evidence feels particularly strong?"

I waited a moment for them to find a place.

"Now, with your partner, will you try asking each other some of these predictable questions, and perhaps using some of the thought prompts, to rehearse the thinking you could add to your letter? Really rehearse what you might write, and try to explain your thinking, so your words are as strong as the evidence you've included."

Kennedy listened to her partner read aloud that chocolate milk has nine essential nutrients, including calcium and vitamins A and D, and then asked Sarah, "Why did you include this evidence?" Sarah thought for a moment. "I included that because that's a lot of healthy stuff. It feels important to let people know that there is good stuff in chocolate milk, stuff that kids need to grow and be healthy. And it's not just one thing that kids need. It's a lot of them."

After a bit, she added, "How is it changing your thinking? What's it all add up to?" Sarah responded, "Well, everyone focuses on one ingredient—sugar. And, I get it, too much sugar is bad for you. But people need to think about more than one ingredient when deciding if something is healthy or not. Chocolate milk seems unhealthy because of the extra sugar, but when you look at what else it has, it isn't so bad at all. In fact, seems to me like kids should be drinking more of it."

I leaned in and said to Kennedy, "You should tell Sarah, 'Quick! Write that down!'"

Reconvene students and highlight the work of a successful partnership discussion, then offer a tip to extend students' transference and independence with this skill.

After a bit, I convened the students.

"Writers, you have a lot of strong thinking to add to your letters now, so I want to give you some feedback. Kennedy listened to Sarah read part of her letter, and then rather than wait for her to think about what to say next, Kennedy went ahead and asked her some of these questions—and Sarah had a lot more to say! So you can ask each other these questions during partner talk, or when you're writing alone, just ask yourself. Then take a moment to write your new thinking.

"The other tip I'll give you is that when one question or prompt doesn't lead you to develop your thinking, just try another one, or think of a different question. It's not any specific question or prompt that is magic. It's that you work hard at explaining your *own* thinking about the topic and what your evidence is making you think."

LINK

Send your writers off, reminding them to be sure to always analyze their evidence whenever they are writing from research and suggesting they start fresh with a new draft.

"Okay, writers, let's get you off to writing while your thinking is fresh. You've learned a ton of strategies to make your arguments strong and your pieces grow stronger and more convincing each day. Yesterday you redrafted, incorporating all your evidence into your letters. Now, you might take some time to reread and revise those drafts." I pointed to the chart "How to Write an Argument." "As you reread and revise your work, remember that whenever you are incorporating evidence into your writing, it's important to analyze and explain that evidence. Your voice matters! If you find places that were all evidence and no analysis, grow some thinking. You might grab a revision strip, write down your thoughts, and tape it onto your draft. You might find you need more room than that because you have too many ideas to write just a sentence or two. If that's the case, put a star on your draft to note that you want to add your thinking there, and then open your notebook and write your ideas down. Go to it."

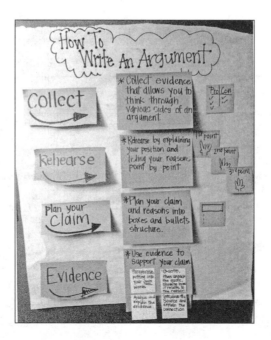

How to Write an Argument

- Collect evidence that allows you to think through various sides of an argument.
- Rehearse by explaining your position and listing your reasons point by point.
- Plan your claim and reasons into boxes-and-bullets structure.
- Use evidence to support your reasons.
  - Paraphrase, putting it into your own words.
  - Quote, and then unpack the quote, showing how it relates to the reason.
  - Introduce the source and explain the connection.
  - Use "set-up" language to prop up your sources (transitional phrases).
  - Analyze and explain the evidence.

Marking Up Writing for Important Parts
Claim, Evidence, and Thinking

LOOK OVER STUDENTS' WORK. You'll see who is especially struggling with the challenge of explaining evidence. You might also sift through the final pieces from the research unit to see who, by the end of that unit, was still simply plopping quotes into their writing without setting up or unpacking those quotes. Those writers will probably need your support here.

As you look at student writing, don't be deceived by volume. You will be looking, this time, for evidence of the writer's *thinking*. Look for what students have done to unpack the evidence they include. Often this work can be deceptive. Paragraphs can be packed with vital, accurate information that links to the point. So at a glance it could seem as though the argument has been made and the writer has made his point. But if you look more closely, you may see that some of these writers are recounting information only. Take Daniel's work, for example (see Figure 6–2). His draft is packed with information but light on analysis or reflection, such as this passage:

> I think chocolate milk should be banned from schools, because of the huge amount of sugar and how many carbohydrates it has. White milk in the schools has 14 grams of sugar, fat free chocolate milk has 20 grams of sugar, and fat free strawberry milk has 27 grams of sugar, which is equal to 8 ounces of Coke. In the article, "Schools may ban chocolate milk over added sugar" it says, "Chocolate milk is soda in drag" and "If you have flavored milk, that's candy." Also it says, "It works as a great treat at homes but it doesn't belong in schools." According to a video on NBC News called "Milk Dud: Schools rule out chocolate milk," it states that if a child drinks chocolate milk every day for breakfast and lunch, in a year they would have 15 pounds of sugar, which equals more than 100 cans of soda. This is why I think schools should ban chocolate and flavored milk from schools.

MID-WORKSHOP TEACHING
Whittle Away Everything that Doesn't Support the Point

"Writers, let's pause for a moment. Getting just the right balance of quoted text and your own thinking is tricky. Many of you are including large blocks of quotations from articles, and sometimes those quotations go on for so long that they dwarf the other parts of your writing—like your thinking! It's hard for me, as a reader, to figure out your point. There are too many points!

"Michelangelo, one of the most famous artists in all of history, once described how he went about taking a block of marble and turning it into a sculpture—say, of a lion. He said, "I just carve away anything that doesn't look like a lion, and I'm left with a lion." In a way, you need to do that same work. Imagine that the part of the quote that supports your argument is the lion and you need to cut away the rest of that quote.

"Let's say I am arguing that chocolate milk should be banned from schools because the sugar in it makes kids hyperactive. I found this quotation to help. Think for a second about what you'd carve away. What isn't exactly helping my point?"

> "Chocolate milk is soda [dressed up]," said Ann Cooper, the head of nutrition services for the Boulder Valley School District in Louisville, Colorado. They do not allow flavored milk in their schools. "It works as a treat in homes, but it doesn't belong in schools."

"Yes, the point about chocolate milk being dressed-up soda is not my lion. I should cross it out. I think that I should keep this: 'It works as a treat in homes, but it doesn't belong in schools.' That totally fits my argument that the sugar in chocolate milk makes kids hyperactive, which might be okay at home, but not in school. So I'm going to cut away everything that isn't that lion. Make sure that you, too, are whittling quotations down to what's essential!"

Daniel
6/01

Throught our country, in schools, there has been a debate whether to ban chocalate and flavored milk, or not to. I think that chocalate milk should be banned from schools. One reason is that chocalate milk has a lot of sugar and carbohydrates. (close to in an 8-ounce serving) Also, kids drink too much of it, it isn't very healthy, and when talking about chocalate milk, we should take a note of obesity.

I think that chocalate milk should be banned from schools, because of the huge amount of sugar and how many carbohydrates it has. White milk in the schools has 19 grams of sugar, fat-free chocalate milk has 20 grams of sugar, and fat-free strawberry milk has 27 grams of sugar, which is equal to 8 ounces of Coke. In the article "Schools may ban chocalate milk over added sugar", it says, "Chocalate milk is soda in drag" and "If you have flavored milk, that's candy". Also, it says, "It works, as a great treat at homes, but it doesn't belong in schools. According to a video on NBC News called "Milk Dud: Schools rule out chocalat milk, it states that if a child drinks chocalate milk ever day for breakfast and lunch, in a year they would have 15 pounds of sugar, which equals to more than 100 cans of soda. This is why I think schools should ban chocalate and flavored milk from schools.

I also think that schools should ban chocalate and flavored milk. Kids drink too much of it, and in "Schools may ban chocalate milk over added sugar" it says, that according to the industry-backed Milk Processors Education Program 70% of students take chocalate or flavored milk. Chocalate milk isn't very healthy, and it says that it is wrong to say that chocalate milk is a healthy choice. Children should get nutrients and healthy things from other foods too. In addition, when talking about chocalate milk, we should take a note of obesity. In the text it says, "Others note the nations child obesity epidemic and say flavored milk simply needs to go." This also shows why schools should ban chocalate milk.

Consequantely, I think that schools should ban chocalate and flavored milk. It has a whole lot of sugar and many carbohydrates. Also, it isn't healthy may be a partial cause of obesity, and it is drank too much. Many schools already banned chocalate and flavored milk, and I think they did the right thing.

FIG. 6–2 The writing lacks analysis, making it sound less like an argument and more like a retell.

The evidence that Daniel selects supports his point that chocolate milk has lots of sugar, and Daniel gestures toward unpacking the evidence by saying, "This is why I think schools should ban chocolate milk." But really all he has done is restate his overall claim. To make a strong argument, authors interpret each of their pieces of evidence, saying what that evidence means and how it fits with the claim, knitting the pieces of information together.

Here's a simple strategy I practiced with Daniel and some other writers like him. I came to the conference armed with a collection of thin-tipped colored markers, the kind that young (and mature) writers love to use for pretty much any reason. Daniel chose three colors that he liked: purple, gold, and green. He decided that green would be for text evidence, purple would be for his reason, and gold would be for his new thinking and explanations—because his thoughts were like gold.

Focusing just on this one paragraph, I had Daniel underline his text evidence with green. He accomplished that task accurately, proud of his abundant evidence. Then I had him underline his reason in purple. At first, Daniel didn't find a reason in this paragraph. "That's only in my introduction," he said. I showed him how he had, smartly, mentioned his reason right after his restated claim—that chocolate milk has huge amounts of sugar and carbohydrates. "Oh," Daniel remarked. "I was going to make that gold for new thinking." I showed Daniel that really, that statement was his claim again. Daniel then searched for gold and found that his paragraph had no gold, yet. "Oh," Daniel said. "I guess I should try out some of those questions and prompts." He gestured to the chart, "Ways to Push Our Thinking," and began drawing thought prompts from it.

I then pulled Daniel's partner over so they could help each other do this important work.

Sometimes, helping students analyze their writing with a critical lens can be as important as offering another strategy. Daniel didn't need me to teach him an alternative strategy to using the prompts to prime his thinking. He simply needed to become aware that he wasn't doing this and that he could. A simple method such as underlining or boxing out parts of an essay can really help a writer "see" his or her writing more clearly.

Setting the Context for a Quotation

Tell students that once they've chosen supportive quotes, writers work to situate those quotes within a context.

"Writers, you have all focused on selecting quotes that support your evidence (and making sure you choose only those parts of the quoted text are strongest— your lion) and then wrapping your thinking and your voice around those quotes to bolster your argument. Sometimes quoting is tricky because even when you've carved out the lion—the perfect bit of text in support of your argument—for it to make sense, the reader needs more than just a line or two. The reader needs context. It doesn't work to just have a bunch of random lions flying around. They need some ground to stand on, or the quotes won't make sense and won't support your argument.

"The articles from which you are gathering your evidence had to handle this same task. Each of those authors had to think, 'How do I set this up so my reader understands it, it makes sense, and it supports my argument?'

"Instead of just quoting tons and tons, authors first carve out the lion. They choose only those parts of a quoted text that directly support their argument. And *then* they think about how to situate the quote so that it makes sense. Often, authors paraphrase to set the context and then quote just the part that they really want the reader to hear."

Set kids up to work with partners to create a context for quotes by paraphrasing.

"Right now, take a look at your letter with your partner. Look at the quoting you did. And when you notice huge, long quotes, giant chunks of text, think about which parts you might paraphrase and which parts you might quote. And when you notice focused quotes that seem to be floating around without any ground beneath them, think about how paraphrasing might help add context. "

As Angel shared her writing with Alex, he asked, "What part of this did you really want to put in your letter? Like, what are the important lines?" Angel shared that she wanted to quote the line about being able to *unteach* kids to drink chocolate milk (see Figure 6–3). Alex responded, "So then you don't need to quote the stuff about Cooper and others." The two of them tried to find a way to cut out the part they didn't need from the original:

Another reason I think chocolate milk should not be in school because now kids are preferring chocolate milk more than plain milk. In the article is says "Cooper and others argued children will drink chocolate milk so we can unteach them that, Cooper said. Our kids line up for milk."

Another reason I think chocolate milk should not be in school because now kids are preferring chocolate milk more than plain milk. In the article is says" cooper and others argued children will drink chocolate milk so we can unteach them that, cooper said. our kids line up for milk."

FIG. 6–3 This quote needs to be revised to provide only information that is necessary in order for it to make sense to the reader.

Angel suggested, "Maybe I could say, 'Many people think that kids would choose plain milk if they didn't have chocolate milk around. Anne Cooper is one of them. She says . . . and then I could quote her.'" She revised her draft (see Figure 6–4) so it now read:

> Another reason I think chocolate milk should not be in school because now kids are preferring chocolate milk more than plain milk. Many people think that kids would chose plain milk if they didn't have chocolate milk around. Anne Cooper is one of them. She says, "We've taught them to drink chocolate milk so we can unteach them that, Cooper said. Our kids line up for milk."

"So, writers, as you continue quoting, remember that sometimes writers need to paraphrase in order to quote. They need to create a context in which the quotes make sense. And they can often use their own words, summarizing or paraphrasing a bit to do so."

Another reason I think chocolate milk should not be in school because now kids are preferring chocolate milk more than plain milk. Many people think that kids would chose plain milk if they didn't have chocolate milk around. Anne cooper is one of them. She says, "we've taught them to drink chocolate milk so we can unteach them that, cooper said. our kids line up for milk."

FIG. 6–4   Paraphrasing helps to situate the quote so it makes sense.

USE QUOTATIONS SPARINGLY

Writers, when you were young, you learned to use exclamation marks to show excitement. Chances are good that before long, your writing was full of exclamation points—rows of them for some events and big fat bold exclamations for other events. I remember one student telling me he uses one for happiness and a whole row of them for someone's birthday and big bold exclamations when "a guy's dying." When I taught little kids, I always knew that on the day after I taught them to use exclamation marks, I'd teach them to *not* use them—or more accurately, I'd teach them to use them sparingly.

So tonight I want to teach you that quotations, too, are often overused. Think of them as like exclamation marks. They spice up a draft. They add energy and voice. But quotes are like special sauces. You don't want to splatter them everywhere, or they won't be special. Your draft will be weakened by excessive use of quotation marks. So look at the amount of your text that is your own writing, and make sure that at least three quarters of your text is your writing, and if that's not the case, eliminate some quotations and instead, paraphrase (which means talking in your own words about what you have learned). To paraphrase a quotation, reread it, think about what you have learned that matters and how that information connects with what you were already saying, and then talk to your reader about your thinking. If your ideas stand on the shoulders of the person you were quoting, reference that person, but you needn't quote.

Meanwhile, your writing needs to be almost done, so read it over, thinking about other ways to strengthen it, and be sure that the work you bring to school tomorrow represents your best work.

Signed, Sealed, Delivered

Dear Teachers,

Your students are nearly ready to deliver their arguments to the principal—or to whomever you've managed to involve in this issue! It would be tempting to simply take the stack of papers they have written to the principal yourself. Certainly it's most efficient that way. But that would be short-circuiting some of the learning your students could take from this work. Part of the effect of any writing, any communication, comes from the form and format of its delivery. How many of us have agonized over the font for an invitation or rubbed different grades of paper, trying to choose one on which to print a resume? How often have you tried to decide if you should use email or phone, text message or a face-to-face meeting to express yourself? Determining the means of delivery of the message, finding the right format is part of the writing process. The way the message sits in the real world, its design, and the kind of space it takes up (or doesn't take up) affect how it is received by its audience. Today you will set students up to make choices about how their argument will be "published" and how it will be delivered to its audience—in this case, to the principal.

Of course, part of preparing a letter is making sure it is written in the register that is most appropriate to its audience. In this case, writing to the principal of a school will probably call for a great deal of attention to the rules of the "The King's English" grammar and punctuation conventions. Editing to that end, too, could be the work of today.

Before students send the letters—either by hand delivery, post office, email, or another way—you'll want to make copies for students to keep in their writing folders, to use later in the unit and to help set the baseline against which to mark their growth as writers of argument.

At the end of the workshop, after the letters are signed, sealed, and on their way, students can look over the copies of these alongside the Opinion Writing Checklist, as a way to set goals for improvement during the rest of the unit.

MINILESSON

As with any topic, there are many ways to teach children how to consider and choose an appropriate format for their writing. One way is to share a piece of your own writing (not about chocolate milk, that is) executed in several different formats—each a possibility for students to use in their own letters to deliver their message. You could write your letter in an email, you could print the same letter on fancy paper with a matching envelope, you could handwrite the letter on loose leaf with a purple pen, or you could write your letter in a note card. The options are endless, but you'll want to choose only a handful, making sure that the letters are starkly different, both in appearance and in their connotations.

Then, you could ask students to form small groups and set each group up with one version of your letter to consider. Ask them to think or jot notes about how the letter's format and style affect the tone of the text, the way it will be perceived by its recipient. You might ask students to consider, as they do this, how the *author* hopes to be perceived and how the way the letter looks might change this for the reader. This work will become more interesting once students are contrasting different formats.

After a minute, ask groups to pass their version of the letter to the next group, so that eventually, each group has considered each format. Finally, you could gather students for a discussion about what they've noticed. You might write on chart paper (or ask a student to do so) a few of the students' thoughts about each format and its effects on the message. Of course, there is no need for total agreement. There is certainly no right or wrong answer about the best way to deliver any given message. Instead, the idea we hope to convey is that writers have choices about the format, presentation, and delivery of their writing, and those choices affect their message. One student might feel that the friendly feel of a note card is best suited to catch the reader's attention and prove the author's point. Another might feel that the more formal look of a letter typed on stationary with a matching envelope would represent the author more professionally. You may have your own feelings about which format would work best, knowing your principal, but what is important here is not that students choose what *you* think is best, but that they practice weighing their options, thinking about the ways that a letter's format can affect the way the author and the author's message are perceived, and making their own informed decisions.

After the minilesson, students will need to prepare their argument writing in the medium and format of their choice. You may want to ask them to make their decisions before they leave the rug. You'll want, of course, to have made a variety of materials available for their use.

CONFERRING AND SMALL-GROUP WORK

You will probably want to use your conferring time not to augment the teaching point about methods and materials for publishing (students are likely to have chosen their format early on and will be getting started as you begin conferring) but instead to tuck in some editing tips. Through conferring, you can deliver individualized instruction for various levels of editing. You are likely to encounter students who could benefit from the following:

- Reminders about conventions of the modes in which they are writing
  - Writing salutations and closings and indenting for letters
  - Filling in the subject lines and being short in emails
  - Addressing paper envelopes
- Reminders about conventions of English
  - Punctuating quotations
  - Punctuating introductory phrases and words with a comma
  - Citing sources accurately
- Tips about ways punctuation can link evidence to thinking
  - Using a colon to offer examples after a short explanation
  - Using a semicolon to say the same thing again in different words
  - Using parentheses to offer up an informal side comment about the evidence you've just presented
- Tips about using craft to clarify points in an argument
  - Employing metaphor and simile to help the reader understand
  - Drawing strong images with words, to emphasize key points

Opinion Writing Checklist

	Grade 5	NOT YET	STARTING TO	YES!	Grade 6	NOT YET	STARTING TO	YES!
	Structure				**Structure**			
Overall	I made a claim or thesis on a topic or text, supported it with reasons, and provided a variety of evidence for each reason.	☐	☐	☐	I not only staked a position that could be supported by a variety of trustworthy sources, but also built my argument and led to a conclusion in each part of my text.	☐	☐	☐
Lead	I wrote an introduction that led to a claim or thesis and got my readers to care about my opinion. I got my readers to care by not only including a cool fact or jazzy question, but also figuring out was significant in or around the topic and giving readers information about what was significant about the topic.	☐	☐	☐	I wrote an introduction that helped readers to understand and care about the topic or text. I thought backwards between the piece and the introduction to make sure that the introduction fit with the whole.	☐	☐	☐
	I worked to find the precise words to state my claim; I let readers know the reasons I would develop later.				I not only clearly stated my claim, but also named the reasons I would develop later. I also told my readers how my text would unfold.			
Transitions	I used transition words and phrases to connect evidence back to my reasons using phrases such as *this shows that . . . .*	☐	☐	☐	I used transitional phrases to help readers understand how the different parts of my piece fit together to support my argument.	☐	☐	☐
	I helped readers follow my thinking with phrases such as *another reason* and *the most important reason*. I used phrases such as *consequently* and *because of* to show what happened.	☐	☐	☐				
	I used words such as *specifically* and *in particular* in order to be more precise.	☐	☐	☐				

- Making transitions between reasons—and between reasons and thinking—clear with explicit language about the structure of the argument
- Checking accuracy of quotations
- Using the Opinion Writing Checklist

MID-WORKSHOP TEACHING

Your students might enjoy getting a glimpse of the tradition around letters. Emily Post's famous book on etiquette is available, full text, online, at http://www.bartleby.com/95/. Chapter 27 deals with notes and shorter letters, and Chapter 8 deals with longer letters. In this day of email and text messages, it is hilarious and thought-provoking to see how Ms. Post suggests that your language matters. Students might enjoy discussing an excerpt, such as:

> The most formal beginning of a social letter is "My dear Mrs. Smith." (The fact that in England "Dear Mrs. Smith" is more formal does not greatly concern us in America.) "Dear Mrs. Smith," "Dear Sarah," "Dear Sally," "Sally dear," "Dearest Sally," "Darling Sally," are increasingly intimate. (p. 27)

Or, on closings, this is what Ms. Post offers:

> The close of a business letter should be "Yours truly," or "Yours very truly." "Respectfully" is used only by a tradesman to a customer, an employee to an employer, or by an inferior, *never* by a person of equal position. No lady should ever sign a letter "respectfully," not even were she writing to a queen.

Whether your students rank your principal with the queen will be up to them. Who knew that *respectfully* put you in such a dire position? You and your children may delight in some of her gems. The main point, of course, is that writers do take every word seriously, including those of their salutations and closings, and that their awareness of evidence shapes their word choice.

SHARE

After gathering students on the rug and making plans for how and when they will deliver their letters, encourage them to reflect on the process of writing an argument—and on these particular letters. "As we wait for our replies," you might say, "you have a great opportunity to step back and examine (and celebrate) what you've done. You know the opinion writing checklists pretty well by now, and I know that many of you have been looking at those checklists frequently as you write. If you haven't yet started working inside the fifth- and sixth-grade checklists, though, now is a good time to do so."

Then say, "Now is also a good time to notice how your writing has grown since the last time we did this, early in the unit. Your arguments have become much more sophisticated, so you should see a lot of growth!"

Give students time to do this work on their own, and then, if there is time, you might continue, saying, "In small groups, will you look over the copies of the letters you have and talk over what you've done well? If you find something you haven't yet done, ask others in your group if they've done it. If they have, look at their work so that you can get an image in your mind of what that work looks like. It really helps to have a clear picture of what you are aiming to accomplish."

Kennedy's group, for instance, looked at her letter (see Figure 7–1).

Kennedy's group agreed that she had been extra careful in how to punctuate her quotations. In fact, other writers in her group decided to compare how Kennedy had punctuated her quotes with their own punctuation. This led to noticing missing commas and references back to what students had learned about this tricky punctuation. Be alert for which students have written letters that can serve as mentor texts for others, so you can set them up during the share as peer mentors.

Yours,

Lucy, Mary, and Annie

Dear Ms. Granger,

I believe chocolate milk should not be served in schools. Schools should not serve it because chocolate milk contains too much sugar. Also, schools should not serve it because it promotes unhealthy eating habits.

One reason why schools should stop selling chocolate milk is because it has too much sugar. According to famous chef Jamie Oliver, "the sugar is coming and it just ain't stopping." When Jamie showed a school bus full of sugar, he makes you stop and think about how much sugar kids are getting from chocolate milk. It makes me realize that even though one bottle of milk might not have much, if you drink it all the time, it's a lot of added sugar. Also, chocolate milk has more sugar than Coke. In an eight ounce serving, Coke has twenty six grams of sugar and chocolate milk has twenty eight. More sugar than soda! Everyone thinks soda is so horrible. But chocolate milk is even worse. Kids shouldn't drink it and schools shouldn't serve it to them.

Another reason why I believe schools should stop serving chocolate milk is because it promotes unhealthy eating habits. When kids get used to drinking plain milk, they don't drink chocolate milk. When schools stopped serving chocolate milk, milk consumption dropped thirty nine percent. Anne Cooper said, "Children will drink plain milk if that's whats offered. We've taught them to drink chocolate milk, so we can unteach them that." School is a place where we are learning to become better readers, writers, and thinkers. People who are thinkers think about what they are eating and drinking. School should teach kids to think about their drinks and their nutrition. They shouldn't serve kids chocolate milk.

In closing, I think it would be cheaper to serve chocolate milk than juice but long term unhealthy kids turn into unhealthy adults. Would you want that on your conscious?

Sincerely,
Kennedy

FIG. 7–1 Kennedy's final letter to the principal

Taking Arguments Up a Notch

IN THIS SESSION, you'll teach students that when starting a research project, writers think about how to capture the information they need, setting up systems to collect their knowledge and research, thus setting themselves up to write a lot.

GETTING READY

✔ Letter from the principal inviting students to lead panels on whether or not chocolate milk should be served in schools (see Connection)

✔ "Systems Argument Writers Might Use to Collect Research and Develop Thinking" chart (see Teaching and Active Engagement)

✔ "How to Write an Argument" chart

✔ Post-its, index cards, and booklets for note-taking (see Link)

✔ Examples of students' note-taking systems from the online resources (see Conferring)

✔ A sample set of notes enlarged on chart paper as well as Post-its (see Share)

YOUR WRITERS DID IT. They wrote their letters. They sent them to the principal. They'll probably saunter into workshop today thinking, "That's it, we did it. Letters sent, job done." They'll pat themselves on the back, feeling satisfied. And they should feel a measure of satisfaction, of course!

You, though, know from experience that the first salvo in a campaign is usually just that—the opener. Martin Luther King's "I Have a Dream" speech imagined possibility and gave heart to the Civil Rights movement—and many people worked together to forward that dream. Lincoln's Gettysburg Address shaped the argument to end slavery as a national covenant—and then he still had to design a campaign to accomplish that task.

"Today is a chance for your students to develop agency over how they will use their accumulated learning to accomplish their tasks."

Throughout their lives, which we hope will be filled with determination, your students will find that perseverance matters. High expectations matter. Coalitions also matter. To accomplish grand tasks, you usually have to bring people together around shared beliefs. You have to figure out your goals, assemble your gifts, and make your plans. And then you have to work hard to achieve them.

Today is a "stirring up" day and a "step-up" day. It's a chance for your students to feel that pull of planning toward shared goals as you create a higher-stakes argument. It's also a chance for them to develop agency over how they will use their accumulated learning to accomplish their tasks. After all, this is not the first time your students have done research. Nor is it the first time they have written persuasive opinions. They bring a lot to the table.

But they're also ten or eleven, that precarious preadolescent age when sometimes it is easier for a young person to continue to let adults do the work.

This lesson can serve as a moment in time in which you cheerlead, cajole, rally your troops, or use whatever style suits you best to nudge your students a few steps along the path toward independence. One teacher, for example, delivered an impassioned oratory to her students, ending with something like, "Its important to work hard for yourself, but it's also important to pay deep attention to what's going on around you. It's important to make things better not just for yourselves, but for everyone." I was in that classroom, and I was as stunned and humbled and inspired as the children were. I vowed to do better.

Any time you want to do better and do more, it helps to clarify your goals and get your start-up systems in order. For the work your students are doing, that can mean nudging them to figure out the systems they need to get in place for inquiry: note-taking, collecting, and writing-to-think. It can mean nudging them to read their texts more closely and to accumulate more of their thinking. It can mean considering how to use each other as resources, to challenge and support each other's ideas, to hone their thinking together, and to have fun working hard. For efficiency's sake, you might be tempted to tell students which systems are most effective. Remember, though, that there is little time left in fifth grade, and that students will need to make the decisions for themselves. Imagine your classroom as a simulation of the research projects they'll face, and invite your students to innovate.

Taking Arguments Up a Notch

CONNECTION

Tell students their work, their persuasive letters, have called greater attention to the issue and that more work is now called for.

"Writers, I have some exciting news. You know how you sent your letters to Ms. Granger? Just this moment, someone from her office hand delivered a response. I thought we should read it together now." While the children watched, I slit open the envelope and began to read.

Dear Fifth-Graders,

You raise many important issues about the pros and cons of serving chocolate milk in our cafeteria. The question of whether or not to continue to serve chocolate milk to children here is clearly a complicated one.

I've decided that it is too soon to make a decision. More research is needed. Voices need to be heard from both sides. We need to weigh this matter carefully and make our decision based on the strongest, most logical argument.

I've therefore decided to schedule a series of panel presentations just over a week from now, which I hope you will lead. I will be inviting interested parties including some parents and the cafeteria staff of the school.

Before you can present to focus groups such as those, it will be important to engage with the most important research on the topic—you will need to research even more extensively than you have so far. I think it will be important to distribute position papers—argument essays—on that day to help the school community with its important decisions.

Thank you again for your hard work and thoughtful letters—they have helped me understand the scale of this question.

Sincerely,

Ms. Granger
Principal, X Elementary
cc. X, President, Parent-Teacher Association
cc. X, School Lunch specialist

◆ COACHING

You'll need to rope your principal, or someone in the school administration, into supporting this notion or think of an alternative. We did something similar to this in the third-grade opinion writing unit. Children wrote letters to the principal, asking for more magazines for the school library, and when we piloted that lesson, lots and lots of principals agreed to support that request. We saw the impact it made on students when their writing actually influenced the person who is, in their world, the most powerful person of all. That is what gave us the idea for this.

Of course, this current project requires not just financing some magazines, but stirring up a panel of parents, and that can fill anyone with trepidation. You could, of course, adapt the plan. Perhaps the plan you set in motion could be a cross-grade debate on this topic instead. The point is that the event needs to be big enough to recruit students' continued investment in the topic.

I looked at the kids' somewhat awed faces, and my face matched theirs. "Oh my goodness, writers, you have really started something. Your words are being taken so seriously. A series of panel discussions with grown-ups from the school committee and with parent representatives, too? Position papers—based on much more research—in a week? Goodness!"

Stand back from this, using it to talk about the way that speaking out can lead to a life of activism.

I paused a moment, looking at the letter. Then I looked up, serious. "Writers, think hard about what this means. When you are actively engaged in changing something or defending something—engaged in social activism—it's often like this. You start with something small, then others get interested, and pretty soon a whole group of people are working together to create a change you want or to defend something you care about. Whether you are defending a community garden or arguing against school uniforms or raising money for the SPCA, you are always going to find that all of a sudden, you are called upon to do work that feels gigantic.

"Writers, we'll need to think about starting points. I need to know if you are game to participate in the panel, to work on the essays, to say 'Yes.'" I scanned the room and saw a lot of nodding. "This is going to be a lot of work, because what this means is that you start your research over. You put aside the letter—and even the position you defended in the letter—and begin researching the issue much more deeply. I've got more sources you can read, but you'll also need to read outside of school and to search for your own sources. Are you game?"

The children were with me, as I knew they would be.

"Today, I want to teach you that when writers get started on big writing projects, they often start by making sure they have systems in place to gather knowledge and to hold onto all their thinking so none of it gets lost as they research and draft. It will be important for you to do that as well."

❖ **Name the teaching point.**

"Today, I want to teach you that writers think about how to best capture the information they need, and then they dive into research, taking notes in the way that best suits them and best sets them up to think a lot and to write a *lot*."

TEACHING AND ACTIVE ENGAGEMENT

Set students up to recall the systems they have learned for collecting toward essays and gathering research, and invite them to adapt or invent systems for their current work.

"So the question you need to ask yourself, writers, is what systems do you know, or could you invent, that will best let you gather evidence and hold onto your thinking, knowing that you are going to be composing and defending evidence-based arguments? Let's set up a chart to describe some of our systems. You've done a lot of research and essay writing over the years. It makes sense, then, for you to recall systems you've used for collecting research and developing thinking. Quickly, think for a moment, and put a thumb in the air when you've thought of a time when you used a system that worked for you to keep track of text evidence and to develop your thinking."

This may be a bit too much hype for the issue of chocolate milk. If this feels too over-the-top, tone it down. But the truth is that we found that if you can feel comfortable talking this way about defending the cause of chocolate milk, the kids are likely to be with you. This is a far more personal issue for them than we ever imagined. More to the point, though, this world really does need our next generation to grow up as activists—ready to take stands, to vote, to work on behalf of causes.

Depending on your students' past experiences and on their responses to your question, you'll offer a range of support here. You may feel that your class will need more concrete support in remembering or inventing note-taking systems, in which case, you'll probably want to have some examples on hand to stimulate their thinking.

Claire said, "I liked it when I had a folder for each of my reasons when I was working on personal essays." She added, "We filled each one of them up with a different kind of evidence, like stories and lists and quotes and stuff."

"It was a helpful system, wasn't it?" I said. "You were able to move things around as you figured out which things to include and which to leave behind, and as you figured out what sequence you wanted to use." I revealed the title of a chart and added Claire's suggestion to it.

Kennedy jumped in. "And twice we collected stuff in booklets, only just one side of the paper, so we could cut them up when we wanted to figure out how our writing might go. We did that when we wrote literary essays and when we wrote our history reports."

Sasha, who had been wiggling around, hand in the air, could wait no longer. "We also used cards for part of our history research, and we could sort them and move them around." I added these to our chart.

Channel students to consider if one of these systems best lets them gather evidence and hold onto thinking or if another might, or an adaptation of one of these.

I looked at the chart with the students for a moment, pondering. "Hmm. Remember, our question, writers, is this: which systems will let you best gather evidence and develop your thinking? Hold in your mind your final goal—presenting and defending your ideas and evidence to a very informed audience. Does one of these systems seem right for you? Is there another you think would be even better? Turn and talk to your partner."

After a moment I reconvened the students and asked for thoughts.

Sebastian piped up with "I think some of us could use iPads or computers to take notes. There are a lot of systems for taking notes on them."

Ben offered, "We think that we should combine some of these ideas. Like, we could take notes on note cards and then add them to folders. And we can add our own thinking to our cards too, so we don't forget it." I added this idea to the chart.

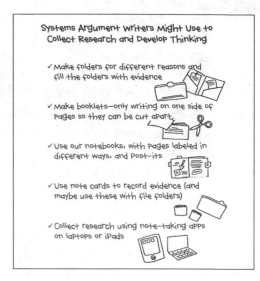

Systems Argument Writers Might Use to Collect Research and Develop Thinking

✓ Make folders for different reasons and fill the folders with evidence

✓ Make booklets—only writing on one side of pages so they can be cut apart.

✓ Use our notebooks, with pages labeled in different ways, and Post-its

✓ Use note cards to record evidence (and maybe use these with file folders)

✓ Collect research using note-taking apps on laptops or iPads

Teachers, if you are in a classroom that has one-to-one devices, and each child has easy access to technology, by all means consider moving children to digital technology. Many teachers and students have used Evernote, which is an easily learned digital application you can use on a laptop or iPad. It lets students take a picture of a text, type their own thinking, or use a stylus to write. And if, as PARCC and Smarter Balanced promise, students in grades 4 and 5 will eventually need to compose extended responses on computers, it's not a bad idea to give students fluency with these tools. Remember that their fluency will be greater than yours.

Still, lots of classrooms depend on paper and pencils. There are advantages to these tools. They don't break or wear out. They don't cost anything. And, in fact, the ability to lay many cards out in front of you, to sort them and move them around, is really helpful even for adult writers.

Your answer to a child like Sebastian, therefore, will depend on your technological readiness in your classroom and your thoughts about paper versus digital systems. Either way, the paper or laptop is just the vehicle. What matters is that writers create systems.

> ### Systems Argument Writers Might Use to Collect Research and Develop Thinking
>
> - Make folders for different reasons and fill the folders with evidence
> - Make booklets—only writing on one side of pages so they can be scissored apart.
> - Use our notebooks, with pages labeled in different ways, and Post-its
> - Use note cards to record evidence (and maybe use these with file folders)
> - Collect research using note-taking apps on laptops or iPads

Before long, each writer had decided the system he or she would use—with most opting for note cards filed into folders or for a variation in the booklets that they'd used in prior units.

LINK

Set writers up to go off and dive deeply into research, using the systems they have decided on.

"Writers, before you get into your research—and I know you are dying to get started—it's worth it to take a moment to get your system organized. I think most of you have decided on a system—like Ben is going to use note cards to record both his research and his thinking, and he's going to keep them in his file folders. Kennedy's going to use a booklet that she can cut up and reorganize later. Whichever system you've decided on (and make sure you've decided before you leave the rug; stick around if you're stuck, and I can help), it will help to take the first couple minutes of workshop time to collect your materials. It should really only take a couple of minutes to get your systems organized, though, so that you can dive into researching and gathering information right away. There is a lot to do before the end of the week!" I gestured to the process chart, to which I had added today's teaching point, as I reminded students of all there was to accomplish that week.

Tools Matter

YOU MAY APPROACH TODAY THINKING that your conferring and small-group time should all focus on the technicalities of note-taking, and it is true that this is infinitely complex, but we want to stress that it is also worthwhile to devote some time to helping students think about their systems of organization so they approach note-taking with ambitious resolve. When writers select their tools, laying them out in preparation for the task ahead, they are assuming the identity of a researcher. They are dressing up for the new role they will play. And when writers think about their tools with each other, they are chatting as writers do. After all, you put a bunch of cooks into a room, and they'll gossip about one oil or another, one whisk brush or another. Put a bunch of writers in a room, and they'll eye each other's Post-its and charts with jealousy.

Do you remember those New Year's days when you resolved to start jogging? The new regimen never could start right away, right? First you needed to buy the new running suit. It is the same for us whenever we start a new book. One can't just decide to write a new book and then presto, you start. No way! The first thing that has to happen is the shopping trip where a new notebook is purchased, and a whole stack of the exactly right pens. Any writer will tell you that the tools matter. Some writers can only write with an extra fine marker pen, or with 11-point Times New Roman font. People have fetishes that function a bit like good luck charms. They bring on the magic, they create the aura. Today's session, then, is only superficially about the tools themselves, and it is actually about the writers in your care. You are helping them assume roles as researchers and rallying them to tackle this upcoming project with great seriousness.

As students prepare to dive back into the research, their writing will be all about synthesis. They'll be bringing together things that don't ordinarily go together. Writing is the preeminent tool for doing this work. It's about mind over matter. It's about layering insight onto information. So today, use your discussions about tools to help writers rethink the note-taking they already did and resolve to do work that is a notch more thoughtful now because they have a second chance to organize the work.

As I pulled up next to Nick, I noticed that he had switched his note-taking system. Originally, when Nick had taken notes, he had used boxes and bullets. His notes had looked like this (see Figure 8–1).

Now, Nick was writing on index cards, and he had folders made out of loose leaf set out in front of him as if he planned to file the cards into the folders. Each of his index cards looked a bit like this one (see Figure 8–2).

I asked Nick to explain his new system of note cards. "Well, after the minilesson, I thought it would be a good idea to set up folders for each reason since I know my reasons. And then I thought I could write my information on index cards and stick them in the folders."

MID-WORKSHOP TEACHING   Maximizing Your Note-Taking System: Researching and Writing *a Lot*

"Writers, now that you've all decided on the systems you'll be using to collect information and organize your notes, it's time to really settle into using that system well—maximizing it. Whether you are using note cards, notebooks, booklets, or a digital system, you want to get a lot done, not tinker with jotting down little bits of information. I know you've started, and all I really want to say to you now is, keep going! Now is the time to research and think and write *a lot*. It will be more helpful to you as you begin drafting if you have piles of note cards filled with evidence and thinking or lots of notes and thinking that you'll cut up and rearrange. If you're having some trouble diving in, you can ask a partner—or simply watch and study, for a minute, someone at your table who seems to have dived in, someone who is up to her elbows in full note cards."

Chocolate milk is bad for kids.

Jamie Oliver TED

- Lots of sugar: as much as a can of soda.
- Serving choc. milk = child abuse.
- 8 tbl. is 1 day's worth of choc. milk.
-

Chocolate Milk is good for you

- Chocolate milk replenishes energy. ▬▬▬▬▬
- Refreshes you and your muscles.
- Replaces lost sweat and sugars.
-

FIG. 8–1   Boxes and bullets are a way to sort information under a claim.

Example 2, Reason 2

Chocolate milk, even in it's improved state, has 31 more calories than white milk.

This is important because white milk is still healthier, but they chose choc. milk, adding up to 14 g. per carton of sugar to their daily diet.

FIG. 8–2   Focusing on one claim and reasons for that claim makes the notes more detailed and analytic.

I complimented Nick on carrying forward his sense that specifics need to be filed under generalizations. Then I added, "Nick, you also learned to analyze the information you gather. You don't have to wait to do that work. You can begin to analyze as you take notes." I asked him to think about the information he had just written. "I jotted these notes," he said, gesturing to an index card, "because it shows that plain milk is still better. Chocolate milk still has more calories and more sugar." I encouraged him to jot that thought down. He added to his index card so it now held information and insight. See more examples of Nick's notes in the online resources.

As you confer and lead small groups, make a special point to invite writers to author their own individual ways of note-taking. In a unit of study such as this one, where the work that students do is largely uniform, there is a real risk that this could slide into an "I say jump and you jump" kind of research project where there is little individual ownership.

Although you'll give writers choices, you'll also want to show them possibilities. If your students have done this work in previous years, you can bring some of that work to your current class. If students haven't done that work yet, recruit a former student or a young friend to work with you, helping you produce examples that show what is possible.

Writers Study Other Writers' Note-Taking Systems and Choose One that Works Best for Them

Make a comparison to an exhibition that stimulates new ideas.

"Writers, lots of times people learn by studying other people's innovations. For example, there is a car show in New York City every year, and thousands of people, including engineers and manufacturers, come to look at the cars and get new ideas. I thought that maybe we could do this same thing now—we could have a sort of "show," an exhibition of some note-taking systems.

"I don't think we will have time today to study everyone's note-taking, but at least for now, I'm going to call on a few of you to go back to your workplaces and set up a display of your note-taking methods. Leave some Post-its beside your work as well, and then the rest of us will come around and study the cool technique you've used, and we'll make lists of things we might try doing as well."

I chose several children (most of whom I'd mentally noted, to make sure that a variety of techniques were being displayed) and asked them to set up their notes.

As some children set up a museum of note-taking, demonstrate to the others how you studied another writers' system, gleaning ideas for how you could classify your own notes.

As those children dispersed, I said to the others, "Let me show you the way one of my friends had taken her notes, and we can start our list of cool ideas just from studying her methods, okay?" I projected an enlarged set of note-book pages. "What I do is I look at what other writers have done, and I say to myself, 'What's something this writer did that might make sense for me as a writer too?'"

I looked carefully at some of the pages. As I did so, I voiced over my responses. "Let's see, this writer seems to collect whatever comes up in the text, but then she marks each of her notes with Post-its that are color-coded: green for notes that support one side of the issue and yellow for those that support another side. That is very cool. I can envision what the pages of my notebook would look like. Yes, that seems like a system that could work for me not just today, but over time." Then I looked up at the children and said, "Are you ready to do similar work? Off you go."

Sugary Drinks Can Be Unhealthy, But is Cow's Milk Unhealthy, Too?
by Mike Ochs

The debate continues as to whether chocolate milk should be served in school cafeterias. Many experts argue that kids shouldn't drink sugary beverages. But some say that kids probably shouldn't drink any cow's milk at all.

C Cow's milk already has some sugar in it, about 12 grams of sugar. Flavored milk can contain up to 30 grams of sugar. These sugars have no nutritional value, says Rip Esselstyn, firefighter, triathlete and author of a dietary cookbook, *The Engine 2 Diet*.

"And because simple carbohydrates are digested so quickly," Esselstyn writes, "any excess sugar is converted into fat." **C**

Not only can simple sugars contribute to obesity, Esselstyn says, but also too much of them can lead to other health problems, such diabetes.

Some cities have started to take action in limiting the amount of sugary drinks people can buy. In 2012, the New York City Board of Health approved a ban on the sale of large sugary drinks. The ban was the first of the kind in the United States.

New York City Mayor Michael Bloomberg was among those people who agreed with the ban. He thought the ban would help New Yorkers live healthier lives.

"This is the single biggest step any city, I think, has ever taken to curb obesity," Bloomberg said. "We believe it will help save lives."

Some experts go even further than just saying that sugary milk is bad for kids. They say that cow's milk itself—with or without sugary flavoring—is also unhealthy.

*all milk These experts say that milk is high in cholesterol and saturated **C** fat. People for the Ethical Treatment of Animals, or PETA, agues that milk can have short and long term effects on health. In the short term, high levels of cholesterol and saturated fat can lead to obesity and diabetes, PETA says. But in the long term, cholesterol and saturated **C** fat can lead to heart disease and cancer.

In 2009, the Physicians Committee for Responsible Medicine (PCRM) also wrote about milk. "Milk's main selling point is calcium, and milk-drinking is touted for building strong bones in children," they **P**

FIG. 8–3 Some students underlined key details noting the side each supports in the margin, with "P" for "pro chocolate milk" and "C" for "con."

Send children off to study each other's systems of note-taking, convening them after five minutes to collect observations and insights that could inform their own note-taking.

After the children browsed for a bit, I reconvened the class and harvested insights from them that they'd learned by studying each other's work.

Ideas for Making Systems More Powerful

- Use colored pens or colored fonts or icons to mark which side of the argument a detail supports.
- Collect information onto Post-its or index cards or digital notes so these can be sorted easily later.
- Use note-taking strategies like pro/con charts or graphs and sketches to show your ideas as you note-take.
- Record the author and title of the article so you don't forget.
- Leave lots of space so you can reread and write what you think beside bits of information.
- Make stars, arrows to show important things and things that connect.
- Don't just collect for one side. Try to be fair and open minded.

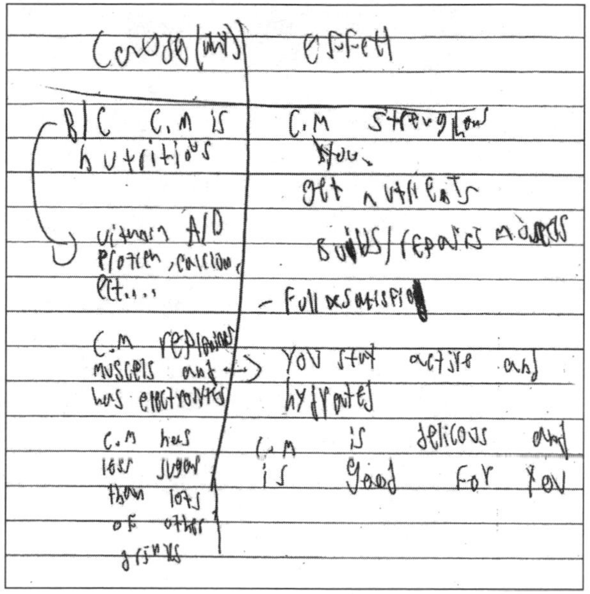

FIG. 8–4   George recorded what makes chocolate milk healthy and how it impacts the human body.

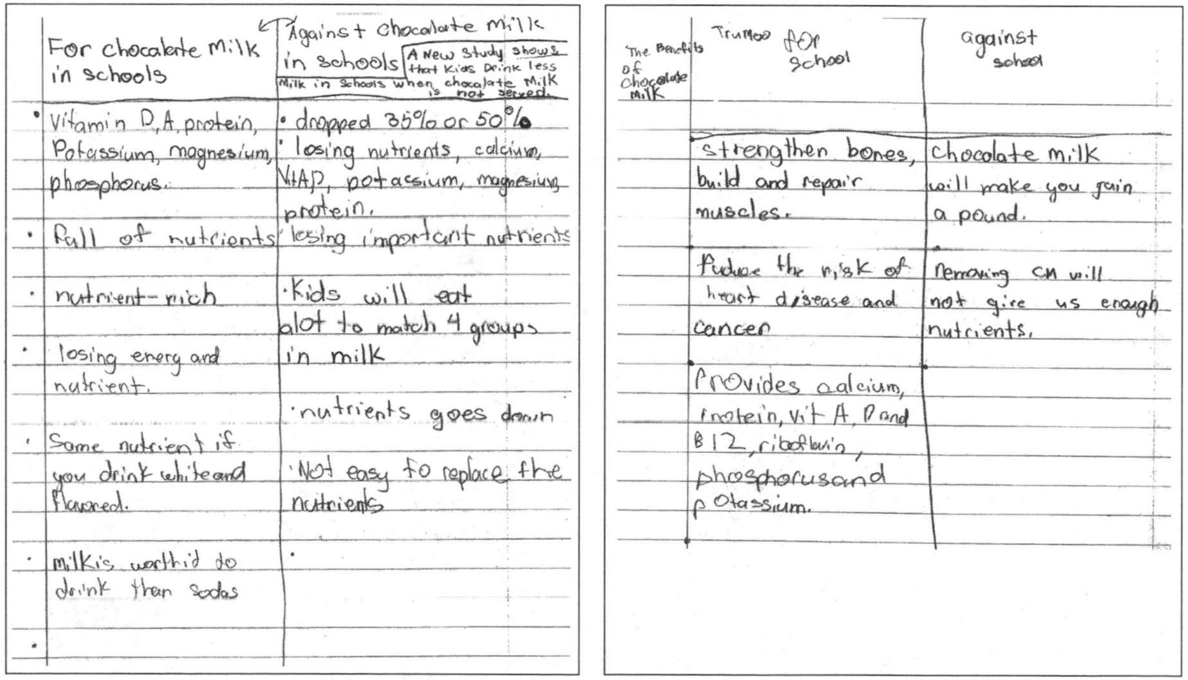

FIG. 8–5   Sam continued using a T-chart to sort his notes, replacing Post-its with a bulleted list.

TIME AND INTENSITY MATTER

A researcher named Malcolm Gladwell has studied what makes people achieve in whatever they are doing—like he studied the Beatles—and he said the one magic ingredient that makes people better is time spent working on something. People who are only so-so just put in half an hour of work. People who become excellent put in tons of time. They know how to turn off the TV and the computer games, and get to work.

Tonight and for the whole of this week, we're expecting that you will not just put in your dutiful homework time. The research you are doing is for real, and you only have a little more than a week to do something significant. So tonight you'll find your own sources, and you'll mine the bibliography you've been given. You can read or you can watch videos. But either way, collect.

Use every technique in the book to not only take notes, but to take note. Turn your mind on so that as you read and take notes, you make connections, ask questions, notice contradictions. Tomorrow we'll talk about the thinking that you did as you researched.

Bringing a Critical Perspective to Writing

To BE BETTER WRITERS, your students need to be better readers. They need to return to their texts and read more closely. They need to do the work named in the world-class reading state standards to determine central ideas and details, to compare and contrast perspective, language, and reasoning. You'll want to recruit your students' willingness to not just read, but to reread closely and analytically. They will discover that rereading, in and of itself, invariably becomes more analytic just because it is one's second (third, fourth, fifth) time working with the text.

In *The Child That Books Built* (2003), Francis Spufford talks about how, as a child, all he wanted to do was read and reread the Narnia books. For him, every other book was just a delay until he could go begin again with Edmund and Lucy. So many readers have a few books like that—books that you return to again and again. It might be *The Lord of the Rings* or *Anne of Green Gables*, *Exodus* or *X-Men*, *Little House on the Prairie* or the Harry Potter series. What's amazing about these books is that it is utterly satisfying to reread them. You think you'd be bored. After all, you already know what happens. Yet somehow, you see new connections and layers and nuances each time. When Anne breaks her chalkboard over Gilbert's head, you grin, knowing that a few years and three books later, they'll be married. When she runs home through the dark woods to Diana's house, you note the early signs of her later determination. Any of the millions (literally) of students who have read Harry Potter will tell you avidly, and in relentless detail, of the small clues and connections they only now see that Rowling laid down in Book One.

It's not just fiction readers who reread, holding in their mind all that they have already found out. It's not just fiction readers who develop a knowledge that allows them to see more because it gives meaning to small details they originally passed over and ignites zillions of tiny connections that they didn't make during their first journey through the text. Powerful nonfiction readers, too, experience these ahas as they reread.

This is particularly the case for nonfiction readers who return to a text after having read a great deal more on the topic. Because they are more knowledgeable, they can add more in between the lines of a text and see more significance in details they ignored during

IN THIS SESSION, you'll teach students that writers bring all that they know about reading critically into writing critically.

GETTING READY

✔ "Chocolate Milk: More Harmful than Healthful" on chart paper (see Teaching and Active Engagement)

✔ Construction paper or Post-it notes, to take notes in the margins of the article (see Teaching)

✔ "How to Write an Argument" chart (see Link)

✔ Example of one point stated two different ways such as "Flavored milk contains as much sugar as soda" and "Drinking flavored milk is like having candy" (see Mid-Workshop Teaching)

✔ Copies of the letters students wrote and sent to the principal as well as notes from Bend I (see Share)

✔ Pencils, pens, or markers for students to underline (see Share)

their first time through the text. They have already constructed many of the big essential ideas about a topic, and so now they are ready to take in more specific information, filing that information alongside the overarching ideas.

"One way that writers become better writers is to become better readers."

Essentially, readers improve their reading with every draft. Their first-draft reading will never be as powerful as their later-draft reading. And one way that writers become better writers is to become better readers. This is the case whether writers are writing poems or memoirs or personal essays or feature articles or, as is the case in this session, persuasive essays. In this session, in addition to reminding your students of all that they know about reading critically, it's important to help them make the link between critical reading and critical writing. Reading and thinking about the texts and other materials students are using as research tools won't automatically translate into critical writing, so we'll need to show them how to take the insights they have as they read with this new, more focused lens, and to translate them into notes—both new pieces of evidence and, most especially, into new ideas and interpretations of the evidence that will help students support their arguments in the context of their persuasive essays.

Bringing a Critical Perspective to Writing

CONNECTION

Tell students about a time when you read a lot of books in a series (or on a topic) and then found that when you returned to reread the first book, you saw much more in it.

"Writers, I'm rereading the Harry Potter books now that I've seen all the movies. I bet you had the same thing happen to you as happened to me. As I watched the last movie, I began to rethink some of the scenes from the first books. So I'm rereading now, and I'm seeing much more in the early books. You've probably had this happen, either with Harry Potter or with other book and television series."

I had Book One with me, and I held it up as I spoke. "I just recently reread the scene in Book One where Harry is at the zoo. Harry is looking at a great snake that is behind glass, when his cousin Dudley mocks him and pushes him into the glass. Harry gets really angry, and suddenly, the glass melts, and this giant snake slides out of the cage! And as it passes Harry, the snake says, 'Thanks,' in a language that Harry can understand.

"When I read that scene the first time, I remember thinking," I deliberately made my voice into a low-key drawl, as if I was somewhat nonchalant about the episode "'Cool, the glass melted. And the snake talked. Very cool. Wonder what that's all about?'"

I made my voice more alert for what came next. "But now that I've read all the other books, I know so much *more*. This time when I read that, I thought: "The glass didn't just melt—that was Harry using his magic for the first time! And the snake didn't speak English. That was the first time Harry understood Parseltongue, the snake language he got when he got some of Voldemort's power. Those are all clues that show how powerful Harry really is."

Debrief, explaining why you'd seen so much more when you returned to reread, in the light of new knowledge.

"Something happened to make me a closer reader the second time. Any thoughts on what that was?" I paused a moment, but didn't actually call on the children, instead I just waited to see the wheels of their minds turning, then pressed on. "I'm sure you are thinking what I'm thinking. What changed was that now I know more, so I saw more in the text. The text didn't change, but I changed, and that made my reading change.

In the next section, we briefly retell a moment from Harry Potter. You could, instead, show the film clip, which is about twenty seconds long and available on video and YouTube. We leave this to your technology preferences! Quick digital references to popular, relevant culture increase engagement, the lever that raises how hard students work.

Watch how this connection gives youngsters an experience that brings home the message of this minilesson.

"It's not that I didn't read carefully the first time. I did—though it's true I was doing so much work just making sense of what was going on that I missed some details. But what's *really* different is that I have now read a lot more, and that means that when I go back to the first thing I read, I see much more in it. I can make connections that were invisible to me earlier."

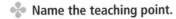 **Name the teaching point.**

"Writers, today I want to teach you that to write well about information, you need to *know* it well. When you know information well—like when you know the Harry Potter series well—you realize that information you read recently fits with (or contradicts) information you read earlier. A big part of writing about information is seeing connections and contradictions between sources of information. The more clearly writers read their sources, the more equipped they are to see those links."

TEACHING

Channel students to reread a familiar text, challenging them to bring their new learning to bear on what they notice. Demonstrate how notes become richer when writers think deeply and use all that they know.

"When you become more expert on a topic, it is amazing how much more you see in a text. This means it is worthwhile to go back to texts you read a while ago and look at them with fresh eyes."

 I revealed an excerpt from one of the first texts we had studied together, saying as I did so, "Let's revisit one of our first texts, 'Chocolate Milk: More Harmful than Healthful.' I'll read it aloud, and let's all look at it, expecting that we will bring more to it. We'll almost be writing between the lines, adding things we know from other texts, seeing more significance than we did the first time. Listen."

> Chocolate Milk: More Harmful than Healthful
> *Schools around the world serve chocolate milk—and kids love it. On a recent Australian newscast . . .*

"Let's stop there. What are you thinking? You could say, 'I'm just waiting, really, for what else it will say.' But if you are a really powerful reader, bringing everything you know to this page, you should already be thinking some things." I left a little pool of silence, expecting some children would notice that this article clearly takes a side on an issue that has ignited strong controversy or noticing, too, this is not an American issue alone. I read on.

> *. . . investigative reporter Chloe Baker interviewed children about chocolate milk. "The only time I get chocolate milk is when I go to school," one student told Ms. Baker, as her friends nodded. In fact, many children only get to have chocolate milk at school—but they get to drink a lot of it there.*

Again I was silent. "What are you thinking?" I asked. "I'm going to try to bring other things I know to this passage. I'm thinking about how some people argue that kids get hooked on chocolate milk when they have it in school, but these

Of course, the same is true of reading any book. It's when you reread and reread again that you see so much more.

kids don't! I wrote a note here based on that thought." I picked up a scrap of construction paper on which I'd written a relevant connection and taped it in the margins of the text, reading it aloud as I did so.

> Some people argue that giving kids chocolate milk in school gets them hooked to it, so they drink it at home, but these kids don't do that.

"What about all that we've learned about the obesity problem? I wasn't thinking about that the last time I read this article. Let's see, how could I write that down?" I murmured to myself (but loud enough for students to hear) as I wrote the following and added it to the margin of the chart.

> If children drink a lot of chocolate milk at school, that's part of the obesity problem. That is a big enough problem without schools adding to it.

I went through the same process and added yet another thought.

> What about other things that are served at school like schools with soda machines and gatorade?

Debrief, highlighting for students how your prior knowledge on this topic, from previous research, has allowed you to think more deeply about what you are reading.

"Researchers, do you see that all these somewhat related ideas come to my mind now, because of all I now know, making that one little text all of a sudden spark so much more thinking in me? Part of the secret behind this is that I *expected* to bring more and to see more to the text this time. This only works if you bring that attitude to it. And once you start paying attention to all of the sparks of ideas that are flying around you, your next step is to put those ideas into words, into notes with full sentences, that will help you add more evidence and more thinking to your essay drafts."

ACTIVE ENGAGEMENT

Channel students to continue reading the same familiar text, working with their partners to bring new knowledge into their reading, to think critically, and to translate their new ideas into notes.

"Let's read a bit more of this, continuing to bring new knowledge to the text." I read aloud the next bit of the text.

> *Jamie Oliver, a food lover and activist, has been leading a campaign against chocolate milk in schools. According to his website, "When kids drink chocolate and strawberry milk every day at school, they're getting nearly two gallons of extra sugar each year. That's really bad for their health."*

> *In an episode of his television show* Food Revolution, *Oliver filled a school bus with 57 tons of sand, representing the amount of sugar American children consume in one week just from drinking chocolate milk.*

The value of being in an immersion study of one topic is that you and the students will know your texts well. Angle your insights, therefore, toward the connections that appeared in your texts. In the text set we assembled, for instance, the significance of obesity and diabetes are raised.

When you shift from the demonstration to debriefing, students should feel the different moves you are making just by the way your intonation and posture changes. After most demonstrations, there will be a time for you to debrief, and that's a time when you are no longer acting like a writer. You are the teacher who has been watching the demonstration and now turns to talk, eye to eye with kids, asking if they noticed this or that during the previous portion of the minilesson.

Ann Cooper, the head of nutrition services for the Boulder Valley School District in Louisville, Colorado, also champions the cause to ban chocolate milk from schools. "Chocolate milk is soda [dressed up]," stated the self-proclaimed Renegade Lunch Lady. "It works as a treat in homes, but it doesn't belong in schools."

"Writers, work together with your partner. What do you notice, think, remember? What are your connections?"

After a few minutes, I called on Roy. "When I first read this article, I noticed the bus full of sugar and I wasn't sure if fifty-seven tons was a lot for all the kids in the whole country." He went on. "But now, I know about obesity being all over the place and diabetes, so I am thinking that fifty-seven tons *is* a lot. And I am thinking that each kid getting two extra gallons of sugar might mean they are in more danger for obesity because two gallons, just from the chocolate milk, is a lot. There is also sugar in ketchup, and it might be two more gallons of sugar."

6/12	A New study shows that kids Drink less chocolate Milk when chocolate Milk is not served in schools
Notes	**Thoughts, opinions, and questions**
chocolate Milk is a very important thing for kids to have. They will be losing those nutrients.	I disagree with the fact of taking away chocolate milk because we need nutrients to survive and milk contains that.
"When flavored milk was not an option many children wouldn't take the white milk." stated Linda Stoll	I understand why kids wouldn't drink it. That is because chocolate milk is more flavored so that's what they want.
Milk has alot of calcium, vitamins and so much more.	why would they take stuff kids need away?
"chocolate milk is just nutrient-rich as white milk." announced stoll	Many people think chocolate milk isnt healthy but they need to understand its important.
As Dietary Guidelines for Americans state for that small added sugar its worth it.	I think Dietary Guidelines for Americans have a point about this opinions.

The Many Benefits of Chocolate Milk	
Notes	**Jottings**
TruMoo CM has less sugar	I think thats an outstanding idea because its healthy with not a lot of sugar
There are many things in kids diets that need to be reduced because they can get sick.	Why would they take away this drinks? We need them
If kids dont get enough nutrients they will need vitiamins	My opinion is many people wont chocolate milk in school so kids get enough nutrients.

FIG. 9–1   These notes reflect the information the writer gathered as well as her interpretation of that information.

"*Wow.* So, Roy, what is super important about what you just did is that you read the same evidence this time as you did last time. Before, the bus had fifty-seven tons of sugar. But now, because you know more, you can spin that evidence, like we talked about. You can show that when you're worried about obesity, fifty-seven tons of sugar is a big deal. How might you write down what you just said as a note that will help you add to your draft later?"

Roy said slowly, "Well, I could say something like, 'Kids don't need those two gallons of sugar from chocolate milk, especially since there's lots of other sugary stuff. They might be more in danger for obesity with all of that sugar. In fact, with all the danger of obesity, it would be great to cut out the fifty-seven tons of sugar Jamie Oliver says kids get through chocolate milk."

Name what students have done in such a way that it is transferable to other topics, other texts, other days.

"I think every one of you noticed more when you reread this text. Every one of you brought in things that you've learned since we first read this article. You tried to make connections and see more importance in the details. This is going to pay off whenever you research—and whenever you are writing something that incorporates research, no matter what form it takes."

You'll notice that again and again, you seize the opportunity to reinforce that the skills students are learning are relevant not just for today, but for all the future moments when they conduct inquiries, compose arguments, or strive to be powerful communicators.

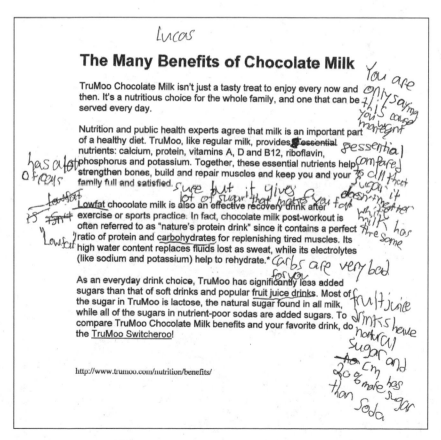

FIG. 9–2   Lucas uses his knowledge of the subject and the source to read critically, talking back to the text in the margins.

Review some of the choices writers might make as they go off to work.

"Writers, as you prepare for your essays and panel presentation, I know you are searching for just the right evidence to support your argument, and you are working on spinning that evidence so it really supports your reasons. Yesterday you all devised (and then honed and revised) your note-taking and information-recording systems, and you dove into using them. Most of you have a great jump on your research. You've got tons of new notes already. Today, you might want to keep in mind this idea that there may be new evidence hiding in texts you've already read—or that you may bring different interpretations to the evidence that you noticed the first time around. As you go on in your research, set yourself the task of rereading texts you read a while ago. With the knowledge you've gained from all your research, you'll see so much more in those first texts, just like I am seeing so much more in the first Harry Potter books. Remember, though, you want to write like the wind. You want to collect as much evidence and develop thinking as possible to set yourselves up for drafting." I added the teaching point to the process chart and set students off to write.

How to Write an Argument

- Collect evidence that allows you to think through various sides of an argument.
  - Set up a note-taking system to organize your research.
  - Reread sources with a critical eye, looking for connections and contradictions.
- Rehearse by explaining your position and listing your reasons point by point.
- Plan your claim and reasons into boxes-and-bullets structure.
- Use evidence to support your reasons.
  - Paraphrase, putting it into your own words.
  - Quote, and then unpack the quote, showing how it relates to the reason.
  - Introduce the source and explain the connection.
  - Use "set-up" language to prop up your sources (transitional phrases).
  - Analyze and explain the evidence.

It can be easy, with today's message about rereading, for students to settle comfortably into doing just that, without translating their reading into concrete notes that include their analysis as well as the original evidence. Remember, this is a writing unit! This is why we keep hitting home on the point that this deep reading in which students are encouraged to bring new knowledge to the texts serves the purpose of taking stronger and more informed collections— resulting in stronger and more informed essays. You'll want to keep an eye out for students who will benefit from an extra nudge in this direction.

Supporting Students Who Struggle to Make Connections across Texts

COMPARING AND CONTRASTING ACROSS MULTIPLE TEXTS is no easy feat, and it will no doubt be more difficult for some students than others. In order to compare, contrast, and evaluate arguments, students must be able to determine the topic a part of a text is addressing, or a point a part of the text is making, and then find that same subtopic or same point being addressed in a section of another text. They also need to hold onto ideas and information over time.

I pulled up next to Angel, who was glancing between two texts with a worried look on her face. "Angel, how are things going for you today?" I asked.

She looked at me, as if to say, "Not great!"

"Okay," she said instead.

"Angel, I'm noticing that you're struggling a bit with where to start today, and I thought I might be able to help. Would you be game for learning a new strategy—one that will help you compare and contrast across texts?" She nodded, without a lot of enthusiasm, and I pressed on.

"Sometimes, when you want to compare what two authors have to say about the same topic, it helps to name that topic first." I scanned over Angel's materials and saw that she had created a section of her notebook dedicated to proving that chocolate milk contains too much sugar. "Let's focus in on the research you are doing around sugar in chocolate milk."

I quickly sketched a chart that looked like this on a sheet of paper, filling in the titles of a few articles I saw strewn on Angel's desk. *(continues)*

MID-WORKSHOP TEACHING
Thinking through Evidence, Point by Point

"Writers, when I research something, I realize that often, what looks like different points are actually the same thing stated differently. For example, in the first documentary we saw, we jotted the point 'Flavored milk contains as much sugar as soda.' After reading the second article, we're jotting another point: 'Drinking flavored milk is like having candy.' Most of you have jotted these as two separate points against chocolate milk, but pay attention! These two points come from different sources and they sound different, but the concept behind them is really the same. Although one source compares it to soda, another to candy, both are ways of saying that flavored milk contains too much sugar.

"As we research, we sometimes have to look beyond the words and the source and ask ourselves, 'What is this point really about? Is this something totally new that I haven't read or noted before now? Or is it a restatement or extension of a point that I've already noted from another source?' If it is a restatement then, we add this onto the point we already have, instead of writing it as a new thing.

"Right now, look over what you have jotted. Think, 'Did I write new points or are they really just restatements or extensions of points I already had?' You may need to reorganize or revise your notes, crossing off duplicate information or moving it to go with existing points.

"In a strong argument, we don't want to be making the same old point in a thousand different ways. We've got to make each new point different from the other points for that side."

	"Chocolate Milk: More Harmful than Healthful"	"The Many Benefits of Chocolate Milk"	"Schools May Ban Chocolate Milk . . ."
Sugar			

"Angel, a chart like this can be really helpful when you are comparing and contrasting the different ways authors talk about something like sugar. It can help to organize your notes and let you see the ways the authors' arguments are the same and different. Let's try to fill this chart out together."

I introduced Angel to a tried-and-true trick: when you are looking for places where an author discusses something in particular, you needn't read the entire article again. Instead, you skim quickly, looking for the relevant word—in this case, for the word *sugar*—and then you circle or highlight the places where you find that word in the text in question. Angel did this quickly and was able to identify a place or two in each text where sugar was discussed. I asked Angel to jot a note or two about what each author had to say about sugar. Soon, her chart looked like this (see Figure 9–3).

"Angel, do you see how helpful it is to use a chart like this? First, we decide on a topic or issue we'll be looking for in our texts. Then we skim, looking for places that talk about that topic and put them alongside each other, keeping track of sources as we go."

"You aren't finished yet. The really important thing is to look across the notes you've made and work to compare and contrast the information you have. Instead of looking for everything, just look for one thing. Like how do the authors agree? Then look for how they disagree."

Angel and I looked across the notes, first for something that each author agreed on. Before long, Angel realized that all the articles agreed that chocolate milk *has* sugar. Not one argued against that. They all agree that chocolate milk has sugar in it.

"Now, let's ask, 'What are the different perspectives they have about that sugar?'" Angel looked across the chart. "Well," she said tentatively, "it's kind of confusing because the 'Chocolate Milk' article says that chocolate milk has 20% more sugar than soda. But the 'Many Benefits of Chocolate Milk' article says that it has *less* sugar than soda and fruit juice." She lit up, "One of them is lying!" Her eyes darted across the classroom like she'd found a scandal and she wondered if others had seen this as well.

"You do need to read suspiciously because everyone does not tell the truth. But sometimes, authors word things in really sly ways so that it is hard to say they are lying. They

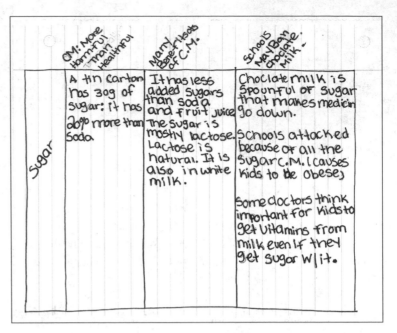

FIG. 9–3 Following one topic across texts helps to compare and contrast information.

just don't really put the whole truth out on the page. Let's look back at the TruMoo article and see what it says." Angel and I reread, noticing that the author claimed that chocolate milk has less *added* sugars, and that the sugar it *does* have is something natural called lactose. Angel, quick to grasp what the author was doing, chimed in: "The author is telling us that chocolate milk has sugar that is natural. Basically I think he's trying to say it is healthy sugar, and to hide that it is *still* sugar."

"Write that down, Angel!" I exclaimed. "Don't let that important thinking fly away!"

Having set Angel well on her way, I reminded her of the strategy we'd practiced and encouraged her to continue on with her work. "Angel, you just learned one way to compare and contrast. You found parts of different texts that discussed the same issue (in this instance, sugar in chocolate milk), jotted some notes in a chart so you could look at the different opinions side by side, and then asked, 'In what ways do these authors agree? In what ways do they disagree?'

"Now, when you write about how chocolate milk has too much sugar, you can acknowledge what other authors have to say (like the fact that most of the sugar in chocolate milk is natural) but disagree with them on how they spin that evidence. This will make you an all-around stronger arguer."

Writers Draw from Earlier Drafts

Tell students that writers often pull gems from earlier drafts into current drafts as they write and revise.

"The poet Donald Hall has an anthology called *String Too Short to Be Saved* (1995). The title comes from Hall's belief that just like some people who save bits of string to use when needed, writers squirrel away observations, quotes, nice phrases, old drafts, photographs, odd statistics, and then when they go to write, they often look over what they've collected to see some new synthesis, some new whirligig that they can assemble.

"Essayists, like poets, collect material, knowing that some of it will end up combined in surprising ways. And certainly one source of material is your prior writing. Many writers have a few topics, or writing territories, that they write about repeatedly. So this means that in an essayist's collection of 'strings' not too short to save, that writer is apt to have some previous writing: letters, speeches, chapters, jottings.

"I'm telling you this because you are in the midst of a writing project, and I'm not sure you are remembering that you have a collection of material that you can draw upon to add richness to your draft. The letter that you wrote earlier may well have some sections that could add to your existing draft. If you find yourself unsure of what else you could do to strengthen your writing, then you might reread the letter you gave to Ms. Granger. It might have a gem in it. Look over your note cards, too, as one may hold important thinking. See if you want to move any of that material into this draft."

Ask students to look across their earlier materials, marking bits that they plan to draw into current drafts.

"Circle or underline the parts that you want to carry forward." I read over their shoulders as they worked, coaching, "Think about your evidence!" and "Any great quotes or statistics you must hold onto? Any important thinking that was better stated? Any big, bold claims? Underline!" I noticed Kennedy had underlined portions of her letter to Ms. Granger (Figure 9–4).

"Writers, your goal is to make each draft stronger than the one prior. Sometimes, to do that, it means carrying forward strengths from earlier drafts, not throwing it all out and starting over. So, as you draft tomorrow, you might want these earlier drafts by your side so you can hold onto the parts that are strong and use them again. Even though you are working within a different genre, writing position papers instead of letters, there are lots of things you can pull from your letters that will help you build a strong argument as you draft your position papers and prepare for your panel presentations."

Dear Ms. Granger,

    I believe chocolate milk should not be served in schools. Schools should not serve it because chocolate milk contains too much sugar. Also, schools should not serve it because it promotes unhealthy eating habits.

    One reason why schools should stop selling chocolate milk is because it has too much sugar. According to famous chef Jamie Oliver, "the sugar is coming and it just ain't stopping." When Jamie showed a school bus full of sugar, he makes you stop and think about how much sugar kids are getting from chocolate milk. It makes me realize that even though one bottle of milk might not have much, if you drink it all the time, it's a lot of added sugar. Also, chocolate milk has more sugar than Coke. In an eight ounce serving, Coke has twenty six grams of sugar and chocolate milk has twenty eight. More sugar than soda! Everyone thinks soda is so horrible. But chocolate milk is even worse. Kids shouldn't drink it and schools shouldn't serve it to them.

    Another reason why I believe schools should stop serving chocolate milk is because it promotes unhealthy eating habits. When kids get used to drinking plain milk, they don't drink chocolate milk. When schools stopped serving chocolate milk, milk consumption dropped thirty nine percent. Anne Cooper said, "Children will drink plain milk if that's what's offered. We've taught them to drink chocolate milk, so we can unteach them that." School is a place where we are learning to become better readers, writers, and thinkers. People who are thinkers think about what they are eating and drinking. School should teach kids to think about their drinks and their nutrition. They shouldn't serve kids chocolate milk.

    In closing, I think it would be cheaper to serve chocolate milk than juice but long term unhealthy kids turn into unhealthy adults. Would you want that on your conscious?

Sincerely,
Kennedy

FIG. 9–4 Facts, quotes, and statistics are compelling evidence to carry forward.

SESSION 9 HOMEWORK

WRITERS PREPARE THEIR NOTES SO THAT THEY CAN EFFICIENTLY BEGIN DRAFTING

Writers, when you draft tomorrow, you want to spend all of your time and energy writing. That means you'll want all your materials for your position paper, your essay, so you know how it is going to go. You'll want on hand the notes you want to use, and any quotes that are underlined in your article. So tonight sort through your materials and get everything absolutely ready, so that tomorrow you'll be able to pick up your pens and write!

Rehearsing the Whole, Refining a Part

WHEN THE POET LUCILLE CLIFTON VISITED Teachers College, she gave us advice that we have held close ever since. She said, "Nurture your sense of what's possible. You cannot create what you cannot imagine."

Time and again this has proved true for us. We find, for example, when trying to help teachers lead powerful writing workshops, that one of the most important things we can do is to work with those teachers' own students, showing the teachers that their students can participate in all the structures of a writing workshop willingly and easily, and they can produce work that is better than the teachers dreamt possible. Just an hour in which we teach the teacher's own students—or those of another teacher, up and down the corridor of the same school—can give the teacher an image of possibility.

But that teaching is especially strong not only if a participating teacher is able to see her students going through the process of gathering for a minilesson, heading off to write, starting in writing, and working intensely for a long stretch of time, but if, in addition, we can help the teacher to begin functioning like a writing workshop teacher, moving among the students to coach into their work, doing whole-class voiceovers to share observations or suggestions, convening informal quick groups and giving them pointers. If we can help a teacher to act like an effective writing workshop teacher for a day, while we are right at her side, setting her up to make some important teaching moves, coaching her along the way, then that teacher leaves that one day of instruction able to plan for tomorrow's teaching by imagining what she will do first, next, next, and able to imagine, too, the student's responses.

As the teacher plays out in her mind how tomorrow's teaching will hopefully go, she'll come to places where the mental movie is blurry, where she's not at all clear how things *do* proceed. Those trouble spots require some extra thinking—some planning.

Just as a teacher monitors her plans for fuzzy parts, a writer can do that as well.

This session helps you to show students that it is helpful to plan one's writing in similar ways, anticipating how the process of writing will go, watching for trouble spots as one makes this mental movie of the work that is to come.

IN THIS SESSION, you'll teach students that writers often plan for and rehearse the entirety of a draft, and then choose a tricky place to focus on as they work.

GETTING READY

✔ Blank sheets of drafting paper, one for each student (see Teaching and Active Engagement)

✔ Two thesis statements, including claims and evidence, from student's chocolate milk letters enlarged on chart paper for the class to refer to as they plan their essays (see Teaching and Active Engagement)

✔ "Body Paragraphs Often Go Like This" chart (see Teaching and Active Engagement)

✔ Example of a student who revises as he writes, crossing out his introduction and then rewriting it before continuing his draft (see Mid-Workshop Teaching)

✔ A conclusion from a sample student essay that students will mine for qualities of strong endings (see Share)

✔ "Techniques for Powerful Final Statements" chart (see Share)

✔ "How to Write an Argument" chart (see Share)

✔ "Powerful Introductions Often Include" list, individual copies for students (see Homework)

Rehearsing the Whole, Refining a Part

CONNECTION

Tell a story about an athlete preparing to compete who envisions and rehearses the whole of her event before beginning.

"Writers, this summer I was obsessed with the Olympics. I know many of you, just like me, could not take your eyes off them! I was especially riveted by women's gymnastics. Gabby Douglas is such a remarkable gymnast! She has such an amazing balance of grace and strength. Every time I watched her, I thought, 'How does she do it?'

"Some of you might remember, the night of the individual all-around competition, when Gabby was in the running for the gold medal. The floor routine was her last event in the competition. The cameras zoomed in, all eyes watching, as she waited on the sidelines to perform. I sat on the edge of my couch wondering, 'What is she going to do?' All of a sudden, Gabby pulled her arms to her chest and turned from side to side. She bent down and jumped up. She put her arms overhead and stretched backward. At first I thought it was really strange. It didn't look quite like stretching. What was she doing? And then, it hit me. She wasn't just stretching, she was warming up her muscle memory by envisioning and practicing her routine. When she tucked her arms to her chest and twisted side to side, she was preparing for her tumbling passes. When she bent down and jumped up, she was warming up her legs for jumps. Gabby was going through her entire routine, thinking about each part, seeing it in her mind, and even practicing some of it. Gabby didn't focus on one move; she focused on her entire performance, start to finish. And it won her the gold."

Liken the envisioning and rehearsing an athlete does before an event to the ways writers envision, rehearse, and plan a position paper before beginning to draft.

"Gabby won her gold in part because she didn't just sit around and wait for the moment when she was going to do her routine, then step up cold to the starting line. Instead, she used a few minutes right before starting to imagine the whole routine, to see herself doing one thing, then the next, then the next. It's like a singer, singing the whole song under his or her breath while waiting in the wings of the stage.

"Writers often do the same thing. Because most good first drafts are written quickly, all in a rush, writers know that right before they pick up the pen and start writing, it helps to imagine what they will do, to picture the process of writing an introduction, a claim, reasons, and to keep on picturing the process of writing a first body paragraph—the works."

The Olympics that featured Gabby were fresh in our minds. In fact, it would be the work of minutes to pull up the clip of Gabby rehearsing her routine and show it to the children. In your classroom, you might choose any recent culturally relevant or mesmerizing event to refer to. Search online for athletes rehearse, *and you will find everything from synchronized swimming to NFL players running through game plans.*

❖ **Name the teaching point.**

"Today, I want to teach you that writers, like athletes, often envision themselves going through the process, accomplishing the feat, before actually getting started. Sometimes, as writers imagine themselves writing the beginning, middle, and end of a text, they realize there's trouble ahead. In those instances, it can help to tackle that bit of trouble before picking up the pen and writing, fast and furious."

TEACHING AND ACTIVE ENGAGEMENT

"Right now, will you take hold of one blank sheet of paper, and in your mind, talking just to yourself, will you touch (or stare at) the top of the page and imagine the work you will be doing there?"

I left a bit of silence, then coached into what students were doing. "Remember that a good introduction will first draw the reader in to care about the topic. You need to think about what's significant about your topic or how it fits with your readers' own lives, or how it is timely."

Again I left some silence. Then I continued a voiceover, quietly coaching. "And in your essay's introduction, you'll write your claim and your reasons. Write that part clear as a bell. You can look at examples others have written to remind you of how a position statement often goes," and I gestured to a chart with some of the position statements the students had written and heard when they were working on their chocolate milk essays.

> Chocolate milk should not be banned from schools because it has nutrients that promote a healthy body and kids drink it.
>
> Chocolate milk should be served in schools. It should be served in schools because it helps children meet their nutritional needs. In addition, it should be served because more children drink milk because of the great taste.

I added, "Before you write your reasons, think if there is a need to order them one way or another. Are they going to be from least to most important?" Again I left some silence. "Thumbs up if so far, you can imagine how your essay's going to go." Almost every writer signaled that he or she was on track.

Then I continued. "So, writers, think about your first body paragraph. You'll start by restating your first reason, and then you'll plop some evidence in. Right now, list the evidence you'll include across your fingers, and think, 'What order might make sense for the evidence?' Again, you might list it least to most important or first in time sequence to last." I left some silence.

"Touch the page where that part of your essay will go, and as you move your finger down the page, write that first body paragraph in the air." As students did this, I called out, "You'll want to include at least one direct quote probably," and "Don't forget that after you include evidence, it helps to unpack it. 'This shows . . . '

When doing this, your intense focus on your own work will lure the kids to do the same. Even if you are not doing anything overtly—not whispering to yourself, not moving your finger down the page—kids can literally see the wheels of your mind work. It's hard to explain why this is true, but we have seen it often. So force yourself to not give covert supervisory glances over the room and to instead pour every inch of your attention into doing the work yourself in a way that creates an incredible demonstration. Once you can feel that the children have stopped glancing up to ask, "What? What should we do?" and have noticed you are not available and have begun to approximate as best they can, doing the work, you can, of course, put down your own imaginings and survey the room so that you sense when to peak again.

You'll notice that we haven't handed out graphic organizers. This is because we believe that most writers make their own stuff, and that simple tools are the best. If you have some children you believe would benefit from pieces of paper with the words introduction *and* body paragraph *labeled on them, you might have these ready.*

"Try it again, and this time, think about whether you are adding transition words between one bit of evidence and another." I referred to a portion of the chart the students had seen earlier.

LINK

Before sending students off, encourage those who need support to stay on the rug, and pair them up with peer tutors.

"Writers, once you have thought about one body paragraph and started the next one in your mind, will you think about whether there is a part of this essay that you think you still need some help on? If so, stay right here on the carpet. But if you have a plan in mind and you are ready to write, fast and furious, give me a thumbs up, and I'll send you back to your seat to get started."

Many students signaled they were ready, and I sent them back, waving with a feeling of great urgency. I collected the others into a huddle and asked, "Who needs help on what?"

When one writer announced he needed help with his thesis, I asked, "Who here feels good about his or her thesis? Can you volunteer to provide some 'emergency thesis care?'"

In this way, I paired most of the children up so they received tutorials from others who also felt insecure and not ready to start. I then met with the tutors, helping them, and soon the group was writing.

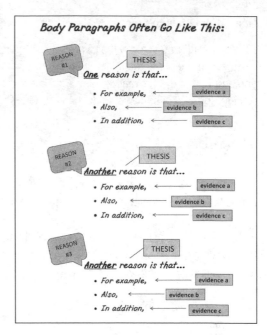

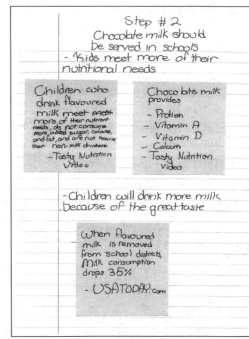

FIG. 10–1   To prepare for drafting, Claire sorted her notes, moving the Post-its under the reasons they supported.

GRADE 5: THE RESEARCH-BASED ARGUMENT ESSAY

Support Students to Write with Focus—Fast and Furious

LIKE US, YOU'VE PROBABLY ENCOUNTERED STUDENTS who need support with volume and fluency during writing workshop. Indeed, at one point or another, most writers struggle to produce writing. When this happens in your classroom even this far along in the unit, empathize with these students, some of whom may be their own harshest critics, and consider possible solutions. In her poem "Spelling," Margaret Atwood writes, "A word, after a word, after a word, is power." You'll want to teach students who struggle with volume that they can become powerful writers by writing.

In many classrooms, it has helped to seat students who struggle with volume together. "Together?" you may ask, thinking the students will distract each other. Certainly, this could happen, but we've found that if you bring students together and tell them frankly that you know getting words on the page can be a challenge and then provide them with quick and periodic support, these same students will progress. We suggest you set students up for success by reminding them of all they have learned. This means that you may seat them near your anchor chart for easy reference, or you may give

---

MID-WORKSHOP TEACHING **Front-End Revision Is Easier than Back-End Revision**

"Writers, can I stop you? Will you stop your writing and look at your work, and will you think about whether the start you've made on your essay is setting you up to do your very best work? Remember that the goal today is to go for the gold. It is to emulate Gabby Douglas. When Gabby planned how her routine would go, when she imagined it in her mind and then went out on the floor to do it, she didn't plan a low-level, just okay performance. She imagined herself doing something better than she'd ever done it.

"If your essay so far has all the pieces in place but it is sort of blah, sort of methodical, then I want you to think whether it will really convince anyone. Think, too, whether this will represent your very best work. If you've gotten an okay start, but it isn't really going for the gold, then pause and go back to imagining your writing. This time imagine yourself doing a fabulous job. Imagine a lead that draws readers in, that gets them to be with you. Once you can picture it, start a new draft, writing fast and furious.

"Ivan's done that already. He had written half a page, with a lead that started like this.

> Lots of kids in school like chocolate milk. I'm one of them. Chocolate milk should not be banned because it has nutrients and it promotes a healthy body.

"Realizing he could do more, Ivan drew a line across the page and started again. Listen to his newest lead.

> Imagine you walk into the cafeteria and there is no more chocolate milk. You say to yourself, "No more chocolate milk! I'd rather die of thirst than drink white milk." There are some schools who are banning chocolate milk. Chocolate milk should not be banned because it has nutrients and it promotes a healthy body. Keep reading to see the advantages of chocolate milk.

"Ivan isn't just allowing himself to do so-so writing. He's reaching for the gold. You can do the same."

---

them individual copies of your class anchor chart. The chart can serve as a reminder and a menu of sorts for the work they will do within the workshop. After you have reminded them of their previous learning, you can help the students to set a goal for the next five to ten minutes. Perhaps you will ask them to mark a spot down the page or to orally rehearse what they will write, and then set them to writing.

Roy, for instance, benefited every day from putting an *X* on the part of the page he was striving to reach, showing that to his partner and me, and then showing off when he reached it. Real writers do this. Steven King talks about trying to write 10 pages a day, even if he feels blocked. Barbara Kingsolver has said the same. Letting young writers know that professional writers make page number goals for themselves gives them a sense of authenticity.

We've found that it can be helpful to appoint one student in the group to cheer the others on. That is, after a few minutes it can be the job of one student to look up and say to the group, "Keep going, get more words on the page!" Then, too, it is important that you come back to check on these students every ten minutes or so to provide quick coaching. By seating the students together, you will have created a group that you can check in with quickly. That is, instead of tracking the progress of four or five students sitting across the room from one another and feeling the need to check in and encourage each of these students, you can come to the one table group and give quick compliments and reminders.

A word of caution: you may be tempted to sit with these students and help them to get started each day, or to have long conferences teaching new strategies to support increased productivity. While this is a natural inclination, we advise, instead, that you ask these students to use what they have already learned in previous lessons to maintain productivity. In part, this is important because conferences in which teachers do a fair amount of talking do not support student productivity, and in part, this is our recommendation because part of what you want to teach this group of students is to find ways to produce writing consistently and independently. It is likely that they need to practice the strategies they have already learned to move toward mastery.

Study a Mentor Conclusion for Qualities of Strong Endings

Engage writers in an examination of a strong mentor conclusion in preparation for writing or revising their own.

"Writers, the author Rose Tremain once said, 'In the planning stage of a book, don't plan the ending. It has to be earned by all that will go before it.' That's true of argument writing as well. The strength of your final statements rests on the strength of your reasoning leading up to your final words.

"Some of you are getting ready to write your conclusions, and a few of you have already started. Let's take a minute to study Jack's conclusion so you have some ideas in mind about writing strong endings. We've been studying Jack's writing throughout this unit, and you are really familiar with his argument at this point. Take a moment to remind your partner what Jack is arguing and his reasons for that argument." The students talked for a moment, and then I gathered them back together. "Let's look at his conclusion. As we look, let's think, 'How did he end his argument?'" I pointed to the conclusion (see Figure 10–3), which was up on chart paper, and read it aloud.

"Turn and talk. Tell your partner specifically what you notice about the way Jack uses his conclusion to bring his argument together." I listened as students talked. One partnership noticed that it was similar to literary essay. The writer emphasized why the claim and evidence matter and left the reader with new insight. I gathered them together and again created a chart using both students' observations and things I wanted to make sure they noticed. The chart looked like this.

---

①

Why Chocolate Milk Should Stay

Schools should keep serving chocolate milk. There should be chocolate milk because kids like it, it gives vitamins, and it gets kids in good habits. Many kids love chocolate milk—it makes them happy to see it in the cafeteria, in their lunch box, at their kitchen table. Research shows that, overall, chocolate milk is pretty good for kids.

Even though some people think it's bad that kids like chocolate milk more than white milk, it's actually especially important that kids like chocolate milk. It turns out that more kids drink milk, when they can get chocolate milk. When you interview a lot of parents, like Katie Couric did, they'll say that their kids only drink milk if they can get chocolate milk. So at least they're drinking milk. In a survey of students in this school, 84% said that they would drink more milk if they had chocolate milk available. Of those same students, 28% said that they wouldn't drink any milk at all unless it were chocolate.

②

Surprisingly, while some think it's just a flavored drink, chocolate milk turns out to have vitamins. A nutritionist from the Dairy Association demonstrates that chocolate milk is a good source of vitamin A, D, E, and calcium. That's a lot of vitamins and they're in something kids actually like to drink! In her information session, the nutritionist is with kids who drink chocolate milk. Their bright teeth and glossy hair illustrates that kids who love chocolate milk will be healthy.

There's one more reason why chocolate milk should be served in schools. It does have some added sugar—that's true. But the famous nutritionist argued that chocolate milk has a lot less sugar and carbohydrates than soda and power drinks like gatorade. So if kids get in the habit of drinking milk in school, then they'll probably skip the sodas outside of school. The chocolate milk that is served in our school, for instance, low fat. So it is a lot better for kids than soda.

It's true that Jamie Oliver, a chef and enemy of chocolate milk, argued that

FIG. 10–2 This essay begins with the kind of strong reasoning that will eventually support the conclusion shown on the next page.

If your students wrote literary essays last year, you might refer to the chart on conclusions from that book, revising it in front of the class to fit argument essays.

Techniques for Powerful Final Statements

Restate claim and reasons.

Emphasize why claim and evidence matter.

Acknowledge the counterclaim and rebut it.

Put in personal experience as insider research.

Add new insight/ leave reader with something new to think about.

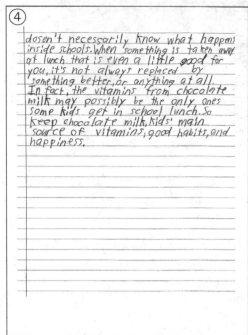

③ chocolate milk does have added sugar. Jamie is a famous English chef who is involved with lunch for kids in schools in Los Angeles. In a shocking video, Jamie shows a school bus filled with sugar to show how much sugar school kids get from chocolate milk. But there are a lot of schoolkids in the U.S, and if you divide that busload up between all the kids, it will not be such a shocking amount. And if you put next to it a bus filled with the vitamins A,D,E and calcium that kids get, the picture might seem very different. That's why we should keep serving chocolate milk at school-maybe it's true that it has a little bit of sugar, but it gets kids to drink milk, it gives them vitamins, and it builds good habits. Personal, insider experience supports this claim. As a fifth grader, this investigator was part of an experiment to ban chocolate milk in his cafeteria. Fifth graders, though, are allowed to go out for lunch. With no chocolate milk, this luncheon seeker started going out for pizza and cake. Gone were all the vitamins and calcium. Jamie Oliver

④ dosen't necessarily know what happens inside schools. When something is taken away at lunch that is even a little good for you, it's not always replaced by something better, or anything at all. In fact, the vitamins from chocolate milk may possibly be the only ones some kids get in school lunch. So keep chocolate milk, kids' main source of vitamins, good habits, and happiness.

FIG. 10–3   This conclusion recaps the main points of the argument and uses a personal experience to refute the opposing argument.

Ask students to either study the draft of their own conclusions or make plans for the conclusion they have yet to draft, incorporating what they know about strong endings.

"You're all in different places with your essays at this point. Some of you have drafted conclusions, and some of you are getting ready to plan them. If you've drafted one already, right now, read it over and think, 'Is this ending worthy of my essay?' If you are not there yet, think about how you might plan for a strong conclusion. You might want to make some notes for yourself." I gave students a moment to read and think.

"Okay, why don't you turn and tell your partner what you think you need to work on to make your conclusion stronger."

Ivan, who had done such strong work revising his introduction, was quick to notice that his conclusion needed the same attention. "This is actually pretty lame," I heard him announce to his partner. I listened in as he read (see Figure 10–4):

I interjected, "Well, you did restate your claim and your reasons. That's a good start." Ivan shrugged his shoulders. "I guess, but that's all I do. There's no voice." I coached him to look back at Jack's conclusion and at the chart. Ivan noticed he could add in more personal experiences as an insider to support his claim like Jack did.

As I moved away to listen in on another conversation, I heard Ivan say, "I'm strong. It's because it's because I drink so much chocolate milk that get so much calcium. Feel my bones!" Ivan put his wrist out. "You just have to exercise a lot, and I do that. So maybe I can talk about how it has helped me to grow strong bones."

CONCLUSIONS

✓ Reconnect to the broader theme or generalization

✓ Make connections to:
- Your thesis and emphasize why the claim and evidence matter
- Yourself and the life lesson you learned or realized
- The author's message

✓ Leave readers with something to think about

After the students talked for a moment, I gathered the class and said, "Writers, remember that you always want to do your best work from start to finish. It's the last words that will ring in your readers' ears, and you need them to be strong. Keep that in mind as you plan for or revise your ending. And let's add 'strong introductions and conclusions' to our chart, 'How to Write an Argument.'"

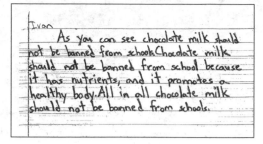

FIG. 10–4   Ivan's conclusion restates his claim and reasons.

How to Write an Argument

- Collect evidence that allows you to think through various sides of an argument.
  - Set up a note-taking system to organize your research.
  - Reread sources with a critical eye, looking for connections and contradictions.
- Rehearse by explaining your position and listing your reasons point by point.
- Plan your claim and reasons into boxes-and-bullets structure.
- Use evidence to support your reasons.
  - Paraphrase, putting it into your own words.
  - Quote, and then unpack the quote, showing how it relates to the reason.
  - Introduce the source and explain the connection.
  - Use "set-up" language (transitional phrases) to prop up your sources.
  - Analyze and explain the evidence.
- Include a strong introduction and conclusion.

WRITING A POWERFUL INTRODUCTION

Writers, tonight I'm going to send you home with a brief list of different things that might go into a powerful introduction. These are things you've done before in essays, and sometimes in information writing, so I'm confident that you'll be able to apply these skills to your argument. Why don't you spend some time writing at least two versions of an introduction, and you can get some feedback tomorrow from your partner. Starting off well will really help bring your readers over to your position and set them up to be convinced by you. Here's a brief list.

Powerful introductions often include:

- Some background information that makes the topic seem important
- A clear description of the sides of the issue so that the reader understands that there are two sides to this argument
- A very clear, explicit, BIG, BOLD, claim! (Makes it totally clear what side you support)
- A summary of your reasons so the reader knows what to expect
- Something catchy that gets the reader engaged, such as a surprising fact or statistic, or a spicy quote
- Something about the author (you) and why the author cares about this topic or what kind of research the author has done to become a trusted authority

Rebuttals, Responses, and Counterclaims

UNTIL THIS POINT, your students have focused their attention on collecting relevant evidence and using it to build a solid argument. It's time to throw a wrench in the works, but a wrench that will help students tighten their arguments, rather than one that derails the machine! It's time to let students in on the fact that the strongest arguments are those that take into account the evidence and opinions of the other side. It is easier to persuade when one knows what one is up against. Teaching students to choose which counterclaims they'll include in their essays, and to offer thoughtful rebuttals, is a crucial element of this unit's work.

This is not easy stuff. Students must not only learn to identify counterclaims, but they must learn how to speak back to them in such a way that their own arguments are strengthened. Anticipating and acknowledging counterclaims can make the author seem more fair and knowledgeable. On the other hand, if an author gives too much air time to the other side, that may weaken the author's own argument. It is easy for inexperienced writers to unintentionally weight the evidence against their side more than the evidence for their side. Or they might get lost in the labyrinth of ". . . on the other, other hand . . ." "Give me a one-handed economist!" President Truman is alleged to have cried desperately one day in the Oval Office, after his financial chiefs answered all of his queries with "Well, Mr. President, on the one hand . . . and then again, on the other hand . . ."

This session can help you offer your students a couple of simple choices for including counterclaims—and rebuttals—in their essays. Your students will be new to this work, and you will be teaching standards well above their grade level. You'll see that the session aims to provide accessible support.

You might play with the idea of counterclaims across your day as well. When students ask you to extend recess or play music while they write or let them go to gym on their own, you can argue, "Well, it's true that . . . nevertheless . . ." Play up this language in reading workshop as well. "Even though Harry Potter is lonely, that doesn't mean he doesn't have friends." You may regret this when your fifth-graders begin using these tactics on you! "It's true that homework provides added time for practice. On the other hand . . ."

IN THIS SESSION, you'll teach students that argument writers strengthen their claims by including evidence-supporting the opposing viewpoint and then offering a rebuttal.

GETTING READY

✔ Excerpt of sample essay on letting dogs loose in the park, enlarged for students to see (see Teaching)

✔ "Phrases to Use to Acknowledge and Rebut Counterclaims" chart (see Mid-Workshop Teaching)

✔ Students' writing notebooks and pencils (see Active Engagement)

✔ "How to Write an Argument" chart (see Link)

✔ Deck of cards with claim and counterclaim (see Conferring)

✔ Copies of sample student essay with counterclaim and rebuttals (see Share)

✔ Pencils to underline student essay with counterclaim (see Share)

✔ "Where Can Argument Writers Address and Rebut Counterclaims in Their Essays?" chart (see Share)

Rebuttals, Responses, and Counterclaims

CONNECTION

Use an analogy from daily life to explain that encountering challenges or resistance can make us stronger.

"Writers, this past month, I've been trying to get stronger. So, I've been lifting weights at the gym. I always pick the same set of comfortable dumbbells, and on any good day, I'd crank out—oh, about fifty bicep curls. Nice and easy, no real sweat. And every day, I've watched, horrified, as the fellow next to me chose really gigantic dumbbells. Every day, sweat would be pouring down his red face, and after about seven or eight bicep curls, he'd look about ready to clang those weights to the ground because they're so heavy.

"I couldn't stand his pain. So yesterday I walked straight up to him, doing my bicep curls, nice and easy, as I said to him, "Sir, don't you think you should be using lighter weights? You look like you're in so much pain!" Writers, he actually snorted at me. "Lighter weights? I'm not here to waste my time *pretending* to exercise. I'm here to get stronger." I think I must have gaped at him like a fish because after a minute, he softened up and explained.

"'If it gives you no resistance,' and he stared pointedly at my super light dumbbells, 'then it isn't really making you stronger. Muscles need to be challenged if you want them to grow stronger. I always tell myself, 'Go heavy or go home.'"

Draw a parallel between your analogy and persuasive writing, explaining that just as encountering challenges and resistance strengthens us in life, an argument is strengthened when it takes on rebuttals that challenge its basic premise.

"I'm telling you this story because I learned something super important that applies to life—and to writing. If we want something to get stronger, we need it to face up to challenge, to resistance. Writers, these past days, you've asserted a claim, then backed it with evidence and quotations. You've been choosing and including evidence that supports your claim. Kind of like my fifty bicep curls with a really light weight, you haven't been encountering much resistance to your claims. Well, guess what? Persuasive writers don't just write about reasons and ideas that support a claim.

"Writers strengthen a claim and show how knowledgeable they are by mentioning the ideas that people raise when challenging the writer's argument. That is, the writer acknowledges counterclaims!

◆ COACHING

Teachers who have been working with Units of Study for Teaching Writing *for a while will no doubt notice that when we use personal stories as metaphors in this new grade-by-grade series, we keep our stories briefer and more to the point than we did in the former edition of these books. This minilesson is a good example. Notice that the students aren't able to spend long thinking about bodybuilding before they are brought back to the point of the lesson.*

"Think about that word; *counterclaims*. You've probably heard the prefix *counter* elsewhere. Right now, see if you can think of a different word that begins with *counter* and if you can figure out what *counter* means as a prefix." I gave the children a moment of silence, then called on a few.

They produced a list: *counterclockwise, counteract, counterstrike;* and a definition: *against.*

❖ **Name the teaching point.**

"Today, I want to teach you that persuasive writers anticipate the counterclaim to an argument and acknowledge that counterclaim. They might use more 'set-up' language, saying: 'Skeptics may think . . . ' or, 'Some will argue . . . ' Then writers rebut the main counterargument."

TEACHING

Using your own writing as an example, demonstrate the way that writers need to imagine the counterarguments someone might produce—counterarguments you'll later rebut.

"When you're arguing or debating something in conversation and someone offers up some information that contradicts your claim—offers a counterclaim—it can make you sweat a little, right? When someone says, 'Yes, but . . . ' and lays out a counterpoint, you have to work harder. If that person has come up with some evidence that doesn't seem to go with your claim, you either have to produce even more evidence supporting your claim, or you have to show that your opponent's spin on the evidence isn't the best one. That work—of arguing in the face of resistance—is called 'coming up with a rebuttal that proves your point.' When you offer a rebuttal, you strengthen your argument.

"Let me show you what I mean. Here's an argument essay I wrote about the issue of letting dogs play loose in the park in the early morning."

I flipped to a sheet of chart paper on which I had written a bare-bones claim-and-supports paragraph and read it aloud.

> Dogs should be allowed to run loose in the park in the early morning. They should be allowed to run loose because they need their exercise. They should also be allowed to run loose because dogs need social time with each other. Above all, the parks are for dogs too.

"So, in this excerpt, the argument is presented nice and easy, the same way I'd crank out fifty bicep curls with a light weight. I have included no resistance against any point I'm making. I am clearly making a point, but I'm not anticipating or taking on what someone with an opposite opinion might argue. I'm not taking on the 'Yeah, buts' out there.

"I want to show you how writers address the 'Yeah, buts' while still keeping their arguments on track. Well, first they've got to think about what those 'yeah, buts' might be, right? One way to do this is to reread your piece, pretending to be someone who disagrees—a cynic, a debater from an opposite side. Watch me try this now."

When you want to show students a new and complex move, it helps to do so on a familiar everyday subject, because the new move, itself, is challenging. By situating that new move in familiar and accessible territory, you provide a scaffold.

Notice that when including your own writing, you can usually make your point by referring to very brief text. This tiny snippet of writing is entirely sufficient for me to make my point. Resist the temptation to bring out a great big long piece of your own writing and spend the entire minilesson time reading it aloud.

You will see in this demonstration, you read a point, then rebut it, then read a second point, then rebut it. It is more typical for one person to make their argument, in full, and then for the other to repeat it. "So you said point 1, 2, 3. Let me talk about them. First, point 1. I disagree because . . . Next, point 2. I challenge that because . . . " You can decide which way you'd rather go.

Changing my tone to a cynical one, I reread the paragraph, pausing after each point to discredit or refute it, beginning each rebutting statement with a dramatic "Yeah, but," "I challenge that," or "I disagree."

> Dogs should be allowed to run loose in the park in the early morning. They should be allowed to run loose because they need their exercise.

Speaking as the cynic, I said, "Yeah, but people need their exercise too. If dogs are running all over the place, they'll get in the way of people who want to exercise."

> They should also be allowed to run loose because dogs need social time with each other.

Again as the cynic, I said, "I disagree. I disagree because it's not important for dogs to have social time. They'd probably fight with each other and get in all sorts of trouble."

> Above all, the parks are for dogs too.

"I challenge that. Parks are for people, not dogs!"

Debrief in ways that extrapolate what parts of your demonstration are transferable to another day and another piece.

Switching back to my noncynical teacher voice, I said, "Writers, did you see what happened here? For every point in the essay, I thought about what the rebuttal might be. My original argument (Dogs should be allowed to run loose in the park in the early morning) is looking a lot weaker after all these rebuttals! I have to do something about these rebuttals if I'm to win my reader back. Countering the rebuttals is heavy lifting, but it makes one's argument stronger. Persuasive writers don't just collect evidence in support of a claim. To make a really strong argument, they need to anticipate, and then rebut—shoot down—counterclaims."

ACTIVE ENGAGEMENT

Rally students to practice acknowledging and rebutting counterclaims in the context of your mentor text.

"Now you try it. Think about the next two claims, and in your notebook, write a passage that I can add into my essay that acknowledges the first counterclaim (I gestured to where I'd made notes of this in the margins of the essay) and then rebuts it. And then, if you have time, do this for the next one as well. Write fast and furious!"

It can be helpful to clarify the way you are alternating between reading a portion of the text and critiquing it. When you are reading the text, you may want to run your finger under those words, and then when you are countering the text, ham up the cynic angle so that students grasp that you are taking on a contradictory voice.

I jotted notes on this in the margins of my argument, which I'd written on chart paper. I did this knowing that later kids would need to recall the counterclaims so they could rebut them.

When I described this work as "heavy lifting" I gestured to suggest that this is work like lifting weights, inferring that it builds muscles, which was the point to my connection. Notice that this continues a message that weaves throughout all of these books—that hard work is important, that success requires effort.

I revealed a chart paper list of sentence starters that could support writers in doing this work.

Phrases to Use to Acknowledge and Rebut Counterclaims

Some people disagree, saying . . . I challenge this. I don't think . . .

Critics argue that . . . While it might be true that . . . , still, all in all, . . .

Others may say that . . . but I argue . . .

Skeptics may think. . . . but I contend . . .

While some might say . . . nevertheless it turns out that . . .

I watched as children wrote, noticing some of these entries in their notebooks (see Figures 11–1 and 11–2).

Then I encouraged students to read these.

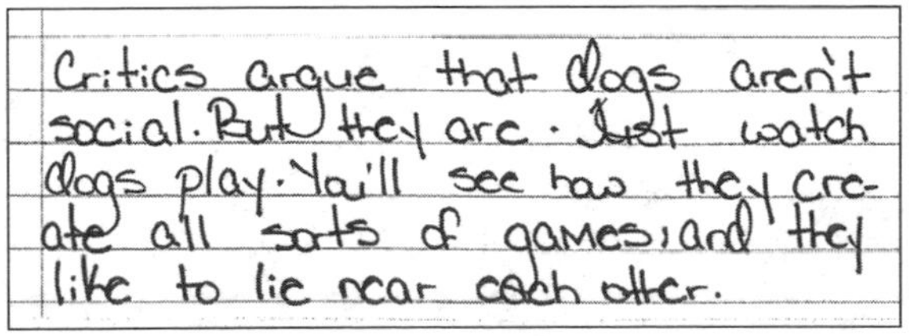

Critics argue that dogs aren't social. But they are. Just watch dogs play. Ya'll see how they create all sorts of games, and they like to lie near each other.

FIG. 11–1   Xavier rebuts with the phrase "Critics argue . . . but . . ."

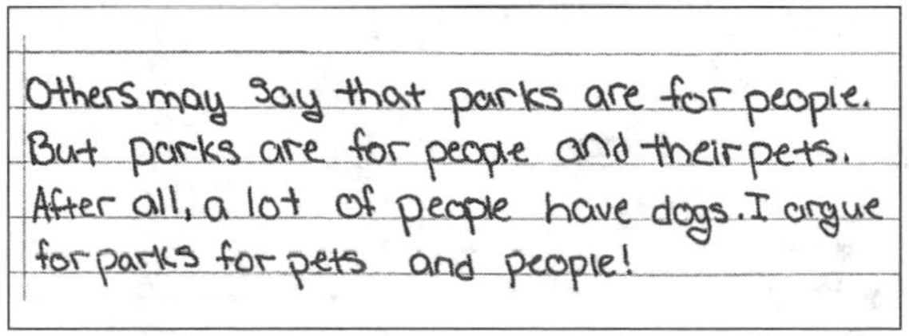

Others may say that parks are for people. But parks are for people and their pets. After all, a lot of people have dogs. I argue for parks for pets and people!

FIG. 11–2   Alex uses the phrase "Others may say . . . but . . ." to build his argument, incorporating the counterclaim.

Teachers, it is crucial for you to realize that eventually, the goal of a counterpoint and rebuttal is not for the writer to simply refute the other person's argument, but for the writer to also give respectful attention to that argument, taking it into account. Eventually, you will look for the writer to say, "Others may claim . . . , and they are partly right. It is true that . . . It is reasonable to argue . . . But on the other hand, . . ." We aren't teaching this now because it adds a layer of complexity to something that is already complex, but you will certainly want to teach this in small groups to your stronger students and to keep it in mind for later instruction.

LINK

Before sending students off, encourage them to try this new strategy and suggest that they might use each other as sounding boards if they need support with envisioning counterclaims.

"Writers, here is the point. You need to imagine how a person will argue against your claim, so that after you make a point, you write something like, 'Some people argue . . .' And then you need to rebut, or respond to, that argument, as you just did. Writers often use phrases like this when rebutting a counterclaim.

"If you're having a hard time envisioning what 'the other side' might say, grab a partner to help you think it through. You might look for someone who is arguing from the other perspective. That person is sure to have some counterclaims for you!"

How to Write an Argument

- Collect evidence that allows you to think through various sides of an argument.
  - Set up a note-taking system to organize your research.
  - Reread sources with a critical eye, looking for connections and contradictions.
- Rehearse by explaining your position and listing your reasons point by point.
- Plan your claim and reasons into boxes-and-bullets structure.
- Use evidence to support your reasons.
  - Paraphrase, putting it into your own words.
  - Quote, and then unpack the quote, showing how it relates to the reason.
  - Introduce the source and explain the connection.
  - Use "set-up" language (transitional phrases) to prop up your sources.
  - Analyze and explain the evidence.
- Include a strong introduction and conclusion.
- Anticipate critics' counterarguments, and acknowledge these in your writing, then rebut them.

Supporting Writers Who Are Ready to Contextualize Arguments within Larger Ideas and Writers Who Need Support with Lining Up Evidence

YOU MIGHT NOTICE a few of your students beginning to do the work of contextualizing their arguments within larger ideas or issues. This is such sophisticated thinking, and it takes some support to maintain control and cohesion. One way to nudge students to incorporate some of that broader thinking is to teach them to include it in a counterargument. And to do that work, you might gather some strong writers to study mentor texts.

Using mentor texts can be especially powerful in small groups. Instead of looking at an entire piece for things your students might notice, isolate your instruction around a smaller piece of text that will focus their inquiry. The most powerful thing about this strategy is that students often notice the things they were probably on the verge of doing. By taking the time to identify it, they can carry on with more confidence.

Find, or create, a mentor text that exhibits craft qualities that you think your stronger writers would benefit from. Even in a small excerpt from a mentor text, there should and will be several things available for them to "find," so the inquiry will be interesting and give them the opportunity to build their independence.

I gathered a small group and showed them the text. In this case, it was one paragraph from a larger essay arguing that people should get their pet spayed or neutered. They had read this text before, but I wanted to draw their attention to this counterargument paragraph. I reminded them of the claim and the two main reasons:

> Pet owners should have their pets fixed.
>
> Reason 1: There are too many dogs and cats and this leads to problems.
>
> Reason 2: Fixing your pet can make them healthier.

MID-WORKSHOP TEACHING
Useful Prompts for Rebutting Counterclaims

"Writers, I see you hard at work, drafting and revising, adding evidence and contextualizing it, and a lot of you are working to think about and then rebut counterclaims, like we talked about in the minilesson. For those of you who are doing that, or may do that soon, I want to let you know a few additional phrases writers can use to rebut counterclaims. I added them to the chart we started earlier."

Phrases to Use to Acknowledge and Rebut Counterclaims

Some people disagree, saying... I challenge this. I don't think...

Critics argue that... While it might be true that, still, all in all, ...

Others may say that... but I argue...

Skeptics may think...

While some might say... nevertheless it turns out that...

"Will you turn to your partner now and just try out one of these phrases or invent a new one that helps you respond to a rebuttal of your argument? You may want to write it down to use later, after you've tried it out a few times. If you try it and feel it works, please take a second to add it to the chart!"

I passed out a half-sheet of paper with the paragraph on it to each student and asked them to read along with me as I read the paragraph aloud. Then I asked them to think about what the writer of the piece was doing *as a writer* to use his or her focused argument to make a bigger point.

> Some people think that this surgery will change their pet's personality. They worry that their interference will make their pet different from who he or she is. These people are misinformed. A pet's personality, just like a person's, is his or her own, and it won't change after "fixing." What will change are some of the annoying and unsafe behaviors. Your pet won't feel the need to "mark" with urine as much. He won't fight other dogs as much. If your dog is a girl, she won't go crazy every few months when she is in heat. Spaying or neutering your pet can actually help you have a happier, better behaved pet. Pets are a big part of our lives. Shouldn't we try to help them be the best they can be?
>
> (adapted from "How to Write an Argument Essay," Belluvue Writing Lab).

After reading, the students talked in partnerships. Kevin and Nicole mentioned:

◆ Writer introduced an idea that hadn't been brought up before (changing personality)

◆ Writer stated what the other side's position was in terms of concerns or "rumors" (afraid it will change their pet)

◆ Writer "taught" or informed the reader (pet's personalities are like human personalities)

Sam and Danielle added to the list:

◆ Writer admitted something, but then turned it to his advantage (changed behavior, not personality)

◆ Writer ended with an idea that seemed bigger than what he started with

You might then coach students to decide which of these they might want to try. Nicole decided that she might add a paragraph addressing the counterclaim. "What are you going to try?" I asked. "Well, I think I could admit something," she replied. I asked her to elaborate on that thought. "I keep saying that chocolate milk is bad, but it's not all bad. It does have some nutrients in it." I coached her to turn that to her favor as the mentor author did. "How could you talk back to that?" I prompted. She looked back at her notes. "Plain milk has the same nutrients. Kids could get them there." She then added a paragraph to her draft (see Figure 11–3) that read:

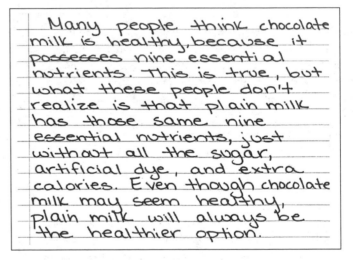

> Many people think chocolate milk is healthy, because it possesses nine essential nutrients. This is true, but what these people don't realize is that plain milk has those same nine essential nutrients, just without all the sugar, artificial dye, and extra calories. Even though chocolate milk may seem healthy, plain milk will always be the healthier option.

FIG. 11–3 This counterclaim admits the validity of counterpoints then turns those points to her advantage.

(continues)

I coached Nicole to look back at the list and think about other moves she might try. She decided she could think about ending with an idea that was bigger than she started with. "How might that sound?" I asked. She paused and thought for a moment. "Well, we're talking about chocolate milk, but it feels like it's really bigger than chocolate milk. I mean we're talking about sugary drinks." She stopped for a moment. I encouraged her to say more about that. "Well," she continued, "maybe this is about all drinks with sugar. We read a lot about how soda has a lot of sugar. I bet I could end with a line about how chocolate milk should be banned, and we should think about all sugar drinks." She then went back to her conclusions and revised it (see Figure 11–4) so it read:

> Schools would be better off if chocolate milk wasn't served. The unhealthy drink would be away from kids. The addictive choice would be gone from school cafeterias. Kids deserve a change. Chocolate milk needs to go, but that isn't the only problem for our kids. Maybe soda needs to go too.

FIG. 11–4   Nicole's conclusion restates her claim then moves to a larger idea, showing the reader the gravity of the debate.

As you send your group back to write, encourage them to imagine significant revisions, trying more than one move they learned from the author. You might even set them up to redraft their arguments. "Writers, sometimes when you learn from another author, you get so many ideas that you just need to start all over," you might say. "If that's the case, grab new loose leaf and redraft. Go to it!"

Where to Include Counterclaims and Rebuttals

Using a strong student piece as a model, rally students to think more deeply about where and how to include counterclaims and rebuttals to strengthen an essay's argument in a balanced way.

"Writers, whenever we are trying to work on a particular aspect of our writing, it's helpful to look at how other writers have handled it. Let's look at this revised essay by Jack to see what he does that we could try, paying attention not only to *how* he weaves counterclaims and rebuttals into his essay, but *where* as well. This is Jack's third revised draft!" I passed out copies of Jack's essay (see Figure 11–5).

"To start, why don't you underline where in this piece he addresses a counterclaim. Once you've done that, think about how he's done it and why he might have chosen to include a counterclaim and rebuttal at that particular point in the essay. Talk with your partner about that." Within moments, students were underlining key phrases and sentences.

Summarize the students' findings about where and how writers include counterarguments and rebuttals.

After students had been underlining and then talking for a few moments, I convened them and summed up what they had almost universally noticed. As I did so, I revealed a chart. As I repeated what the students had noticed, I gestured to the place in Jack's writing where they saw this.

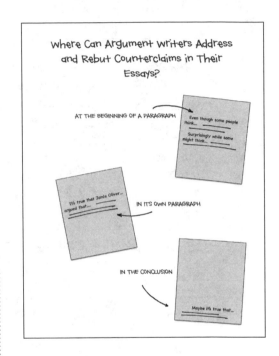

Where Can Argument Writers Address and Rebut Counterclaims in Their Essays?

- AT THE BEGINNING OF A PARAGRAPH
  "Even though some people think . . ."
  "Surprisingly, while some might think . . ."
- IN ITS OWN PARAGRAPH
  "It's true that Jamie Oliver . . . argued that . . ."
- IN THE CONCLUSION
  "Maybe it's true that . . ."

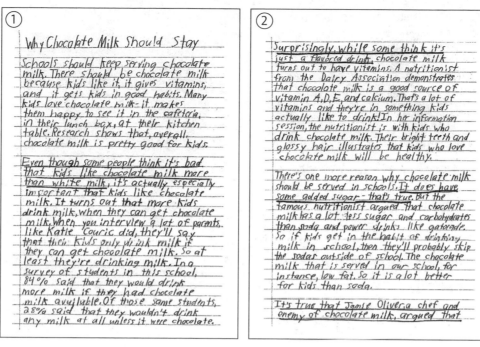

① Why Chocolate Milk Should Stay

Schools should keep serving chocolate milk. There should be chocolate milk because kids like it, it gives vitamins, and it gets kids in good habits. Many kids love chocolate milk-it makes them happy to see it in the cafeteria, in their lunch box, at their kitchen table. Research shows that, overall, chocolate milk is pretty good for kids.

Even though some people think it's bad that kids like chocolate milk more than white milk, it's actually especially important that kids like chocolate milk. It turns out that more kids drink milk, when they can get chocolate milk. When you interview a lot of parents, like Katie Couric did, they'll say that their kids only drink milk if they can get chocolate milk. So at least they're drinking milk. In a survey of students in this school, 84% said that they would drink more milk if they had chocolate milk available. Of those same students, 28% said that they wouldn't drink any milk at all unless it were chocolate.

② Surprisingly, while some think it's just a flavored drink, chocolate milk turns out to have vitamins. A nutritionist from the Dairy Association demonstrates that chocolate milk is a good source of vitamin A, D, E, and calcium. That's a lot of vitamins and they're in something kids actually like to drink! In her information session, the nutritionist is with kids who drink chocolate milk. Their bright teeth and glossy hair illustrates that kids who love chocolate milk will be healthy.

There's one more reason why chocolate milk should be served in schools. It does have some added sugar - that's true. But the famous nutritionist argued that chocolate milk has a lot less sugar and carbohydrates than soda and power drinks like gatorade. So if kids get in the habit of drinking milk in school, then they'll probably skip the sodas outside of school. The chocolate milk that is served in our school, for instance, low fat. So it is a lot better for kids than soda.

It's true that Jamie Olivera chef and enemy of chocolate milk, argued that

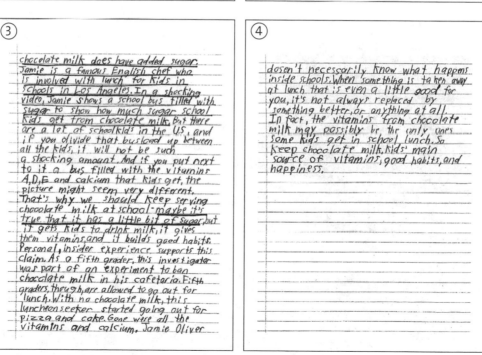

③ chocolate milk does have added sugar. Jamie is a famous English chef who is involved with lunch for kids in schools in Los Angeles. In a shocking video, Jamie shows a school bus filled with sugar to show how much sugar school kids get from chocolate milk. But there are a lot of schoolkids in the U.S., and if you divide that busload up between all the kids, it will not be such a shocking amount. And if you put next to it a bus filled with the vitamins A, D, E and calcium that kids get, the picture might seem very different. That's why we should keep serving chocolate milk at school-maybe it's true that it has a little bit of sugar, but it gets kids to drink milk, it gives them vitamins, and it builds good habits. Personal, insider experience supports this claim. As a fifth grader, this investigator was part of an experiment to ban chocolate milk in his cafeteria. Fifth graders, though, are allowed to go out for lunch. With no chocolate milk, this luncheon seeker started going out for pizza and cake. Gone were all the vitamins and calcium. Jamie Oliver

④ dosen't necessarily know what happens inside schools. When something is taken away at lunch that is even a little good for you, it's not always replaced by something better, or anything at all. In fact, the vitamins from chocolate milk may possibly be the only ones some kids get in school lunch. So keep chocolate milk. Kids' main source of vitamins, good habits, and happiness.

FIG. 11–5 Jack goes point by point, naming the counterclaim and then rebutting it.

"Whenever you write arguments, you'll need to remember that strong arguments usually mention counterclaims and then rebut them—and these are a few of the ways you can include those. Studying other writers' writing would help you learn more ways still, if you needed them!"

THINKING ABOUT AND REBUTTING COUNTERCLAIMS

Writers, you've just learned a few different places you might mention and rebut the counterclaim. Take a minute to reread your essay and create a self-assignment. As you read and think about what you need to do, ask yourself, "Where might I acknowledge the counterclaim?" If you already have the counterclaim in your essay, you might push yourself to think of other ways or places to rebut it. Remember to take spider legs and extra drafting paper home with you so you can make your revisions or redraft.

Evaluating Evidence

ODAY'S SESSION IS CHALLENGING. It opens the Pandora's box of a whole new topic: critiquing evidence. You will be teaching students to weigh the validity of other people's arguments and of their own arguments, using this sort of critique as an opportunity to learn how to strengthen an argument.

Until now, the message to students has been that when writing an argument essay, a writer makes a claim and then supports it with reasons and evidence. You've taught that writers need to "unpack," or discuss, the way the evidence supports the reason. You've even touched upon the fact that evidence itself is usually neutral and needs to be interpreted, explained (or even "spun") so that it can be used to back one claim or another. The fact that chocolate milk has four grams of added sugar can be regarded as a reason to avoid chocolate milk (four grams—so many more than water!), or it can be regarded as a reason to choose chocolate milk (four grams—so many fewer than soda!).

In this session you take students deep into the work of realizing that even if a writer has structured an essay into claims, reasons, and evidence, and even if the argument has cited and unpacked a variety of evidence, this does not mean the argument itself is necessarily a valid one. This session attempts to introduce writers to thinking about the most common problems in arguments—ones they'll encounter in the texts they read and write.

For example, let's think about the chocolate milk debate. If one were to argue that chocolate milk should be banned from all schools because it is bad for kids' health, one could say, "Then are you saying that candy, too, should be banned? Brownies? French fries? Should coffee be banned from the faculty room?" In other words, one form of scrutinizing an argument can be to think, "What follows from this reasoning? What else would then need to change? What are the logical consequences of this position?" In a second example, one could critique the argument that parents need to be told about their teacher's ratings (based on one day's standardized test scores) by taking this to its logical extension and imagining what else would need to be changed. "Shouldn't fireman be rated based on an hour-long test, and shouldn't people be told, also, about those ratings for the firefighters? Police officers? Investment bankers?"

IN THIS SESSION, you'll teach students that argument writers evaluate evidence to ensure that their own arguments are solid.

GETTING READY

- ✔ Playing cards to make a simple house of cards (see Connection)
- ✔ Link to YouTube video of a house of cards collapsing (see Connection)
- ✔ A pack of index cards for each partnership, with the six different model arguments on them (see Teaching and Active Engagement)
- ✔ A demonstration set of the arguments either on the Smart Board so they can be moved or a set of teacher index cards (see Teaching and Active Engagement)
- ✔ "Common Flaws in Reasoning" chart (see Teaching and Active Engagement, Conferring, and Share)
- ✔ Sample student writing that lets the reader know when evidence is problematic (see Share)
- ✔ Students' writing folders with their most current drafts (see Share)
- ✔ "How to Write an Argument" chart (see Share)

In our work for the CCSSO (Council of Chief State School Officers), we've worked with CBAL, a branch of ETS, to pilot tools to help students analyze predictable ways in which arguments are illogical or flawed. It is very challenging to detect flaws in logic (logical fallacies), and many of your students may find this beyond their reach. But there are some underlying concepts that all students will be able to pick up, and that's the work you'll embark on in this session. For example,

---

"This session attempts to introduce writers to thinking about the most common problems in arguments—ones they'll encounter in the texts they read and write."

a lot of young readers and writers (and some adults) expect any nonfiction text to simply "tell the truth." They take these texts at face value. This session will help students progress toward being critical readers and writers who recognize that nonfiction is someone's perspective on the truth and that language sways emotions just as much in argument as it does in narrative. Here, you'll use the metaphor of a house of cards to sharpen your students' alertness to moments when an argument may sound strong but actually be falling apart—like a house of cards.

The work in this session is complex and you might consider it to be above grade level. But it is important work that is often not taught at all, so we encourage you to take it on. Politicians build cases during campaigns and the people evaluate the arguments, then vote. Attorneys build cases and the juries evaluate them, then decide guilty or not guilty. Business people create arguments about what is and is not going to raise standards, then the public agrees or disagrees. Teaching kids to evaluate arguments sets them up be active agents of their own destiny—and ours too.

Evaluating Evidence

CONNECTION

Gather the writers in the meeting area and explain the meaning of the expression "a house of cards" as you model building one.

"Writers, give me a nod if you have ever heard the expression 'a house of cards.'" A few students nodded. "Well, for those of you who haven't, it's an expression that really means something with an unsound or not strong foundation." Quickly, I placed two cards on the desk next to me and balanced a third card on top of these. "Look how these two bottom cards support this top card. I bet I could keep going and keep building this house. I could build it five or even more tiers up. But here's the thing, writers. No matter what, this will always be a house built out of cards. And that means it is weak. If I take one of the cards away," as I spoke I pulled out one of the bottom cards, "the whole thing will collapse."

Teachers, you can show a house of cards on your computer or Smart Board if you want. If you really want to recruit your students' interest, allow them to actually see the house collapse. Search for a video of a house of cards falling down. There are multiple examples of this on sites such as YouTube.

Harken back to the work students did last year in essay writing by connecting the analogy of the house of cards to the analogy of essay writing as construction.

"In fourth grade you learned that essay writing is a bit like constructing a building. Essayists cement together a variety of reasons and evidence to create an essay just like builders cement together all kinds of materials to create a building. But now you are ready to learn one of the most important things there is to know about the construction of an essay, and that is this: without a solid foundation of reasons and evidence, your entire argument will collapse. Instead of a strong building, you'll realize you've built a house of cards. If you've built a house of cards, this means that no matter how tall your building may be, it will always be weak at its foundation."

CBAL argues that the ability to analyze others' arguments is crucial to the skill of constructing a logical argument. Students aren't used to analyzing warrants, or reasons, of text, however, so we introduce this work almost as a mind game, to hold their interest and engage their reasoning.

❧ Name the teaching point.

"Writers, today I want to teach you that some reasons and evidence are better than others. Some reasons and evidence are stronger and lead to valid arguments, and some are weaker and can create invalid arguments. To be sure you provide the strongest possible reasons and evidence, it helps to keep asking the question, 'How do I know?' and be sure that you can give precise, exact answers."

In The Skills of Argument (1991), Kuhn argues that being able to answer this question (How do I know?) is critical to the success of an argument. She says, "An inability to answer the 'How do you know' question suggests that the assertion should not have been made" (44).

TEACHING AND ACTIVE ENGAGEMENT

Let writers know that practicing evaluating the reasoning of others can help writers to evaluate their own reasoning as well as learn predictable problems that can lead to flawed reasoning.

"You've seen TV shows where someone goes to court and his lawyer makes an argument, saying, 'My guy didn't do it and I can prove this because he, one, has an alibi, and, two, he has a witness.' And then the lawyer from the *other* side takes the stand and rips apart the first argument. 'That alibi was for the wrong time. The witness isn't believable because . . .'

"Lawyers spend much of their time evaluating cases and weighing evidence to get as close to a valid judgment as possible. When any of you argue about anything, you need to do this same lawyer-like thinking, and you need to do this thinking to test the strength of your own argument as you work on it, so you can make it stronger and stronger. Today I'm going to teach you some of the tricks for doing this.

"The first skill is to learn to evaluate the arguments of others. To evaluate someone's argument, you don't just think about whether you happen to already agree with their conclusion. Instead, you ask a key question. You ask, 'How do you know?' You decide *not* if an argument is your cup of tea, but if it is defensible, if the person has supported it in a responsible way (whether or not it is your cup of tea).

"Researchers have found there are a couple of problems that one sees in many arguments, and if you know to check for these problems, it can help you review someone else's argument with a lawyer's eyes. But instead of just telling you what the common problems are that make many arguments weak, I'm going to give you a bunch of reasons around an argument so that you can rank whether those reasons are strong or weak. As you do this, be on the lookout for some of the common problems in many people's arguments. You'll see those problems in these arguments.

"When someone makes a case, remember you judge it by asking, in your mind, 'How do you know?' If the person's argument doesn't answer that question, it is not strong. You don't think whether you agree, but whether the person has supported his or her argument. Arguments that are invalid have weaker reasons. They are like the houses of cards.

"So, keep asking, 'How do you know?' of the person making the argument, and if there is no real way that the person who made the argument has answered the question, that argument is weaker. Are you game to test some arguments?" Heads nodded.

Involve writers in ranking reasons—good, bad, okay—for arguments you provide.

"Here is the situation: people in a town gathered for a town meeting to discuss whether it is a good idea for the town to build a skateboard park. People spoke for both sides. I'm going to hand each partnership a pack of 6 index cards, each with an argument on it that people made, and the arguments are sometimes for and sometimes against the skateboard park.

"Okay, go through your cards together and weigh the arguments." I watched as children started reading over and discussing their cards.

Person A: "We shouldn't have a skateboarding park. Our town needs money for other, more important things. Our football team needs new uniforms, for example. If we build that skateboarding park, our team will be embarrassed on the field."

Person B: "We shouldn't have a skateboarding park. I know someone who skateboarded all the time and so he stopped doing his homework and started getting bad grades and this shows everyone who uses it will get bad grades."

Person C: "We should have a skateboarding park. I had one in my town when I was growing up and I loved it. All the kids will love it like I did."

Person D: "We should have a skateboarding park. All these people who are saying we shouldn't are just cranky and trying to deny our kids a little fun."

Person E: "We should have a skateboarding park. Right now kids who want to skateboard use the sidewalk and that's dangerous. Only last week, I saw an older woman almost being run over because skateboarders were on the sidewalk."

Person F: "We should have a skateboarding park. Skateboarding is exercise and it gets kids involved in a healthy activity. It's better than having them just sit around with nothing to do or get into trouble."

Coach into partnerships to help students to weigh evidence as they rank, and to remind them that this work is meant to illustrate common ways many people's arguments fall apart.

I pulled up to listen as Natalie and Kennedy talked over a few of the reasons. "Person C really enjoyed skateboarding when he or she was a kid. I think that's pretty good evidence," Kennedy said as she moved the statement into the "good" pile.

I interjected, "How do you know?"

Kennedy looked at the card. "Well, this Person C did it herself so she knows skateboarding is fun. That's evidence."

"How do you know that this reason shows that the skateboard park is best *for the town*?" I kept pressing them.

Kennedy hesitated. "Oh! Right. Just because one person did, that doesn't mean that everyone will."

Person A takes for granted that everyone buys into the idea that football is more important than skateboarding. But that assumption is not supported by evidence. There is no answer to the question, "How do you know?"

Person B makes a generalization. He assumes that what happens in one particular example will happen to everyone.

Person C generalizes from a personal example and assumes that what happened to him- or herself will happen to everyone.

Person D's argument attempts to discredit the character of critics rather than discrediting the quality of the critics' argument.

Person E takes one particular example and applies it to everyone—the same as B and C.

Person F links two events as if they are causal. He suggests that if kids don't skateboard they'll get into trouble, but there is no evidence that lack of exercise causes trouble.

"Writers," I said. "I want to remind you I wrote these arguments because they illustrate really common weaknesses in many people's arguments, and if you know what those weaknesses are, sometimes you can see them in your own writing as well."

Kennedy moved the card from good to okay. "So, it's not the best evidence, but I still think it's not terrible."

"Keep ranking. Use the questions and also the claim itself to help you test the reasoning, and remember you are questioning, 'How does the arguer support the precise words in her claim?'"

Channel the writers to discuss the reasoning that led them to evaluate the argument as strong or weak.

"Writers, in a minute, we'll talk about the choices you made in sorting and ranking these arguments, but what I am most interested in hearing about is *why* you made these choices. Will you look over what you have sorted and think about ways this work might teach you about common problems in many people's arguments?" After a minute, I said, "Okay, writers, will you share some of the main ways you learned that people sometimes make their arguments weaker? Turn and talk."

Reconvene the writers and share some of what you heard as you model sorting some of the demonstration index cards.

"Writers, I'm going to share some of what I heard, and if you and your partner also said this, will you give me a thumbs up?

"So, some of you were noticing that some arguments had a flaw because they gave evidence about what one person did and used that example to assume that's what *everyone* would do." Some thumbs went up. "Person C did that when he said what he loved growing up and assumed that's what *all* kids would love, right? And Person B did that when he assumed that because he knew someone who happened to be a skateboarder and got into trouble at school, that meant that *all* kids who skateboard would get into trouble at school. So we could say they had a flaw of using a specific example to prove their point. This is a flaw we see a lot. Let's start getting some of these observations down." On a chart I wrote:

> Common Flaws in Reasoning
> * Generalizing (assumes specific example will be true everywhere)

Here I am deliberately choosing to share what I've heard rather than elicit because I want to steer the students toward common logical fallacies and carefully provide the language used to describe these.

"Now, I also heard you saying that another flaw you noticed was that the argument tried to convince by talking badly about *the people*, not their arguments." Thumbs went up.

"Yeah, so Person D is saying that the people are cranky, which doesn't mention the quality of their arguments at all, right? It just totally goes away from discussing evidence and facts. So we could add that to the chart."

> • Discrediting (insults people's character rather than taking issue with their points)

"Another flaw I heard was that some of the arguments just assumed consequences would happen when there was no evidence that they would. Person B did that, right? By assuming that kids who skateboard will get bad grades.

> • Assuming Consequences (implies cause-and-effect relation-ship that isn't proven)

"The last thing I heard people saying was that some people were basing their whole argument on a conclusion that they are framing as true for everyone when it might not be. Like how Person A is basing an argument on a premise that football is more important than skateboarding. If that isn't true, the whole argument falls apart, right?" I added these to the chart.

> • Questionable Assumption (argument founded on something that might not be true)

Teachers, you might consider how to incorporate this work across the curriculum. Consider how the level of your current events curriculum would be raised if students began to study speeches given by politicians for flaws in logic. Discrediting the character of the other side might be something they see. Or you might have students spend time in the day studying advertisements, looking at the assumptions behind these, and considering the flaws in those assumptions.

Common Flaws in Reasoning

• Generalizing
   assumes specific example will be true everywhere

• Discrediting
   insults people's character rather than taking issue with their points

• Assuming Consequences
   implies cause-and-effect relationship that isn't proven

CAUSE   EFFECT

• Questionable Assumption
   argument founded on something that might not be true

LINK

Help your writers make the connection between reading arguments critically and reading and revising their own arguments for flaws in reasoning

"Writers, you just did some really close reading work. That work, of reading over parts of an argument and really analyzing its logic, is not something you'll want to save for reading other people's arguments. You'll want to apply those same lenses to your own writing! No house of cards for you. When you find one of these flaws, stop! Get out some paper and rewrite that part. I imagine I'll see you reconsidering parts of your argument or reading your evidence more suspiciously."

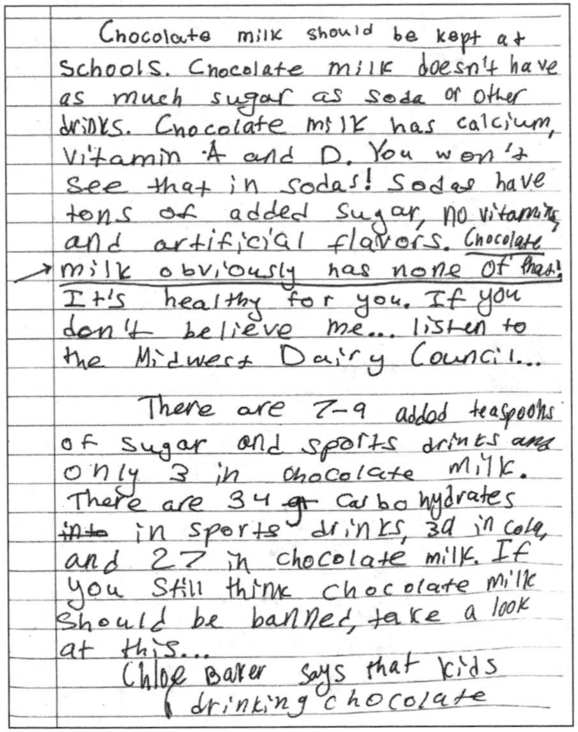

> Chocolate milk should be kept at schools. Chocolate milk doesn't have as much sugar as soda or other drinks. Chocolate milk has calcium, vitamin A and D. You won't see that in sodas! Sodas have tons of added sugar, no vitamins, and artificial flavors. Chocolate milk obviously has none of that! It's healthy for you. If you don't believe me... listen to the Midwest Dairy Council...
>
> There are 7-9 added teaspoons of sugar and sports drinks and only 3 in chocolate milk. There are 34 g carbohydrates into in sports drinks, 3d in cola, and 27 in chocolate milk. If you still think chocolate milk should be banned, take a look at this...
> Chloe Baker says that kids drinking chocolate

> milk at school everyday earns it an out-of-control problem. An out of control problem that there are getting vitamins A an D, Calcium and only 3 teaspoons of added sugar? (compared to 9 teaspoons). And there Chloe Baker goes, saying that 39 grams of carbohydrates is healthier than vitamins.

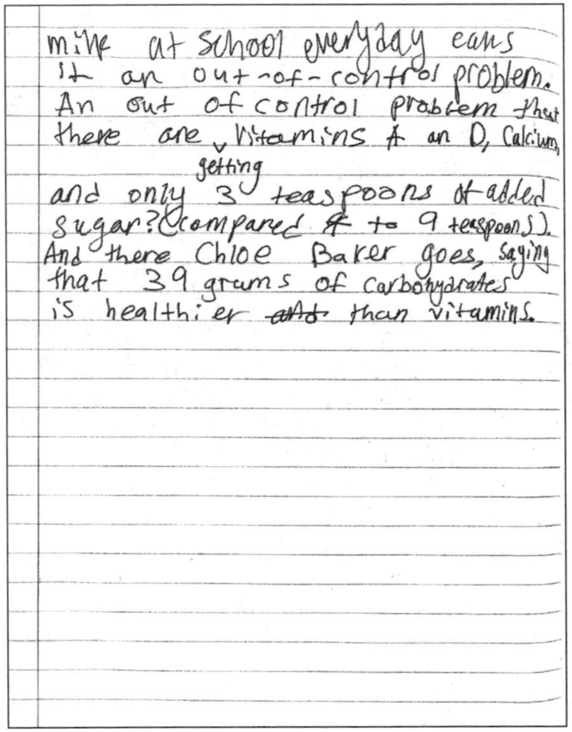

FIG. 12–1   This writer noticed she leaped to a flawed conclusion, saying that chocolate milk does *not* have artificial flavors and added sugar when, in fact, it does. She marked that spot for revision.

Analyzing Logic in Claims and Counterclaims

WHILE CRITICAL, THIS WORK CAN BE CHALLENGING, so don't be surprised if you notice some children struggling with it. In fact, anticipate it. One of the first predictable problems you may see is writers who have difficulty transferring what they have done in the lesson to other texts and contexts. To help writers with this, you might pull a small group and involve them in creating predictable flawed arguments that people might give for the topic they are currently researching.

To do this, you might gather writers around the chart constructed during the lesson and ask them to consider how arguments with these flaws would go on the topic of chocolate milk in schools. You might first give an example of what you mean, perhaps explaining what a flawed argument using "assuming consequences" reasoning would look like.

After modeling with one such argument, you might ask the group to work in partnerships to create a flawed argument depending on the reasoning of giving one specific example and generalizing that to all people. Writers might come up with a reason like "I drink chocolate milk and I'm not overweight or sick. So kids will be fine." As writers learn what illogical arguments look like, you can keep pushing them to think of what exactly makes it not hold up. Then you can remind them to check their own research, and any reasoning they hear throughout their life, for these pitfalls.

For writers who seem to grasp how to recognize flawed arguments in others but do not grasp flawed arguments of their own, you can coach them to continue to ask the question "How do you know?" of their own reasoning, involving them in considering what further evidence would be needed to really support their reasoning and how to go about getting that evidence.

Getting students into the habit of automatically looking for the assumptions that others are making can help them to be more critical in their own lives and perhaps better prepare them to be active citizens.

MID-WORKSHOP TEACHING Be on the Lookout for Flawed Arguments—and if Necessary, Return to Research

"Writers, may I have your attention for a moment? I noticed Norah doing something fabulous that I think you might find helpful. Norah noticed she had a flaw in her argument. She discovered that she had taken one case and made it seem like that would happen everywhere. She used the example that milk consumption dropped in one school when the school stopped serving chocolate milk to show that it would happen in all schools. When Norah realized her argument was flawed, she returned to her research. She looked for stronger evidence. She found a study that showed in several schools milk consumption dropped when chocolate milk stopped being served. And then, she grabbed a slip of paper and started revising that paragraph. She wrote the whole thing over and taped it onto her original draft. As you think about your argument, when you find areas that have flawed reasoning, return to research, find more compelling evidence, then revise your drafts."

You'll likely also find that several of your students thrive when evaluating reasoning. These students pore over their position papers, analyzing their own logic and revising when necessary. You might encourage them to extend this thinking to the counterclaim, teaching them to tackle the opposing side's views by spotting weaknesses in the logic of the argument. "Writers," you might say, "one way to rebut the counterclaim is to analyze the argument the opposing side is making, looking for flaws in the reasoning. If you find flaws, talk about them in your paper. You might say, 'Some people think . . . but if you look carefully at the argument you will see . . . '" Then, coach children to return to their papers, studying the counterclaim they plan to address. Ask them to look at the logic, and, if they find flaws, use those to bolster their own argument.

Unpacking the Strengths and Weaknesses of Evidence for Readers

Rally students to study the draft of a student who has added his thinking about how evidence used in a counterclaim is problematic, thus exposing its weakness.

"Writers, can I have your eyes and attention? I know you are drafting, and I want you to have as much time as you need to write, but I want to quickly point out some work my former student Jack did that I think might be helpful for you to study. In this piece, Jack is doing that work we did yesterday, of being the cynic. He actually loves chocolate milk, as you know, but he was imagining what critics might say for a rebuttal, and that made him really look closely at the reasoning of his sources, making sure to let his readers know when and how some evidence is problematic. When I talked with Jack, he told me that he thought he had spotted a problem in one of the texts. When I asked him what it was, he said, 'You know how in mysteries the author throws in a few false clues to get you off track? Well, I think I found some red herrings in this video on chocolate milk.'

"I'm going to read a little bit of his piece to you, and I want you to listen to how Jack realized this evidence is problematic.

"Here's the part of Jack's piece where he wrote about the reasoning of Ms. Dobbins, the woman from the Mid-West Dairy Organization" (see Figure 12–2).

"Writers, Jack thought that the children were put into the video to look healthy and adorable and get viewers off track. He explained that so that readers will be alert to that problem in the evidence and be more critical of it. We should include the idea of red herrings as well. I'll add it to our list of common flaws in reasoning."

> The nutritionist from the Dairy Association (Dobins?) claims that chocolate milk has essential nutrients and vitamins and it dosen't have as much sugar as alot of flavored drinks for kids. She also postitions herself as a mom and has her kids with her—and the kids look really healthy. They are good avritisments for chocolate milk- possible even red herrings.

FIG. 12–2   Jack problematizes evidence, weakening the counterargument and strengthening his own.

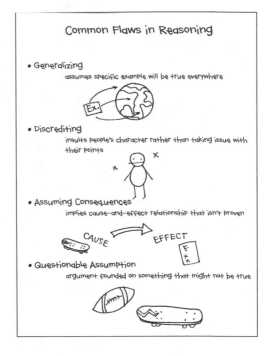

Ask students to study their own drafts through this lens, looking for places where they might unpack the strengths or weaknesses of evidence for readers.

"I'm betting that you can all find places in your drafts where you might be able to look more closely at how sources spin their evidence. Remember, read with the lens of what someone might say who was rebutting. You might notice more then. Be a cynic!

"Will you quickly look over your evidence right now and point to one spot where you can explain further, or where you can see how someone might rebut it by attacking the logic? Share with the person next to you!" The room erupted into conversation.

Kennedy looked at her draft. "I talk about Jamie Oliver and that school bus. All that really made me think about how much sugar is in there. But maybe that's a red herring." She stroked her chin with her hand and thought for a moment. "What do you mean by that?" Natalie asked.

"Well, it is a lot of sugar. But, how long does it take to drink *that* much sugar? Didn't the video say that that was a whole city worth of kids? Or the country?" They flipped back through their notes. "Yea, that's all of L.A. That's a big city. It seems like this is trickier than I thought. I have to really think about what someone might say from the other side."

"Okay, writers, so remember that you want to help lead your reader to see your thinking as you build your argument. And a big part of that is letting your reader see the strengths or weaknesses of the evidence as you see them so the reader can follow your thinking and know you are aware of possible counterarguments. I'm going to add that to our process chart. Let's keep flash-drafting. Write your arguments as soundly as you can. Go to it!"

How to Write an Argument

- Collect evidence that allows you to think through various sides of an argument.
  - Set up a note-taking system to organize your research.
  - Reread sources with a critical eye, looking for connections and contradictions.
- Rehearse by explaining your position and listing your reasons point by point.
- Plan your claim and reasons into boxes-and-bullets structure.
- Use evidence to support your reasons.
  - Paraphrase, putting it into your own words.
  - Quote, and then unpack the quote, showing how it relates to the reason.
  - Introduce the source and explain the connection.
  - Use "set-up" language (transitional phrases) to prop up your sources.
  - Analyze and explain the evidence.
  - Show your reader the strengths and weaknesses of your evidence.
- Include a strong introduction and conclusion.
- Anticipate critics' counterarguments, and acknowledge these in your writing, then rebut them.

STAYING ALERT WHEN REASONING SEEMS TO BE COMMON SENSE

Writers, during our mystery reading unit, you learned to read mysteries suspiciously, searching for clues about "who dun it?" Today, will you reread all of the evidence you've already been reading, only this time, will you reread the texts suspiciously, noticing ways the authors of the articles (and the videos) use flawed logic? Notice little sly moves the authors have used to manipulate you into believing what they want you to believe. Remember, Jack noticed that the children on the pro-chocolate milk video put out by the American Dairy Association look totally healthy. The children are posing as if they are the woman's kids, but they probably are actors. If her kids didn't look healthy and fit, do you think they'd be on this video? No way!

So read suspiciously, with a lawyer's eyes, looking for holes in the logic in these articles. And if you find yourself questioning some of what people have argued, be sure you insert a passage about that into your essay. You know how to use flaps and added-on half sheets of paper to make your writing grow, right?

A couple of tips are: whenever something seems to be presented as common sense or natural, that is time for you to be alert because it's likely the author might be giving flawed reasoning. So, for example, if you read something like "As an everyday drink choice, TruMoo has significantly less added sugars than that of soft drinks and popular fruit juice drinks," you might nod your head and think, "Yes, right. Well, that makes sense."

Two: beware of slippery statistics! One of you suggested it would be worth looking at serving size in Ms. Dobbins's math! Numbers can be manipulated, researchers! Now, tonight, don't just glide along saying, "Sure, sure." Instead, stop yourself. Say to yourself, "Wait, stop! Is that author just trying to appeal to what everyone thinks is good, to trick you into buying this product?" Writers, when authors try to make it seem like something is obvious or just makes sense or everyone just feels this way, that is a time to be on high alert.

Flavored milk versus white milk: What's the difference?
Q&A with Dr. Sarah Jane Schwarzenberg, co-chair of MN-AAP's pediatric obesity taskforce

1. Why is chocolate milk a factor in the pediatric obesity epidemic?

The simple answer is that it is higher in calories than plain milk with the same fat content. The difference is about 50 cals/8 oz. That may seem small, but a child drinking one carton each school day (5 days/week) will gain one pound in 14 weeks FROM CHOCOLATE MILK ALONE. *You'll gain 13 and 2/3 of a pound in a school year from C.M.*

In fact, many children are drinking 2-4 cartons of this milk each day, and it is not the only unnecessary calorie-dense product they are given. *Some kids could triple and double it*

2. By removing chocolate milk from schools, some people are concerned that kids won't drink any milk and won't benefit from the calcium, Vitamin D and other nutrients they need. What are your thoughts on this? *These two have natural sugar and they probably won't offer that.*

If children are offered juice, pop, fruit drinks, etc, as an alternative to plain milk, they will drink them instead of plain milk. If they are offered water as an alternative, they will likely drink plain milk. There are many important changes that must be made in children's diet if we are to reduce obesity and reduce the risk of heart disease and cancer in the future. *Kids don't realize it but drinking chocolate milk gives a better chance of diseases and cancer* Ideally, children would eat more vegetables—but providing them with Ranch dressing and melted cheese to get them to eat them creates nutritional disaster. We want them to eat more fruit, but adding caramel coating to entice them increases obesity. Similarly, bribing children to ingest calcium and vitamin D, etc, by providing them with a high-calorie sweet beverage simply trades one nutritional problem for another. *Like adding chocolate syrup to milk*

If we are panicked that kids aren't getting enough of a nutrient, we should give them a vitamin, not sugar them up.

FIG. 12–3   On the lookout for slippery statistics, Lucas does the math!

Appealing to the Audience

ADVERTISING AGENCIES KNOW THE SIGNIFICANCE OF AUDIENCE. They do market research to find out what kind of music their buyers listen to, what values they share, what kind of life they yearn for. With this knowledge in hand, ad agencies shape their ads to their audience. Tommy Hilfiger makes its polo shirt for urban teenagers—kids who are *Twilight* readers, Beyonce fans. J. Crew markets their polos to college youth and young parents. Chances are, the basic model for those polo shirts is nearly the same, made in the same factory even, but each company spins its shirt so it seems to go with a lifestyle.

Everyone knows something about angling toward audience appeal. When an eleven-year-old wants to stay up later, she knows to say to a parent, "Because I want to *read*."

"Hundreds of small victories over bedtimes, meals, and electronics lie behind children's knowledge of how to persuade adults who care for them."

Staying with a grandparent on the weekend, that same student might say, "Because I want to *spend more time with you*." Somehow that child knows that for a busy parent, the concept of more time together, late at night, is not necessarily that appealing. The concept of the quiet child huddled over a book is. It is not a matter of manufacturing a reason to get what the child wants so much as it is a matter of selecting the one reason among many that the audience will respond to.

In this session, your children will have an opportunity to practice targeting specific audiences. Chances are that your students will know how to do this work intuitively. They'll know the lingo for persuading parents versus peers. Hundreds of small victories over

IN THIS SESSION, you'll teach students that writers think carefully about their audience and then tailor their arguments to particularly appeal to that audience, conducting an inquiry into how this might be done.

GETTING READY

✔ A buzzer and a bell (see Teaching and Active Engagement)

✔ "Ways to Sway an Audience to Take Your Stance" chart (see Teaching and Active Engagement, Mid-Workshop Teaching, and Share)

✔ "How to Write an Argument" chart (see Link)

✔ Sample student writing that uses vocabulary that's just right for the audience (see Mid-Workshop Teaching)

bedtimes, meals, and electronics lie behind children's knowledge of how to persuade adults who care for them. Teach them to notice *how* they do that, to see the persuasive techniques they use to address certain audiences. Invite them to imagine, then, what would change when they try to persuade other audiences, from nutrition experts to teachers to principals.

Within this work lies some of the craft of persuasion that this session aims to teach your students. When writers incorporate knowledge of their audience, they are able to be more deliberate with which examples they choose, which vocabulary, and which references, allowing them to tailor a piece so that it strikes close to the hearts of intended readers.

Because the very next session will be students' panel presentations, you will want to be sure to explain to them that time (and focus) is of the essence. You will also want to have done the footwork beforehand to set the panel presentations up. It will be helpful for you, before today's teaching, to read through tomorrow's session, which clearly describes the prep work you'll need to do to organize the panel presentations and set your students up to succeed. You'll need, for example, to select and secure audiences to attend students' panel presentations and to decide how the panels will differ, which kids will present to which audiences, and how. You'll need to make sure to explain the logistics to students as well, so that they can envision how the presentations will go. You might want to do that at another time during the day, since today's lesson is chock-full.

Appealing to the Audience

CONNECTION

Tell students that just as lawyers think carefully about the jury to whom they are presenting and tailor their arguments accordingly, writers of arguments think carefully about the audience for their writing and tailor it accordingly.

"Writers, hands up if you've heard the expression 'jury of one's peers.'" A scattering of hands went up.

"In America, when someone is on trial for breaking the law, that person is guaranteed a jury of peers, which means a group of people who represent a broad spectrum of the population, particularly of race, national origin, and gender. That's to ensure the trial is fair. But here's the part I want you to think about: when a lawyer is defending someone, she needs to think about all the different kinds of people who are sitting on the jury—anticipating what will sway each one of them to vote for her client's innocence. In other words, that lawyer has got to think about her audience.

"So what does this have to do with all of you and with whether or not chocolate milk should be allowed in school?" I asked.

"A lot, in fact. Up until now, you've been working hard to determine what you, yourselves, believe about the role of chocolate milk in school. And it's clear to me that this class has in it some very enthusiastic chocolate milk advocates and, on the other hand, some serious chocolate milk naysayers. You've pulled off quite a feat by compiling evidence into well-crafted arguments. But—now comes the hard part. Now you have to figure out how to convince not only yourselves, but your audience as well."

When teaching reading or writing, it is often helpful to go outside the topic to make your point, and then say, "It's the same way when you read or write." You'll see that we do this repeatedly.

Explain that students will be presenting their arguments to different audience groups and that their arguments will be more effective if they tweak their arguments to appeal to the group to whom they present.

"In just days now, some of you will present to other kids in our school. Some of you will present to your parents. Some of you will present to the cafeteria workers. And some of you will present to the principal, Ms. Granger. Representatives from those groups will judge the various arguments and cast votes." I revealed a chart letting kids know to whom they would present their argument. "That's a whole range of people to convince! And I can bet that you are already thinking about how you might need to tweak your arguments to appeal to each audience. So right now, let's think about how we're going to pull this off."

Teachers, in this session we created groups and chose an audience for children. You might decide to let students choose their own audience. You could put up chart paper with different audiences on top, and children could sign up, creating their own groups.

✤ **Name the question that will guide the inquiry.**

"The question we'll be exploring is: What persuasive techniques help us address—and sway—a particular audience?"

TEACHING AND ACTIVE ENGAGEMENT

Reenact several ways a particular argument might go, asking students to determine which spin is most effective for that particular audience.

"To answer this question, I want you to observe a little reenactment of something I witnessed in another school recently. Who wants to be my volunteer?" Lots of hands shot up. I called on Sarah.

"Sarah, you sit here, on my chair. You'll be the principal of the school. Not our principal, Ms. Granger, but the principal of this other school, Ms. Woods. Here—put on these glasses and my scarf. That's better. You look official now."

To the class I said, "Now I'm going to be the kids I saw that day. Pay close attention to how I go about trying to convince the principal that recess should be longer. Jot notes if it helps."

I handed Sarah a buzzer and a bell. "Sarah, if you aren't convinced, ring this buzzer. That will be your way of saying, 'Aaaannnh' or giving me a thumbs-down. That will mean I didn't convince you. But if I argue in a way that you, as Ms. Woods, the principal, feel convinced that recess should be longer, then go ahead and ring this bell. That 'ding, ding, ding' will be your way of giving me a thumbs-up. To the group, I said, "Everyone else, put on your best observation hats!"

Slouching my shoulders, I said in my best whiny little kid voice, "Ms. Woods, recess should be longer because it's fun for us to play. And we want to play for more time. So can it be longer, please?" I gave Sarah the signal that she should decide how I'd fared as an arguer. Gleefully, Sarah rang the buzzer.

"Bzzzz," I said, imitating the buzzer sound. I gestured for the kids to imitate it as well.

"Thumbs-down for that one. Here I go again," I said. Again, I slouched my shoulders, and this time, I said, "Ms. Woods, if recess were longer, kids could do the stuff that kids like to do, like play ball and run around and hang out with our friends, and stuff. You know, we deserve to have extra time 'cause we work so hard."

Sarah hit the buzzer and, on cue, the class and I called out, "Bzzzz."

Straightening my shoulders and losing the whine in my voice, I turned to Sarah, looked her in the eye and said, "You know, Ms. Woods, if kids had a longer recess time, we'd be more productive when we returned to the classroom. First, we'd get out all that pent-up energy we build up from sitting all day, and so we'd be able to concentrate on our work. Another thing is recess is an important time to make friends, and when we have friends, we're happier in school. That helps us do better. And finally, sometimes we play games that involve reasoning skills—like capture the flag—so even though it looks like we're just playing, we're actually doing thinking that helps us in some subjects in school."

Invite children to observe as you and a child in the class role-play a recent exchange you witnessed at another school between one class of kids and their principal, whom they were attempting to convince that recess should be longer. As they watch, children should investigate the techniques used to sway the principal.

Use your voice as well as your language to dramatize the difference in your argument and to emphasize persuasive techniques.

I looked at Sarah, who gave the bell three enthusiastic taps. Gesturing to the class, I led them in a chorus of "Ding, ding, ding!"

"Whew!" I said, wiping my forehead. "I convinced Ms. Woods."

Debrief. Elicit from the child volunteer one thing you did that swayed him to your side. Begin a chart of ways to sway an audience.

Then, resuming the role of teacher, I said, "Sarah, tell us just one thing I did or said that swayed you to believe kids should have a longer amount of recess."

"You talked about school."

"Be more specific," I prompted.

"Well, umm, you convinced me that recess would help kids do better in school."

"Yes, and as a principal, you're most interested in . . . " I let my voice trail off.

"Kids doing well in school!" Sarah sang out.

I gave Sarah a thumbs up and said, "So one essential way to sway an audience is to angle your argument so that it addresses things that that particular audience cares about. Let's start a chart of ways to convince an audience of what you believe." On a piece of chart paper, I wrote:

Persuasive Techniques to Sway an Audience

- Focus on what your audience cares about.

Set children up to talk in partnerships about their observations. Elicit responses to add to the chart.

"Everyone, quickly turn and tell your partner what else you noticed me doing to convince 'Ms. Woods' just now."

After a few minutes, I reconvened the group and solicited responses. Like Sarah, the kids noticed that when I switched from making the argument about me to making it about both me and the person I was trying to persuade, I succeeded. They noticed that supplying reasons that supported whatever the audience most cared about (in this case that kids perform well in school), also strengthened my attempt to persuade. Making comparisons to other alternatives was another persuasive technique.

Soon our chart looked like this.

> ### Persuasive Techniques to Sway an Audience
>
> - Focus on what your audience cares about.
> - Show how your audience will benefit, telling several specific ways.
> - Use a confident, persuasive (not whiny) voice.
> - Make comparisons that emphasize your point/help your audience visualize.

Set children up to continue investigating what sways an audience, this time working in partnerships to think about first one audience, then another, then another.

"Writers, let's return to our chocolate milk in school debate. It's your turn to do a little role play now. We're going to move quickly through three scenarios, so be ready to switch roles when I call out a new one.

"This is how it will work. Partner 1 will begin as the panel *of kids.* Partner 2, you'll be the person presenting one side of the topic. You can pick either side. When I say 'Go,' Partner 2, do your best to present the information to convince a panel of kids that chocolate milk in schools should stay or go. Partner 1, you have an equally important job. It's up to you to notice what works to sway you to Partner 2's belief. When Partner 2 does or says something convincing to you in your role as a kid, give him or her a quiet 'Ding, ding, ding!' Jot notes so that we can add to our chart.

"Okay, go!"

As children worked in pairs, I listened in. Most kids had decided to defend keeping chocolate milk in school—even if they had been keen proponents of ousting it up until now. The focus was on having choice and on being able to have a little treat and on the fact that chocolate milk added energy to get kids through the school day. Noticeably absent was mention of nutrition, something few kids cared about. On the other hand, some children did mention weight and personal appearance as being important to some kids.

After a few minutes I called out, "Switch roles! Partner 2, you are now the panel of parents. Be ready to take notes and to give Partner 2 a 'ding, ding, ding,' when he or she says or does something to sway you as a parent."

Again, I circulated around the meeting area. This time, lots of kids were arguing for ridding schools of chocolate milk. Their attention, by and large, was on nutrition and health. Kids cited the rise in obesity and in diseases caused by sugar and fat. Those who argued for chocolate milk this time argued for its "easy nutrition in a bottle" and said that it helped kids like school, which helped them pay attention.

Emphasize the fact that the panel is comprised of kids because your point will be that persuaders alter their argument in order to take into account the audience. Soon the audience will switch to being a group of parents.

As partners worked, I voiced over, "Partner 2s, remember that you are parents, not kids. Partner 1s, you need to convince Partner 2s as parents." I then mentioned that if we had had more time, we could have repeated the process once more, with Partner 1s as the panel made up of the principal (Ms. Granger) and school administrators. But we cut that short.

Debrief. Collect children's observations about what worked to sway them.

I reconvened the class to cull their thinking. "Writers, thumbs up if this role play was fun." Lots of thumbs shot up. "Thumbs up if it was sometimes hard to get into the head of a particular panel." Expectedly, again a lot of kids signaled yes. "Thumbs up if this exercise got you thinking about specific techniques you can use to angle your writing so that it's more convincing to a particular audience." About two thirds of the class raised their thumbs.

"Hmm. Let's add to our chart on ways to sway an audience. Maybe your new observations will get people thinking about what to do next."

Xavier offered, "I noticed that when my partner talked about things that I know about—like athletes who were in Refuel Chocolate Milk ads, I related to those athletes, and I felt more convinced. I feel like I work as hard as those athletes when I do sports, so the examples were really good for kids who are also athletes. That's when I was listening as the panel of kids. I don't know if parents or principals would know about those ads—or kids who weren't athletes."

Claire added, "Yeah, and quotes helped, too. Like when I was the parent, it felt impressive to hear something that the Surgeon General said."

Ivan said, "Sarah created a terrifying picture. If we didn't get chocolate milk, she made it seem as if we would all die."

Persuasive Techniques to Sway an Audience

- Focus on what your audience cares about.
- Show how your audience will benefit, telling several specific ways.
- Use a confident, persuasive (not whiny) voice.
- Make comparisons that emphasize your point/help your audience visualize.
- Use references that the audience will understand.
- Cite people the audience respects/trusts.

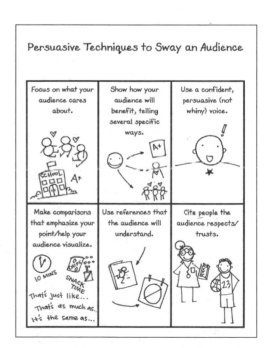

LINK

Send children off to revise their drafts, drawing on what they learned about both audience (today) and other elements of persuasion (on prior days).

"Writers, I wouldn't be surprised if your minds are in overload right now with everything you've been learning, not just right now, but also the past few days. Before you return to your seats, you may want to take a moment to review some of the charts we've made together as a way to get ready to do your best writing. Some of you may focus on bringing out a more critical perspective in your essays, others of you may be focused on coming up with counterarguments to strengthen your writing, and some of you may be weighing how powerful your evidence is, and of course, I hope that all of you will also think about audience as you work. Ask yourself, 'What can I add to my draft that will angle it to get that group of people on board with what I believe?' Okay, off you go!" As students returned to their seats, I added today's teaching point to the process chart.

How to Write an Argument

- Collect evidence that allows you to think through various sides of an argument.
  - Set up a note-taking system to organize your research.
  - Reread sources with a critical eye, looking for connections and contradictions.
- Rehearse by explaining your argument and listing your reasons point by point.
- Plan your claim and reasons into boxes-and-bullets structure.
- Use evidence to support your reasons.
  - Paraphrase, putting it into your own words.
  - Quote, and then unpack the quote, showing how it relates to the reason.
  - Use "set-up" language to prop up your sources (transitional phrases)
  - Introduce the source and explain the connection.
  - Analyze and explain the evidence.
  - Show your reader the strengths and weaknesses of your evidence.
  - Include evidence that will sway your audience.
- Include a strong introduction and conclusion.
- Anticipate critics' counterarguments, and acknowledge these in your writing, then rebut them.

Understanding Your Audience

THIS WORK HINGES ON KNOWING YOUR AUDIENCE. You need to know who you are writing to or talking to, and to know the audience not only by name or by face—but by what they care about. It will be easier to think through how to appeal to some audiences than others. Principals are clear authority figures; kids know they want students to work hard. They interact with them often. The head of food services might be more difficult.

It will be hard for kids to think through how to argue their point with audience in mind if they don't understand the audience. In such a scenario, kids are apt to continue writing what makes most sense to them and what feels most compelling to know. This means that if youngsters don't know the specific concerns that their readers will bring

to the page, they're not apt to angle their arguments differently because they've taken audience into account. If you see this, you might teach students to ask questions that will help them get to know their audience before crafting an argument. They might ask questions like, "What is their job?" "What role do they have in the world?" and then "Using what you know about their place in the world, what might they want and why?"

Once students have wrapped their minds around who they are presenting to and what that person might care about or want to know, you might set them up to practice making their cases, creating a role-play scenario similar to the one from the lesson. Writers could work in partnerships; one partner presents his case while the other

---

MID-WORKSHOP TEACHING   Choosing the Right Words for a Particular Audience

"Writers, eyes on me for a moment. I was just talking to Nick about his argument against chocolate milk in schools. Nick is going to present to a panel of kids, and he's worried that it will be a hard sale to convince them that chocolate milk should go.

"I asked him what might help, and he said, 'You know, more kid like stuff. Like that girl reporter who talked about bullies as wack. Remember?'

"He was referring to the little scene I created for all of you early on in this unit, when you were working on adding quotes to your writing. I asked what, in particular, Nick liked about the word *wack*, and he said, 'It's just, it's true, and she doesn't try to fancy it up. She just says it straight. Plus they are writing for kids, and that's words kids get.'

"I realized that Nick was onto something. I said, 'Oh, so you mean she really knows her *audience*! That is a really strategic move, to use words that will be just right for your specific audience! I don't think Ms. Granger would appreciate being told that

chocolate milk is wack, but this reporter is talking to kids. And you will be too. There are kids on your panel.'

"Nick is absolutely right that finding the perfect words is one really good way to appeal to an audience. *Before*, his writing sounded formal and was full of adult-like language. That might have worked well to convince Ms. Granger or parents, but maybe not kids. After we talked, he started adding in words that he knew other kids would 'get,' like chocolate milk is 'yummsters!' Now Nick feels much more confident about presenting to his panel.

"Let's add vocabulary to our chart. As you continue to revise, you might think about the words you're writing and how they will affect your particular panel." I added "choose vocabulary that's just right for your audience" to our chart while the students got back to work.

---

serves as the audience. When the argument feels like its missing the target, the audience makes a buzzing sound, and the writer tries again, revising his case to better suit the listener. When it feels convincing and compelling, the audience dings the bell, and partners switch roles.

Then, too, for the children who seem to be breezing through this work, you might push them to think about the many roles their audience might hold and how that could affect their argument. So, the principal might also be a parent. "How would that shift your argument? What evidence could you add or what would you revise in your work?" you might ask. Push these students to think about the many hats that any one person wears and then craft a more nuanced and complex argument as a result.

Your writers might find themselves in a sea of evidence, believing their audience needs to hear all of it to be convinced. If that's the case, you might also push your students to think about their sources. Students can lay out all their evidence, look across it and think, "Which of these sources would my audience find most credible?" Nicole was preparing for her presentation to school administrators. She was planning to convince them that chocolate milk should not be served in schools because it has too much sugar. In her draft, Nicole cited Jamie Oliver, referencing the bus full of sand that represented the sugar kids drink in flavored milk. In her notes, she had a quote from a doctor saying chocolate milk has more sugar than Coke.

I put the index card with the quote on her draft next to the paragraph where she cited Jamie Oliver. "When you write an argument, there will be many compelling pieces of information like the two you have here. In this case, writers think about the source. They think, 'Who is my audience most likely to listen to?' You have evidence from Jamie Oliver and you have evidence from a doctor. Who is your audience most likely to listen to?" She thought for a moment. "Well, I think the doctor. School administrators want kids to be healthy, and if a doctor is saying that, they'll probably agree." I

> According to Stephen Burns MD and Associate Professor at the University of Washington, "While Coke has only about 26g of sugar in an 8 oz serving, chocolate milk has 28g of sugar in one 8 oz serving."

FIG. 13–1   Naming the source and providing background compels the reader to support the argument.

coached her to take out a revision strip and jot the information she plans to include in her essay (see Figure 13–1).

After she wrote the quote on the revision strip, she noted that the quote was all numbers. "True," I agreed. "That's a really smart thing to notice. Numbers are one type of evidence. Do you think this kind of evidence will sway your audience? If you think so, you might consider adding more evidence like that." She immediately started rummaging through her notes and found one that said kids gain about five pounds a year from chocolate milk.

"I'm going to add this too because I think principals listen to numbers." She added the following line.

> Chef Jamie Oliver, a health activist and philanthropist, says kids gain about five pounds a year from chocolate milk alone.

Part of writing a complex and nuanced argument is considering the tone and voice of the piece in addition to what is being said. After students explore the many roles the audience might hold, you might coach them to think about not only what they will say, but also how they will say it. You could set out two or three different essays, all with the same thesis but written to different audiences. Children can compare and contrast the essays, thinking, "How does the author make his point known in each one? How does the voice shift depending upon the audience?" Then they could return to their own writing, studying it through the same lens, thinking about how they can revise their piece so both the content and tone match the person who will be listening intently.

Getting to Know Your Audience Even Better

Ask your students to work in their panel groups to brainstorm together ways they might most effectively convince the audience to whom they will present their argument.

"Writers, you'll see that I've put signs in each of the corners of our room with names of the people you'll be addressing soon." Pointing to the various signs, I said, "Kids are by the art supplies, parents are by my desk, Ms. Granger and other school administrators are by the library, and cafeteria workers are by the closet. Quickly and quietly, will you go to the corner where your audience is located." I gave them just a few seconds to do this, and soon they had dispersed to the four corners of the room.

"We've been talking in general terms about how to convince an audience, but in just a few days you'll be presenting your findings to a *particular* audience. I thought it might help if those of you on the same panel spent just a few minutes brainstorming how to convince parents or Ms. Granger or kids or the cafeteria workers. Pretend you're in a marketing meeting. Ask yourselves, 'What is going to especially hook my audience?' You might look at the chart we created. But you might also think about what you know about your audience. What does this group care about? Worry about? Appreciate? What will draw this group in? Go ahead and discuss."

After a few minutes, I reconvened the group.

Ask students to reflect on the process of considering an audience and to make plans for how they will, as a group, consider their audience as they present.

"Writers, what did you discover during this process? Anything surprising? Turn and tell the person sitting next to you." I solicited some responses.

Chloe said, "I realized that I don't really know my audience that well. I'm on the cafeteria workers panel, and I don't know much about the people who work in our cafeteria."

"Me, too!" Kennedy chimed in. "My panel is the school administrators, and even though we talk to them in the hallways, it's not like kids know those people so well."

"Hmm, I wonder whether you might need to do a little more research. Only this kind would be centered on getting to know your audience. If you had more time, you might try having conversations with your audience—or even conduct interviews with them to learn more.

"Right now, why don't you take a couple of minutes to make a plan for how you are going to ensure that you are speaking directly to your audience in your essays and presentations. Jot a few notes to yourselves if you like."

FOLLOWING THROUGH ON PLANS

Writers, tomorrow you are going to share your position papers with your target audience. You want to provide the most convincing argument possible. You've just made a plan for work you need to do before you go in front of your audience. Tonight your homework is to follow through on your plan. If you just realized you need to know more about your audience, conduct some research, read articles or talk to school or family members. If you need to add research and revise your essay, do so.

A Mini-Celebration

Panel Presentations, Reflection, and Goal-Setting

ear Teachers,

Today marks a slight departure from other sessions. Although you will teach a minilesson, just as you do every day, the one today will be extra mini. Its function will be to set students up for the big work of the day—the panel presentations. Today when you say "Off you go!" you won't be sending students off to write at their seats. Rather, you'll be dispersing them to their various locations around the school (or around the classroom, if you prefer), where they will be presenting their positions on chocolate milk in school to a variety of preselected audiences. After the panel presentations, you will gather students together to reflect on their presentations and their writing process as argument writers and to set their goals for Bend III of the unit.

Today's session will require a fair amount of preparation. You will need to select and secure audiences to attend students' panel presentations, decide where the panels will meet, which kids will present to which audiences, and how.

If you decide to spread your panels throughout the school, perhaps one might take place in the cafeteria with the "nutrition specialists" (aka the cafeteria staff and school nurse or PE instructor), a second in the principal's office with a few key school administrators, a third in the auditorium with parents, and a fourth in the gym with kids from other classes. Of course, if you spread out the panels this way, be sure you can recruit facilitators for each one—perhaps other teachers or adult volunteers.

You'll need to consider, too, the logistics of the panel presentations themselves. To give these an official feel, you might, in advance of this day, print and staple each group's position papers and then put out a few on display for the audience to peruse, perhaps side by side with the sources children drew on to support their arguments. Each panel of students might then give short oral presentations in defense of their positions; two or three kids can represent each side, taking turns to offer just a few key points. Once both sides have presented, there could be time for questions from the audience. Although these panels won't function as formal debates, by now children will have learned enough about debate to engage in a little lively back-and-forth, should their panel discussions lead to this (you may want to prepare them for this possibility so that they hone their debate skills, anticipate questions and counter-arguments, and are prepared to respond and rebut).

Finally, you'll need to determine how the argument "winners" will be decided and what the outcome will be. You might select a committee made up of one member of each audience to vote, post-panels, for the most convincing side. In the event that the pro-chocolate milk side is successful, the school might allow those students to advertise their findings in a public way, perhaps posting posters in the cafeteria (or distributing letters to classrooms) promoting the benefits of drinking chocolate milk. Or the pro-chocolate milk students might present their findings on an additional panel one day in the cafeteria, to any kids or teachers passing by. On the other hand, if those kids arguing against chocolate milk are declared more convincing, perhaps the school might, in fact, ban chocolate milk from the cafeteria for the remainder of the year, and those students could hang or distribute materials explaining why. Of course, neither side may "win." Another possibility is that panel members themselves work on a position that they can both agree on, such as posting the calories and added sugar content of chocolate milk or distributing fliers or only banning it for the school's youngest (grades K–2) students, with the explanation that kids that little don't yet have the maturity to make such an important health decision. (Of course, this might incite an unfavorable reaction from primary students, but then, that might be an opportunity for yet another form of argument-based writing!)

However you decide to publicize your decision, be sure to tell your class that the outcome will only be in effect for the remainder of the year. That way, next year's fifth-graders can tackle this same issue in a similar forum, and you also won't instigate a schoolwide rebellion!

However you decide to operate your own school's work around these panels, bear in mind that your fifth-graders have worked diligently to prepare for today, so it's important that the symposium itself maintain that feeling of rigor and the conviction that its outcome matters. Above all, your goal is to convey to students that their voices carry weight; that they have the power to argue—and to effect change.

MINILESSON

As soon as children are gathered on the rug, tell them that today's minilesson will be a quick setup for the bigger work of today—the panels! You might say something like, "Writers, let's not waste one minute, because very soon each one of you will be presenting your findings to an audience. The research and writing and thinking you've put into this very important topic is no small feat. Give yourselves a quick pat on the back!"

Then say, "Here's the thing, though. All that hard work you've done to prepare for today's panels will be for naught if you don't give equal care to how you present yourself today. 'You've heard the saying that a person needs to 'dress the part.' You know how to do that. If you go to a wedding, you dress for that occasion. If you go on a hike, you dress for that occasion. Today you need to dress for the role of being a member of a panel, a symposium. I don't actually mean you need to dress for this part—none of you can rush home and get on a new outfit before our panels begin—but today," and this would be your teaching point, "I want to teach you that when people are part of a panel—when their goal is to convince an audience

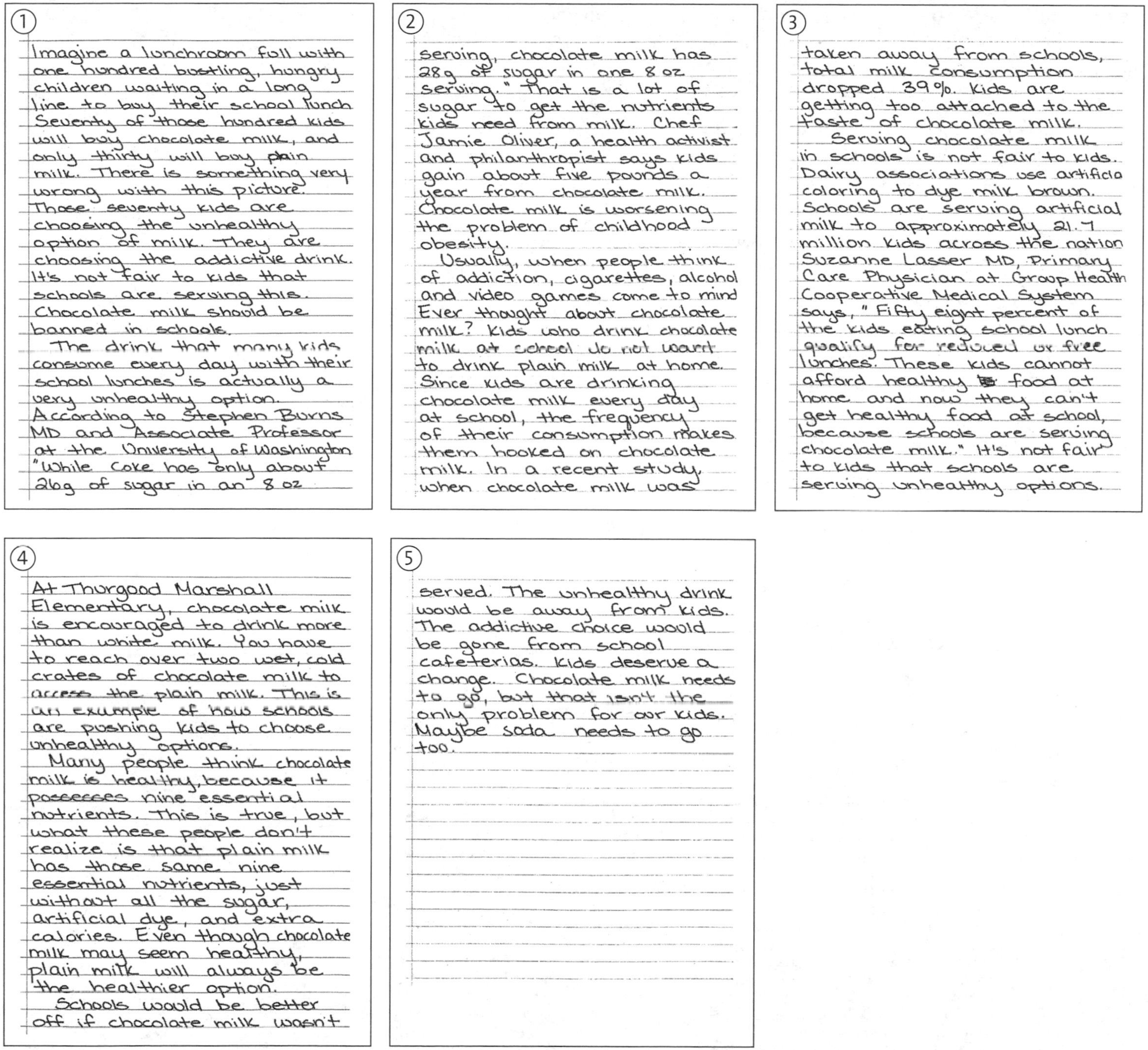

1

Imagine a lunchroom full with one hundred bustling, hungry children waiting in a long line to buy their school lunch. Seventy of those hundred kids will buy chocolate milk, and only thirty will buy plain milk. There is something very wrong with this picture. Those seventy kids are choosing the unhealthy option of milk. They are choosing the addictive drink. It's not fair to kids that schools are serving this. Chocolate milk should be banned in schools.

The drink that many kids consume every day with their school lunches is actually a very unhealthy option. According to Stephen Burns MD and Associate Professor at the University of Washington "While Coke has only about 26g of sugar in an 8 oz

2

serving, chocolate milk has 28g of sugar in one 8 oz serving." That is a lot of sugar to get the nutrients kids need from milk. Chef Jamie Oliver, a health activist and philanthropist says kids gain about five pounds a year from chocolate milk. Chocolate milk is worsening the problem of childhood obesity.

Usually, when people think of addiction, cigarettes, alcohol and video games come to mind. Ever thought about chocolate milk? Kids who drink chocolate milk at school do not want to drink plain milk at home. Since kids are drinking chocolate milk every day at school, the frequency of their consumption makes them hooked on chocolate milk. In a recent study, when chocolate milk was

3

taken away from schools, total milk consumption dropped 39%. Kids are getting too attached to the taste of chocolate milk.

Serving chocolate milk in schools is not fair to kids. Dairy associations use artificial coloring to dye milk brown. Schools are serving artificial milk to approximately 21.7 million kids across the nation. Suzanne Lasser MD, Primary Care Physician at Group Health Cooperative Medical System says, "Fifty eight percent of the kids eating school lunch qualify for reduced or free lunches. These kids cannot afford healthy food at home and now they can't get healthy food at school, because schools are serving chocolate milk." It's not fair to kids that schools are serving unhealthy options.

4

At Thurgood Marshall Elementary, chocolate milk is encouraged to drink more than white milk. You have to reach over two wet, cold crates of chocolate milk to access the plain milk. This is an example of how schools are pushing kids to choose unhealthy options.

Many people think chocolate milk is healthy, because it possesses nine essential nutrients. This is true, but what these people don't realize is that plain milk has those same nine essential nutrients, just without all the sugar, artificial dye, and extra calories. Even though chocolate milk may seem healthy, plain milk will always be the healthier option.

Schools would be better off if chocolate milk wasn't

5

served. The unhealthy drink would be away from kids. The addictive choice would be gone from school cafeterias. Kids deserve a change. Chocolate milk needs to go, but that isn't the only problem for our kids. Maybe soda needs to go too.

FIG. 14–1   Nicole's position paper in favor of banning chocolate milk from schools

in some way—they rise to the occasion. They dress the part. Specifically, they stand up tall, they speak in a loud, clear voice, they don't fidget or giggle, and they greet and engage politely with the audience."

Next, launch into a combined teaching and active engagement in which you quickly demonstrate first presenting poorly (hunch over your paper, mumble, flop your arms every which way, launch into a fit of giggles) and then presenting clearly, with some formality (stand up straight and make eye contact with kids each time you look up from your paper; read in a clear, loud, steady voice). Then set children up to work in partnerships to have a go at this themselves. One partner can be the audience and the other, the presenter, and then they can switch roles. Channel your students to try out first what not to do and then what to do. This whole role play should move quickly—thirty seconds for a role. Say something like, "Partner 1, you're the terrible presenter. Partner 2, you're the audience. Go!" And then, "Stay in the same roles, but Partner 1, now be a successful presenter. Go!"

Once children have practiced this way, make sure they each have their position papers, and then send them off to their panels. Ideally, there will be an adult on hand to help moderate each panel. Meanwhile, you may want to circulate between panels. Because you will want these to feel as formal as possible, and because they may take place in various spots around the school, you won't interrupt the panels for a mid-workshop teaching or confer with children. You may need to coach in a bit from the sidelines, as needed.

① Chocolate Milk is Good,
And Good for You

By Xavier

For years, people have been arguing about whether or not chocolate milk is good for you. Some people think it's bad because of the sugar and fat in the milk, but research shows that chocolate milk is actually good for you. It helps your body fend off fat, it has nutrients that your body needs, and it gives you energy, especially after exercising. Chocolate milk is good for your body.

Chocolate milk helps your body fend off fat. Researchers at Penn State have been studying how cocoa makes the fat from chocolate milk break down. They have found that the cocoa makes the fat in chocolate milk breaks down in our bodies before it has time to be absorbed. "Compounds in cocoa inhibit the activity of the pancreatic lipase enzyme," says researcher Josh Lambert, which stops the body from digesting the fat. That means that chocolate milk helps your body fend off fat that it doesn't need. This means that you don't gain a lot of weight after drinking chocolate milk.

Chocolate milk has nutrients that are good for your body. This is important because the nutrients it has are the

② nutrients that you don't get enough of, and the nutrients that your body needs the most. Chocolate milk has nine nutrients that your body needs: protein, calcium, vitamins A, B2, B3, B12, and D, phosphorous and potassium.

Researcher and Medical Doctor Keith Ayoob says, "Removing nutrient-rich chocolate milk creates unintended consequences for kids' nutrition." They won't get enough of the missing nutrients in chocolate milk, and they might drink soda or other drinks that have way more sugar and calories and less nutrients.

Also, 71% of parents agree that drinking chocolate milk is a perfect way to give kids nutrients. They think that if you take chocolate milk away, then kids won't get the nutrients that are critical to their bodies. Chocolate milk gives you nutrients that your body needs.

Chocolate milk is a great way to give you energy. After you drink it, your muscles refuel with the protein, and you can exercise more and longer after you drink it. "Protein is instrumental in rebuilding muscle damaged from a tough workout," says Jill Barker of the Montreal Gazette. A lot of people agree, and even pro athletes are drinking chocolate milk after their workouts.

"Small exercise studies have found that chocolate milk can help boost endurance after intense workouts," says

③ reporter Allison Aubrey of NPR. This means it gives you energy. Laboratory testing has shown more than once that athletes get more energy for a longer period of time from drinking chocolate milk compared to Gatorade.

"I think in years past, you would have been a little bit strange if you drank chocolate milk immediately after a run. But now it's absolutely mainstream," says runner Dan DiFonzo. This is important not only because it helps top athletes, but it can also help active people, and could become one of the top sports drinks in the world.

Some people think chocolate milk isn't good for your body because it has too much sugar. British celebrity TV chef Jamie Oliver even appeared on *Jimmy Kimmel Live!* to try to show that chocolate milk is pretty much soda because of all the sugar it has. However, most of the sugar in chocolate milk is natural, not added. While the added sugar is not necessarily good for you, the cocoa helps your body fend off the fat and use the protein so you don't gain as much weight compared to drinking Gatorade or other sports drinks.

Chocolate milk is healthy, and it helps your body. You don't gain a lot of weight from it, it has nutrients that are really important, and it gives your muscles energy so you can rebuild your muscle strength and continue to perform really well.

④ Chocolate milk could grow to be one of the healthiest drinks in the world - if it isn't already!

FIG. 14–2   Xavier's position paper in favor of chocolate milk in schools

Some of your coaching might be nonverbal cues to children. For example, Nicole was presenting to the principal and assistant principal. As she began to read (see Figure 14–1), her lip quivered a bit and her voice wavered through the first line. I stood up tall and made a fist, gesturing strength. She cleared her throat and began again, this time with conviction. After Nicole finished, the principal asked, "If we take away the chocolate milk, how will we make sure that kids get their nutrients? According to your argument, we've gotten them hooked and now they won't drink plain milk." Nicole looked at me, unsure if she should take the question. I gestured for her to go ahead and answer, giving her a thumbs up and a grin before moving on to the next panel.

Once the panel presentations have concluded and the whole class is back in your room, you'll want to lead a share that sets children up to do two very important things. First, quickly reflect on the work they've done that culminated in their presentations, thinking, "What worked especially well?" and "What might they have done differently?" Second, revisit the Opinion Writing Checklist, and consider which of these they have within grasp and which they might cultivate going forward. That is, you'll want children to set goals for the next bend, taking stock both of what they do especially well—where their argument writing talents lie—and of areas they might stand to improve. Children will need to draw on both as they pursue new projects with greater independence in the final stretch of this unit.

To prepare for this share, you will need the Opinion Writing Checklist for Grades 5 and 6. You might put your copy on the overhead projector and quickly explain the categories, then hand out clean copies of the checklist to students. Writers can then either work with partners or alone to reflect on these categories within their argument essays. Certainly, they can consider their oral presentations as well. Which categories of argument-writing skills do they think they have under their belts? Which categories need more work? Students can use the colors to mark parts of their essays that correspond to that category, making marginal notes to themselves related to strengths, weaknesses, and goals.

Then they can consider which categories could stand some attention as they move on to their next project. Each child might jot down a few concrete goals for themselves for the final stretch of the unit and as argument writers. These should feel meaningful, so encourage students to give them some attention and

Opinion Writing Checklist

	Grade 5	NOT YET	STARTING TO	YES!	Grade 6	NOT YET	STARTING TO	YES!
	Structure				**Structure**			
Overall	I made a claim or thesis on a topic or text, supported it with reasons, and provided a variety of evidence for each reason.	☐	☐	☐	I not only staked a position that could be supported by a variety of trustworthy sources, but also built my argument and led to a conclusion in each part of my text.	☐	☐	☐
Lead	I wrote an introduction that led to a claim or thesis and got my readers to care about my opinion. I got my readers to care by not only including a cool fact or jazzy question, but also figuring out was significant in or around the topic and giving readers information about what was significant about the topic.	☐	☐	☐	I wrote an introduction that helped readers to understand and care about the topic or text. I thought backwards between the piece and the introduction to make sure that the introduction fit with the whole.	☐	☐	☐
	I worked to find the precise words to state my claim; I let readers know the reasons I would develop later.				I not only clearly stated my claim, but also named the reasons I would develop later. I also told my readers how my text would unfold.			
Transitions	I used transition words and phrases to connect evidence back to my reasons using phrases such as *this shows that*	☐	☐	☐	I used transitional phrases to help readers understand how the different parts of my piece fit together to support my argument.	☐	☐	☐
	I helped readers follow my thinking with phrases such as *another reason* and *the most important reason*. I used phrases such as *consequently* and *because of* to show what happened.	☐	☐	☐				
	I used words such as *specifically* and *in particular* in order to be more precise.	☐	☐	☐				

to capture their goals in ways that feel lofty yet specific enough to be measurable down the line. Rather than record, "I want to work on reaching my audience," a child might write, "I want to find a deeper way to connect with my audience. I'm going to try to ask questions during interviews that help me better understand my audience so that I can write an essay with details that really reach and sway that audience."

This whole day—and certainly this final component—should feel celebratory. Truly, your children have much to be proud of. And now they are positioned to hone their skills yet further in this next bend, to continue to draw on their talents and passions, and to work with greater independence on projects of their own choosing—ones that will be close to their hearts.

Enjoy!

Lucy, Mary, and Annie

Argument across the Curriculum

ear Teachers,

Typically, in these letters we suggest work that can take place within the writing workshop to further the work of the unit. In this letter, however, we will suggest that you might make time in other parts of your day to strengthen your students' skills in argument.

We developed this idea in a think tank, which we mentioned before, comprised of staff members of the Teachers College Reading and Writing Project and a team from CBAL, which is a research and development arm of Educational Testing Services. Working together with funding from the CCSSO (Council of Chief State School Officers), we've been studying ways to strengthen students' work in argument writing and ways to use learning progressions to support and track that growth. As part of this, we've talked about the fact that although many students grow up immersed in a culture of storytelling, few grow up within a culture of argumentation and debate. Yet, with the adoption of world-class standards, argument writing (and really, argument reading) have moved front and center as priorities for students' literacy development.

We've come to believe, then, that it would be advantageous to students if we found opportunities throughout the day to immerse them in a culture of debate, or argumentation (in the best sense of that word). And we believe that it would invigorate the school day to find many opportunities, often, for students to take and defend positions, to learn from argument and counterargument. The research is clear that if students have opportunities to do the work orally that we hope they will learn to do as writers, this is advantageous to them.

SETTING UP A DEBATE ABOUT A TEXT IN CLASS

We recommend, therefore, that you might start a whole-class read-aloud by letting students know that instead of listening to develop ideas about the characters and the story, you're asking students to instead listen with an argument in mind, weighing which position they want to take on in that argument. You could decide to read aloud a familiar text, asking students to experience that text differently than usual, or you could work with a new text. If for example, you choose to read aloud "Stray," a short story from *Every Living Thing*, by Cynthia Rylant, you might say "Some see Doris as *strong*, while others see her as *weak*," and ask your students to listen in a way that allows them to decide which position they will take and why.

Help Students Create an Argument as You Read Aloud

As you read, you will want to nudge students to think deeply by pausing in selected spots to react ("Whoa! Big stuff!") and to ask students to stop and jot, drawing on their knowledge of note-taking, or to turn and talk, pushing themselves to think as deeply as possible about the argument at hand. When selecting spots to pause, be sure to choose ones where the text could be supporting either of the positions. If you have a hunch that one position might be far more popular, you might strategically pause at places where the evidence can be seen to be more in favor of the underdog position. That is, if I know many in the class might say that Doris is strong, I might purposefully ask them to stop and jot at moments where she may not be acting with as much strength. You might offer prompts like the following to nudge students to turn and talk or to stop and jot.

- "Let's stop here to think about what we know about _____ so far. What position are you starting to take on the character so far? Make some notes to yourself. Jot, 'So far, I am taking the position that . . .'"

- "Are you thinking about that question? What position are you taking right now? What reasons and evidence have you gathered? Tell your partner what position you are taking and why."

- "Now that we've finished reading, what are you thinking? What position do you take? Look over your notes and get ready to choose a position. You can revise or add to your notes. Do that now."

After you finish reading the text (or part of the text), give students a few minutes to consider the argument you posed at the start and make their decision. Position A or position B?

Let Students Know How a Debate Goes and Begin!

We generally use a format that is similar to the structure of formal debates but differs in ways that offer more scaffolds. Our intention is to give students time to plan with others who take the same position, and also to create an urgent, intense, engaging process that supports students becoming more at home with the positioning and conversational moves that are integral to debate.

To start this process, ask your students to take sides on the initial question. How many think Doris is strong? How many think Doris is weak? With a show of hands, you can see if your groups are roughly equal, and if they are not, you'll need to recruit some of your stronger students to tackle the more challenging job of defending a side they don't actually support, which is an important skill to develop. In any case, we suggest that you form two groups that are equal in size, with those who agree with position A lining up in front of your right arm and those who agree with position B lining up beside where you are gesturing with your left arm. Eventually, when you repeat this protocol using other texts, you may ask students to also choose to stand in the middle station if they feel they could argue either side, allowing you to position them where you need them. In any case, on the first day of engaging in debate, we suggest that the two lines turn to face each other so that each person in a line can shake hands with the person in front of him or her from the other line, forming opponent teams of two.

You might quickly overview the major parts of the upcoming process with students.

Steps Involved in Arguing about Texts

Analyze text(s), gathering evidence and ideas so as to take a position.

Caucus with those who share your position to plan what your claim, evidence, and reasons will be, referring to the text.

State your case in front of your opponent. Explain your position with reasons and evidence.

Say back your opponent's best point.

Caucus with those who share your position to plan a point-by-point rebuttal of your opponent's position.

Rebut each point from each opponent.

Conclude by reminding listeners of your most compelling points and perhaps most compelling rebuttals or by developing a shared position.

Now the debating begins! We suggest keeping students aware of time by announcing when it is each opponent's time to speak and when there is only a bit of time left in a part of the process. Set a time limit on the time they have to debate (and keep this very brief) as this can help to push them to be more organized and efficient in the way they lay out their case.

Expect that this process may not be one that is smooth sailing the first time your students experience it. Like anything, repeated practice will help your students to get stronger and stronger. Before long, this can be a familiar routine in your classroom, the same way that argument can become a familiar element across your curriculum.

Coaching to Raise the Level of the Arguments

If your students can manage the above process of debating with aplomb, here are a few ways you can teach into their work to raise the bar.

Teach them to strengthen the organization of their arguments. As students plan their initial position and reasons, you could coach them to remember the structure of essays, reminding them that the boxes-and-bullets structure that has been so helpful to them in organizing their essays can also be helpful in debate. The box (which you can also illustrate as the palm of your hand) might represent their position and the bullets (which you can illustrate by tapping your fingers), their reasons. As students cite evidence by drawing on the text, you might coach them to think whether there are categories to their evidence or whether some should be saved for last.

Teach them to consider counterarguments as they plan. You might say, "Look for holes in your own evidence and shore it up—like you are defending a castle that you know has a weak spot. Imagine you are defending your castle against attackers. Picture your enemy's strategy and your weak spots. That's where you want to put archers or build a high fence. You want to anticipate and counter what someone might say against you as you lay out your case."

Teach them to be strategic about presenting evidence. You might say to students, "Some evidence is stronger than other evidence. Think over the evidence you laid out to support your position. You are probably realizing that there was at least one piece of evidence that was the best. Maybe it was the most powerful; maybe it showed exactly the point you wanted to make; maybe it was the hardest for someone else to argue against. Point right now to the piece of evidence you have that is the best. Well, I want to give you the tip that you want to be strategic about how and when you give this evidence. If this is, let's say, your secret weapon, when you do use it? Right up front? Or do you hold it back and wait 'til the end to use it? You want to think about how you will lay out your evidence and be strategic about when you use it."

Teach them to connect evidence to the point. If students seem ready for more coaching, you could tell them, "You don't want to just lay out your evidence, like just blah, blah, blah and lay it right at your opponent's feet. Instead, you want to connect each piece of evidence to your point or points. You want to make sure that there is no way that your opponent will be able to say that your evidence does not prove your point. So here are some moves I have added to the chart to help you do that kind of work.

This shows that . . .
This means that . . .

Teach them to rebut each of the opponent's points systematically. Another bit of advice you could offer could go like this: "The goal is to poke holes in your opponent's argument, and there are some specific tips I want to give you to help you to do this.

"The first is that you want to address each of your opponent's main points and then show how each of those points is a problem. It's like your opponent is standing on a table and you want to knock out each of the legs so your opponent is left standing on nothing. To do this, you can show how your opponent has overlooked something or is not showing the whole story. You might use some prompts like":

- So your point seems to be . . . but that doesn't explain why . . .

- So you are claiming that . . . yet that overlooks . . .

- So you are saying . . . However, what about the fact that . . . ?

Concluding the Debate

You might conclude the debate by having the opponents become partners and work together to create position C, a more nuanced statement that each partner can agree with and argue for with reasons and evidence that fits most of the story. You might even ask them to flash-draft an essay (either in tandem or independently) of this new position.

You might also set students up for a second round of debate by offering some tips, now (assuming you did not do this already) to raise the level of the work. They might hold another debate the next day, this time on another text or topic.

DEBATING ACROSS THE CURRICULUM

Of course, this debating does not have to take place only during read-aloud. Your students could debate across the curriculum. Imagine watching your students argue the merits of being a Loyalist or a Tory in social studies. Imagine them arguing over which hypothesis is more likely to be proven correct in science!

You might also get students ready to argue by creating situations for debate over everyday matters, such as letting them choose the next class field trip, for example. "Should we go to the zoo or the museum?" you might ask them, and let them argue to decide. Once they decide, of course, they can work to persuade different audiences—administration, parents, other classes—that their choice should be accepted. The possibilities are endless, and all of this argument work will, in the end, strengthen students' listening and speaking skills, their ability to argue and to evaluate others' arguments, and of course, their ability to develop written argument.

HOMEWORK

Writers, Margaret Thatcher once said, "I love argument, I love debate. I don't expect anyone just to sit there and agree with me, that's not their job." You love argument, you love debate. Tonight for homework, don't just sit there and agree with people at home. Argue! Think of someone you could talk to (a sibling, parent, or neighbor) then pick a topic you two could debate. You might debate whether or not you should get a new pet, or which animal would make for the best pet. You might debate which is the best dinner, or, whether or not you should have homework. The possibilities are endless!

Each of you will take a side, state your claim, support it with reasons and evidence, and refute the counterclaim. Remember to use what you know about writing arguments. Weigh your evidence. Think, "Is this a logical argument or do I have flaws in my reasoning?" And, consider your audience—use your tone of voice, language, and evidence to sway them.

Then, once you've participated in this debate, flash-draft an essay in which you state your claim, forecast your reasons supporting that claim, and then add researched reasons in a separate paragraph. Provide the same evidence in support of each reason as you did in the debate. The flash-draft should require no more than twenty minutes of fast and furious drafting.

To great debates,

Lucy, Mary, and Annie

Taking Opportunities to Stand and Be Counted

IN THIS SESSION, you'll teach children that argument writers stand up for what they believe in, drawing on all they have learned to build a strong case.

GETTING READY

✔ Story of a time something bothered you, so you gathered research and made an argument, fighting until you caused circumstances to change (see Teaching)

✔ Students' writer's notebooks and pencils (see Active Engagement, Conferring, and Share)

✔ "How to Write an Argument" chart (see Share)

B Y NOW, YOU'VE BECOME ACCUSTOMED TO THE FINAL BEND in most units providing students with a time to work with more independence on the kind of writing they have just studied, with your support. This bend, then, is no exception.

For the last portion of this unit, you let students know that argument is a life skill, not just a school skill. Encourage students to see the real-world payoff to the skills they have been developing, and channel them to imagine, organize, embark on, and carry out an independent project using argumentation to advocate on behalf of issues they care about. Not only will students be choosing their own topics, but they will be choosing their audience and the genre of argument writing that best suits their project. Some students will be writing to bring others along in their thinking, in which case a persuasive essay is likely to be the best fit. Some students will be writing to convince someone in particular, in which case a persuasive letter is the best fit. Still others will be presenting an argument to a concerned group, in which case a petition is the best fit. All of these genres are ones that have been introduced in earlier grades in these units of study. They are all, essentially, argument essays adapted to a specific audience. Mostly, you'll reinforce that now that students have honed their argument skills they can deploy those skills in many types of writing and speaking, for many purposes.

In teaching, the real-world nitty-gritty challenges are ever present, and frankly, this final bend in the unit is replete with them. The reason that we suggested all students inquire into the pros and cons of chocolate milk for the bulk of the unit was because we are fully aware that it's nigh impossible for you to marshal resources—especially texts that offer conflicting perspectives—on the twenty-eight or so topics that your kids will choose when you invite them to choose issues that matter to them. Some of your students will be able to find their own texts on the topics they select, but we're well aware of how complicated that is. You'll see, then, that because we're aware that finding texts will be challenging for some students, we help students select topics on which they have personal expertise, and we channel them to use surveying and interviewing and observation as well as reading to learn different perspectives of the topic. These methods of investigative research are also important and will balance text-based research in many types of argument writing.

"We want to end the unit by giving students a chance to write about topics that get their blood boiling or their sense of justice offended."

So, yes, this last bend in the unit is a bit messy. Expect students to bite off more than they can chew, to take on a topic that makes you antsy, to slip somewhat as they strive to be independent and daring. We hope the bend is not only messy, but also more than a bit inspiring, exciting, and significant. We want to end the unit by giving students a chance to write about topics that get their blood boiling or their sense of justice offended. We want to help them take what they've learned and use it to speak up, to make change, to learn to be heard.

At the same time, of course, we also aim to take students' argument writing skills up a notch or two, giving them a chance to practice and become more at home with writing point and counterpoint, with weighing the validity of their argument, with writing in ways that appeal to an audience—in short, with the more advanced work of writing arguments.

Taking Opportunities to Stand and Be Counted

CONNECTION

Stand back for a moment to review what your students have done, and then use their past success to propel them toward a future project that has scope and significance.

"Writers, between your panel and the debate we did the other day, the work you have been doing is significant. You've all done a great job. Because of your thinking, debating, and writing, you've made all of us look at texts differently, and at chocolate milk differently.

"You may have thought, writers, that the past few weeks were all about chocolate milk. And that issue was certainly the focus of your arguments. But as I watched you research and argue, I have realized that, actually, you have been learning to become effective activists, to become people who fight hard to make changes in the world. Now that you've made people look differently at chocolate milk, I'm thinking you can use your writing to make others in your community think differently about other things as well. That's huge."

❖ Name the teaching point.

"Social activists fight to make change. They get involved with things they know and care about, do their research, and then write or speak to affect the ways others see that same topic. To become social activists, you need to use all the skills you've learned up until today to argue for things that matter to you."

Your job sometimes involves being not a teacher, but a preacher. Today you will rally students to use their writing for a purpose. You need to teach this lesson with unwavering confidence and commitment, as if you are totally sure that your students each care deeply about a particular cause and are eager to use writing to advance that cause. Your confidence will bring students along.

World-class state standards were designed so that students would spend their K–12 years developing the skills that are important in college. And it is certainly true that the most rigorous colleges ask students to read in order to argue the merits of one position or another. But we resist the idea that a child's entire K–12 education is preparation for college. We embrace the genre of argument writing not just because this is important preparation for college, but also because this is important to life in a democracy. This nation needs educated, critical citizens who can carefully review evidence, who can be open-minded, suspending judgment until listening to all sides, and who can argue forcefully and effectively. The goals for this unit, then, go far beyond that of college preparation.

TEACHING

Recall an earlier story you told about using writing to make a difference, and point out that that one incident was just one of many times when you've written to effect change. Tell the story of another time.

"Do you remember the story I told you about trying to influence where I went to high school? That was an issue that mattered to me, and so I gathered research and presented my case, and in the end I was able to change my parents' thinking and switch schools. In my life, there have been lots of times when I've found causes and concerns that need to be addressed, and I've used the skills you all are developing.

"Writers, here's a true story. When I was in college, I lived in a dorm building that's over a hundred years old. So while it is architecturally very beautiful—old buildings usually are—it had antique plumbing. One day I found some mold growing on the wall. So I complained to the building owner, but no one came to check. So I complained again and a guy came, poked around, mumbled something and left. Two weeks went by with no action from Housing. That mold kept spreading and becoming more grotesque, and actually developed fuzzy little spore sacs. I know because I inspected it with a magnifying glass. I started feeling a little wheezy too. When I visited the doctor, he wanted to know, 'Was there something new in my environment that might be causing an allergic reaction?' I told him I suspected it was the darn mold, and he nodded, a little shocked at the fact that I was living in such conditions.

"Well, that was it! I realized it just wasn't right. This had gone on long enough. I also realized that things could get even worse! That night, I borrowed a classmate's camera, zoomed in on that mold and took some gory close ups. I had found my argument!

"I went into the room next to mine and checked that wall—and found that there were beginnings of mold there too. I talked to that neighbor and photographed her wall. I went back to the doctor and interviewed him about the harmful effects of such a mold on a person's health. I Internet-searched fungal infections. I fished out the official complaint note I had sent to the Housing Office. And once I had all this evidence with me, I began to write."

Explain that when you wrote to make a difference, you not only did make change, but you also began a lifetime of writing for real-world purposes. Overview other times you've used writing to make a difference.

"Writers, the good news is that I was moved to a new room fast, and they returned three months' rent. But the better news is that I have never stopped writing about things that need to be changed in my world. I learned to collect evidence and use it to argue for action. When a professor said I didn't have the right experience and background to sit in his class, I fished out evidence of all my relevant experience—recommendation letters from old teachers, evaluation reports that showed how good I was—and wrote to him, arguing to be given just one chance. When my school wouldn't give me funds for our classroom library, I researched statistics that showed the effects of reading on performance in state tests. I researched websites that sell used books for half price. I researched wasteful expenditures in the school that could easily be cut down. And I wrote to the school board, arguing for the money. Writers, I got the money.

"The reason I'm telling you all this is that I want you to see that when I looked around me, *at my life*, I noticed stuff that was *not right around me*, that had gone on *for quite a while*, and that was something worth researching and arguing."

This is a long, detailed story. You may decide it is too long—too detailed—and it might be. But on the other hand, details make a story, and they are as important when you are teaching a minilesson as when you are writing a narrative. One of the important things to realize is that the qualities of good writing are also qualities of good minilessons.

You'll notice that these stories do not emphasize the entire process of writing an argument. There is less of a focus on weighing the evidence, less on considering alternate points of view, and more of a focus on writing to convince. You may decide to tell a story that highlights something a bit different. We were aware that we were focusing above all on the purposes of writing and felt that at this point, stirring children to want to write for real-world causes was our most important mission.

Teachers, we're writing from our experience and you may want to do the same. It's great if you can think of your own narrative about a time when you conducted research to affect change, noting the steps that you took and naming different pieces of evidence that you gathered. In the next session, you will share the research (photographs, articles, interviews, etc.) that you collected so be sure to pick a topic for which you have, or could gather, those samples. On the other hand, you may decide to borrow our example, devoting your time to your students' work rather than to digging up old photos and letters.

ACTIVE ENGAGEMENT

Channel students to list a few possible topics for the next argument piece they'll write and then to plan one of those topics.

"So my question to you today is this: What is it that you want someone in your world—someone in your life—to think differently about or do something about? What would you like to change? What little or big thing at home?" I paused for two seconds, a brief pool of silence for children's minds to wander home in. "What little something—or big something—that you notice on your way to school every morning?" Again, I paused slightly to allow children to imagine the bus ride or carpool. "What about during school assembly? In the courtyard? At the playground? In the halls? During class? After school? On your team?

"Now that you've found your argument-writing voice, you can take any issue and argue to change it. In silence, for a minute, I want you to list things you've experienced or observed that you want to argue about and change."

After another two minutes, I called out, "You've got great ideas for argument essays. Now, try jotting some boxes and bullets for one or two of these ideas. Imagine you were planning an argument right now. How might it go? Write a plan." While students wrote, I read over their shoulders. I noticed that Caroline's notebook looked like this:

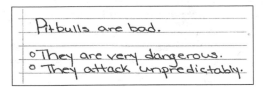

FIG. 16–1 The reasons support the opinion and build upon each other.

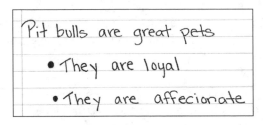

FIG. 16–2 Caroline's partner took the opposing position.

LINK

Disperse children with partners to rehearse for the writing they'll soon do. Suggest they write essays in the air to each other as a way of trying out different possible plans for their essays.

"Writers, you just wrote down some issues that you care about, and you jotted some notes in boxes-and-bullets form. Right now, will you take your partner to a quiet spot in the room, and will you rehearse your favorite idea by giving a little argument speech about it, using your boxes-and-bullets plan? Try one idea and another. This technique is really helpful for exploring possible ideas. It's almost as if you imagine the essay, as a way of making sure your idea is a good one."

Teachers, it will help to pause between your words, inviting children's minds to scan these familiar, frequented areas. Leave blocks of silence. Your goal is to inspire introspection, to get children's minds wandering to the dining rooms and back alleys, to Grandma's and to the dentist's—places where the issues closest to them might be hiding, places that you or I, their teachers, can't reach.

Don't be afraid to expect students to produce topics and plans quickly. We've taught this lesson often, and you'd be amazed at how quickly students generate topics and plans.

After children talked for a bit, I asked them to stop and listen. "Writers, before you actually start flash-drafting your essay, will you take a minute to think about your claim, about the idea you are advancing? Oftentimes writers start with something really general. 'I think fifth-graders should plan their own graduation.' Or 'Littering is bad.'

"Almost always, a claim is stronger if it is more specific. To make it more specific, it helps to say your claim out loud a bunch of times, until you've found a way to say exactly what you mean. Will you try that now? Just write your claim, and then write, 'In other words . . . ' and write it again." I suspected that Caroline would benefit from some support with making her claim more specific, so I circled back to check in with her. I read over her shoulder.

> Pit bulls are bad.
> In other words, they are very dangerous.

I coached leanly, "Why does all this matter? What feels most important?" She tried it one more time, adding the following line to her notebook.

> In other words, people shouldn't have them as pets. They should be banned.

After students did this for a few minutes, I said, "Circle the claim that seems most specific and most accurate, one that you think you could produce evidence to support. As you go back to work, you're going to want to be considering what audience is the best fit for your topic. Who are you trying to convince? And that will help you decide what form your argument will take. Are you writing a letter, to convince one person in particular? A petition, to convince a lot of people to make something happen? A position paper or editorial, to help sway a lot of people's opinions about a big idea? Keep all of that in mind as you rehearse and draft! Okay, back to work! I'm sure you will need a few more moments for rehearsing before you switch to your writing work. Don't forget to use the tools in the room to help you." I pointed to the chart "How to Write an Argument" as the students began.

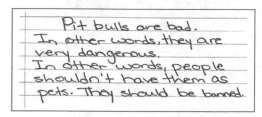

FIG. 16–3 Caroline is narrowing her claim. The first try at a claim is still general and overlaps with one of the reasons, while the second is specific and will focus the research and argument.

We realize that this is a longer and more involved link than usual, but we recommend taking the extra time here to support students as they launch into this brand-new work. Taking the time to help them get focused early on will pay off! Also, teachers, remember that it will help to keep in mind that one of the ways to support students at all ability levels is to allow students who are less proficient to write about less focused claims. These are easier to support.

Finding a Topic and Planning Your Essay with Audience in Mind

YOU MIGHT ANTICIPATE THAT SOME OF YOUR WRITERS will need additional support as they get started. There might be some who struggle to come up with a topic. Thinking about things they want to change might prove difficult. If so, you might teach them to look back through their notebooks and study their entries from personal narrative and memoir. They might look through their entries thinking, "Is there a topic I tend to write about a lot? Is an issue hiding in there?"

For example, when I coached Nate to look back through his notebook, he noticed a small moment about track tryouts. "I remember that. It was terrible. It shouldn't be like that!" he exclaimed as he skimmed the entry. "*Everyone* should get to be on the track team." I coached him to say more: "What exactly felt so terrible about track tryouts?"

"Well, kids should all get to run. Activity is good for kids. And when you get cut, it hurts your self-esteem. Plus, it feels weird when some kids get to run and some don't. It makes things competitive." I then channeled Nate to write his claim and reasons in his notebook (see Figure 16–4). He wrote:

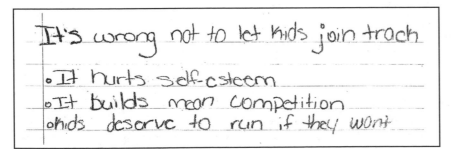

FIG. 16–4   The bullets are all reasons supporting the claim, making them parallel bullets.

MID-WORKSHOP TEACHING
Writers Plan with an Eye on the Deadline

"Writers, eyes up here," I said. "If you are going to be a researcher and an advocate not just in school but throughout your whole life, you can't just fix your vision on glorious, big goals. Have you heard of the saying that a person shouldn't be so heavenly minded that they are no earthly good? Well, to live the life of being an advocate, you need to be of some earthly good. You've got high-minded ambitious goals. But, to pull those goals off, you need to make very practical, down to earth plans.

"Usually, a writer starts with a timeline, with a deadline. Specifically, I'm going to ask all of you to finish your writing five days from today. So you have four days to research, write, revise. You're going to need, right now, to figure out what to do right now so that you get your writing done by the deadline." Use the chart to help you think about the steps you need to take, and then get started on them." I gestured toward the familiar chart, "How to Write an Argument."

"Nick has started flash-drafting his essay already. When I asked Nick if he knew enough to write, he said, 'I'll never know enough! Writing it will help me figure it out.' That is exactly the purpose of flash-drafting, writers—to help you see where you are with your argument. So don't delay too long until you take that next step! You might already be ready, right now, to think about the evidence you've gathered so far, the ideas you have, and quickly, jot a boxes-and-bullets outline. If you want, jot two different boxes and bullets and pick the one that is stronger. This should be no big deal for you by now! Go ahead."

You might also find a few students who quickly latch onto a topic but struggle to put their boxes and bullets together. They might have overlapping bullets, and you will need to coach them to find reasons that are not two ways of saying the same thing. Sometimes a simple, "What else?" moves children into different thinking. Others might need to do some quick research to find more than one reason to support their claim.

You might, as well, find some students who will benefit from support with using what they know about their audience to guide genre choice from the very beginning. You might coach those students to decide whether a letter, a petition, or an editorial essay will be the most effective way to sway their audience's opinion. One point you might make is that it's worth thinking about choosing the audience for whom their letters will have the most impact. For example, if I want to change the rules about letting dogs loose in my local park, I wouldn't write to the president, but I might write to a city councilperson or create a petition for local dog owners.

To help students think beyond the letters and position papers they wrote so far in the unit, gather them together and explain how you are thinking about where your argument could make the greatest difference. You might even invite them to help you decide whether a letter to the editor, a petition, an article for the local community paper, or a letter to your council person, would do the greatest good. Then show them how you research your audience. If you are writing to a council person, you might try to find out if any have pets! You might figure out if local vets would let you leave a petition in their offices or if there is a blog online for local dog lovers.

Then let your students work together to brainstorm their own possible audiences, and do some research on finding addresses and any possible details about that audience. With that knowledge in hand, they can begin to tailor their arguments and position their work in a specific niche.

Writers Take Charge of Their Writing Lives and Plan Their Next Moves

Remind students that they are in charge of their writing lives and that they need to call on all they know to plan their work, including planning next steps for themselves.

"Writers, each of you has chosen something to write about that for some reason has you stirred up. In this class we have someone advocating for girls and boys to have one soccer team and someone advocating that kids shouldn't have to try out for track, that everyone should be included. We've got a researcher speaking out for a dance party just after graduation, and we have someone else speaking out against that idea. Many of you have been writing quick drafts, getting down all that you can as fast as possible.

"Remember, you are your own job captain. There's a famous line from a poem by Walt Whitman, that goes, 'Oh Captain, my Captain!' So I say to you, 'Oh Captains, my Captains, what will you do?

"You need to be thinking, 'What should I do next?' For example, remember earlier that after you'd started writing just a bit of an essay, you stopped, drew a line under what you'd written, and thought about whether you were going for the gold or not. Was it your best? You might decide to do that again.

"Then, too, you might have been writing today and gotten to a place where you need information and evidence. You might be saying to yourself, 'I need to figure out if my opinion is warranted, and if it is, to get some convincing evidence.'

"You may find that what you really need to do tonight is to engage in some conversations, notepad in hand to capture quotes. You may need to do some research on the Internet. You might need to recall your own experiences as a researcher. Remember that these three kinds of research: gathering information through primary sources, text-based research, and researching your own experience, can each help you support your argument.

"You are the captain of your writing. You need to decide what you need to do next. Take a moment and do that now." I made sure everyone could see the process chart as they made their plans.

How to Write an Argument

- Collect evidence that allows you to think through various sides of an argument.
  - Set up a note-taking system to organize your research.
  - Reread sources with a critical eye, looking for connections and contradictions.
- Rehearse by explaining your position and listing your reasons point by point.
- Plan your claim and reasons into boxes-and-bullets structure.
- Use evidence to support your reasons.
  - Paraphrase, putting it into your own words.
  - Quote, and then unpack the quote, showing how it relates to the reason.
  - Introduce the source and explain the connection.
  - Use "set-up" language (transitional phrases) to prop up your sources.
  - Analyze and explain the evidence.
  - Show your reader the strengths and weaknesses of your evidence.
  - Include evidence that will sway your audience.
- Include a strong introduction and conclusion.
- Anticipate critics' counterarguments, and acknowledge these in your writing, then rebut them.

REMEMBER TO INCLUDE SPECIFICS AND REBUTTALS

Arguments are like information writing, in many ways. They need to be built with bricks of information. You all have chosen topics you know a lot about, but this doesn't always mean you remember to include precise, specific information. Reread what you wrote today and look to see whether you included bricks of information—statistics quotes, facts, lists, details. Locate the places in your draft where you need more specific information.

And then, find the necessary information you don't already have. Among other things, you will need to learn about other sides to the topic. If you have a certain view on pit bulls, you need to research views that are different than your own. Strong arguments, as you know, include counterclaims and rebuttals! So, what would those who are against you say? And what would you say back to them? You will certainly want to include the details of that in your writing as well.

Once you've gathered more research, reread your draft to see where that information belongs, and then write a new draft—at least of those sections—including the information.

Everyday Research

IN THIS SESSION, you'll teach children that argument writers find some of the most persuasive evidence in everyday life.

GETTING READY

✔ Evidence that you used to support the persuasive writing that you shared with the class in session 16 (see Connection)

✔ Chart paper and marker (see Teaching)

✔ Students' writing notebooks and pencils (see Active Engagement)

R IGHT NOW, YOU MAY BE CONCERNED about coordinating a whole class full of kids writing *evidence*-based arguments when each one has chosen his or her own topic. When students were all writing on a shared topic, you were able to support students' writing with quotes and statistics. But what do you do *now*?

It won't be hard to round up a few resources from the library and the class computer for some students' topics. (And you can collect files of articles over the years.) But mostly, we suggest that you acknowledge and accept the fact that finding resources will be a challenge, realizing that this will always be true in real life as well, and we hope you teach into this challenge.

Today, then, you'll want to teach your persuasive writers to be proactive researchers and evidence gatherers. You won't have premade text sets or prefabricated resource folders to hand them. The topics are too real, too urgent, too personal: the right to have a puppy, permission for slumber parties, rules about cell phones in school, policies regarding admission into selective middle schools, bringing a loved one home from the nursing home. Some relevant texts may offer evidence for topics such as these, but students will probably also need to generate evidence from their own lives. That is, researching these sorts of topics can also mean interviewing, surveying, and observing—field work.

In this session, you'll teach your writers to hunt for and mine everyday sources—the stuff that when documented becomes primary sources such as the letters, photographs, and interviews they research in social studies and science. You'll help them use interviewing, surveying, studying photographs and other documents, observation, and yes, firsthand experience as sources of information. Research leads writers into hospitals and factories, into the rain forests of Brazil, into war-torn neighborhoods. To write persuasively about a topic, a writer often goes straight to the people who are directly concerned with this topic and interviews them straight on. Or takes along a camera as well as a notebook. Your students will need to learn to do the same, with the topics closest to them. Whom will they ask? What scene will they describe firsthand? How will they cull the evidence, the details, they need from their lives? This is the work of a writer.

Everyday Research

CONNECTION

Share the evidence you used to write the persuasive letter you cited in the last session.

"Writers, take a look at this. Don't freak out. I know it's a little gross." I showed a picture of a moldy wall to the class, fully expecting the collective "Ewww" that came from the assembled fifth-graders. "I'm not going to tell you what that is. And I have some more things to show you.

"Now, take a look at this." I replaced the photograph of the mold with a medical report from my doctor, where I had highlighted the telltale respiratory symptoms. "What is this?" I asked, waiting until a few children called out that it was a doctor's report. "What does it say?" I prompted children to notice the highlighted symptoms.

"And this is important to look at, too." I replaced the doctor's report with a typed-up transcript and read it aloud, quickly and expressively.

Me: When did you first notice the mold?

Abigail: I've been in this room for a year and a half now, and it reappears every couple of months. Someone from Facilities will come down and replaster the wall but it just grows back.

Me: So replastering is obviously not the solution.

Abigail: No. This building is ancient. There's a busted pipe behind that wall for sure and it's leaking. Facilities isn't taking it seriously enough.

Me: Have you complained?

Abigail: I've lost count of how many times I've complained.

As mentioned earlier, you can, of course, appropriate this story and share any yucky images you'd like of mold and stained walls. Or, think over any time you were an activist, or wished you had been, and gather artifacts. Your real sense of courage—at having to switch schools, at being cut from a team, at seeing a garden bulldozed—will fuel the authenticity of your demonstration.

Debrief. Explain that being a successful researcher often means leaving the desk and seeking out bits of evidence that exists in the world.

"I just showed you a photograph, a doctor's report, and the transcript of an interview. And I bet you recognized where they were from, right?" I nodded as many kids called out that all of the items related to the letter I'd written about my dorm room wall.

"That letter was one of the most persuasive pieces of writing I have ever authored. Here's the thing I want you to notice. I didn't just sit at my desk to write it. I had to go out and do research, and I did that not just by reading, but also by meeting people, by going places, by talking. Of course, I also did use print sources. For example, I used the Internet to research fungal infections of the lungs. But a big part of my research involved collecting quotes from Abigail (another student who had the same problem in her room), taking compelling photographs of the mold itself, and talking to the doctor."

❧ **Name the teaching point.**

"Writers, today I want to teach you that writers turn the world upside down to collect the information they need to clarify their writing and strengthen their arguments. As writers discover and collect information from their environment, they are thoughtful and deliberate as they decide what to include and how to include it."

TEACHING

Give students an overview of the minilesson, explaining that soon they will have time to plan the research they are going to do straight away—today—as they gather information for their writing.

"For today's minilesson, I want to tell you a story and give you some tips, and then later in this minilesson I'm going to give you some time to do a bit of planning. You'll be planning the real-life research you need to do—and that is research you need to do today and this evening. You have no time to waste!"

Tell a story about a time when people were taught to write by being taught to engage in research—local, primary-source research, involving interviewing and observing.

"The man who most influenced the way that writing is taught to kids is a man named Don Graves. He isn't alive anymore, but his ideas are! Anyhow, one day Don Graves was asked to teach teachers how to teach writing. After school, the teachers gathered in the school library at Union Street School in Hamburg, New York. Don Graves walked in, but instead of giving the teachers a talk, he got *them* to do the same sort of thing you all need to do. He gave small groups of teachers each an envelope. Inside one envelope, a group read, 'Mr. Jeffery has run the school's furnace for 18 years, and he's noticed a lot of changes in ways people use heat. He's expecting to talk to you at 3:10.' In another envelope, instructions directed people to Mrs. Eaton, who lived just alongside the school and had a collection of antique dolls. Another letter said, 'You can learn a lot about what teachers are told to do, and what teachers value and don't value, by looking in the trash can by the mailboxes and by teachers' desks. Do a study of the things that teachers in this school are throwing away, and use that study to help you grow ideas about things teachers are being told to do.'

The goals for today is to inspire children to conduct their own research, seeking multiple sources of information to support their claims. As you share your own story of conducting research, emphasize that researchers not only go out into the world to gather evidence, but also seek out multiple sources, gathering a variety of information.

This is a true story, of course. Don Graves was the first researcher to study children as writers, and his research opened the field of children's writing. He'd been a pastor before becoming a professor and a researcher, and many found his research to be inspirational.

"My point to you is that often researchers decide to write about topics that are grounded in their own life, and researchers know that it isn't always that easy to do a computer search and turn up relevant information. Sometimes, the best source of information is right before your eyes—in your friends, your teachers, your principal, your family, in the police and shopkeepers and crossing guards and librarians in your town."

Share some tips about how to make primary research especially productive, stressing the value of collecting precise, specific, dense information.

"I'm going to give you a few tips that can help you when you research information that is right before your eyes." As I talked, I jotted quick notes on chart paper.

"One. Details matter! You can't record every detail, so choose the best ones, the kind that will really make your readers see or feel something specific about your topic. If you interview someone, record some of the specific words the person uses. If you notice an announcement that was sent home, get the exact words for at least part of the announcement. As the researcher Roy Peter Clark says to journalists, 'Don't forget to get the name of the dog.'

"Two. Once you get one piece of information that feels important and interesting, try to get others that go with it. So if you get the star track player to tell you whether he thinks there should be track tryouts, then get the newest, greenest member of the team to tell you what he thinks about the same topic, and the track coach, and the principal. Instead of having each person talk about something different, when you get one thing that seems like it will be a part of your writing, get other stuff that feels related.

"Three. Remember that numbers can persuade as much as details. When you write, 'Out of the five people interviewed, four were in favor of track tryouts,' you impress the reader because you actually have some statistics behind your claim. Four out of five can also be expressed as a percentage—80%. That is a high statistic. It tilts the argument in your favor. Sometimes surveys and statistics can be researched, but at other times, writers go out and conduct a survey and calculate the numbers and percentages they need to quote.

"You'll probably discover other things that you find are making your research really productive as you start doing it. If you discover something, let us all know about it!"

ACTIVE ENGAGEMENT

Channel writers to plan for the research they are about to do.

"So, writers, I'm going to give you a few minutes to do some planning. Will you make yourself a to-do list, jotting down places you can go, people you can talk to, documents you can secure, surveys you can conduct, that will help you become an expert on your topic?"

As children jotted, I looked over their shoulders. Nicole had put her topic at the top of the page and was jotting her list (see Figure 17–1).

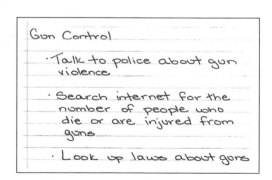

FIG. 17–1   Nicole's plan includes seeking a variety of information from authorities on the topic.

After a few minutes, I said, "Talk with each other, Talk, specifically, about what you can do—in really practical terms—today and this evening, because you don't have long to get this research done."

LINK

Remind writers of the many kinds of evidence they might rely on to do their research, including nonprint sources.

"Writers, I began this minilesson with that story from my own life—about the evidence I used in my letter of complaint, collected from sources that were staring me right in the face. All of you have selected topics that are meaningful to you, ones that come straight out of your own personal experiences or passions or concerns. That means that you have a wealth of evidence on hand to bolster your arguments. Use it! Whether you find a petition or professional records or take photos, or conduct interviews or give surveys to people who are in some way connected to your issue is up to you. You will want to use all of your sources—quickly! And, of course, you can also read up on your topics. There are many, many ways to research a topic, and often the best, most persuasive sources are looking us in the face. Off you go!"

Coaching into Students' Search for Primary Evidence

THERE ARE SEVERAL WAYS TO OFFER YOUNG WRITERS more support in searching for primary evidence for their arguments. You might begin by teaching students to conduct effective interviews. Start by coaching them to prepare an interview protocol. "Researchers don't just go out there and start thinking up questions on the spot," you'll tell kids. "Preparation for an interview begins as the desk, before you even meet with your interviewee." Show children that writers draft a list of possible questions before going out in the field. These are questions that will elicit information that is most relevant to the topic, of course. Teach them prompts to elicit more information from an interviewee, for example, "Could you say a bit more about that?" or "Can you give me a specific example?" or "Why do you think that is so?" To facilitate this teaching, you might simulate an interview in class with a colleague or set students up to interview each other. You might play interview clips in which pros such as Oprah or the now-retired Larry King ask questions, setting children up to notice how these pros elicit information. Do their questions appear prepared? How do they get the interviewee to say more? How do they change from one question to the next? Another question you'll want your writers to consider is "Who should they interview?" Explain that the voice of the stakeholders is the most relevant. Who does this argument concern? Who does it affect? Who is the neutral bystander?

Unlike Oprah, your young writers won't just be conducting an interview for some live audience. They'll be transcribing what the interviewee says to write about later. This is no small challenge. Coach children to jot quick notes in shorthand, or allow them to take along a friend as a "scribe" or even a portable voice recorder if they have one. Once they have the script of an interview all written out, you'll coach them into selecting only the most quotable phrases to use in their writing. You might use mentor texts to demonstrate how an interviewee's voice can be used to strengthen a point that the writer is already making—or how, in fact, studying the transcript can help us come up with even more points in favor of an argument. *(continues)*

MID-WORKSHOP TEACHING
A Short Project Can Lead to Many More

"Writers, look up here for just a second. David McCullough, a researcher whose work I've been reading lately, often spends *five years* writing a book about one topic—topics like the Brooklyn Bridge or the Panama Canal or former president Harry Truman. At a speech he made at the New York Public library, he said that people wonder whether it feels claustrophobic to work for five years on one subject. His answer was this: 'One subject?' Think about it: Is the Brooklyn Bridge, the Panama Canal, one subject? It isn't one subject. It's a thousand subjects. And the magic, the sense of adventure, comes from not knowing where you're headed.'"

"I'm telling you this for a reason. We only have a few days left of this unit, so you are going to have to compress your findings in just a few days into an argument. But here's the thing: as you conduct surveys and interviews, and as you read up on your topics, you may find that there's so much more you want to know—and to write about—on this one topic. If that happens to you, today, or at any point during the remainder of this unit, do this: jot yourself a note in your notebook. Maybe you can even have a page devoted to this. And on that page you can jot any new threads you want to explore on this topic after this research is completed. Writers do that all the time. They get ideas that may not go in this one project, but that they can shelf for another, longer project. Who knows? Some of you may become researchers like David McCullough, who spend five years on a topic like bullying in schools or how teams are decided, or who gets to be in the school play."

You might encourage children to conduct more than one interview, urging them to select people from both sides of an argument to quote. "Allow the reader to see that you've researched the people on both sides of your claim," you'd teach. Of course, this means teaching them to refute quotations from the opposite party. Each argument will have more than one stakeholder. While arguing about school policy, for example, they'll want to get the voice of the parent, the teacher, and the principal as well as the voice of the student.

If your students are up to the challenge of conducting mini-surveys, by all means, encourage them to prepare and conduct this form of primary research. Surveying consists of three distinct phases: designing questions, collecting answers, and then analyzing these. Students will need help with all three. As they design their survey questionnaire, they'll need to think up the questions most pertinent to their argument and decide the mode of answers they'd like (yes/no or multiple choice). Will they insert a comments section at the end? To simplify the process, you might prepare a simple survey questionnaire template for students to use. Next, they'll need to collect answers, to go out into the field and invite relevant people to take their survey. Confer with your writers to determine that they have the resources to actually do this fieldwork. For example, will they need you or a parent to supervise? If you are net-savvy enough, you might show them how to conduct online surveys (through sites such as surveymonkey .com), possibly under your supervision. Remember that the focus of your unit is writing, not data collection, so you'll keep this surveying process simple and easy. Analyzing the results of a survey and then incorporating these into an argument will also require coaching. You'll want to model or mentor ways to insert survey findings into actual writing: "In a survey conducted at (insert place), x out of y people said 'Yes' to . . . " or "X percent of the people responded that. . . . "

Since the topics chosen for this bend are centered largely on students' own lives, writers can rely on personally experienced anecdotes as primary evidence. You might ask students whether they have a personal story about this topic that will serve as a strong persuasive example. In other words, the story ought to sway the reader.

This is not the first time that writers will be inserting a mini-narrative into an expository text structure. Help students recall earlier teaching about how to use the power of a small story to illustrate a point: use of dialogue, details, pacing, starting at a strategic point in the timeline of the event.

Writers Include Their Journeys of Thought in Their Drafts

Let students in on the fact that when writers include questions, realizations, and discoveries in drafts, they anticipate things readers want to know.

"Here's a last bit of advice for today. Watch yourself learning about your subject. Pay attention to your questions and your confusions. Put even your questions and confusions on the page because—and this is important—because your questions and confusions will be your readers' as well. Pay attention, too, to your dawning ideas, to your realization that one thing leads to another, because your readers want to experience those same dawning realizations. You'll very likely write about how you started to learn about a topic, then felt a mental itch, became curious, began researching, discovered information, weighed the sources of information.

"So, researchers, remember that your questions, your trails of thought and discovery, all of those could be important to your research—and they may be of interest to your readers as well, as you'll be writing as an insider on this topic. Turn to your partners and share what you've done so far. And be sure to share your questions as well."

> First of all, if you don't wash your hand, you'll get sick because the germs growing or spreading in your body. If you accidentally ate a food that is licked by someone, you can get sick and also your stomach will be infected, it can make you vomit. If you are sick, do not touch any objects and living things. If you did, the germs would spread on objects and living things. Animals will get sick or a germs on objects that is touched by someone will be sick, too. I understand some people may think that by washing their hands too much cause body don't know how to fight back. You need a little soap so your body know how to fight back.

FIG. 17–2 Anthony begins to show his reader that handwashing affects the invidual and society at large.

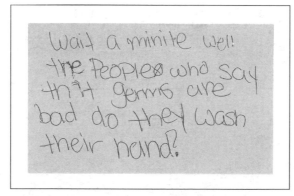

> Wait a minite wel! the peoples who say that germs are bad do they wash their hand?

FIG. 17–3 Jennifer jotted her question on a Post-it and stuck it on her draft as a reminder to follow the line of thinking.

CONTINUE COLLECTING INFORMATION!

Writers, I don't need to tell you your homework. I'm sure you were already setting yourself tasks as researchers. Some of you might want to survey teachers or students about your topic. You might design one important question, and use it in a survey with lots of people, keeping track of how many yes or no answers you get, so you can use that data in your writing! Or you might want to call someone to arrange an interview or a visit. Or you might want to interview some friends. The important thing is to get more information and more viewpoints. As you gather this information, try putting it straight into your rough draft.

Taking Stock and Setting Writing Tasks

ear Teachers,

It is quite likely that your workshop will now seem disorderly! That's predictable. That's what happens when young writers begin to work independently. They're not all in sync. So while one writer is taking notes, another may be researching fresh texts, another may be adding thinking or quotes to a draft, and a fourth is perhaps a bit adrift, out of sync with the smooth movement of the class.

Now is when it will be really important to keep your sense of humor and your sense of focus, so you can lean on the one and inspire the other. Many of your children will step up and astound you with their productivity and drive. And yet, their "eleven-year-old-ness" will still emerge. "What are you doing!?" may be on the tip of your tongue as two of your children inch their way through a one-page article, underlining every single line with a yellow highlighter, as if every word were gold.

Sort out when your writers need reminders of rituals and strategies they've learned. You can use voiceovers, or guidelines written onto the top of your whiteboard, or notes dropped onto writing spaces that remind students of all they know. "Chisel out your lion." "Don't forget the name of the dog." "Evidence needs to be spun." "Think who your readers will be and appeal to them."

In planning today's session, the question becomes "When the work is more individual than usual, what can you teach to the whole combined class that will be useful to them all?"

MINILESSON

At this point, it is probably important that students take a moment to assess their progress toward their deadline and to consider the question of how their draft is coming along, holding in their minds their visions of what they want their final piece to look like, asking questions such as "Have I added in my quotes?" "Have I added my thinking to my evidence?" "Have I tried out an introduction or conclusion?" "Have I been *writing*?"

You may begin the lesson by telling a very brief cautionary tale of a time in college when you researched a paper and left all the writing until the end, only to find yourself swamped by your notes, and challenged by putting all your thoughts into words in the time you had left. You might relate how, another time, you forgot to check your sources, and were up all night double-checking them at the end. You could then suggest that students consider the state of their drafts, holding in their minds their visions of what they want their drafts to include and asking themselves how close they are now to that vision.

After giving students a moment to assess, you might say something like, "Today I want to teach you that as any writer moves toward a deadline, the writer takes stock of his or her draft often, making sure that the draft is coming along and making sure to leave time for significant revision as needed."

During your teaching, you will want to demonstrate for students how you can do this sort of taking stock. You might use your own writing, or you may choose to use a student's writing as a model. As you read the draft you can ask, "What parts of my argument have received more of my attention? Have I worked on an introduction? A conclusion? In my reasons and evidence, have I worked to spin my evidence so it supports my reasons? Have I inserted important quotes, chiseling out just enough to sharpen their force?" You can use any tools in the room to help you come up with questions. The "How to Write an Argument" chart might be one of the most useful for this.

As you channel students to reflect, self-assess, and plan, be sure you remind them to look at the Opinion Writing Checklist for sixth grade, using it as a source of goals for themselves. Demonstrate your process of reading over your draft, looking for and finding work that you want to do next. Jot to-do sticky notes that spell out your next steps, such as "develop conclusion," and paste those to your draft so you'll know exactly what tasks you want to set yourself to bring your writing closer to your vision. After your demonstration, be sure to pause and explain what you have done, debriefing your work.

You might pull out the anchor chart as well as the checklist. Then, too, students can look at mentor texts and use them to jog their minds. For example, the text that Jack wrote and students studied early in the unit could be revisited now.

Opinion Writing Checklist

	Grade 6	NOT YET	STARTING TO	YES!
Structure				
Overall	I not only staked a position that could be supported by a variety of trustworthy sources, but also built my argument and led to a conclusion in each part of my text.	☐	☐	☐
Lead	I wrote an introduction that helped readers to understand and care about the topic or text. I thought backwards between the piece and the introduction to make sure that the introduction fit with the whole. I not only clearly stated my claim, but also named the reasons I would develop later. I also told my readers how my text would unfold.	☐	☐	☐
Transitions	I used transitional phrases to help readers understand how the different parts of my piece fit together to support my argument.	☐	☐	☐
Ending	I wrote a conclusion in which I restated the main points of my essay, perhaps offering a lingering thought or new insight for readers to consider. My ending added to and strengthened the overall argument.	☐	☐	☐
Organization	I arranged paragraphs, reasons, and evidence purposefully, leading readers from one claim or reason to another. I wrote more than one paragraph to develop a claim or reason.	☐	☐	☐
Development				
Elaboration	I included and arranged a variety of evidence to support my reasons. I used trusted sources and information from authorities on the topic. I explained how my evidence strengthened my argument. I explained exactly which evidence supported which point. I acknowledged different sides to the argument.	☐	☐	☐
Craft	I chose words deliberately to be clear and to have an effect on my readers. I reached for precise phrases, metaphors, analogies, or images that would help to convey my ideas and strengthen my argument. I chose *how* to present evidence and explained why and how the evidence supported my claim. I used shifts in my tone to help my readers follow my argument; I made my piece sound serious.	☐	☐	☐

During the active engagement, you may ask students to use their own writing to practice with you this on-the-run assessment of what writing work is still needed. If a few students don't have much of a draft yet, make this a wake-up call, and suggest they set themselves the task of drafting immediately, even leaving the meeting area early to continue that urgent work.

To wrap up this lesson, you might tell students that writers tend to do this kind of taking stock by looking at their actual draft often, and to remember now and forever more that writers set themselves *writing* tasks. You will want to remind them that today's lesson presents just one of many strategies to keep in mind as they head back to their own work.

CONFERRING AND SMALL-GROUP WORK

As students learn to construct arguments independently, they will encounter predictable challenges. One of the most significant of these will be when their draft suffers because their knowledge is limited. You'll notice this challenge when you see writers structure their essay well but struggle with elaboration. Or they develop one reason well, but the next reason is unsupported.

When you see writers who need more to say in order to write more, you might start by saying, "Argument writers often find themselves needing to get more information for one part of their argument. One thing writers can do is to list their reasons and then their sources of information for each reason." Once students have done this, you can encourage them to mine more information for reasons that are underdeveloped. If some reasons have no sources, you may need to help students imagine who they could interview, or quickly find a text for that student.

All of your conferring, however, may not arise from a sense of students' needs. Their strengths can also be on your mind. You might invite writers to offer seminars to other writers. You could, for instance, make a chart on the board of some writing work, such as "engaging introductions, spinning evidence, thoughtful conclusions, inserting juicy quotes," and you could invite students (whom you may have tapped beforehand) to offer conferences or small groups with other writers, where they use their own writing as a mentor text, and perhaps do some guided practice. Many students lean easily into "what if you did . . ."

Another way to frame these seminars would be to think of the big work of argument writing, which you described when last you worked with the checklist at the end of Bend II. This includes structuring your writing so your claim is obvious and your reasons and evidence are clear; thinking through the logic and reasoning of your argument so it is as sound as possible; considering the social appeal—the audience—and

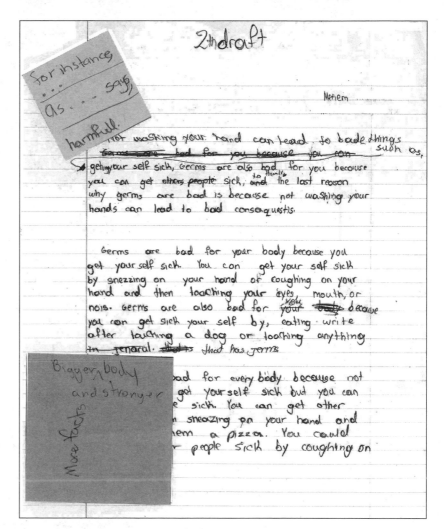

FIG. 18–1   Meriem set goals for transitions and elaboration.

tailoring examples, references, and vocabulary to that audience. If you wanted to add a fourth aspect, it would be editing for conventions so that your writing is as convincing and clear as possible. Students who are particularly good at one of those aspects of argument could look over drafts and mentor other writers.

MID-WORKSHOP TEACHING

Chances are, your students may need some practice with anticipating other positions and developing rebuttals in their writing. You might invite partnerships to stage on-the-run, quick debates, where they imagine counterclaims to their arguments and then try to refute them. You might say something like, "When you get good at argument, you sometimes switch sides for practice, taking the opposite position, so that then you can try to rebut that position in your own argument. Then while your thinking is fresh in your mind, you get out your draft and jot your ideas on it."

SHARE

During the share today, ask students to reflect on the extent to which their writing meets the expectations of the sixth-grade checklist. If most of those goals are met, you can encourage students to record other goals that they've also met. You could add a goal or two as well. For instance, you might add on that writers provide some background about the issue to develop a context for the reader. Or you might add a point about really addressing your audience with specific examples, references, and vocabulary that would provide social appeal, or about really distinguishing the particular claim from the claims that others might make. Your students could annotate their own drafts with the parts where they see they have reached their goals and the parts where they want to do even better.

HOMEWORK

You might say, "Writers, at the start of the unit in Session 3, you studied Cecilia's essay. You took it home and marked it up with labels. You found examples of where the text matched the sixth-grade goals, and stuck the label beside those places. Do you remember that? When you annotated Cecilia's essay, I told you that later in the unit, you were going to do that same work with your own pieces. Tonight for homework, that's what you are going to do. I copied the sixth-grade goals (as well as a page of fifth-grade goals) on sticky labels, and I'm going to ask you to annotate *your own* essay. Look for places in the text that exemplify the goal, and stick the matching label next to it. As you do this work, think, 'What do I see? What work might I still need to do?'"

Gook luck,

Lucy, Mary, and Annie

Using All You Know from Other Types of Writing to Make Your Arguments More Powerful

ear Teachers,

You will always want to begin planning for any day's teaching by thinking first about the work that your students are apt to be doing. Today your students will probably be setting themselves the task of making their arguments as powerful as possible. This means that today you will presumably want to give them both more direction and more time to do this work. Of course, you will want to study your students' work to see what final lessons you want to teach to help them grow as writers within this unit. There are any number of possibilities we can imagine.

You may want to look across students' drafts to be sure they are making use of all that you have taught. We hope that you will see that your students' arguments are well struc-tured, with clear claims, reasons, and evidence; well thought out, with valid reasoning and connections; and angled to address a particular audience. If you see, instead, that your students are not making use of all that you have taught, then by all means, go back and reteach and remind students that they are meant to carry work forward, transferring and applying what they have learned to fulfill their potential and be as convincing and compelling as possible.

MINILESSON

For today's minilesson, we suggest that you show how argument writers employ small moments in their writing to make their point. You might begin by reminding students of all the ways they have used small moments in essays in previous units this year and in years past. You might say, "Writers, I know that for years now in writing workshop you have included small moments in essays. So the question I have for you is, Why do essay-ists include small moments? Think for a moment, then turn and tell your partner your ideas." Chances are, your students will recall that essayists often include small moments as examples of their ideas. The moment brings to life the issue that their essay deals with. Some students may offer other ideas, such as that small moments stir up the reader's emotions or get to the heart of why they care about this issue or illustrate the writer's stance.

It is important to explicitly recall earlier teaching so that students expect to transfer and apply what they've learned in prior workshops. You might say something like, "Today I want to remind you that whenever you are doing one type of writing, such as argument, you can still use everything you have learned from other types of writing to reach your audience. In particular, your storytelling craft can be a persuasive technique."

Of course, you'll then want to show students how to do this work. It's always engaging for the students to see you write and to hear your writer's voice. For instance, you might say, "Writers, watch me do this work. When I think about the ways that argument writers use small moments to make their point, there are two main techniques they often use. One technique is to include an invented or imagined moment. That's where the writer says something like 'Picture this . . .' or 'Imagine this . . .' and then creates a vivid scene that will stick with the reader. Another technique is to comb through your research for a true small moment and tuck part of that moment into your essay, as an engaging way to present evidence."

Next, you might demonstrate one of these techniques. Choose the one that you think might be most challenging for your students, so that you leave the easier one for them to practice in the active engagement. You might, for instance, say, "My position is that the school should allow teachers to bring well-behaved dogs into class. One of my reasons is because good dogs help children focus. Well, I have a true story to back that up. Like you, I've been looking for people to interview, and so I called my friend who teaches in Seattle, who brings her dog to class, and I asked her to tell me about one moment when the dog helped a child focus. And she did! So I might tuck that small moment into my essay. Listen for what you know about small moments. Really listen for the storytelling craft that you know so well." Then write-in-the-air, as if you are composing in front of the children. Pause a bit, to make it plausible that you are composing this small moment in the moment!

> One reason that teachers should be allowed to bring well-behaved dogs into school is because the dogs can help children focus. For instance, at Pathfinder School, young Sadie finds her reading partner, Fletcher, an eight-year-old black Labrador. "Settle down," Sadie says, "it's time to read." And Fletcher does. First, he waits for Sadie to choose her book. Then, he waits for Sadie to lean against him. Then, for the next hour, dog and child read together. "This story is sad," Sadie says at one point, tears running down her cheeks. Fletcher licks her face. Sadie keeps reading. Fletcher helps her to focus. With Fletcher as her partner, Sadie could read forever.

Invite your children to share what they noticed about small moment writing, such as using dialogue to enliven the scene, introducing characters, and story structure. Point out, as well, how you connect the point of the story back to your reason.

During the active engagement, your students will probably be jumping out of their skins, dying to create an imagined moment when Fletcher helps a student focus. "What if . . ." you can ask. You could also tell students one of your other reasons, so that they are more likely to create original moments. Have them work with a partner to create a moment that could make your point for another one of your reasons, then, such as that teachers should be able to bring dogs to school because they help keep people calm. Start them off with "Picture this . . ." If you need to prompt more, you could add, "Picture this. You're late to school or you hear raised voices or you wake up angry and go to school angry." Your children should have no trouble imagining a scene of how a dog calms everyone who comes to school. Make sure to debrief how these two techniques, telling a moment from a real story and telling an imagined scene, allow argument writers to call on storytelling craft as a persuasive technique.

After some practice, you might direct students to look at their own work. They might look at their drafts and notice places they could put in imagined stories. Or they might look back at their research for real stories. Looking back over her articles, Caroline noticed there were several stories she might use of pit bulls attacking people. "I could talk about the boy who got his eyebrow bitten off by a pit bull, or I could tell the story of the woman whose dog attacked her," she said to her partner. I nudged her to pick one and try telling part of a story to her partner, then writing some of it in her notebook. She told her partner:

> Once, for example, a boy was coming home from school. He saw a dog at a fence. He didn't see the "Beware of Dog" sign. "Good dog," the boy said, as he reached through the fence. Then . . .the dog bit him! It was a pitbull, and it had been trained to bite.

To end this lesson, you might tell students that always, writers lean on all they know about writing, especially the skills they have honed over many years of practice. Send them off with a reminder that they can use what they're powerful at from *any* type of writing, including poetry, information writing, narrative, and opinion writing, whenever they write. As children transition to independent writing, add today's teaching point to your process chart (see next page).

CONFERRING AND SMALL-GROUP WORK

Today you may want to have studied students' work and come up with a few small groups before the workshop begins, so that you can address a few different themes that may be coming up as students do this work. You may instead move around the room, including all students in quick table conferences to address as many needs as possible. We've listed some predictable conferences below, as well as a few to extend the powers of your strongest writers.

• Help them to find a real and important audience for their argument. When a student is writing that everyone should be able to try out for track, for example, it may be more effective to target the Parent Teacher Association than the track coach. Thinking about influence and how an audience might join the cause can help writers choose more specific audiences.

How to Write an Argument

- Collect evidence that allows you to think through various sides of an argument.
  - Set up a note-taking system to organize your research.
  - Reread sources with a critical eye, looking for connections and contradictions.
- Rehearse by explaining your position and listing your reasons point by point.
- Plan your claim and reasons into boxes-and-bullets structure.
- Use evidence to support your reasons.
  - Paraphrase, putting it into your own words.
  - Quote, and then unpack the quote, showing how it relates to the reasons.
  - Introduce the source and explain the connection.
  - Use "set-up" language (transitional phrases) to prop up your sources.
  - Analyze and explain the evidence.
  - Show your reader the strengths and weaknesses of your evidence.
  - Include evidence that will sway your audience.
  - Tell imagined, or true, stories.
- Include a strong introduction and conclusion.
- Anticipate critics' counterarguments, and acknowledge these in your writing, then rebut them.

- Teach students to engage their readers by thinking harder about their audience. Are they writing for adults or their peers? What kinds of things does their audience care about? What examples would particularly sway them? You might pull a few students into a group and provide some guided practice in tailoring vocabulary, examples, and references or comparisons to a particular audience.

- Help students rehearse and revise the reasoning in their arguments by pulling small groups into debates. Invite students to listen hard for logic, for how valid the argument is, for possible counterpositions, and for ways to rebut those positions. Have students rank and sort their most important points and then compare these to the points they make in their essays.

- Invite your poets to consider language. Some of your writers might be very skilled poets. You might invite these writers to try writing about their subject in a few poems, and then invite them to weave some of that poetic language into their argument or to set some lines as prologues or epilogues to their essays, as Elie Wiesel and other writers have.

- Remind students that writers are accurate with their quotes and citations. Some writers may want to review how to punctuate dialogue and how to cite their references. Demonstrate how to use parenthetical references or endnotes.

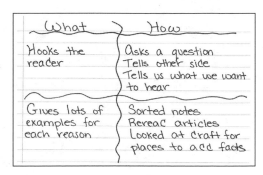

FIG. 19–1 Listing several moves the author made in the "How" column creates a repertoire of strategies for students to use in their own writing.

MID-WORKSHOP TEACHING

Invite students to recall what they learned from studying mentor texts in the past as a pathway toward raising the level of their own writing. Have on hand a few well-chosen texts. You might have some student writing that exactly matches the type of writing your students are doing. You might also seek published articles and essays where one piece of the text seems accessible to young writers and gorgeous in its craft. Box out the parts that you think would be productive to study. Then, during your mid-workshop teaching, remind your writers that it is almost always worth looking at something other writers have done well to get ideas for revision. You don't have to do a full-on demonstration of how to study mentor texts. Simply remind them to use what they know about studying what an author does to get ideas for their own writing.

SHARE

At the end of this workshop, we recommend you celebrate the ways students have made their writing more powerful. As we've suggested in prior units of study, a symphony share would work nicely here, or you may decide to have students share their learning in small groups. However you decide to celebrate their work, you'll want to highlight students independently forging ahead in a variety of ways.

HOMEWORK

You could say, "Writers, tonight, please study the mentor text I'm giving to you, thinking about the work that author did that you might try. I have copies of Cecilia's essay for you. As you read through it, find examples where you feel the argument is particularly strong. Then think, "What did Cecilia do to make it that strong?" Jot some notes as you do this. Write down what the author wrote and the steps you imagine she took to create that part. Then, use your notes to revise your writing, trying some of the work Cecilia did in your own piece. Tomorrow you will share with your partner the work you did."

Teachers, see Figure 19–2 (on the following pages and also available in the online resources) for a printable sample essay you might use. You might decide to use a published piece or a different student text. Whatever text you use it should be accessible to kids and rich in craft.

Sincerely,

Lucy, Mary, and Annie

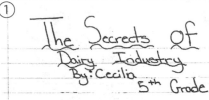

① The Secrects Of Dairy Industry
By: Cecilia
5th Grade

Have you ever read a nutrition facts table label on a chocolate milk carton? Most likely you have. Dairy companies tell us that chocolate milk is healthy and delicious. They tell us that it helps us refuel our bodies during a workout. That is what we want to hear. But is it the truth? No one has ever seen a commercial or read an advertisement for chocolate milk stating that chocolate milk is filled with fat, sugar, and calories. Dairy companies give us what we want to hear, but not necessarilly the truth. It's the only way to mask the fact that chocolate milk isn't healthy. They want us to by their products, and if schools stopped serving chocolate milk, they would lose

② a lot of money. So what's the point in telling us the truth, anyway?

Chocolate milk isn't healthy. Although it has few vitamins, chocolate milk is also packed with sugar, fat, and calories. Chocolate milk has eight table-spoons of sugar in one of the eight ounce cartons they serve in schools! That's one tablespoons per ounce! A child drinking one carton [of chocolate milk] each school day will gain one pound in 14 weeks from chocolate milk alone... many children are drinking 2-4 cartons per day... "says Doctor Sarah Jane Schwarzenberg of MN-AAD's pediatric obesity task force. This may not seem like a lot, but in one year, a kid would gain five extra pounds, and in ten they would gain fifty. Recently, Jamie Oliver filled a wheelbarrow with sugar to represent the amount of sugar a kid gets from drinking

③ chocolate milk every day for a year. Ann Cooper calls chocolate milk "soda in drag". Even the "Got Milk?" corporation admits that chocolate milk has 31 more calories than white milk. Some very active kids can burn off the calories and fat with exercise, but most kids aren't very active. A lot of kids are overweight, and still drink chocolate milk. No matter how many vitamins, the bad stuff outweights them in chocolate milk.

Dairy companies want us to buy their products. ALL companies want us to buy their products. This is what's in their heads: money. NOT the health of American kids. The dairy industry has sponsored several studies in favor of chocolate milk. "Studies sponsored by the dairy industry show that when this happens overall milk const consumption drops..." says Dana Woldow. The dairy industry

FIG. 19–2   Cecilia's essay demonstrating the sixth-grade standards

④ Sponsored this and many others studies because they want to show us that chocolate milk should be kept in schools, and if chocolate milk is kept in schools, schools will buy it from them. Many dairy companies, such as the Mid-Atlantic dairy association." These commercials are just ways to get us to buy their products, and it's working. But it needs to stop working.

If schools stopped serving chocolate milk, the dairy industry would lose a lot of money. Flavored milk accounts for 70% of milk served in US schools. This means that if the schools stopped serving chocolate milk, dairy companies would lose sales to schools. Overall milk consumption drops 37% when chocolate milk is removed. This means that sales to schools would also drop 37%,

⑤ resulting in money loss for the dairy industry. To them, there's no point in telling us the truth when they'd lose all that money by doing so.

It's true that many people who know about the amount of sugar, fat, and calories chocolate milk has still believe it's healthy. They think so because of the vitamins. But kids can get vitamins in plenty of other tasty and nutritious foods. Kids shouldn't depend on chocolate milk for health.

Although dairy companies give us what we want to hear, the truth is more important. Sure, it has vitamins, but it still isn't healthy. They The only reason they tell us that it is because they want us to buy their products. If we stopped, they would lose a lot of money. But if The Dairy Association admitted admitted that chocolate milk isn't

⑥ healthy, kids in our country would be overall healthier. They need to think about the futures of American children. And if dairy companies aren't telling us the truth, what other food companies might also be lying?

FIG. 19-2 (Continued)

Evaluating the Validity of Your Argument

IN THIS SESSION, you'll teach students that argument writers strengthen their claims by making sure their evidence doesn't depend on flawed reasoning.

GETTING READY

✔ Excerpts from an essay on school uniforms enlarged for students to see (see Teaching)

✔ Chart titled "To Increase the Validity of an Argument, Writers Alter Their Language and Tone" (see Active Engagement)

✔ Chart paper and marker (see Active Engagement)

✔ Students' writing folders with their most recent drafts (see Active Engagement)

✔ "Common Flaws in Reasoning" chart (see Link)

✔ Excerpts from mentor teacher essay on dogs running loose in the park (see Share)

WHEN I WAS IN SCHOOL, debates were something that only an exalted group of seniors did within the exclusivity of their club. Members of the debate club stood around in blazers, attacking the ad hominem, exposing the logical fallacy. I felt pretty certain they could quote the law in Latin.

It wasn't until years later that I realized attacking an ad hominem didn't require donning a blazer and posing at the rostrum. All it needed was a certain mental vigilance (some would even call it common sense). I had never been in the Debate Club but I could spot when a person tried to win an argument by attacking another's character rather than their logic. I could sense when someone talked about an individual case as if that could support a sweeping generalization. Or when they tried to divert attention from the real argument by harping about an irrelevant detail. While I couldn't name the logical fallacy, I could certainly recognize when one was made.

We are wiser about school curricula today. Many people will agree, for instance, that debating does not need to be reserved for elite schools and classes, or that it needn't be only an extracurricular activity. Many will agree that debating needs to be part and parcel of the mainstream curriculum for all students. When young people aren't given opportunities to spar with each other over differences of opinion, then their muscles for eventually writing arguments aren't as well developed as they could be. More importantly, children who do not participate in any sort of oral debating may miss out on chances to learn, early on, a habit of logical thinking.

Earlier, in Session 12, you began the all-important work of teaching children to frame their arguments in a way that relies on sound logic and avoids blanket statements. You'll extend that work today, teaching them to make their logic foolproof, to present evidence in a way that makes it defensible. You'll show writers that to do this, they don't really need to discard the evidence they have or try to dig out something even more compelling. Sometimes all they need to do is to frame the evidence in language that is precise and does not generalize.

Evaluating the Validity of Your Argument

CONNECTION

Explain that a truly persuasive essay makes a "believer" out of the reader.

"Writers, I've been watching you all scribbling away. I've glanced over a few shoulders and spoken to a few of you (I'll get to the rest of you today), and I see you writing about the *real* stuff—stuff that matters in your lives. And I'm also noting that you can be pretty persuasive when you set your minds to it. As you work at persuading your reader, however, remember that you don't just want this reader to *consider* your point of view. You want to convert the reader, make a believer out of him or her. You want the reader to end your essay and think, 'Yes! I agree with every word.' That reader shouldn't have a doubt left in his or her head but that you are one hundred percent correct in all you've claimed.

"Achieving that level of persuasiveness is not easy. You can't just charm the reader with a cute story or move them with an emotional reference or bowl them over with a few facts. To achieve that level of persuasiveness where the reader is helpless putty in their hands, writers have to be clever about the way they present their evidence. They don't just gather, gather, gather evidence and then plop this evidence into the essay. They test the logic of this evidence from *every angle possible* and make sure that no holes can be poked through it.

"We've already looked at some common flaws in reasons. There's one in particular that is really common, and I'd like to revisit it."

❖ **Name the teaching point.**

"Today, I want to teach you that truly persuasive writers word and present their evidence in a way that is incontestable. One way they do this work is to make sure that they are not presenting specific evidence as being true for all times and occasions—unless it is."

TEACHING

Share a simple example of a text that generalizes evidence, inviting students to notice the flaw in the logic.

"Writers, look at this point that I picked out of one persuasive essay." I flipped to a sheet of chart paper, where I had copied an excerpt.

You might be thinking, "I've said this before! Don't they know this?" The journey from personal opinion and preference to evidence-based, researched argument is not accomplished in just an essay or two, though. It is one of repeated practice, consistent reminders, calibrated coaching. Because your students chose topics they are personally interested in, expect some slippage. Their very vehemence may lead them to eschew logic for passion, and you'll need to coach them to incorporate both.

Our school should force kids to wear school uniforms. One reason is that they're cheaper. "We have to spend more money buying different clothes for kids to wear to school everyday," complained a parent.

Let's analyze this evidence. Can we poke holes through this logic? Can we say, 'Sorry writer, but I don't agree with Mr. Parent.' Turn to your partner and share why you might disagree."

After allowing thirty seconds for partners to buzz with each other over the statement, I intervened. "Yes! I heard you poke holes through this logic. You were not convinced! Some of you said that uniforms can be more expensive, especially if they include extra stuff like ties and badges and sashes. Some of you said that parents could just make kids wear the same regular clothes. So this quote—this evidence—is contestable. It hasn't really persuaded us, has it?

"The solution is not to discard this evidence or to try and find other evidence. The evidence can work! But to truly persuade us, the writer has to set it up differently. He can't just say, 'Uniforms are cheaper.'"

Demonstrate that generalizations can be removed if we word and present evidence differently.

I flipped to the next page of my chart pad, where I had copied more of the essay, and read it aloud, underlining some words as I read them.

Uniforms are <u>usually</u> cheaper for parents <u>in the long run</u>. Kids <u>often</u> feel pressure to wear the latest fashion and not to wear the same things often. This <u>can cause</u> a strain for parents. "We have to spend more money buying different clothes for kids to wear to school everyday," complained <u>one</u> parent.

"Writers, notice that this paragraph is careful not to say that uniforms are always cheaper. It uses words like *usually* and *in the long run*. It doesn't say, 'This definitely causes a strain' but that it *can cause* a strain. The writer isn't pretending that this quoted parent is representative of all parents out there. He calls him *one* parent. The reader is reassured that the writer admits there are more. As a result, this writing is more *honest*. It isn't claiming that this point is 100% true everywhere, every time.

"No one likes a know-it-all. We like honest, humble people, right? Readers, too, will believe a writer who is honest and humble. A writer who states evidence but acknowledges that this may not *always* hold."

ACTIVE ENGAGEMENT

Reiterate the previous teaching with a second, quick example.

"Let's look at a little more of the same essay supporting uniforms. Again, see if you can poke holes in this logic or if it is convincing." I flipped to the next page.

Because in the lesson students are evaluating small changes to language, you'll notice that in the share, we emphasize revising larger swatches of their essays through extensive elaboration. You want to evaluate your workshop sessions through the lens of elaboration, asking, "Have my children written enough today?" If the minilesson leads to extensive reading or thinking work, that may be fine—if it is balanced by a mid-workshop that leads to more writing, to homework that requires a lot of writing, and if this is followed by a day of drafting.

Picture a schoolyard of uniformed kids, shirts tucked in, hair pulled back from faces, eyes bright and eager to learn. Now imagine the same kids in short-short skirts, pants that hang low, and punk hairstyles. Which look do you think is the best one? I'm sure you'll agree that it's best for students to wear uniforms.

"Turn and talk. Test the argument by asking three question prompts." Turning to the chart paper, I quickly jotted:

How do you know?
Is that always true?
Is that true for everyone?

The children talked, and then I said, "I agree that this writer is trying to make us think uniforms are great by painting uniformed kids positively and the ones in regular clothes in negative ways. This writing also makes those 'everyone' statements, which is stereotyping. Not all kids out of uniform will be wearing really short skirts or low-slung trousers."

Demonstrate that the careful selection of words can remove stereotypes.

"How could this writer fix the picture so that it doesn't stereotype against *all* nonuniform wearers? Talk with your partners, rewriting it in the air." I listened in for a bit, and then set to work on chart paper, writing this:

Picture a schoolyard of uniformed kids, a sea of blue shorts and white shirts. This <u>may be a bit boring</u>, but it <u>can feel</u> comfortable <u>for many</u>. Now picture the same yard full of kids in regular clothes. <u>Chances are</u>, a few kids' clothes will be ones adults don't love—the skirts too short, the pants too low-slung—but many clothes will be appropriate. <u>The good and the bad</u> thing will be that the kids will have chosen their outfits . . .

"Writers, many of you suggested something more like this. You are right that the writer still paints a picture in the reader's mind. But this *writer* seems much more balanced. It feels like this writer has considered both sides of the story. Instead of pretending that something is true always, he uses phrases like 'Chances are that . . . ' and 'The good and bad thing will be . . . '"

Remind students that writers test for logic by asking, "How do you know?" Add that a second question to ask is "Is this always true?" Share examples of words that can be used to remove generalizations.

"Writers, remember that earlier, when writing about chocolate milk, we talked about not building a house of cards. And we learned that to check if an example or evidence is solid, we ask, 'How do you know?'

"We'll add another question to that list: 'Is this always true?' And if our evidence doesn't hold true for every occasion, we make sure to alter our language to reflect this by adding responsible words. Then our tone will be more believable.

To Increase the Validity of an Argument, Writers Alter Their Language and Tone

- IF IT ISN'T ALWAYS TRUE, IT MIGHT BE TRUE . . . often, some-times, usually, frequently, in many cases, in many instances, on many occasions, commonly, ordinarily

For example, instead of "Parents prefer uniforms."

"IN MANY CASES, parents prefer uniforms."

- IF IT ISN'T TRUE FOR EVERYONE, IT MIGHT BE TRUE FOR . . . many, most, countless, innumerable, a multitude of people, numerous people, scores of people, diverse people

For example, instead of "Kids feel the pressure of having to keep up."

"MANY kids feel the pressure of having to keep up."

A more measured, careful tone can often be more persuasive than an impassioned, inflammatory one. 'Uniforms can be helpful' is more persuasive than 'school uniforms will save lives and increase happiness!'"

LINK

Rally students to use a variety of lenses when critiquing their own writing.

"Writers, you'll probably find that not only in writing, but in life, being precise with your language is a good idea. It's actually more convincing to say 'mostly' than 'always,' or 'many' rather than 'everyone.' As you go off to write, this is going to be one good lens for critiquing your own writing. You know other ways to critique your argument as well, including all of these common flaws in reasoning." I gestured to the chart we had made earlier, "Common Flaws in Reasoning."

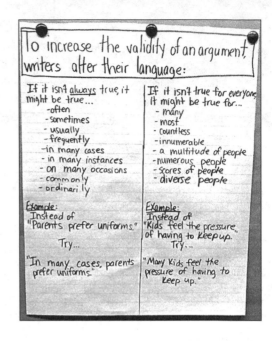

Common Flaws in Reasoning

- Generalizing (assumes specific example will be true everywhere)
- Discrediting (insults people's character rather than taking issue with their points)
- Assuming Consequences (implies cause-and-effect relationship that isn't proven)
- Questionable Assumption (argument founded on something that might not be true)
- Red Herring (gets readers off track)

The main thing for today is to finish your writing. Make sure you are clear about whether you are drafting a persuasive essay or letter or speech or petition. You may want to again analyze a mentor text for ideas for what to do in your writing, or you may want to get a tutorial from someone in class whose writing you admire, or to use the checklist to think about how to set specific goals for your remaining time.

"Before you go off, quick, out of all those choices, or anything else you had in mind, think—what do you most want to accomplish today?'"

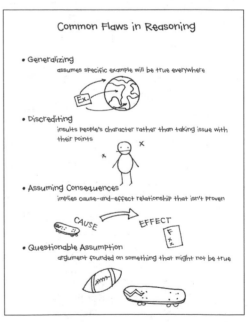

Playing Devil's Advocate and Spotting the Biased Sample

YOU MIGHT DECIDE TO RATCHET UP THE LEVEL OF PEER WORK by teaching some strong students to play devil's advocate. Explain that a devil's advocate challenges another's argument—not because he disagrees with it, but to force the arguer to further strengthen it. That is, you could teach partners to listen to each other's essays critically, challenging every point, forcing the writer of the essay to defend her position. You might even have students play this game in a small group, with more than one person playing devil's advocate and more than one person defending the side of the essay being read aloud.

You'll want to teach that the devil's advocate listens carefully for holes in an argument's validity and points these out. While there is much to teach in the field of logic, it is easy to overwhelm students with talk of logical fallacies. Instead, you'll want to teach just one or two ways an argument's validity might be challenged. You'll want to simplify these fallacies by using easy-to-understand terms and providing several examples so that children learn to identify them in each other's—and ultimately their own—arguments. Warn students to expect that many new points will turn up while playing devil's advocate, points that hadn't been anticipated when the essay was originally written. Coach writers to jot these points down so that they may consider them at length later because it may not be possible to answer each point at the precise minute when it is raised. Often, the writer will have to research and refine a response.

I started, for example, by teaching Ari and his partner to watch out for the general to specific example, when the writer really means a specific, unique example, but speaks in generalities.

Squarely facing two devil's advocates in his small group, Ari began reading his essay in support of zoos (see Figure 20–1).

Sometimes endangered animals are in trouble in the wild because there isn't enough to eat. For example, Tom French, who won a

MID-WORKSHOP TEACHING
Quick Debates to Test Accuracy and Precision

"Writers, Claire and Nick were just hotly debating the accuracy of their reasons and evidence—and they aren't even researching the same subject. But what they realized is, even if you haven't shared the research, you still can listen for *how* someone argues and be suspicious when they use words like *always*, *every time*, *definitely*. You can call people on that.

"Doing a quick debate for a few minutes with your partner is a great way for you to test your language. Partners, you can help each other be even more precise and accurate. Go ahead, have a quick debate, and listen for when your partner exaggerates or stereotypes. Be skeptical!"

Pulitzer Prize journalist, studied elephants in many zoos, and he wrote a book about them. It's called ZOO STORY. It turns out that there are too many elephants in South Africa. There isn't enough food for them and there isn't enough food for the rhino, because elephants eat all the trees. So when elephants get moved to zoos, it might save their lives and it might help some other animals too. Tom French shows that in zoos, there are clinics with experts who will care for the elephants.

I nudged his partner, who asked Ari to read again, pondered, then asked, "Any zoo? Isn't that a generality? Do you mean any zoo is okay, or just specific kinds of zoos?"

Eventually, Ari moved from "We should support zoos" to "We should support good zoos like the one in San Diego," making his claim and reasons more clear, more specific, and more foolproof. "Overall, it seems like zoos are a good idea, as long as they take good care of the animals. They can rescue endangered animals, and they can breed them so they won't be so endangered," he wrote. I then gathered Ari and his partner and asked if they felt comfortable teaching this work to another partnership of strong writers, using Ari's work as a demonstration text. Taking a few moments to rehearse their lesson, Ari and his partner then eagerly set out to teach. Asking partnerships to reteach what you've taught creates a ripple effect in your writing workshop.

> Sometimes endangered animals are in trouble in the wild because there isn't enough to eat. For example, Tom French, who won a Pulitzer Prize journalist, studied elephants in many zoos, and he wrote a book about them. It's called Zoo Story. It turns out that there are to many elephants in saut Africa. There isn't enough food for them isn't enough food for the rino, because elephants eat all the trees, So when elephants get moved to zoos, it might save their lives and it might help some other animals too. Tom French shows that in zoos, there are clinics with experts who will care for the elephants.

FIG. 20–1 Though the example is specific, it is used as a generality, creating flaws in reasoning.

Writers Add Detailed Explanations to Defend Their Position

Demonstrate reconsidering a part of your argument where you made blanket statements, and develop a detailed explanation to sharpen your position and explain your thinking.

"Writers, bring your arguments to the meeting area." I waited for students to gather, then started. "Writers, sometimes when you find yourself making exaggerated statements, like 'All parks should allow dogs' or 'Everyone loves dogs,' it's not enough to just fix up a few words. You actually have to write a more detailed explanation of your thinking. Let's look at my argument, for instance. In this one part, I had written":

> Dogs should be allowed to run loose in the park in the early mornings because all dogs like to socialize with each other. They like to play with each other, not just run on a leash.

"Well, I just tried a quick debate with Nick, and he caught me right away. 'You can't say *all* dogs like to socialize,' Nick said. 'Some dogs fight, or are afraid of other dogs.' He's right. I could change that *all* to *most*. But that's not really enough work, writers, because then I'm just backing away from my position. I really did mean that all dogs need some free time, some time to be with other animals. So while Nick was right that I can't use the phrase I had, I need to do more important work than just change the word. I really need to explain my thinking. So I might cross out that part and try putting everything I was thinking into words. It might be something like":

> Dogs should be allowed to run loose in the park in the early mornings because most dogs need some free time. They need to make their own decisions about who to play with, when to run and when to wrestle with another dog. Even if they decide NOT to play, at least they'd be making their own decisions. That's why dogs should be allowed to run loose sometimes—so they can be free for just a few minutes.

"It's not perfect yet, but writers, do you see how I didn't just accept that I have to change my language? I thought hard about what I really meant, and I added a more detailed explanation."

I gestured at the students' arguments. "You can do this too, writers. Sometimes you do want to simply change a word here or there to be more convincing. But other times, you want to add a more detailed explanation of your thinking. Don't give up your position too easily!"

ALTERING LANGUAGE AND ADDING DETAIL

Writers, in just a few days you will be publishing your essays. You want your arguments to be solid, airtight, without flawed reasoning, and with strong positions. Tonight for homework, recall what you know about composing powerful arguments, and write a new draft of your essay. You'll copy some portions of your existing draft, and change other portions. Think about places where you might change your language to make it more persuasive, more logical and credible. Then, too, think about places where you really need to add a more detailed explanation of your thinking. Above all, think about how *best* to defend your position.

Paragraphing Choices

W HEN KIDS THINK ABOUT GRAMMAR, they often think of it as fixing mistakes. They may fix their capitalization or their spelling, or add quotation marks. Usually, they'll do this work at the end of the writing process, in a burst of editing. Adult writers do this kind of editing as well, and it's worth thinking about what happens when we do. We read over important emails, use our spell-check if it's available, and if not, we may even substitute a word we know how to spell for one we don't. (Recently I was writing an email and wanted to use the word *soiree*. But I wasn't sure how to spell it—and so I substituted the word *party*. "Sorry you'll miss the party" didn't sound nearly as elegant, but I was pretty sure I had spelled *party* correctly.)

In the urge to be correct, students too will make substitutions. They'll use the smaller word or the smaller sentence or the simpler form of dialogue so that they won't risk being wrong. One small part of today's session, therefore, will challenge your students to use the strategies they know to fix up their writing, to be risk takers with their language, and to rely on each other and their tools to the best of their ability to help catch mistakes.

The bigger focus for today, though, is those significant grammatical choices writers make that affect readers' understanding and ease in following ideas—choices that are not just quick fixes, but instead, are thoughtful decisions. Decisions about when to paragraph, what to end paragraphs with, making verb tense choices, and considering the artful fragment fit into this category. It's tempting to try to teach all of these in one big editing blob, but chances are slim that your students will really learn the deep, move-toward-more-thoughtful-choices approach that you are hoping for if you teach that way. Instead, today you will give them the opportunity to focus on one grammatical choice—choices about expository paragraphs—watching you model how a writer makes careful decisions. It is important for young writers, and it merits time for them to really see *how* and *why* writers do this work.

IN THIS SESSION, you'll remind students of editing strategies they know and will also teach them strategies writers use to make decisions about nonfiction paragraphs

GETTING READY

- ✔ Editing Checklist, used and built upon across the year, enlarged for students to see (see Connection)

- ✔ Excerpt from essay on dogs in classrooms, written out on chart paper (see Teaching and Active Engagement)

- ✔ Colored markers (see Teaching and Active Engagement)

- ✔ Students' writing folders with their current drafts and pencils or markers (see Share)

Paragraphing Choices

CONNECTION

Set your students up to recall what they know about editing, and use a reminder chart to turn them to strategies for how to edit versus what to edit.

"Writers, as you get ready to publish your argument essays, I know that you have been searching for real audiences for them. So Nate is sending his letter to the track coach, the Parent Teacher Association, and the principal! Claire is sending her letter about bike lanes to the city council. Nick is sending his essay about gun control to the paper as an editorial. Of course, you want your writing to be as perfect as possible, so that nothing will distract from your argument. That means . . . editing! You know a lot about editing, so quickly, turn and tell your partner, what are a few things that you know you really want to double-check and fix up as you get ready to publish?"

As the students talked, I flipped to an editing checklist.

One of the jobs you want to do in the connection is to heighten students' engagement. Sometimes you use stories, metaphors, activities, popular culture to increase their engagement. For today, you rely on something simpler, but no less powerful: personal connections.

Editing Checklist

1. Does this make sense? Are any words or parts missing?

2. Are all my sentences complete? Have I checked for run-ons and fragments?

3. Have I used correct capitalization (for names and the beginning of sentences)?

4. Have I used commas and quotation marks for dialogue?

5. Have I checked to see that all my verbs and subjects agree? Are my verbs in the right tense (past, present, future)?

6. Do the words all seem to be spelled right? Do they look right? Have I checked any I'm uncertain of?

7. Have I checked for frequently confused words (to, too, two; there, their)?

8. Have I paragraphed and indented?

9. Have I written with voice?

"Writers, let me have your eyes up here, please. The things you're talking about now are things that you should double-check. That's the writer's life. When your work matters, you double-check. Especially with the way some of you write on your phones now, texting fast and furious, with all sorts of shortcuts. You'll forget how to spell some words, or you'll write fast and get something wrong. So before you send your writing to audiences you care about, go back over it and look at your capitals, your spelling, your commas, and your punctuation for quotations. Our chart might help you.

"These are *quick* fix-its, writers. The only choices you have to make about them will be when to do this work and how you'll go about it.

"But there are grammar choices that you'll need—and want—to think more deeply about, those which qualify as important writing choices. One of these is when to make a new paragraph in your writing."

✤ **Name the teaching point.**

"Writers, today I want to teach you that nonfiction writers often use a paragraph to introduce a new part or a new idea or new reason. Nonfiction writers also use paragraphs to help the reader with density—they think about how much information a reader can handle at one time."

TEACHING

Demonstrate, using a mentor text that you have set up with very clear markers for paragraphing, such as transitional phrases.

"Writers, I'm sure you remember that when you worked on narratives, you learned that writers use paragraphs to introduce a new character, a change in the setting, or a change in time. The paragraph in a story is kind of like a signpost for the reader that something is changing. Well, it's the same in nonfiction writing. Your paragraphs are like a signpost to the reader, saying, 'Pay attention! Something is changing!' Readers need these signposts.

"Let's try this work together. I'm going to reread part of my argument about having dogs in schools. Watch as I reread with the lens of paragraphing." I flipped the chart paper over, revealing what I had written.

> In some schools across the country, you'll find dogs in the classroom. Yes, dogs! Sometimes these dogs are official therapy dogs. Other times they are simply well-trained dogs, who have permission to be in school. District Two should allow teachers to bring well-trained dogs to school. The district should allow dogs because they help children stay calm, they help children focus, and they can help with school safety. One reason District Two should allow dogs is because they help keep children calm. This fact may seem surprising, but research shows that dogs help lower anxiety and make people calm. According to <u>The Seattle Times</u>, "being around dogs actually lowers people's blood pressure and even their heartrate." This is important because school can get a little chaotic. Having animals that help calm us all down could be really helpful.

A good time to tackle paragraphs, whether you are writing narratives or expository text, is just before kids clean up their final drafts. If kids are typing, it's helpful to look at a clean copy in order to box out paragraphs. When they're handwriting, they'll need to consider all their additions and insertions. You probably want to make your demo text look like your students'; that is, if they have Post-its and spider legs, you should, too, so you can read across them to consider how to chunk your final piece.

Another reason District Two should allow dogs is because they help children focus. It turns out that children will read and even do math better when they have a dog nearby. In fact, for some kids, it's better to sit right on the floor by the dog.

"Just looking at that much text with no white space is hard, right? It's just too dense. It's hard for readers to follow. So, what to do? How do you break this into paragraphs? Well, we said that nonfiction writers use a paragraph any time a part changes, like when the text moves from an introduction to a supporting reason, or when there's a new idea or reason."

I stared at the text, running my finger over the sentences for a moment. "Well, the first part of an essay is usually an introduction. This whole thing isn't the introduction, though. Some of this is my reasons and evidence. So let me read over the start." I paused part way down the page. "I guess I would put a paragraph right after 'help with school safety.' That's really the end of my introduction. I know because right after that I say 'One reason,' and that's clearly when I begin to talk about my reasons and evidence."

I used a marker to box out that paragraph.

ACTIVE ENGAGEMENT

Call on students to help you figure out where to paragraph, and then ask one student to explain his or her paragraphing decisions.

"Writers, will you help me see where else I should paragraph? You know to use a paragraph to introduce a new part, or a new idea or reason. Turn and talk to your partner. Where should I introduce a new paragraph, and why?"

As the children talked, I walked among them, encouraging them to explain to each other *why* a paragraph should go where it would. I also found a partnership who could model this explanation. Then I reconvened the students.

"Writers, Kennedy and her partner were explaining where they think I should put a new paragraph. Kennedy, why don't you share with us? Come on up here, and use the marker if you'd like."

"Well," Kennedy said, grabbing a marker with alacrity, "you have a paragraph for the introduction now." She pointed to the part of the text that was boxed in green. "And that means this next part, that starts with 'One reason' is the beginning of the paragraph. We looked for where that paragraph would end. At first we couldn't figure out where it would end. But then we saw where you say, 'Another reason.' So we think the second paragraph should be from 'One reason' to just before 'Another reason.'" Kennedy boxed the second paragraph in red and the beginning of the third one in yellow (see Figure 21–1).

"That was a smart strategy, Kennedy, to look for where the next paragraph would begin, if you weren't sure where this one would end. Looking for obvious clues like transition phrases is a really good idea."

There are various ways to indicate paragraph revisions on a rough draft. Editors often use a paragraph symbol or two backslashes. For children, boxing paragraphs out often helps them really see the length and balance of their paragraphs, and it helps them visualize the content the paragraph encapsulated. If your students are word processing, expect to teach them how to use the return key, and indent paragraphs. On many digital state tests, students can only paragraph by hitting the space bar, and often you are unable to recognize their paragraphs. Skipping a line helps.

Teachers, instead, you might consider handing out copies of your text and asking students to box it themselves.

LINK

Debrief the work that students might do as they prepare for publication, and remind them to turn to each other for help.

"Okay, writers, as you bring your arguments to publication, make sure they are as strong as possible in every way. That means reviewing your logic, double-checking your spelling and punctuation, and figuring out where you want to insert paragraphs. One more tip: you'll have to be careful to include all your insertions as you get your piece ready for publication. Some of you want to type or record your piece. Remember, writers help each other. You're so lucky to write in a community of writers. If you feel unsure about any of your fix-it work or your choices, reach out to another writer."

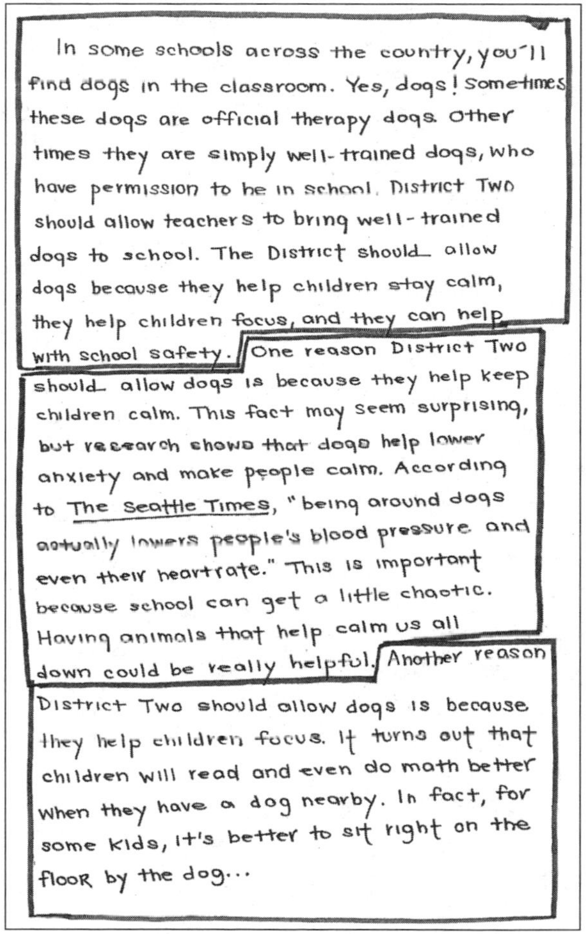

> In some schools across the country, you'll find dogs in the classroom. Yes, dogs! Sometimes these dogs are official therapy dogs. Other times they are simply well-trained dogs, who have permission to be in school. District Two should allow teachers to bring well-trained dogs to school. The District should allow dogs because they help children stay calm, they help children focus, and they can help with school safety. One reason District Two should allow dogs is because they help keep children calm. This fact may seem surprising, but research shows that dogs help lower anxiety and make people calm. According to The Seattle Times, "being around dogs actually lowers people's blood pressure and even their heartrate." This is important because school can get a little chaotic. Having animals that help calm us all down could be really helpful. Another reason District Two should allow dogs is because they help children focus. It turns out that children will read and even do math better when they have a dog nearby. In fact, for some kids, it's better to sit right on the floor by the dog...

FIG. 21–1   The transitional phrases make clear the different parts of the piece, and set the text up for the lesson on paragraphs.

Sorting Information within Paragraphs

TRAIN STUDENTS' EYES TO PULL BACK FROM THE IDEAS AND DETAILS of the text and focus instead on its overall structure. Writers ought to be able to see where the claim is situated (often at the very top), and they ought to be able to move their finger down this page to point/count out where each new point of supporting evidence begins. An ability to look beneath the trimmings and see the solid beams, to really see the architecture of a piece of writing, is the true hallmark of a craftsman.

Even though your students have only had a few days to conduct their research, they are apt to have tons of it at their fingertips. They have grown stronger at crafting arguments and will want to incorporate multiple pieces of evidence for each reason. Often this can lead to paragraphs (like the one used in the minilesson) that are dense and hard to read. In the information writing that they did previously, students learned that new pieces of information went into their own paragraphs. You'll want to carry this teaching forward, reiterating that paragraphs are like containers. They help sort information into small, separate categories; they also help the reader's eye take in chunks of information instead of being overwhelmed with an unsorted barrage of merged-up words.

With some students' writing, you might realize that paragraphing isn't as simple as indenting to break up stretches of text. Sometimes in children's expository writing, an absence of clear paragraphing can be symptomatic of deeper organizational issues. Despite plenty of practice in previous reading and writing units, some children may still not have internalized the basic organizational boxes-and-bullets template. In such cases, expect to see disjointed bits of information clumped together, ideas that don't flow logically from each other, the absence of clear topic sentences or irrelevant details cropping up without warning. If you have more than one such case in your room, don't waste another minute before calling these children together into a small group to reexplain the claim-and-supports structure of basic essay writing.

MID-WORKSHOP TEACHING
Writers Are Daring, and They Are Problem Solvers

"Writers, can I have your eyes for a moment? I know you're busy editing, fixing up, inserting paragraphs." I waited until the children looked up. "I want to tell you about something funny that just happened with Claire and Sarah. Claire had a line in her essay where she talked about bike lanes, and she said they were important because lots of bikers got hit by cars. She said that right now, a biker could find himself in a massacre! But then Claire realized she didn't know how to spell *massacre*. She was just going to take it out and instead write 'accident with a lot of people.'

"Claire and Sarah were helping each other edit their essays. When Sarah saw that Claire had crossed out *massacre*, she asked why. Claire explained that she'd tried to look the word up in the dictionary, but there was no m-a-s-a-k-e-r! Writers, it's true that dictionaries are better for looking up what a word means than for looking up how to spell it. But persevere. You know a lot of strategies. Sarah helped Claire try them all. They wrote the word out different ways. They asked other writers' advice. They tried looking it up those ways—and they finally found it!

"Be daring, writers. Dare to use big words you don't know how to spell. And be a problem-solver, like Sarah. Use everything you can think of to figure out those spellings and to solve your editing challenges."

Explain that each paragraph forwards its own distinct idea and that it flows from the paragraph before it in a logical sequence. You might confer with students to help them see bits of ideas and information that seem to "go together" and show them how to sort this into a distinct paragraph.

Some students' writing may appear, at first glance, to be well paragraphed, but closer inspection might reveal that the ideas in each paragraph are not distinct. In this case, you might reiterate previous teaching about topic sentences, that these are often (though not always) placed at the very start of a paragraph and that they sum up the main idea of the entire paragraph. You might even set up a basic "paragraph outline" for their essays, explaining that paragraph one will forward a claim and provide a summary of basic evidence for this and that subsequent paragraphs

(two, three, and/or four) will each elaborate one bit of evidence. Counterclaims can be tackled in a separate paragraph. If your writers have lots of details to insert for each bit of evidence, by all means, teach them to create multiple paragraphs for each point or supporting evidence. Keep reminding students to paragraph when they introduce new evidence.

Of course, you'll also remind students of all they have learned regarding paragraphing in narrative. "When you wrote memoir, you learned that you might start a new paragraph when a new person is speaking, there is a new time or place, or to highlight a part of the story that is particularly important. Now, you are using stories in your essays. Carry forward what you have learned." Then direct students back to their drafts and have them use colors to box out paragraphs as you did in the lesson.

Writers Collaborate, Using a Variety of Ways to Help Each Other Edit

Set students up with methods for editing in a community of writers.

"Writers, could you bring your pieces to the meeting area please? Writers, as you get ready to publish, I want to remind you that it is so helpful to have someone else read your piece and help with editing. There are two different methods for this work. One method is to have your partner read *your* piece aloud. Your partner will use your punctuation to guide his or her voice, slowing down for commas and paragraphs, speeding along when there is no punctuation or pause. Listening to your piece be read aloud will help you notice tiny things like missing punctuation and bigger things like missing words!

"A second method of editing in collaboration is to have your partner read with a pencil in hand. It's really hard to notice mistakes in our own writing. Your eye just moves right along, thrilled with your own ideas. But someone else can underline words that might be misspelled, put a question mark in the margin when something seems to be missing, and help box out paragraphs.

"Let's take some time to do this right now, writers. Find your partner. Set yourself up to read each other's pieces aloud, and to read and mark them up. Really help each other. Writers depend on each other to clean up their work." Looking over students' shoulders, I saw Ivan helping Sarah with her paragraphing, and Claire reading her partner's piece, pausing to say, in her own voice, "I think you might need . . ."

SESSION 21 HOMEWORK

PREPARING FOR PUBLICATION

Writers, when you are in school, partners help you. When you are at home, siblings, guardians, or friends help you. As you work on your essays tonight, seek out help. Ask someone, maybe even your neighbor, to read your piece aloud to you, noting your punctuation. Or, sit side by side and underline missing punctuation and misspelled words together. Or call each other and read your pieces. In middle and high school, you might have to find your own study partners or turn your friends into partners. Practice this now!

Remember that tomorrow is the celebration so your essays need to be ready for publication. Use all that you know about the writing process, and writing arguments, and helping each other to prepare your essay.

Celebration
Taking Positions, Developing Stances

 ear Teachers,

This letter marks our final word with you. The work you did in this unit of study, though, is work that we hope will inform your instruction in other units and across content areas. Taking real-world stances, arguing and defending positions, and developing logical, coherent arguments are skills that students will call on again and again in their academic and professional lives—and perhaps in their personal lives as well! In this letter we offer suggestions for how to support students in transferring and applying the work that they have done in this unit to their future endeavors.

As your students share their writing and reflect on their knowledge of argument, you will want to consider how to maintain an attitude of continuous striving and empowerment. Your students have made remarkable strides as argument writers. Capitalize on their prowess, and solidify their skills, perhaps by offering opportunities to argue in social studies and science. Imagine your students conceiving of history or science not as a series of inevitable events, but as a series of debatable decisions. If you do this work, remind students that they know how to argue well—and send them off to research, write, debate, and revise about climate change, greenhouse gases, westward expansion, and so on. If you are the teacher of these disciplines, unroll your charts! If you have colleagues who teach content, invite them to look at student work and teaching charts, and see if you might coauthor a version of the unit that is set in social studies or science.

The fact is that you have taught your students to argue, and that is a powerful, transferable skill set. It's also one that they can keep getting better at. Positioning yourself as a continual learner is part of what makes expert tennis players, piano players, litigators—anything. For your celebration, we invite you to set your students up to share their writing, reflect on their skills, and study some "great debaters" with an eye toward the future. If possible, you want to spread this out over two days so you can include a final on-demand piece as part of your celebration of writers' strengths, in addition to your celebration of writers' pieces.

You might first set your students up in small groups to share their arguments with each other. Invite them to read as if they are giving a speech, using what they learned from their panel presentations to make eye contact, emphasize their points, and stir their audience. Have peers jot down one or two points they found particularly convincing, or phrases they particularly liked, as feedback for writers. Writers like to know when they have been effective.

Ask students to decide, as well, where they want their piece to live. Do they want to do anything more with their essay? You, of course, can keep it as simple as putting them up on the wall, but by now your students know a lot about targeting particular audiences, and they may know more about digital possibilities than you do. Encourage them to go beyond the work of the unit. Do they want to post their essay somewhere particular in school? Address it and mail it? Post it online? Make a podcast? A class blog? This could be the work of five minutes, or it could be ongoing independent work for some of your activists. Today, they can get that work going.

Next, you might consider inviting students to flash-draft a persuasive essay. Tell them to bring any text or material they want, and explain that they'll have a chance to show off their proficiencies as argument writers, on any topic. Then, the next day, after students write, give them their very first, beginning-of-the-year, on-demand opinion piece and invite them to compare the two pieces, checklist at hand, and mark signs of progress. You, and they, are sure to see evidence of growth.

 Finally, you might gather your students to watch a scene from the film *The Great Debaters* (2007) or another film argument scene you find inspiring. We particularly like the scene in *The Great Debaters* where the young students from Wiley College defend civil disobedience against the Harvard students who rebut their claim. Set students up with notebooks as they watch, and have them jot notes. You might invite them to keep two columns: what they notice these debaters doing that they learned to do as well and what they notice that they'd like to do next time (stuff we do now/stuff we want to do next).

Then you might convene a grand conversation about *The Great Debaters* as a final closing and allow your students to discuss their ideas with minimal to no input from you. See what they come up with. You might allow one student to record the class's ideas on a chart and let them call on one another. Finish by noting all that your students have done, your pride in their accomplishments, and your faith in their ability to continue to grow.

Well done!

Lucy, Mary, and Annie

Here are some samples of finished student pieces. You can also find them in the online resources.

No Track Tryouts

P.S. 6 Parents, Teachers, Coaches, and Kids! I call on you to change the policy that kids have to try out for track. It's wrong to not let kids join track because it hurts their self-esteem, because it builds a nasty sense of competition, and because all kids deserve to run if they want.

Some pooh-pooh the idea that kids' self-esteem gets hurt. But picture this: Sonia goes to track on Monday. It's the pre-cut practices. Sonia suffers sometimes from asthma. She has to rest sometimes so she can breathe. Sonia goes to track on Tuesday. Already she feels stronger. Wednesday, Sonia runs hard, stopping to rest only once. Thursday, Sonia dashes into homeroom. "I can't wait to run today" she thinks. Then she sees the letter on her desk. The team made its cuts. She's been cut. How do you think Sonia feels? I'll tell you how she feels, she feels TERRIBLE. She feels slow and horrible. She feels like everyone is staring at her, feeling sorry for her. She wonders if she'll ever be good enough. And the truth is—her school didn't think she was good enough to participate. Schools are supposed to make you stronger, not destroy your self-esteem.

Not allowing kids to join track also makes kids competitive with each other. In one survey, 18 out of 20 kids said that they would rather make the team than stay friends with each other. In an interview with a student who made the team, this source said, "I don't really hang out with any of my friends now who didn't make the team. They don't have the red shirts, or run with us. I don't know, I just don't see them anymore." You might think that competition would bring out the best in kids, and maybe it does when they're older, but in elementary school, it makes kids mean and lonely.

The most important reason not to make cuts for track is that all kids deserve to run. For goodness sakes! We're nine and ten years old. Isn't this the time when we should be learning skills and getting stronger? A lot of people say that it's 'just sports, that's how it is.' But we're not pro-ball players. All of us deserve to exercise and get faster. And there's no other time or place for us to run at school if we don't run with track. By the time we get home, it's mostly dark. At school, only the track team is allowed to leave the grounds to run. The gym is too small. All of us deserve this gift.

Change this policy, P.S. 6. Give us the fast legs and strong bodies we all deserve. Let us ALL be the runners we want to be.

---

① P.S. 6 Parents, Teachers, Coaches, and Kids! I call on you to change the policy that kids have to try out for track. It's wrong to not let kids join track because it hurts their self-esteem, because it builds a nasty sense of competition, and because all kids deserve to run if they want.

Some pooh-pooh the idea that kids' self-esteem gets hurt. But picture this: Sonia goes to track on Monday. It's the pre-cut practices. Sonia suffers sometimes from asthma. She has to rest sometimes so she can breathe. Sonia goes to track on Tuesday. Already she feels stronger. Wednesday, Sonia runs hard, stopping to rest only once. Thursday, Sonia dashes into homeroom. "I can't wait to run today" She thinks. Then she sees

② the letter on her desk. The team made its cuts. She's been cut. How do you think Sonia feels? I'll tell you how she feels, she feels TERRIBLE. She feels slow and horrible. She feels like everyone is staring at her, feeling sorry for her. She wonders if she'll ever be good enough. And the truth is— her school didn't think she was good enough to participate. Schools are supposed to make you stronger, not destroy your self-esteem.

Not allowing kids to join track also makes kids competitive with each other. In one survey, 18 out of 20 kids said that they would rather make the team than stay friends with each other. In an interview with a student who made the team, this source said,

③ "I don't really hang out with any of my 'friends' now who didn't make the team. They don't have the red shirt, or run with us. I don't know, I just don't see them anymore." You might think that competition would bring out the best in kids, and maybe it does when they're older, but in elementary school, it makes kids mean and lonely.

The most important reason not to make cuts for track is that all kids deserve to run. For goodness sakes! We're nine and ten years old. Isn't this the time when we should be learning skills and getting stronger? A lot of people say that it's 'just sports, that's how it is.' But we're not pro-ball players. All of us deserve to exercise and get faster. And

④ there's no other time or place for us to run at school if we don't run with track. By the time we got home, it's mostly dark. At school, only the track team is allowed to leave the grounds to run. The gym is too small. All of us deserve this gift.

Change this policy, P.S. 6. Give us that fast legs and strong bodies we all deserve. Let us all be the runners we want to be.

FIG. 22–1   Nate's essay against track tryouts

The Viscious and Terrifing Breed: Pit Bulls

There is a sweet little pit bull looking at you so innocently but the next time you blink you see the pit bull fiercely biting you. Pit bulls are vicious pets that are very violent and dangerous. I think these dangerous pets should be banned because they can seriously hurt people and attack someone unpredictably. And so, these pit bulls cannot be tolerated within our communities anymore!

Pit bulls are very dangerous noted as the most dangerous dog in America. These pets have been in every fatal dog attack. One of the attacks is a pit bull fiercely attacking a nine year old boy. Another 12 year old girl had a huge piece of her eyebrow clawed out by a pit bull. "Children should be able to walk to school without worrying a pit bull might attack them," Tamara Vostock said in the article Ban Pit Bulls: Local City May Be Next (she is also the author of the article.) The Supreme Court had even said, "Pit Bull attacks, unlike attacks by other dogs, occur more often, are more severe and are more likely to result in fatalities."

Pit bulls have been attacking people unpredictably. One attack was on a pregnant woman that was attacked and killed by a pit bull, her family pet, when her husband was out. The woman was bitten over and over again. By noon, when her husband returned, he found his wife lying on the floor with their two year old pit bull on top of her. These pit bull attacks keep on happening. According to DogsBite.org, a chart shows that pit bulls have attacked 826 children and attacked 687 adults. They have also wounded 1,093 people and killed 207 people.

On the other hand, some people believe pit bulls are good for children. They get along nicely and are always very playfull. They show love and care to each other. But that is wrong. According to the article Toddler Recovering After Dog Attack, a pit bull attacked a child when she was walking in her backyard. She suffered through her wounds on the right side of her face and stomach. Another child that was a 4 year old girl was attacked by her family pet, a pit bull. This isn't how pit bulls and children should get along and it definitely shows how they are not good for children.

Pit bulls are the most violent animal living today. Would you want to have a pet that can suddenly attack you one day? There are even more attacks pit bulls cause that are happening today. If we don't ban these violent animals, these attacks will keep on going and will be unstoppable! Ban pit bulls! If we do, many people would be saved from these attacks. Your life could be saved. Make the right choice and ban pit bulls now!

1

The Viscious and Terrifing Breed: Pit Bulls

There is a sweet little pit bull looking at you so innocently but the next time you blink, you see the pit bull fiercely biting you. Pit bulls are vicious pets that are very violent and dangerous. I think these dangerous pets should be banned because they can seriously hurt people and attack someone ~~bred~~ unpredictably. And so, these pit bulls can not be tolerated within our communities anymore!

Pit bulls are dangerous noted as the ~~most~~ dangerous dog in America. These pets have been in ~~every~~ fatal dog attack. One of the attacks is a pit bull

2

fiercely attacking a nine year old boy. Another 12 year old girl had a huge piece of her eyebrow clawed out by a pit bull. "Children should be able to walk to school without worrying a pit bull might attack them," Tamara Vostock said in the article Ban Pit Bulls: Local City May Be Next (she is also the author of the article.) The Supreme Court had even said, "Pit Bull attacks, unlike attacks by other dogs, occur more often, are more severe and are more likely to result in fatalities."

Pit bulls have been attacking people unpredictably. One attack was on a pregnant woman that was attacked and killed by a pit bull, her family pet, when her husband was

3

out. The woman was bitten over and over again. By noon, when her husband returned, he found his wife lying on the floor with their 2 year old pit bull on top of her. These pit bull attacks keep on happening. According to DogBite.org, a chart shows that pit bulls have attacked 826 children and attacked 687 adults. They have also wounded 1,093 people and killed 207 people.

On the other hand, some people believe pit bulls are good for ~~people~~ children. They get along nicely and are always very playfull. They show love and care to each other. But that is wrong. According to the article Toddler Recovering After Dog Attack, a pit bull

4

attacked a child while she was walking in her backyard. She suffered through her wounds on the right ~~too~~ side of her face and stomach. Another child that was 4 year old girl was attacked by her family pet, a pit bull. This isn't how pit bulls and children get along, and it definitely shows how they are not good for children.

Pit bulls are the most violent animals living today. Would you want to have a pet that can suddenly attack you one day? There are even more attacks, pit bulls cause that are happening today. If we don't ban these violent animals, these attacks will keep on going, and will be unstoppable! Ban pit bulls! If we do, many people would be saved from

5

these attacks. Your life could be saved. Make the right choice and ban pit bulls now!

FIG. 22–2 Caroline's essay against pit bulls as pets

Pit Bulls, The Side That Is Right!

Cute pit bulls lined up, adorable faces, all looking their best for you! That is pit bulls trying to do what you like when you would like. Pit bulls like to love not attack, unless you train them to, and they should be kept as house pets. How would you feel if everyone wanted to destroy you? I believe pit bulls should be kept as house pets because pit bulls are very affectionate and very loyal. Pit bulls should be allowed to keep their rights to be pets like all other animals. They did not hurt us, why should we hurt them?

Pit bulls are very affectionate, they love to give kisses. For most pit bulls, "attack," "destroy," and "hit" are not in their dictionary. They would never try to attack anyone. If they were to attack, they would attack in kisses. Pit bulls will always be what they are, affectionate and have the right to be alive. They are very loving to their owners and would never try to hurt them. For example, an eleven-year-old pit bull saved eleven people from a building on fire. He woke up people living there, being a heroic dog. Because of this eleven people are still living. Sadly, the heroic dog Chaos didn't make it out alive. If a dog saves people, we have to save them too.

Pit bulls are very loyal. They will always protect you and your family. They will stand by you whenever you need help. For example, a dog named Weela was very protective of Gary. Weela saved Gary's life. Weela got bitten on the face by a rattlesnake. This all happened because Weela pushed Gary out of the way saving his life. Later on, Weela saved thirty people, twenty-nine dogs, thirteen horses, and one cat. What a pit bull! Without them, the population of people and animals would decrease. Not only are pit bulls loyal to their owners, but they are also loyal to everyone around them.

Despite my argument, some people still feel that pit bulls can be dangerous. You can turn your back for about one minute and leave your pit bull alone with your child and before you know it an attack may occur. However, Pit Bull dogs are made for fighting. That is very true, but some dogs do not fight and instead they listen to their owners. Just because some dogs are bad the media does not have to focus on the bad side of dogs. The media should know that not all dogs are fatal, pit bulls aren't either.

I think that pit bulls should be allowed to live. "All dogs and animals should be created equal!" Many other people should think so too because if just one person violated the law it doesn't mean all people have to die, just the person who committed the crime should have to pay the price. All I'm trying to say is just because many pit bulls are violent and have mental thoughts to fight, not all pit bulls are bad, some are heroes.

FIG. 22–3 Alessandra's essay in defense of pit bulls